Heidegger Reexamined

Edited with introductions by

Hubert Dreyfus
University of California, Berkeley

Mark Wrathall
Brigham Young University

Contents of the Collection

Volume 1
Dasein, Authenticity, and Death

Volume 2
Truth, Realism, and the History of Being

Volume 3
Art, Poetry, and Technology

Volume 4
Language and the Critique of Subjectivity

Heidegger Reexamined

Volume 4
Language and the Critique of Subjectivity

Edited with introductions by

Hubert Dreyfus
University of California, Berkeley

Mark Wrathall
Brigham Young University

NEW YORK AND LONDON

Published in 2002 by
Routledge
270 Madison Avenue,
New York, NY 10016

Published in Great Britain by
Routledge
2 Park Square, Milton Park,
Abingdon, Oxon OX14 4RN
www.routledge.com

Routledge is an imprint of the Taylor & Francis Group.
Copyright © 2002 by Taylor & Francis Books, Inc.

Transferred to digital printing.

All rights reserved. No part of this book may be reprinted or reproduced or utilized in any form or by any electronic, mechanical, or other means, now known or hereafter invented, including photocopying and recording, or in any information storage or retrieval system, without permission in writing from the publisher.

10 9 8 7 6 5 4 3

Library of Congress Cataloging-in-Publication Data

Heidegger reexamined / edited with introductions by Hubert Dreyfus, Mark Wrathall
  p. cm.
  1. Heidegger, Martin, 1889–1976. I. Dreyfus, Hubert L. II. Wrathall, Mark A.
B3279.H49 H35228 2002
193—dc21   2002005873

ISBN 978-0-415-88518-8 (POD set)
ISBN 978-0-415-94041-2 (set)
ISBN 978-0-415-94042-9 (v. 1)
ISBN 978-0-415-94043-6 (v. 2)
ISBN 978-0-415-94044-3 (v. 3)
ISBN 978-0-415-94045-0 (v. 4)

Contents

vii   Series Introduction
xi   Volume Introduction

1   The Ego and Dasein
     Jean-Luc Marion

33   Can There be an Epistemology of Moods?
     Stephen Mulhall

53   Die Rolle der Sprache in 'Sein und Zeit'
     Cristina Lafont

72   *Destruktion* and Deconstruction
     Hans-Georg Gadamer

85   Derridian Dispersion and Heideggerian Articulation: General Tendencies in the Practices that Govern Intelligibility
     Charles Spinosa

99   Heidegger on Logic
     J. N. Mohanty

128 The Conditions of Truth in Heidegger and Davidson
     Mark A. Wrathall

149 Heidegger and the Intentionality of Language
     Roderick M. Stewart

157 Overcoming Metaphysics: Carnap and Heidegger
     Michael Friedman

193 Logic and the Inexpressible in Frege and Heidegger
     Edward Witherspoon

219 The Other Minds Problem in Early Heidegger
     Harrison Hall

227 Philosophy after Wittgenstein and Heidegger
     Charles Guignon

251 Meaning Constitution and Justification of Validity: Has Heidegger Overcome Transcendental Philosophy by History of Being
     Karl-Otto Apel

271 The Question of the Subject: Heidegger and the Transcendental Tradition
David Carr

287 Heideggerean Postmodernism and Metaphysical Politics
Robert B. Pippin

309 Acknowledgments

Series Introduction

Martin Heidegger is undeniably one of the most influential philosophers of the 20th century. His work has been appropriated by scholars in fields as diverse as philosophy, classics, psychology, literature, history, sociology, anthropology, political science, religious studies, and cultural studies.

In this four-volume series, we've collected a set of articles that we believe represent some of the best research on the most interesting and difficult issues in contemporary Heidegger scholarship. In putting together this collection, we have quite deliberately tried to identify the papers that engage critically with Heidegger's thought. This is not just because we wanted to focus on "live" issues in Heidegger scholarship. It is also because critical engagement with the text is, in our opinion, the best way to grasp Heidegger's thought. Heidegger is a notoriously difficult read—in part, because he is deliberately trying to break with the philosophical tradition, in part, because his way of breaking with the tradition was often to coin neologisms (a less sympathetic reader might dismiss it as obfuscatory jargon), and, in part, because Heidegger believed his task was to provoke his readers to thoughtfulness rather than provide them with a facile answer to a well-defined problem. Because of the difficulties in reading Heidegger, however, we believe that it is incumbent upon the commentator to keep the matter for thought in the forefront—the issue that Heidegger is trying to shed light on. Without such an engagement in the matter for thought, Heidegger scholarship all too often devolves into empty word play.

So, the first and most important criterion we've used in selecting papers is that they engage with important issues in Heidegger's thought, and do so in a clear, non-obfuscatory fashion. Next, we have by and large avoided republishing articles that are already available in other collections of essays on Heidegger. We have made exceptions, however, particularly when the essay is located in a volume that would easily be overlooked by Heidegger scholars. Finally, as our primary intent was to collect and make readily available work on current issues and problems arising out of Heidegger's thought, we have tried to select recent rather than dated articles.

In selecting themes for each volume, we have, in general, been guided by the order in which Heidegger, over the course of his career, devoted extended attention to the problems involved. Thus, the first volume contains essays focusing on Dasein—the human mode of existence—and "existential" themes like authenticity and death, because these were prominent concerns in the years leading up to and immediately following the publication of *Being and Time* in 1927. The second volume centers on Heidegger's account of truth, and his critique of the history of philosophy, because these were areas of extended interest in the 1930s and 1940s. The third volume is organized around themes indigenous to the 'late' Heidegger—namely, Heidegger's work on art, poetry, and technology.

But this is not to say that the volumes are governed by a strict notion of periods in Heidegger's work. In the past, it has been commonplace to subdivide Heidegger's work into two (early and late) or even three (early, middle, and late) periods. While there is something to be said for such divisions—there is an obvious sense in which *Being and Time* is thematically and stylistically unlike Heidegger's publications following the Second World War—it is also misleading to speak as if there were two or three different Heideggers. The bifurcation, as is well known, is something that Heidegger himself was uneasy about[1], and scholars today are increasingly hesitant to draw too sharp a divide between the early and late. So while the themes of the first three volumes have been set by Heidegger's own historical course through philosophy, the distribution of papers into volumes does not respect a division of scholarship into early and late. We have found instead that the papers relevant to an 'early Heidegger' issue often draw on Heidegger's later work, and vice versa.

The last volume in the series is organized less by Heidegger's own thematic concerns than by an interest in Heidegger's relevance to contemporary philosophy. Given mainstream analytic philosophy's preoccupation with language and mind, however, this volume does have two thematic centers of gravity—Heidegger's work on the essence of language, and his critique of modernist accounts of subjectivity.

In its focus on Heidegger's relevance to ongoing philosophical concerns, however, volume four merely makes obvious the intention of the series as a whole. In his 1925–1926 lecture course on logic, Heidegger bemoaned the fact that people "no longer philosophize from the issues, but from their colleague's books."[2] In a similar way, we believe that Heidegger is deserving of attention as a philosopher only because he is such an excellent guide to the issues themselves. We hope that the papers we have collected here demonstrate Heidegger's continuing pertinence to the most pressing issues in contemporary philosophy.

NOTES

[1] Writing to Richardson, Heidegger noted: "The distinction you make between Heidegger I and II is justified only on the condition that this is kept constantly in mind: only by way of what [Heidegger] I has thought does one gain access to what

is to-be-thought by [Heidegger] II. But the thought of [Heidegger] I becomes possible only if it is contained in [Heidegger] II." William J. Richardson, "Letter to Richardson," in *Heidegger: Through Phenomenology to Thought* (The Hague: M. Nijhoff, 1963), 8.

[2] *Logik: Die Frage nach der Wahrheit, Gesamtausgabe* 21 (Frankfurt am Main: Klostermann, 1995), 84.

Volume Introduction

This volume is organized around the theme of Heidegger's reception in contemporary philosophy. No single appraisal has been more responsible for the main stream analytic reaction to Heidegger's work than Carnap's dismissal of Heidegger's philosophical claims as metaphysical pseudo-sentences. For many years, if Heidegger was mentioned at all by an analytic philosopher, it was only to repeat facilely Carnap's critique. As Michael Friedman shows, however, both Heidegger and Carnap share a common starting point in the Neo-Kantianism prevalent in the German-language philosophy of their time. By exploring in detail the Carnap/Heidegger controversy, Friedman shows how a more subtle and substantive engagement between analytic and continental thought might be possible.

Many of the papers in this volume use Heidegger's work to achieve such a productive engagement. Edward Witherspoon shows how there is room for a constructive encounter between analytic and continental philosophy by turning to the heart of the superficial analytical dismissal of Heidegger's work—his views on 'the Nothing.' Witherspoon argues that, properly understood, Heidegger's investigation of the Nothing reveals an effort at thinking about the inexpressible foundation of logic similar to that of Frege. Charles Guignon shows Heidegger's parallelism with another of the founders of analytic philosophy, Wittgenstein, while Mark Wrathall connects Heidegger's work on truth with the truth-conditional semantics of analysts like Donald Davidson.

Perhaps the most fruitful areas for exploring Heidegger's relevance to contemporary philosophy are found in his views on language and his critique of subjectivity. The linguistic turn in mainstream Anglo-American philosophy intersects in intriguing ways with Heidegger's own emphasis on language. Heidegger's philosophy, in some ways, is quite congenial to the analytic view that all issues in philosophy are best tackled by a study of how we talk about these issues. As Hans-Georg Gadamer, Christina Lafont, and Karl-Otto Apel point out, Heidegger was an early advocate of the view that language plays a fundamental role in the constitution of the world. At the same time, Heidegger rejected unequivocally the view of language generally employed in the analytic philosophy of language. Heidegger would see the analyst's emphasis on the philosophy of mind or, indeed, the way analysts tend to conflate language and mind, as a vestige of the modern subjectivism that he was trying to overcome.

Christina Lafont, on the other hand, reviews Heidegger's explicit account of language presented in *Being and Time*. To make sense of this account, she argues, one must read between the lines to see that Heidegger accords to language a 'transcendental' role in the constitution of intelligibility—a transcendentalism which Lafont argues is problematic.

John Stewart situates Heidegger's thought on language vis-a-vis contemporary disputes over reference, and explores the consequences of this view of language for a Heideggerian account of intentionality in the philosophy of mind. Stewart's essay connects up in interesting ways with the essays in volume one that deal with the nature of Dasein and Heidegger's account of intentionality. The reader is referred back to the articles by Brandom, Haugeland, and Dreyfus for further discussion of these topics.

Heidegger's interest in language was manifest already in *Being and Time*, where section thirty-four was devoted to showing how language "has its roots in the existential constitution of Dasein's disclosedness."[1] This means that Heidegger did not believe language could be treated as the most fundamental level for analyzing human existence. To the contrary, it is itself grounded in our practical mastery of our world, and the understanding of being that this practical mastery presupposes. There is, as the essays in this volume make clear, considerable debate over how such an account of language is meant to work, how it bears on contemporary accounts of language in analytic philosophy (Stewart and Wrathall), and even whether it is consistent with other features of Heidegger's thought (Lafont).

There is a widespread sense among scholars that Heidegger's views on language changed in important ways in the decades following the publication of *Being and Time*. In particular, he seems to have acknowledged in his later work a more central constitutive role for language in our experience of the world: "because language is the house of Being," Heidegger wrote, "we reach what is by constantly going through this house."[2] On the face of it, this clearly seems to be a mediational view of the role of language—that is, the view that all our actions in the world are mediated through linguistic categories. On the other hand, it is equally clear that Heidegger doesn't understand language—the thing that is mediating our access to the world—on the representationalist model of mainstream philosophy of language. Even in the late Heidegger, language is not understood in terms of a representation of the world, but rather as a way of being oriented to the world. The late Heidegger is quite clear that if language is the house of being, this does not mean that the things we encounter in the world are our constructs. To the contrary, language, Heidegger says, "speaks us," which means that the 'language' he is talking about is the opening up of a world that makes ordinary talk possible: "Language speaks by saying; that is, by showing. Its saying wells up from the once spoken yet long since unspoken saying that permeates the rift-design in the essence of language. Language speaks by Pointing, reaching out to every region of presencing, letting what is present in each case appear in such regions or vanish from them."[3]

Heidegger's views on language also have important consequences for how we understand the role of the logical analysis of language. Heidegger offered a number of lecture courses[4] in the decades before and after the publication of *Being and Time* on the topic of logic in the broadest sense—"the theme for logic is discourse in regard to its most basic sense: to let the world and human existence [*Dasein*] be seen."[5] Although Heidegger was not a logician, J. N. Mohanty shows that Heidegger's philosophical view of logic is worth taking seriously. Mohanty reviews and appraises Heidegger's main theses about logic.

Heidegger's analysis of language has relevance not just to the analytic tradition, but also to the deconstructive tradition in philosophy. Hans-Georg Gadamer and Charles Spinosa both address aspects of the contemporary deconstructive critique of Heidegger. Gadamer reviews Heidegger's path from his recognition of the constitutive role of language in our experience of the world to his efforts in the destruction of the metaphysical tradition. If language is co-constitutive of the world, and our language is shaped by the conceptuality of the metaphysical tradition that has closed off an authentic experience of existence, then, Heidegger reasoned, the most pressing task for philosophy was a poetic effort at breaking our language free of the conceptuality of metaphysics. Gadamer argues, however, that this destructive move opens up two possible courses—one is the Derridean project of deconstruction, which would finally destroy metaphysics by undermining even Heidegger's philosophical project of seeking the meaning of being. The other path, the one Gadamer prefers, is a return to dialogue, which would reappropriate the metaphysical project. Spinosa, on the other hand, sees the point of conflict between Heidegger and deconstruction as turning on their respective understandings of the way background practices tend to function in the production of intelligibility.

Of course, there is a broader issue behind Heidegger's disagreement with contemporary philosophy of language and the elevation of logic as a scientific method. Heidegger sees these disciplines as inheritors of the errors of the modern view of subjectivity. The idea of a subject is the idea of an entity which has certainty and transparency regarding its own states, but knows other entities only through its representations of them. The implications of this story, familiar since Descartes, can be traced out in two directions. With regard to ourselves, it supposes that we can have a clear, certain, and distinct grasp about every essential feature of our being. With regard to knowledge of things acquired through perception, it entails that we can never have a certain grasp of their existence or nature. Several articles in volume two reviewed Heidegger's critique of the skepticism this produces about our knowledge of the external world and the discoveries of the natural sciences.

We also have a number of articles detailing and criticizing Heidegger's attack on the notion of a self-transparent subject. Jean-Luc Marion addresses in general the achievements and limits of Heidegger's attempt to break out of the Cartesian tradition, which understands the self as a subjective ego cogito. At stake is a non-subjectivistic, non-mentalistic account of human being. Other articles address specific implications for the way we think about the philosophy of mind that follows from Heidegger's rejection of Cartesian subjectivity. Harrison Hall tackles the age-old Cartesian worry about our ability to know other minds. The problem dissolves once being-in-the-world is properly understood. The Cartesian view of the mind, as is well known, also has important consequences for epistemology—not least of which is the privileging of cognitivism in matters epistemological. Stephen Mulhall takes up this problem on the basis of the Heideggerian idea that disposedness (*befindlichkeit*) is one of the constitutive features of Dasein. This is to say that the human way of being always finds itself disposed to the world in a particular way. The ontic manifestation of disposedness is mood. The centrality of mood to the disclosedness of world, Mulhall shows, entails a revised assessment of the privileged status accorded cognitive states.

But modernism is not without its defenders. David Carr and Robert Pippin argue that there are significant ways in which Heidegger's account of modernity has gone astray. They also contend that these errors in Heidegger's historical account of modernity highlight weaknesses in his response to the shortcomings of the metaphysical tradition. Carr reviews Heidegger's rejection of all philosophy since Descartes as a metaphysics of subjectivity. Carr argues, however, that Heidegger has, in two important respects, overlooked the transcendental tradition in modern philosophy, exemplified by Kant and Husserl. These transcendental philosophers, Carr argues, in fact affirmed the transcendence of the world, and thus cannot be fairly characterized as reducing all existence to existence for a subject. Second, these thinkers deny that the self has a foundation-giving self-transparency in thought.

Robert Pippin argues that Heidegger's counter-Enlightenment reaction to modernity misunderstands the modern opposition to dogmatism and affirmation of self-grounding rationality (of which idealism is the most extreme exponent), and thus overreacts or mis-reacts to the shortcomings of modernity. In particular, Pippin argues that we can acknowledge the possibility of an unescapable historicism and lack of rational grounds, without thereby mystifying it. The result will be "a modernity necessarily unending and unsettled," but in which we need not give up on the rationalist ideal.

Like Pippin, Karl-Otto Apel believes that a central appeal, as well as a central difficulty, of Heidegger's history of being lies in its relativizing and historicizing of meaning and knowledge. Also like Pippin, Apel argues that the situatedness and historical contingency of the way our language mediates our knowledge need not force us to give up the ideal of validity. The alternative to Heidegger's destruction of transcendental philosophy, Apel suggests, is the "regulative ideal" of "a consensual justification of validity claims."

NOTES

[1] *Being and Time*, trans. John Macquarrie and Edward Robinson (New York: Harper & Row, 1962), p. 203.

[2] "What are Poets for?" in *Poetry, Language, Thought*, trans. Albert Hofstadter (New York: Harper & Row, 1971), p. 132.

[3] "The Way to Language," in Martin Heidegger, *Basic Writings*, revised and expanded, ed. David Farrell Krell (San Francisco: HarperSanFrancisco, 1993), p. 411.

[4] See, for example, the 1925 course *Logic. The Question concerning Truth*, in *Gesamtausgabe*, vol. 21 (Frankfurt am Main: Klostermann, 1995), and the 1928 course *The Metaphysical Foundations of Logic*.

[5] *Gesamtausgabe*, vol. 21 (Frankfurt am Main: Klostermann, 1995), p. 6.

3

The *Ego* and *Dasein*

1. The Figure of Descartes within Heidegger's Path

Just as it is self-evident that Heidegger did not cease to confront Nietzsche, Hegel, Kant, or Aristotle, so his relation to Descartes can appear to be secondary. Thus, neither the commentators of Heidegger nor, to be sure, the historians of Descartes insist on the relation, when they do not ignore it altogether. Whatever the—bad or all too understandable—reasons for this misappreciation, they cannot lessen one massive fact: if only chronologically, Descartes appears already at the beginning of Heidegger's career and occupies it almost all the way to its end. If we stick to the texts already available in the present state of the publication of the *Gesamtausgabe* (in 1985), and unless we are forgetting something, the extreme evidence of a debate with Descartes intervenes as early as 1921 and right up to 1974.

In the course that he gives as *Privatdozent* in Freiburg during the winter semester of 1921–22, under the title of *Phänomenologische Interpretationen zu Aristoteles: Einführung in die phänomenologische Forschung* [*Phenomenological Interpretations of Aristotle: Introduction to Phenomenological Research*], a course therefore prior to the Marburg period, Heidegger does not treat Aristotle so much as he outlines a whole introduction to phenomenology; however, that introduction does indeed approach a philosopher: but instead of Aristotle, it is Descartes. Examining in fact "the metaphysics of the *I* and the idealism of the *I* [*Ich-metaphysik, ichlicher Idealismus*]," first in its Kantian and phenomenological forms, he ends up finally at Descartes, whose limits he already very clearly marks:

> The "*sum*" is, to be sure, also first for Descartes, but it is precisely here already that the failure lies: he does not stop there, but already has the pre-conception of the meaning of Being in the mode of simple observation [*Feststellung*] and even of the indubitable [*Unbezweifelbaren*]. The fact that Descartes was able to deviate toward the posing of a theoretical question

of knowledge and even that, from the point of view of the history of spirit [*geistigeschichtlich*], he inaugurated it, simply expresses [the fact] that the "*sum*," its Being and its categorial structure, were in no way a problem to him, but that the significance of the word "*sum*" was [for him] understood in an indifferent sense [*indifferenten . . . Sinn*], absolutely not related [properly] to the *ego*, formally objective [*formal gegenständlich*], uncritical and unclarified.

Already with this outline of an interpretation, Descartes appears as having privileged the ego in its certitude and as having assumed the *sum* without any real mediation: in other words, the mode of Being illustrated by the *sum* remains caught in its supposedly obvious, common, and indisputable sense and is therefore thought in fact on the basis of the acceptation of *esse* that is suitable to objects. Descartes privileges the question of the ego (hence the establishment of a theory of knowledge) and remains silent on the question of the *sum* (hence an objectivizing interpretation of all *esse*). Paradoxically, under the gaze of the young Heidegger, Descartes already poses the question of the mode of Being of the *sum* precisely by remaining silent on it in favor of a question concerning the status and the power of the *I*: "the weight of the question is placed immediately, without any motive and following the traditional standpoint, upon the 'I,' whereby the meaning of the 'I' remains essentially undetermined [*unbestimmt*], instead [of being placed] upon the meaning of the 'am.'"[1] Right away the essential is marked out: the *I* in the "I think" of the "I think, therefore I am," must be determined on the basis of the meaning of Being, and not on the basis of its own meaning as *I*.

The confrontation with Descartes, outlined so early, unfolds largely during Heidegger's stay in Marburg. In fact, that stay both opens and closes with a course explicitly dedicated to Descartes. That of the first winter semester of 1923–24 (still unpublished) undertakes an introduction to modern philosophy (*Der Beginn der neuzeitlichen Philosophie*); it must have evoked the figure of Descartes, at least if one accepts the testimony from the last course given in Marburg, in the summer of 1928: "This class, during the summer semester of 1928, set itself the task of assuming a position opposed to Leibniz. . . . The first semester of 1923/1924 risked taking the corresponding position with Descartes, which is then surpassed in Sein und Zeit (§§ 19–21)." We should underscore that the last course not only confirms that the first was dedicated to the study of Descartes and also that it thus anticipated nothing less than *Sein und Zeit*, §§ 19–21, but also itself concerned Descartes inasmuch as he persists in Leibniz, who, "like Descartes, sees in the *I*, in the *ego cogito*, the dimension from which all the fundamental metaphysical concepts must be drawn. One attempted to resolve the problem of Being as the fundamental problem of metaphysics through a return to the subject. However, in Leibniz as well as in his predecessor [i.e., Descartes] and successors, this return to the *I* remains ambiguous because the *I* is not grasped in its essential structure and in its specific mode of Being."[2] From these texts, which frame the stay at Marburg but also precede it, it is necessary to conclude— and all the more so, no doubt, insofar as others will come to confirm this clear preoccupation—that Heidegger discerns from the beginning of his "path of thinking" the decisive importance of Descartes; but he does not see it where, following the tradition, his contemporaries saw it—in the establishment of the ego at the level of transcendental or quasitranscendental principle. He locates it, on the contrary, in what Descartes hides behind the evidence and the dignity of the *ego cogito*—in the indetermination of the way of Being of that ego, whose *sum* remains so indeterminate that it falls under the hold of the mode of Being of objects. Heidegger interrogates the *ego cogito* no longer concerning the cogitative origin of its primacy, but first concerning the ontological indetermination of its *esse*, and thus concerning what it conceals of itself and not what it proclaims of itself. This concealment, originally located in the indetermination of the Being of the *I*, in some way calls first for a phenomenological examination—since phenomenology bears above all on what, of itself, does not show itself. Thus the conversation with Descartes marks more than do other confrontations Heidegger's strictly phenomenological point of departure.

But it characterizes just as well his last texts. Sticking to a narrowly chronological criterion, one could stress the fact that Descartes remains an essential preoccupation right up to the end. (1) In 1969, the second seminar at Le Thor recalls the historial position of Descartes: "What happened between Hegel and the Greeks? The thought of Descartes"; or: "With Fichte we witness the absolutizing of the Cartesian *cogito* (which is a *cogito* only in the measure that it is a *cogito me cogitare*) in an absolute knowing."[3] (2) In 1973, the Zähringen seminar carries to its highest point the interpretation of the Cartesian ego on the basis of the question of Being: " . . . subjectivity itself is not questioned as to its Being; indeed, since Descartes it is the *fundamentum inconcussum*. Throughout all modern thought, issuing from Descartes, subjectivity consequently constitutes the barrier to the beginning of the question in search of Being."[4] (3) In 1974, one of the very last texts, *Der Fehl heiliger Namen* (*The Lack of Divine Names*) again signals this "barrier" in taking up again the theme of the first Marburg course: "At the beginning of modern thought are / According to the order before any clarification of the matter of the / thought of the treatises on method: / from Descartes the *Discourse on*

3

Method and the / *Regulae ad directionem Ingenii.*"[5] If only chronologically, Heidegger's thought does not cease to encounter that of Descartes, in a confrontation at least as constant as those that tie Heidegger to Nietzsche or Aristotle. This textual datum, which will be confirmed by the great number of instances concerning Descartes in the mature works, nevertheless does not suffice to clarify the encounter between Heidegger's thought and Descartes's. At the very most it allows us to establish the fact of that encounter and to require an understanding of it. The abundance and constancy of the Cartesian references will themselves become intelligible, moreover, only to the extent that concepts come to motivate and justify them. What conceptually identifiable reason leads and therefore constrains Heidegger, from the beginning to the end of his path, to argue over and with Descartes?

2. The Phenomenological Motif of the Original Confrontation

At the very moment Heidegger was expounding and critiquing Descartes at Marburg, Husserl was expounding and agreeing with Descartes at Freiburg, in a course during the 1923–24 winter semester, from which the work *First Philosophy* issues: even when he happened to maintain a "false theory," the "philosophical genius" of Descartes led him to sow the "seeds of transcendental philosophy."[6] In fact, Husserl had not awaited that date (nor, a fortiori, the *Cartesian Meditations* of 1929) to place Descartes at the center of his reflection; well before the *Ideen*, the Göttingen lectures had done so in 1907, after, to be sure, other texts.[7] At least in its Husserlian form, phenomenology had already before Heidegger tied its destiny to that of its interpretation of Descartes, in such a way that nothing phenomenological could any longer be decided, regarding principle, without a discussion with Descartes. Such as Heidegger encounters him, Descartes already has the status of a phenomenological motif, if not the rank of a phenomenologist. For Heidegger, through the intermediary of Husserl, Descartes first appears positively as a phenomenologist. In other words, the authority of Husserl, especially after the reversal of 1907, invested Descartes with a phenomenological dignity of such a kind that any discussion concerning Descartes amounts to a discussion with Husserl; more exactly, any discussion of the Cartesian theses that were legitimated by Husserl is equivalent to a theoretical discussion of Husserl himself. The equivalence between Descartes and (Husserlian) phenomenology can thus be developed in two absolutely opposed directions; either Descartes is a phenomenologist because he anticipates Husserl; or else Husserlian phenomenology is not fully phenomenological because it remains imprisoned by uncriticized, even undiscerned, Cartesian decisions. Very early on, Heidegger will follow the second direction: his departure from the Husserlian interpretation of phenomenology is carried out through a critique of the Cartesian presuppositions in it. Descartes will undergo a critique, but a critique that is addressed also and first at Husserl, who is all the less a phenomenologist insofar as he remains more a Cartesian. Descartes thus arises as the nonphenomenological motif in Husserl.

Thus, in the summer of 1925, the *History of the Concept of Time: Prolegomena* attempts an "immanent critique of phenomenological research" by examining how the latter determines pure consciousness. In other words,

> Our [i.e., Heidegger's] question will be: Does this elaboration of the thematic field of phenomenology, the field of intentionality, raise the question of the *Being of this region*, of the *Being of consciousness*? What does *Being* really mean here when it is said that the sphere of consciousness is a sphere and region of *absolute* Being? What does *absolute Being* mean here? What does Being mean when we speak of the Being of the transcendent world, of the reality of things? . . . Does phenomenology anywhere really arrive at the methodological ground enabling us to construct [*stellen*] this *question of the meaning of Being*, which must precede any phenomenological deliberation and is implicit in it? . . . As the basic field of intentionality, is the region of pure consciousness determined in its Being, and how?![8]

One should notice that here, in 1925, Heidegger addresses to Husserl and to the region of consciousness the same question and, in fact, the same critique that he addressed already in 1921 to Descartes and to the *ego cogito*: to establish the epistemological priority of the ego and of consciousness is an achievement, but it does not free one from having to determine the ego's mode of Being. Descartes is repeated with Husserl, not only positively with the illumination of the condition for any certitude in knowledge, but also negatively, with the forgetful evasion of the mode of Being peculiar to originary certitude. To be sure, Husserl encountered and noted, between consciousness and the reality of the world, "an unbridgeable difference of essence [*ein unüberbrückbar Wesensunterschied*]," "a veritable abyss of meaning [*ein wahrer Abgrund des Sinnes*]." But for all that, can he see therein only the divergence from "a necessary and absolute Being [*ein notwendiges und absolutes Sein*]"? In short, in order to think an epistemic divergence is it sufficient to name an ontic-ontological divergence, as if from the irreducibility of consciousness to what it constitutes there ensued, for this very reason, "the principial difference among ways of Being, the most important that there is in general, that between *consciousness* and *reality* [*die prinzipielle Unterschiedenheit der Seinsweisen, die kardinalste, die es überhaupt gibt, die zwischen* Bewußtsein *und Realität*]"?[9] It would have been necessary that Husserl not at all restrict himself to repeating the epistemic terms of the opposition—the absolutely certain because knowing consciousness, opposed to the reality that is contingent and relative because known—and undertake to elaborate the respective ways of *Being* of the two terms; but he reasons, in order to outline these two ways of Being, within a pair—certitude, contingency—that belongs entirely to the mode of Being which is solely that of the reality of the world, and which therefore has to do entirely with Being understood as permanent subsistence in the present. Like Descartes, Husserl is confined within the Being of the reality that is proper (or rather *im*proper) to consciousness, such that he evades the supposedly principial question of its way of Being; for its epistemic primacy, consciousness thus pays, so to speak, the price of an implicit but total submission to the way of Being of reality, and therefore of the world. Husserl carries out such a desertion of the question of the Being of consciousness only by relying explicitly on Descartes. Indeed, he cites Descartes textually in order both to define and to obscure consciousness' way of Being: "Immanent Being is also indubitably in the sense of absolute Being, in that in principle *nulla 're' indiget ad existendum* [*Das immanente Sein ist zweiffellos in dem Sinne absolutes Seins, dass es prinzipiell nulla 're' indiget ad existendum*]."[10]

Several remarks are necessary here. (1) Husserl undoubtedly does claim to define consciousness' way of *Being*, since he deduces absolute Being from immanent Being. (2) In order to reach his end, he cites the authority of Descartes, *Principia Philosophiae*, I, § 51: "*Per substantiam nihil aliud intelligere possumus, quam rem quae ita existit, ut nulla alia re indigeat ad existendum* [By *substance* we can understand nothing other than a thing which exists in such a way as to depend on no other thing for its existence]."[11] The meeting between these two thinkers certainly owes nothing to chance, since, already in agreement in recognizing the epistemic primacy of the ego, they meet again to define its way of Being by substantiality. (3) Husserl, however, modifies Descartes's formula: he omits *alia* in "*alia re*" and accepts *res* only between quotation marks: "*nulla 're.'* " Why? Obviously because *alia* (*res*) would imply that consciousness was itself and first a *res*; but Husserl undertakes here precisely to oppose consciousness to *realitas*; therefore, in defiance of any philological probity, he must modify what, in the quotation from Descartes, would implicitly extend *realitas* to the *res cogitans*, in order to retain from it only the application of substantiality to the ego. (4) This adjustment and therefore this difficulty already prove that Husserl utilizes in Descartes an insufficient and unsuitable definition; and in fact, for Descartes substantiality covers not only the *res cogitans* but even (although not without difficulties) all of the *res extensa*; therefore, it contradicts—far from confirming—the Husserlian privilege of consciousness: "*... substantia corporea et mens, sive substantia cogitans...* [... corporeal substance and mind, or thinking substance ...]" (*Principia Philosophiae*, I, § 52).[12] A second contradiction might be added, moreover: all finite substance, thinking as well as extended, admits, for Descartes, a radical indigence with regard to the ordinary support of God; because of this, substantiality, which the ego must share with extension (first disagreement with Husserl), has only a relative validity (with respect to God) and not at all an absolute validity (second disagreement with Husserl). (5) These gaps do not call into question Husserl's intimate familiarity with Descartes; they prove, on the contrary, that the fundamental convergence had more power than any divergence in detail.[13] Such an exemplary encounter—Husserl citing Descartes to attempt to determine consciousness' way of Being—could not have escaped the attention of Heidegger. In fact, the same course from 1925 points out Husserl's formula and identifies it with precision as a reprise of Descartes. It can then stigmatize the ontological insufficiency of the reprise: immanence, indubitability, and absoluteness in no way allow one to think the *Being* of consciousness: "This third determination—absolute Being—is not in its turn such that it determines being itself in its Being, but such that it grasps the region of consciousness within the order of constitution and assigns to it in this order a Being that is formally anterior to any objectivity."[14] The Cartesian definition does not allow one to ground the difference of regions—which is ontological. Heidegger reduces to nothing the effort and the textual adaptations that Husserl imposes on Descartes's formula; here, it is Heidegger who defends the orthodoxy of the Cartesian text, precisely because it is conceptually opposed to Husserl. And what is more, Heidegger continues: not only does Husserl lose his way in reprising and forcing an unsuitable answer from Descartes, not only does he shy away from the authentic determination of consciousness' way of Being by believing himself to satisfy such a determination through the simple reprise of Cartesian certitude, but he goes astray even more radically in assuming a Cartesian question that he has not legitimated phenomenologically.

> Husserl's primary question is simply not that concerning the character of the Being of consciousness [*nach dem Seinscharakter des Bewußtseins*]. Rather, he is guided by the following concern: *How can consciousness in general become the possible object of an absolute science?* What guides him primordially is the *idea of an absolute science*. But this idea, that *consciousness*

must be the region of an absolute science, is not simply invented; it is the idea which has occupied *modern* philosophy ever since *Descartes.* The elaboration of pure consciousness as the thematic field of phenomenology is *not derived phenomenologically by going back to the things themselves* but by going back to a traditional idea of philosophy (nicht phänomenologisch im Rückgang auf selbst gewonnen, *sondern im Rückgang auf eine traditionelle Idee der Philosophie*).[15]

Let us measure the scope and acuity of Heidegger's critique of Husserl. (1) The question of the way of Being of consciousness receives no answer, because Husserl remains dependent on Descartes. (2) Husserl, evading the authentically phenomenological difficulty of the Being of consciousness, privileges the nonphenomenological ideal of a certain science of consciousness; we are therefore not far here from the parricidal declaration put forth by the same course: "In the basic task of determining its ownmost field, therefore, phenomenology is *unphenomenological!*"[16] (3) If Husserl distances himself from phenomenology, he owes this to the persistence in him of the Cartesian ideal as *mathesis universalis* and *universalissima sapientia,* defined already in the *Regulae.*[17] Far from guiding him along the phenomenological path, as Husserl thinks, Descartes played the notable role—from Heidegger's point of view—of *holding* Husserl *back* on the phenomenological path; between Husserl and full phenomenology, thus between Husserl and Heidegger, stands Descartes, a unique obstacle and stumbling block. The "affinity" that unites Husserl with Descartes[18] therefore designates a unique phenomenological obstacle, which phenomenology must surmount in order to remain itself; henceforth, in order to advance along the phenomenological path that Husserl leaves, Heidegger will have not only to leave Husserl but to "destroy" the one who held Husserl back—Descartes himself.

Thus can we better understand why Descartes occupies so much of Heidegger's attention: the chronological importance of the debate that he provokes ensues from the phenomenological radicality of the question that he poses—precisely by not posing it. To think Descartes means, for Heidegger, certainly not to repeat the establishment of the ego, as was attempted, each in his own way, by Hegel, Schelling, and Husserl, or even to overturn it like Nietzsche, but to destroy it in order to make appear, as the phenomenon that it hitherto concealed, the mode of Being of the ego (or of what is supposed to take its place) such as it is distinguished from the mode of Being of inner-worldly beings. Destroying the ego is not reducible to abolishing it ontically, but undertakes to free its ontological dignity—in short, destroying the *ego* opens access to *Dasein.* In this sense, within Heidegger's thought Descartes has no other privilege than that of the obstacle par excellence that prohibits the ontological fulfillment of phenomenology by blocking it with the ego and by thus masking *Dasein*.

3. The First Omission: The Indetermination of the "Ego Sum"

In 1927, and consistent with what has been outlined since 1921, Descartes intervenes in *Sein und Zeit* as "a supreme counter-example." A counterexample, exactly an extreme countercase (*Gegenfall*) of the ontological problematic of worldhood, Descartes therefore pushes phenomenology to its final extremity by failing to recognize the way of Being of the beings of the world; but this being the case, he calls into question—such as we shall see—the way of Being of all beings, beginning with *Dasein*. Indeed, "since the interpretation of the world first begins with an intra-worldly being, in order then to lose sight completely of the phenomenon of the world, let us try to clarify ontologically this point of departure by considering perhaps the most extreme development to which it ever led [*in seiner vielleicht extremsten Durchführung*]," namely the Cartesian ontology of the world. In this extremity, moreover, it is also a question of "the phenomenological destruction of the '*cogito sum*,'" which Heidegger announces, as the third part of his debate with Descartes, after §§ 19–20, just outlined in § 21 and put off to the unpublished "Second Part, Division 2."[19] In fact, the reproach addressed to Descartes applies to two omissions, that with respect to the world, and that also with respect to the ego, whose two ways of Being are missed equally, if in different ways. It is necessary to remark, moreover, that the reproach made to Descartes precedes the famous analysis of the *res extensa* from §§ 18–21,[20] where there is only a first confirmation, appearing first with regard to the *cogito sum*, already in the introduction to *Sein und Zeit*; this one holds, let us stress, for the entire plan announced in § 8, and therefore also for the unpublished part. The principle that institutes subjectivity within all of modern philosophy displays two characteristics: it claims to announce an absolutely certain beginning and, at the same time, it misses the thought of Being by masking the *esse* in the *sum* which is itself still left unthought under the shadow cast by the ego, which is alone thought in evidence: "In the course of this history, certain privileged domains of Being have come into view and have served as the primary guides for subsequent problematics (the *ego cogito* of Descartes, the subject, the *I*, reason, spirit, the person). But these domains, consistent with the complete omission [*Versäumnis*] of the question of Being, remain uninterrogated as to Being and the structure of their Being." Or again:

In taking over Descartes' ontological position Kant made an essential omission [*ein wesentliches Versäumnis*]: he failed to provide an ontology of Dasein. This omission was a decisive one in the spirit of Descartes' ownmost tendencies. With the "*cogito sum*" Descartes had claimed that he was putting philosophy on a new and firm footing. But what he left undetermined [*unbestimmt*] in this "radical" beginning was the mode of Being of the *res cogitans*, or more precisely the *meaning of the Being of the "sum"*. The elaboration of the implicit ontological foundations of the *cogito sum* is what marks the second stage along the path of the destructive return toward the history of ontology. Our interpretation not only proves that Descartes had necessarily to omit [*versäumen*] the question of Being in general, but it even shows why he was able to suppose that the absolute "Being-certain" of the *cogito* exempted him from raising the question of the meaning of Being of that being.[21]

Several remarks become unavoidable here. (1) In its § 6, *Sein und Zeit* questions Descartes first and above all with regard to the meaning of the Being of the *sum*; or rather, the Cartesian omission of the meaning of Being in general is indicated first and above all in the *ego cogito*; only the order of the first part and the absence of the second can give the reader the feeling that, within his debate with Descartes, Heidegger privileges the doctrine of the *res extensa*. With regard to this, one is dealing only with a particular failure (to think the phenomenon of the world), which is inscribed in the universal failure to think the way of Being of beings and, to begin with, of *Dasein*. (2) Nevertheless, the *ego cogito* and the *res extensa* offer to the phenomenological destruction undertaken by *Sein und Zeit* the case of two comparable "omissions": Descartes fails to recognize the ego's way of Being because he sticks to the certitude of its existence, without distinguishing a particular epistemic category from an ontologically determined existential; and if he sticks here to certitude, it is because he limits himself to transposing it into the ego starting from the domain where he first experienced it epistemically, the object of methodical science, extension. For if epistemically the object depends on the ego according to a tacit and undefined ontology (a gray ontology, let us say), the ego borrows from the *res extensa* in order to carry out its own interpretation through certitude. In all cases, the two "omissions" go hand in hand, displaying the same insufficiency: the indetermination of the meaning of Being. (3) The two dimensions of this single insufficiency anticipate exactly the two regions distinguished by Husserl: the absolute region of consciousness, on the one hand, and the relative region of worldly things, on the other. And just as Descartes fails to think them as such, so Husserl fails to think their respective meanings of Being. It is therefore suitable to take up and to specify the two failures of which *Sein und Zeit* accuses Descartes as integral parts of the "destruction" of the history of ontology and therefore, positively, to understand them again as a breakthrough beyond the phenomenological obstacle presented by Descartes.

Habitually taken as the thinker of the *cogito sum*, Descartes could therefore more properly be characterized by a radical inability to think that very same *cogito sum*, or at least to think the *sum* on the basis of the *esse*; on the contrary, Descartes reduces *sum* to *cogito* and *cogito* to *sum*. The ego itself is characterized only by an epistemic determination—that of the absolutely certain first principle which renders possible the certain knowledge of other beings. The extension of certitude, which goes from the known being back to the knowing ego, satisfies the generalized requirements of method only by leaving proportionally indeterminate and shadowy the question of the meaning of Being for the ego. The more that epistemic certitude invades ever more extended domains of being so as to render them homogenous as so many *cogitata*, the more the whole of being betrays the deep indetermination in which it is left by the forgetting of any interrogation concerning what, each time, Being means for each being or each domain of beings. This first affects the ego, which, by absorbing, so to speak, the *esse* in the *sum* and the *sum* in itself, assures in itself only its own ontological failure. This indetermination marks the first and radical omission of Descartes: ". . . a total ontological indetermination of the *res cogitans sive mens sive animus*"; or again: "Descartes, to whom one attributes the discovery of the *cogito sum* as the point of departure for modern philosophical questioning, examined—within certain limits—the *cogitare* of the *ego*. On the other hand, he leaves the *sum* totally unelucidated [*unerörtet*], even though he posits it just as originally as the *cogito.*"[22] By stigmatizing such an indetermination, Heidegger in no way contests, however, the certitude of the knowledge of the ego as *cogito*; it is even very remarkable that he never engages in the debate, as common as it is facile and lazy, to call into question the certitude of the reasons that end up demonstrating the first, absolutely indubitable and necessary existence of the *ego* as *cogito*. Heidegger contests an entirely different point—namely, that epistemic certitude, which delivers the ego as the first certain object for the knowledge that, finally, the ego itself *is*, should suffice to determine ontologically the ego's characteristic way of Being. Through his very silence on this point, Descartes postulates the univocity of certitude (which keeps the same meaning and the same validity when it goes from known objects back to the knowing subject); that univocity is founded (like, moreover, the medieval *univocatio entis*) only on a deep indetermination. Or better: the certitude remains not only ontologically undetermined, but above all indifferent to the question bearing on the ways of Being of the meaning of Being. Descartes first claims that certitude applies in the same sense to the whole (nevertheless heterogeneous) series of *cogitatum-cogito-ego*; then he postulates that, just as the *cogitatum* is, ever since the gray ontology of the *Regulae*, supposed to find the correct determination of its mode of Being in certitude, so the ego requires no determination of the meaning of its Being other than, again, certitude alone. The certitude of the *ego cogito* therefore does not abolish the indetermination in it of the *sum* and of the *esse* but rather reinforces that indetermination. The evident certitude of the ego allows Descartes only to desert any interrogation of the mode of Being implied by that very certitude and leads him to consider the meaning of its Being as self-evident, evident by itself. "*Nota est omnibus essentiae ab existentia distinctio*," he responded to Hobbes.[23] Descartes thus not only omits the question of the meaning of Being of the *sum*; he masks this omission itself, in blinding himself with the epistemic evidence of the *cogito*. Descartes's first omission is accomplished by omitting itself.

This omission of the omission nevertheless decides the ego's way of Being, precisely because it does not explicitly determine that way of Being: if Descartes does not think its *sum* as such, he will think it implicitly on the model of intra-worldly being, following a "reflection [*Rückstrahlung*] of the understanding of the world on the explication of *Dasein*," for "*Dasein* . . . is inclined to fall [*verfallen*] upon the world where it is and to interpret itself reflectively [*reluzent*] on the basis of that world."[24] The way of Being of intra-worldly being thus becomes, precisely because there lacks any approach to the meaning of Being of the ego, the pole of attraction and of interpretation of the way of Being of intra-worldly being. The Cartesian ego (like, moreover, its substitutes and derivatives within the metaphysical tradition, up to and including its Husserlian avatar) differs essentially from *Dasein* in this: it is not according to its proper way of Being, and therefore it is not thought according to its proper way, but, first and always, it runs aground on intra-worldly being and imports upon itself intra-worldly being's improper way of Being. It is certainly an ego only by not being according to its Being—epistemic certitude, ontologically undetermined. The Cartesian ego is lost the very instant it finds itself and precisely because it finds itself in the mode of certitude.

4. The Second Omission: The Permanence of Intra-Worldly Being

The impropriety is here doubled, for just as the Cartesian interpretation of the ego omits its way of Being and also fails to understand this first omission; just as the absence of that interpretation delivers the ego to engulfment in the mode of Being of intra-worldly beings to which it nevertheless does not in principle belong; so finally the interpretation of the mode of Being of intra-worldly beings omits, in Descartes, the phenomenon of the world so as to substitute for it the univocal and minimal subsistence of presence-at-hand (*Vorhandenheit*). According to an analysis that is as well known as it is ambiguous and ephemeral,[25] the worldhood of the world is manifested less by the subsistence of beings present-at-hand (*vorhanden*) than by their play in the capacity of equipment that is manipulable and ready-to-hand; in this play, beings are defined by that for which they can serve (*um zu*), in a finality that, under the diverse aspects of interest, of utility, of function, of organization, etc., ultimately depends on "what it is all about" (*Bewandtnis*), and therefore on *Dasein* itself, which thus opens the world in its worldhood. The subsistence of being present-at-hand (*Vorhandenheit*) follows from *Zuhandenheit* only through the reduction and impoverishment of being ready-to-hand to the sole requirements of theory; the object required by the theoretical attitude must only remain, isolated as an atom of evidence, permanent as a perfect subsistence, neutralizing all finality as purely objective. The object of the theoretical attitude is obtained through reduction, abstraction, and method; it does not precede the being that is usable and ready-to-hand, but follows from it through impoverishment and elimination. That operation, which thus reverses the phenomenological preeminence of *Zuhandenheit* over *Vorhandenheit*, results from Descartes. The privilege that method accords to mathematical knowledge in fact does not rest for him on some intrinsic excellence of that science, but on its aptitude for reaching the certitude and permanent subsistence of an object; the primacy accorded to mathematics results, according to Descartes, from the privilege, immediately conceded to permanent subsistence alone, of certain objectivity as the sole meaning of intra-worldly being.

> What has a mode of Being of the kind that measures up to the Being that is accessible to mathematical knowledge *is* in the proper sense. That being is *what always is what it is*; this is why what constitutes the real Being of beings experienced in the world is that which has the character of *constant remaining* [*des ständigen Verbleibs*], as *remanens capax mutationum*. . . . Far from allowing the mode of Being of intraworldly beings to be given beforehand by those beings, Descartes, on the contrary, prescribes to the world its "veritable" Being on the basis of an idea of Being (Being = constant Being-present-at-hand [*Sein = ständige Vorhandenheit*]) that is no more legitimated in its own right than it is unveiled in its origin.

The permanence of being as an object present-at-hand, "*ständige Dingvorhandenheit*,"[26] establishes the meaning of Being of intra-worldly being only by degrading it in an acceptation that imposes certitude upon it, at the expense of the phenomenality of the world. The interpretation of being in general as permanent subsistence present-at-hand (*Vorhandenheit*) does not only omit the meaning of the Being of the ego by leaving the *sum* in it undetermined as such; it omits also and to begin with the meaning of the Being of intra-worldly being, of which it nevertheless claims to assure perfect knowledge. The two omissions come together in a common and more originary failure to think the Being of *any* being.

What assessment can the historian of philosophy—if at least, by a fragile hypothesis, he can be isolated from the philosopher—give of such an analysis and "destruction" of Descartes? Without launching into a more ample discussion that it would be necessary to carry out in another framework, we shall stick to three remarks.

1. Heidegger confirms that the *ständige Vorhandenheit* obfuscates and occupies the meaning of Being by raising the Cartesian interpretation of the *res extensa* as *substantia*, itself reduced to what *remanet* (= *verbleibt*) in any reduction.[27] This reference is obviously very exact; however, it masks another reference, which attributes permanence (*remanet*) first and directly to the ego before the *res extensa* itself; for, before asking "*Remanetne adhuc eadem cera?*" and responding "*Remanere fatendum est,*" thus before encountering the *res extensa* (which, it is necessary to repeat, does *not* intervene in the analysis of the piece of wax), Descartes had already reduced the ego to the *cogito* " . . . *ut ita tandem praecise remaneat illud tantum quod certum est et inconcussum.*"[28] If permanence characterizes certitude as the (missed) way of Being, then it would have to intervene already with the first certitude, and, in fact, it does indeed intervene with the existence of the ego; thus it is with respect to the ego that it would have been necessary to carry out the diagnostic of permanent subsistence: each time that it thinks, the ego remains. To miss such a Cartesian reference is surprising on the part of one who knows Descartes as precisely as Heidegger, and all the more insofar as this first remaining confirms, far from weakening, the whole thesis put forth by *Sein und Zeit*: *Vorhandenheit* does not determine only intra-worldly being, but flows back, through reflection (*Rückstrahlung*), upon the ego itself and closes all access for it to its true Being. One might respond, and quite rightly, that §§ 19–21, treating worldhood only such as Descartes misses it, did not have either to know or to mention a text treating the *Vorhandenheit* of the ego. However, even if one accepts this response, another question arises: Did Heidegger have to use the remaining of the ego, in the Second Part, Division 2, dedicated to the "ontological foundation of Descartes' 'cogito

sum' "?²⁹ Within this hypothesis alone, he would have taken more from a text that backs him up at the very moment when, apparently, he ignores it.

2. The omission of the meaning of Being in general is indicated in the Cartesian texts by the insufficiency of the doctrine of substance. On the one hand, Heidegger notes pertinently, substance is reputed as not affecting us directly, "... *non potest substantia primum animadverti ex hoc solo, quod sit res existens, quia hoc solum per se nos non afficit.*"³⁰ Thus, the investigation concerning substance turns straightaway toward an investigation concerning its principal attribute, while substance itself remains in principle unknown in itself. There follows a fundamental "equivocity" of the term,³¹ which confuses its ontological acceptation with its ontic acceptation, so as to evade all the more easily the complete desertion of the first and take refuge in the treatment of the second. The debate, to which Descartes gives priority, concerning the distinction between finite and infinite substance only reinforces the fundamental orientation toward the solely ontic acceptation of *substantia*; in no way does the Cartesian treatise on *substantia*, in *Principia*, I, §§ 51–54, take up the discussion, which is ontological at least in intention, of οὐσία by Aristotle in *Metaphysics* Z. This reproach of Heidegger to Descartes seems to us essentially justified.

The debate becomes deeper in a second critique, which is less visible but more important. In submitting the ontological to the ontic in *substantia*, Descartes necessarily confuses the ontological difference: "The ontic being substituted for the ontological, the expression *substantia* functions sometimes in the ontological sense, sometimes in the ontic sense, but most often in a confused ontico-ontological sense. But what is harbored in this imperceptible difference [*Unterschied*] of signification is the inability to master the fundamental problem of Being." To this *grundsätzliches Grundproblem*, Heidegger adds a note in his personal copy, a simple phrase, *ontologische Differenz.*³² A decisive addition! For it reveals that by obscuring the ontological within *substantia* Descartes first gave rise to the aporia wherein Husserl was supposed to be caught when he imagined himself able to distinguish substances (or "regions") solely by ontic criteria, without undertaking to distinguish their respective modes of Being (ontologically). It reveals, next, that Descartes failed to confront the difference between Being and beings, which alone would have allowed him to establish ontologically the distinction between beings or substances. The convergence of these two omissions—of the meaning of Being of the *ego*, and of the meaning of Being of intra-worldly being— flows finally from the original evasion before the ontological difference. The reintegration of Descartes within the history of metaphysics, through what *Sein und Zeit* as yet names only the "destruction of the history of ontology," had, moreover, to finish by revealing in him the essential trait of metaphysics: the failure to recognize the difference between Being and beings. Since in *Sein und Zeit* this difference remains implicit, though really at work, it stigmatizes Descartes only under the form of the two omissions of the meaning of Being of beings. That, however, is sufficient to bring out the ontologically Cartesian genealogy of Husserl's phenomenological insufficiencies—which it was a matter of showing.

3. Could one not, however, object to the analysis of *Sein und Zeit* that Descartes does indeed elaborate a thought of the world? Is not the worldhood of the world set up as an explicit problem to begin with when the *ego* asks itself whether it is alone in the world, "*me solum esse in mundo*,"[33] and then when it undertakes to prove the existence of the world in the Sixth Meditation? From these two references, one must on the contrary draw an argument in favor of the thesis of *Sein und Zeit*. In the first case, the ego reaches other possible beings only starting from itself, that is, from the *ideae* that it can have of such beings; thus representation determines them in advance as certain objects, and therefore according to subsisting persistence (*Vorhandenheit*), with God constituting no exception to this determination and, symptomatically, the other person finding in it no free place.[34] In the second case, the very fact that the "existence of the external world" must be proved constitutes—more than the absence of convincing proof which Kant deplored in taking up the Cartesian plan[35]—the real phenomenological "scandal"; for the world can owe its existence to such a proof only inasmuch as it is first reduced to the level of a representation that awaits actuality, that is, the level of *Vorhandenheit*. To prove (or not) the existence of the world presupposes that one has already neglected the worldhood of the world—its appearance within the phenomenological horizon.

The two omissions in Descartes therefore constitute only one—to have grasped "the Being of 'Dasein' . . . in the very same way as the Being of the *res extensa*—namely, as substance." Thus he determines Kant: "'Consciousness of my *Dasein*' means for Kant a consciousness of my Being-present-at-hand [*Vorhandensein*] in the sense of Descartes. When Kant uses the term '*Dasein*' he has in mind the Being-present-at-hand of consciousness just as much as the Being-present-at-hand of things [*sowohl das Vorhandensein des Bewußtseins wie das Vorhandensein der Dinge*]."[36]

5. "Dasein" as a "Destruction" of the "Ego"

Descartes's two omissions of the thought of the meaning of Being lead back therefore, in the end, to a single inability to think the Being of beings without recourse to *Vorhandenheit*; that inability itself results from the failure to recognize the ontological difference—at least understood according to its negative formulation: "Being can never be explained by beings."[37] The ego is set up by Descartes, and after him by Kant no less than by Hegel, as a being which is privileged to the point that it must account for all other beings and take the place of any meaning of Being in them; in short, it must guarantee them ontically and legitimate them ontologically. But at the same time, and in an increasing measure, its own meaning of Being remains, first of all, completely undetermined. The indetermination of the *ego cogito* in its mode of Being overruns all the other beings and deprives them of any ontological solidity—"the ontological groundlessness [*ontologische Bodenlosigkeit*] of the problematic of the Self [*Selbst*] from Descartes' *res cogitans* to the Hegelian concept of spirit." In other words, "if idealism signifies tracing every being back to a subject or to a consciousness having the distinctive privilege of remaining *undetermined* [*unbestimmt*] in their Being and of being able at the very most to be characterized negatively as 'non-things,' then that idealism is no less naive on the methodological level than the crudest realism."[38] Consequently, what separates Descartes (and those whom he made possible) from the question concerning the meaning of Being is exactly equivalent to what separates the *ego cogito* from *Dasein*. *Dasein* maintains within itself an echo of what the *ego* [*cogito*] already exhibits: *Da-*, here, in this unique place where all the rest can then take place; but with the *ego cogito* the rest has the status only of *cogitatum*, because I limit myself, or rather *I* is limited in the capacity of ego, to *cogitare*; on the contrary, starting from *Dasein*, the *Da-* accords to the rest of being nothing less than *sein*, nothing less than to be. There where the ego gives to be thought, or rather to make itself be thought (or even to make itself simple thought) without ever giving Being in a determinate and determining sense, *Dasein* gives Being by determining the way of Being of the other beings, because it itself, in advance and according to its privilege, determines *itself* to be according to its own way of Being. To be sure, the ego is, but it is without thinking about it, since it thinks only about thinking its thinkable things, whose respective ways of Being it does not establish any more than it is itself determined in its own way of Being; in thinking itself as being only through and for the exercise of the *cogitatio*, it masks, through the epistemic evidence of its nevertheless ontologically loose existence, and then through the certitude of the other subsistent truths, the total absence of decision concerning the Being of beings, which are reduced to the level of pure and simple *cogitata*. *Ego cogito*, not *ego sum*, nor *Dasein*—the very formula that Descartes privileges betrays what indetermination disqualifies it ontologically and the two omissions that it commits. From this point on, the whole interpretation of Descartes by *Sein und Zeit* would have to be thematizable within the sole opposition between the *ego cogito* and *Dasein*, consistent with the declaration of principle that "the *res cogitans*, which does not coincide with *Dasein* either ontically or ontologically. . . ."[39]

These oppositions remain to be developed. According to the first, ontically, the *res cogitans* does not coincide with *Dasein*; indeed, the *res cogitans* has only an ontic consciousness of itself (from the point of view of *Dasein*), whereas *Dasein* is not identified (from the point of view of the *res cogitans*) as being itself another *res cogitans*. Although Heidegger never presents this opposition explicitly, it can nevertheless be reconstructed, in at least three ways.

1. The ego is a *res* that shares the *realitas* of intra-worldly beings, whether they be present-at-hand or ready-to-hand; on the contrary, "the Being of *Dasein* was at the same time delimited in relation to [*abgegrenzt gegen*] modes of Being (Being-ready-to-hand, Being-present-at-hand, reality [*Zuhandenheit, Vorhandenheit, Realität*]) that characterize the being that is not to the measure of *Dasein*."[40] The *res* of the ego leads to the Husserlian impossibility of distinguishing effectively the region of consciousness from the region of the world; on the contrary, *Dasein* does not count among the real terms, nor does it admit anything real in itself, because it precedes and renders possible the mode of Being of reality.

2. The ego is defined by the absolute primacy in it of the theoretical attitude; it is born from doubt; but this very doubt becomes practicable only inasmuch as every immediate, urgent, useful, and necessary relation has disappeared: ". . . no conversation . . . no cares or passions," ". . . *curis omnibus exsolvi*." On the contrary, "scientific research is neither the only, nor the closest possible mode of Being of this being [i.e., *Dasein*]"; indeed, *Dasein* relates to the world in the mode of preoccupation, which manipulates and utilizes beings as ready-to-hand, and therefore without the least disinterest; the theoretical attitude befalls *Dasein* only after the fact and as through subtraction: "In order for knowing [*Erkennen*] to become possible, as a circumspective determination of the present-at-hand [*des Vorhandenen*], there must first be a *deficiency* in our preoccupied having-to-do with the world."[41] *Dasein* is not limited to maintaining the theoretical attitude, in rejecting the so-called "natural" attitude (in fact, the preoccupation that makes use of being inasmuch as ready-to-hand), but assures and passes beyond both, because, more radically, it is *Dasein* that, ontologically, first renders them possible.

3. Finally, the *res cogitans* is confined to the domain of the *cogitatio* and relegates to other *res* that of *extensio*, according to an almost irremediable caesura; consequently, the *res cogitans* escapes space, which it also

lets escape. *Dasein*, on the contrary, because it is not first defined by the representation of present-at-hand (*vorhanden*) being, does not exclude a fundamental spatiality. The "spatiality of *Dasein*" has to do with the de-severing (*Entfernung*) through which it abolishes the distance of a being with respect to itself; such a nullification of distance, and thus a de-severing, modulates the original ecstasy of *Dasein*, its Being-in-the-world. As opposed to the subject of idealism, issuing from the *ego cogito*, "the 'subject,' if well understood ontologically, *Dasein*, is spatial."[42] *Dasein* is neither nonextended in the way of the *ego cogito*, nor is it extended in the way of the material *res*: it is spatial, or, in other words, not nonextended. Thus, *Dasein*, by refusing to take on the common title of *res*, is not restrained in face of the *res cogitans* but on the contrary surpasses it, in not being limited either to the theoretical attitude or to nonextension. It is perfectly confirmed that, taken as a being, *Dasein* does not coincide with the *res cogitans*.

But, as the "ontic characteristic of *Dasein* consists in the fact that it *is* ontological," its ontic opposition to the *res cogitans* can only prepare the ontological distinction that distinguishes it from the *res cogitans* (this time on the basis of itself and not at all of the *res cogitans*). No doubt, the *res cogitans* can claim, like *Dasein*, a multifarious "primacy," but not such an "ontological primacy." On at least three points the opposition between them becomes irreducible.

1. In *Dasein*, its Being is at issue; it is peculiar to this being to have to decide on its mode of Being and, in that decision, not only is *its* (mode of) Being at issue, but *Being* as such, and therefore the mode of Being of other beings, which themselves do not have to decide on the one or the other.[43] *Dasein* maintains with itself a surprising relation of uncertainty: far from assuring itself of itself in knowing itself as such, it knows itself only in admitting what play is at play in it—the play of its Being or more exactly the play of Being put into play, always to be decided in the case of this privileged being. *Dasein* knows itself authentically only by recognizing itself as an undecided and all the more uncertain stake, which will never and must never be rendered certain. *Dasein* plays—in the sense that wood has play: it maintains a gap, an articulation, a mobility, in order that the fold of Being, everywhere else invisible, should unfold, turning on that being like a panel on a hinge. Such a play, in the end beyond both incertitude and certitude, decidedly opposes *Dasein* to the *ego cogito*. No doubt, Heidegger is textually wrong to characterize the *ego cogito* as *fundamentum inconcussum*; however, Descartes does indeed aim in it at a "*fundamentum, cui omnis certitudo niti posses*," at some "fairly solid foundations"; and Descartes does indeed wish it to be unshakable: "*minimum quid . . . certum et inconcussum*"; it is even notable that he thinks it

according to the persistence of *Vorhandenheit*: "*quid firmum et mansurum*"; even more, the ego itself immediately takes the form of a foundation, or better an autarchic and sufficient fund: "a fund that is entirely my own."[44] In thinking itself, the ego takes hold of itself as full owner; not only is incertitude overcome, but the certitude of the *fund*, henceforth definitive, will be extended to every other *cogitatum* to come; the ego, to be sure, decides itself, but in order to abolish all play in the certitude of self; and if in the future the ego decides other beings, it will be in order to reduce them, as so many *cogitata*, to its own certitude. Thus *Dasein* opens a play, that of the Being of other beings, through its own, there where the ego closes all incertitude, first in itself, and then in the *cogitata*.

2. *Dasein* exists, but existence is defined in its turn as possibility: "*Dasein* always understands itself in terms of its existence, in terms of a possibility of itself to be itself or not to be itself." To exist means: to be outside of oneself, in such a way as to be only in the mode of being-able-to-be, in accordance with the stakes that essentially establish *this* being in a fundamental play with its Being, and therefore with Being itself; existence implies the ecstasy of *Dasein* outside of itself in the play of Being on which it is up to *Dasein* to decide. When the *res cogitans* grabs hold of itself with certitude in saying "*ego sum, ego existo*,"[45] it immediately interprets its *sum*, and therefore its Being, as an existence. Is it a matter of the existence that characterizes *Dasein*? On the contrary, specifies Heidegger: "if we choose existence to designate the Being of this being [i.e., *Dasein*], this term does not and cannot have the ontological signification of the traditional term *existentia*; *existentia* is ontologically [exactly] tantamount to Being-present-at-hand [*Vorhandensein*], a mode of Being that is essentially foreign to the being that has the character of *Dasein*." Is it necessary to prove that Descartes in fact understands *existentia* as the counterpart simply of possible essence, which it abolishes in certain and univocal permanence? He himself does not even define existence, insofar as he considers it as self-evident. "*Neminem enim unquam extitisse tam stupidum crediderim, qui prius quid sit existentia edocendus fuerit, antequam se esse concludere potuerit atque affirmare.*"[46] For the *ego cogito, existentia* means entrance into *Vorhandenheit*; for *Dasein*, existence signifies exit from self and transcendence with regard to *Vorhandenheit*, in order to enter into the possibility that, definitively, it is.

3. Finally, "it belongs essentially to *Dasein* to be in the world." Contrary to its Husserlian limit, intentionality is not restricted to the theoretical attitude because the relation to the world does have to do first with the constitution of things; intentionality is broadened and radicalized to the point of opening the *I*, immediately and from itself, to something like a world; thus alone can the Being of other beings be

at issue in a being. This critique of Husserl, which in an important way motivated the publication of *Sein und Zeit* and which runs throughout the whole work, is also valid against Descartes, by virtue of the "affinity" that unites them. Descartes, indeed, reaches the *ego cogito* on the hypothesis of its independence with respect to the whole possible world; the ego appears in fact when and on condition that the beings of the world disappear under hyperbolic doubt; the ego is thus defined as "a substance whose whole essence or nature is simply to think, and which does not require any place, or depend on any material thing, in order to exist."[47] Thus Heidegger is perfectly well founded in speaking (with regard to Husserl and Kant, and thus also with regard to Descartes) of a "worldless I [*weltlose Ich*]," of a "worldless subject [*weltlose Subjekt*]."[48] The classic difficulties of an opening to the world in Cartesianism do not have to be recalled here; they would sufficiently confirm the diagnostic given by Heidegger. Thus *Dasein* in no way rediscovers itself in the *res cogitans*, since the ego could be defined on the basis of *Dasein* as its strict reverse: the being for whom its own Being is *not* an issue. Reciprocally, *Dasein* could be defined, on the basis of the *ego cogito*, as its reverse: the being that is *not* inasmuch as it thinks (itself). *Dasein* therefore maintains with the *ego cogito* a relation of "destruction."

6. "Dasein" as a Confirmation of the "Ego"

Such a relation of "destruction," however, would not make any sense if there were not in the ego, such as it limits itself to thinking, already an ontology; for the "destruction" always bears on "the history of ontology." It is therefore necessary to presuppose for the ego a metaphysical situation, which inscribes it within the history of the ignored ontological difference; there follows a reexamination of the case of the *ego cogito* such as it still deploys a figure of the Being of being, although in an obscure and forgetful mode. But this historical (or rather historial) presupposition would not have any legitimacy if the *ego cogito* could not establish its ontological pertinence, even inauthentic and obfuscated, no longer in the course of the history of ontology but in the "new beginning"; if only to maintain its hermeneutic role toward and within metaphysics, the *ego* must keep in itself a reserve and potentiality of Being. It remains to be examined, therefore, whether *Sein und Zeit* does justice, if only partially, to these two postulations of the *ego cogito*.

From the—dominant—point of view of its "omission," the Cartesian ego is absolutely denied the manifestation of the meaning of Being, a property that characterizes *Dasein* alone. The ontico-ontological antagonism between the *ego cogito* and *Dasein* appeared clearly enough (§ 5 above) that, without insisting on it or weakening it, we would nevertheless counterbalance it with the remark of another relation between these same antagonists. To be sure, the *ego cogito* presents itself to *Dasein* as its most rigorous adversary; and yet *Dasein* would not have such an urgent need to destroy it if *Dasein* did not find in it, as in a delinquent outline, some of its own most characteristic traits: indeed, *Dasein* cannot not recognize itself in at least four characteristics of the *ego cogito*, according to a rivalry that is all the more troubling insofar as the similitudes only sharpen it.

1. *Dasein* "does not have an end [*Ende*] at which it just stops, but it *exists finitely* [*existiert endlich*]"; finitude is not added as if from the outside to an existence which, thus, simply would not have an indefinite (*endlose*) duration; it essentially determines *Dasein*, which is only for a term, its own death, according to a temporality of the future; marking Being-toward-death, finitude opens access for *Dasein* to its characteristic ecstatic temporality, according to the privilege of the future, in opposition to the temporality of *Vorhandenheit*, which privileges the present as remaining. But the *ego cogito* is just as well characterized by finitude: "*cum sim finitus*";[49] this finitude does not have only an anthropological function (the ego has to die, it lacks several perfections, etc.) but a quasi-ontological function; indeed, finitude alone provokes doubt, and thus opens up the *cogitatio*, which in its turn establishes the beings of the world as so many *cogitata* to be constituted; the finitude of the ego thus directly determines the meaning of Being for beings other than the ego. The pertinence of this *rapprochement*, of course, remains hidden to and by Heidegger, since he envisages the finitude of the ego only within the horizon of "the anthropology of Christianity and the ancient world"[50] and reduces the relation between finite substance and infinite substance to an efficient production, so as to deny Cartesian finitude an originary validity. It nevertheless remains that the ego can establish both itself as *cogito* and, indissolubly, the beings of the world as *cogitata*, only because it *is* according to an essential finitude; moreover, Heidegger's later meditation on the *cogitatio* (representation, *Vorstellung*) will continually develop this implication. Therefore, *Dasein* confirms the ego according to finitude.

2. There is more: *Dasein* is that being for whom Being is an issue only on the express condition that that Being be its own, in person: "its essence lies rather in the fact that in each case it has its Being to be, and has it as its own [*es je sein Sein als seiniges zu sein hat*]"; or again: "That Being which is an issue for this being is in each case mine. . . . Because *Dasein* has *in each case mineness* [*Jemeinigkeit*], one must always use a *personal* pronoun when one addresses it: 'I am,' 'you are.' "[51] *Dasein*

could not be itself, namely the one to whom it characteristically belongs to put itself into play as a being with Being for its stakes, except in a personal capacity; no one can play the role of *Dasein* in place of anyone else; the function of *Dasein* does not allow any failure to appear; even if it is a "you are" that is the *Dasein*, this *you* will itself also have to say "I am"; *Dasein*, even and especially played by another than myself, is played in the first person because it must be played in person. Thus, even if *Dasein* does not say *ego cogito* to begin with, it can say *-sein* only by saying "ich bin," and therefore "*ego sum.*" *Dasein* therefore inevitably speaks, at least once, *like* the *ego cogito*: "*ego sum*," "I am." This meeting appears absolutely decisive. Indeed, Descartes did not simply inaugurate the tie between *cogitatio* and existence in a "subject"; he tied them in a "subject" that itself is always interpreted (in the theatrical sense of the term) in the first person, or better, as a character (*persona*, also theatrical) that one must perform in person (still theatrically) by assuming the function of an "I"—by *saying* "I," "hoc pronunciatum, *Ego.*"[52] The successors of Descartes will tend, on the contrary, to eliminate this involvement of and with the ego; either by replacing the first formula with another, which no one any longer has to perform exclusively: "*Homo cogitat*" (Spinoza); or else they will abolish it, either by subtraction (Malebranche), or by generalization (Leibniz). Descartes is distinguished, therefore, not only by the necessary relation between the two simple natures (*cogitatio* and *existentia*), but above all by the performance of their necessary tie by the irreplaceable ego. Existence befalls man only inasmuch as he thinks, but above all inasmuch as he thinks in the position of the ego. Thus Descartes approaches fairly well the irreplaceability that characterizes *Dasein*. Therefore, *Dasein* confirms the ego according to mineness (*Jemeinigkeit*).[53]

3. The finitude and irreplaceability of *Dasein* befall it as the being for whom its Being is an issue; that way of Being falls to it by virtue of its Being-toward-death, for death is its ownmost, its most absolute, and its least surmountable possibility; indeed, "death [is] the possibility of the pure and simple impossibility of *Dasein.*"[54] For its death, *Dasein* finds itself exposed to its own and final impossibility, as much because death remains to us ontically inconceivable (unimaginable), as because death puts an end to the possibility that *Dasein* is (even more than to its possibility to "do" this or that thing). Now, the *ego* knows a similar paradox, not, to be sure, with regard to its death, but with regard to its freedom; for possibility opens up, in Cartesian terms, with the free will, the only infinite formally in the finite *res cogitans*. This free will uncovers its impossibility when it confronts the divine omniscience and omnipotence, which annihilate the very notion of the possible; in such a meeting, the *ego cogito* does not only confront the impossibility of (free)

possibility, which nevertheless imposes itself according to theory; it also meets the possibility of impossibility, since it decides, in the practical order, to act as if it could act freely, even though it does not understand how it can. In each action, the *ego cogito* comports itself as if it were free and as if the impossible (an event not necessarily predetermined by God) again became open to the possible. The possibility of the impossible can therefore be understood of freedom as of Being-toward-death. Thus, *Dasein* confirms the ego again according to the possibility of impossibility.

Even if one admits that these convergences rest on indisputable textual bases, it would nevertheless still seem dangerous, or even specious, to pretend to draw from them as a consequence an essential homogeneity between the ego and *Dasein*. No formal similarity seems to counterbalance the critique bearing on the ontological indetermination of the *ego cogito* supposedly established in principle by Descartes: "What he left undetermined [*unbestimmt*] when he began in this 'radical' way, was the kind of Being which belongs to the *res cogitans*, or—more precisely—the *meaning of the Being of the 'sum.'* " A "complete ontological indetermination [*völlig ontologische Unbestimmtheit*]" not only gives rise to a "non-determination [*Nichtbestimmung*] of the *res cogitans*," but it even leaves "the *cogitationes* ontologically undetermined [*unbestimmt*]." If ontologically the ego and *Dasein* differ as the undetermined and the determined, is it not necessary simply to conclude that, from the strictly ontological point of view of *Sein und Zeit*, they differ absolutely?

4. But it is precisely this indetermination that, far from leading to an opposition without mediation, will suggest a fourth convergence that draws the ego near to *Dasein* at least as much as it first seemed to separate them. For *Dasein* itself—and this is precisely why the existential analytic is required—frees itself only slowly from an inevitable indetermination. Thus, when it is a matter of responding to the existential question concerning the *who* of *Dasein*, the suspicion immediately arises that "the ontological horizon for the determination of the being that is accessible in pure and simple givenness remains fundamentally undetermined [*unbestimmt*]." Even more, "the Being of *Dasein* remains [itself] ontologically undetermined [*unbestimmt*]"[55] insofar as the sole determining phenomena of anxiety and care do not intervene. Therefore, the indetermination that is denounced in the *ego cogito* concerns *Dasein* just as much—at least provisionally, until the analysis of anxiety; to escape ontological indetermination remains a formidable task, whether one is dealing with *Dasein* or the ego, to the point that the final section of *Sein und Zeit* (§ 83) could allow one to suppose that a sufficient determination of the horizon of givenness has not yet been attained.[56] But there is more: the indetermination put forward against the ego and affecting

Dasein as an insufficiency can also receive a positive phenomenological characterization at certain decisive moments within the elucidation of *Dasein*. In other words, the indetermination can sometimes become an ontological determination, when it manifests the disappearance of any determination of *Dasein* by beings. Such a reversal can be located in at least three circumstances.

1. During the experience of *anxiety*, *Dasein* suffers an absolutely indistinct mood, for "that before which anxiety is anxious is totally undetermined [*das Wovor der Angst ist völlig unbestimmt*]. Not only does this indetermination [*Unbestimmtheit*] leave factually undecided what intraworldly being threatens, but it signifies that in general it is not intraworldly being that is 'relevant.' " Anxiety therefore deploys a mood that is "totally undetermined" (in the very terms first put forward against the ego) whereby *Dasein* no longer confronts this or that being, but precisely the impossibility of identifying any being in face of which to flee; the fact that no determinate being can any longer come to determine anxiety as a specific fear determines the nothing as such; thus, "the peculiar indetermination of that alongside which *Dasein* finds itself in anxiety comes to expression: the nothing and the nowhere."[57] In short, through the ontic indetermination of anxiety, *Dasein* reaches its ontological determination; its transcendence with regard to being is accomplished only through radical ontic indetermination (the nothing); only thus can it be determined in its Being.

2. In Being-toward-death, the indetermination reappears in an indisputably phenomenological function. Indeed, death implies, precisely so that and because it is certain, a temporal indetermination: "Along with the certainty of death goes the indetermination [*Unbestimmtheit*] of its *when*." It is precisely the conjunction of the certainty of death with its indetermination that opens it up as the possibility of *Dasein*: "*Death, as the end of Dasein, is Dasein's ownmost possibility—non-relational, certain and as such indeterminate [gewisse und als solche unbestimmte], not to be outstripped.*" This indetermination—of dying—"originarily opens in anxiety," because it is equivalent to the "*indetermination [Unbestimmtheit] of being-able-to-be*," such as it characterizes and therefore determines ontologically the being that can be resolute because it exists—"the indetermination [*Unbestimmtheit*] that rules a being that exists." Not to be determined amounts, for *Dasein*, to being only in the mode of existence, through resoluteness and according to possibility—in short, it is equivalent to being determined ontologically.

3. In the analysis of conscience as call and care, the phenomenological "positivity" of indetermination is explicitly recognized: "The indetermination and indeterminability [*Unbestimmtheit und Unbestimmbarkeit*] of

25

the caller [*Rufer*] is not nothing, but a *positive* characteristic." In fact, it is resoluteness itself, such as it frees and sums up all the prior existentials, that imposes an essential indetermination—that of existence as such: "To resoluteness necessarily *belongs* the *indetermination* [*Unbestimmtheit*] that characterizes any factically thrown Being-able-to-be of *Dasein*. Resoluteness is sure of itself only as decision. However, existentiel *indetermination*, being determined in each case in decision alone, possesses its *existential determinateness* [*existentiale Bestimmtheit*] from resoluteness."⁵⁸ One must therefore hold as established that the ontic indetermination of *Dasein* assures it, precisely, its ontological determination, as the being that decides *itself* with nothing of beings. *Dasein* decides *itself* through its own resoluteness only inasmuch as nothing of beings determines it and inasmuch as it does not determine itself as a being. Related to the initial objection made to the ego, what does the "positive" indetermination of *Dasein* signify? At the very least it signifies that the debate is not played out between indetermination and determination, but between, on the one hand, an ontological indetermination (ego, ontically determined) and, on the other hand, an ontic indetermination (*Dasein*, ontologically determined by this very possibility). The opposition therefore concerns two indeterminations; the one, ontic, positively assures *Dasein* of determining itself in its Being, while the other, ontological, negatively leads the ego not to be determined in its Being. But does this conflict suffice to disqualify the ego definitively? Nothing is less sure, as soon as it belongs essentially to *Dasein* to give itself first as the *They* and to miss itself as such. Everything happens henceforth as if, even in its indetermination, the ego were miming *Dasein*, in the way that the *They* mimes, in the inauthentic mode, the authentic *Dasein* to which it essentially belongs.

Thus ego and *Dasein* meet according to finitude, *mineness*, the possibility of the impossible, and indetermination. That their similarities remain separated, or even opposed, according to authenticity and inauthenticity does not suffice to alienate them one from the other—since this final opposition belongs entirely to the existence of *Dasein*. It does not seem so easy to decide phenomenologically between the ego and *Dasein* as strict strangers. But what mime still unites them?

7. The Repetition of the "Ego"

What are we to deduce from these conditional confirmations? No doubt that the "destruction" of the *res cogitans* would never have shown such an urgency, already with the introduction to *Sein und Zeit*, and then throughout the whole work, if *Dasein* had not been able to recognize itself so easily therein; the ego appeared to *Dasein* like a failure, but first as its own failure, and therefore above all as a danger whose fascination imposes its norms and against which it is necessary to resist better than did Husserl. In the ceaseless struggle to mark *Dasein* off from the *ego cogito*, *Sein und Zeit* therefore had step by step to locate the *ego cogito*'s insufficiencies, highlight its decisions, and invert its orientations; such a confrontation, as warlike as it is, cannot avoid a sort of mimetic rivalry, where the victor sometimes appears, under some aspect, to be vanquished by the vanquished. In short, the *ego cogito*, precisely because *Sein und Zeit* does not cease to reject it, there appears all the more enigmatic in itself and all the more intimately tied to *Dasein*. The analytic of the one, because it advances only with the "destruction" of the other, confirms its undecided validity. This paradoxical conclusion could indeed have first been that of Heidegger:

> If the *ego cogito* is to serve as a point of departure for the existential analytic, there would have to be not only a reversal [*Umkehrung*], but even a new ontologico-phenomenologico-phenomenal confirmation (*Bewährung*) of its tenor. The first statement would then be "sum," in the sense of "I-am-in-a-world." As such a being, "I am" in the possibility of Being toward various attitudes [*cogitationes*] as [so many] modes of Being alongside intra-worldly beings. Descartes, on the contrary, says that *cogitationes* are present-at-hand [*vorhanden*] and that in them there is conjointly present-at-hand an *ego* as worldless *res cogitans*.[59]

It is amazing that at the end of the preparatory analytic of *Dasein* and after the essential part of its "destruction" of Descartes, Heidegger still outlines the possibility of a retranscription of the analytic of *Dasein* in the terms—to be sure, displaced and reinterpreted—of the Cartesian ego. Its historial figure doubtless must have exercised a powerful fascination in order that, surviving its historical avatars and its phenomenological critique, it should still be referred to. The confirmation here accorded the *cogito sum* can be justified phenomenologically only if, in a way still to be determined, the formal statement consigned by Descartes can be rendered manifest under the aspect of another phenomenon than that to which Descartes, and therefore also Kant and Husserl, limited themselves. Concerning the possibility of such a confirmation of what nevertheless has just suffered a reversal, it can be a matter only of repeating, in a non-Cartesian mode, Descartes's *ego cogito sum*. As strange as it may appear, the plan of such a repetition has nothing of the *hapax* about it, not only because *Sein und Zeit* attempted to see it through, but also because even the last seminars still formulate it: "The paragraphs dedicated to Descartes in *Sein und Zeit* constitute the first attempt to exit from the prison of consciousness, or rather no longer to reenter it. It is not at all a matter of reestablishing realism against idealism, for by limiting itself to assuring that a world exists for the subject, realism remains a tributary of Cartesianism. It is rather a matter of managing to think the Greek meaning of the ἐγώ." To overcome the ego in the direction of the ἐγώ was no doubt what Heidegger undertook topically by commenting on Protagoras and stressing his irreducibility to Descartes.[60] But had he not, beforehand, accomplished this more radically through the analytic of *Dasein*—a non-Cartesian and perhaps already more than Greek ego?

And in that case, must one not recognize definitively that in *Sein und Zeit*, in the "destruction" of the ego's Cartesian acceptation, the ego not only does not definitively disappear, but is born for the first time to its authentic phenomenological figure? Even more, would not the "new beginning" be inaugurated with the declension of the ego according to the not metaphysical, but existential, requirements of *Dasein*? It is therefore necessary to examine how the ego-hood of the ego can attain its phenomenological—that is, its non-Cartesian—legitimacy.

Given *Dasein*: How does it differ essentially from the beings that are not in its mode? In the fact that it is the being for whom its Being is an issue, that is, the being for whom Being is in each case its own. But, since "the Being which is an issue for this being in its Being is in each case mine," it is necessary to admit that "the claim of *Dasein*, in accordance with this being's characteristic *mineness*, must always speak the *personal* pronoun: 'I am,' 'you are.' " Because it brings the Being in it into play, *Dasein* can only put *itself* into play, and therefore it can express itself only in person, since it can bring itself into play only as an *I*: "I myself am in each case [*bin ich je selbst*] the being that we call *Dasein*, and I am so as a being-able-to-be for whom it is a matter of Being that being."[61] Here, the possibility of saying "I am," and therefore of declining *Being* in the first *person* results from *Dasein*'s property of bringing itself *in person* into the play of its own Being. The *I* would have neither interest nor legitimacy if, in the capacity of an "existential determination of *Dasein*," it did not have to be and could not be "interpreted existentially," that is, if "'I'-hood and ipseity were not conceived existentially." But these two terms do not remain equivalent, as if the one could be substituted for the other. On the contrary, their existential interpretation demands that "the self [*Selbst*] which the reticence of resolute existence unveils be the originary phenomenal ground for the question of the Being of the 'I.' Only the phenomenal orientation concerning the meaning of the Being of authentic being-able-to-be-oneself [*Selbstseinkönnen*] puts the meditation in the position of being able to elucidate what ontological right might be claimed by substantiality, simplicity, and personality as characteristics of ipseity [*Selbstheit*]."[62] Selfhood (ipseity, *Selbstheit*) alone renders possible, through its absolute coincidence with self, what might be expressed by no matter what *personal* pronoun, and it therefore assures the *I* of any possible "I am" its authentic possibility; if the Self did not determine the *I*, no being would be such that it might in itself bring itself into play in its very Being—precisely because no *same* would then be accessible. Conversely, in its position as They, *Dasein* claims to stick to the *I*, itself the mere "appearance of a Self [*scheinbare Selbst*]."[63] The I can therefore say "I am" with perfect existential legitimacy only if it is reduced to the essential phenomenon of the Self (*Selbst*). But the Self becomes visible and given only in the phenomenality of care (*Sorge*); indeed, "the expression 'care of self' [*Selbstsorge*] . . . would be a tautology";[64] in all care, it is indeed precisely of itself, with respect to other beings, that *Dasein* takes care: it cares only for itself, or rather all care concerns itself with other beings only by virtue of the care that the Self thus shows to take of itself. In this context, the "I am" finds a proper phenomenological site—it puts into operation the Self's care of itself, according to care as the Being of *Dasein*. The "I am" intervenes, therefore, in order to mark the mineness of *Dasein*—"I am in each case myself [*bin ich je selbst*] the being that we call *Dasein*, and I am so as a being-able-to-be for whom that Being is an issue."

Next it intervenes more precisely in order to develop the phenomenon of debt (*Schuld*): "But where will we find the criterion for the originary existential meaning of the 'in debt' [*schuldig*]? [Answer:] the essential here is that the 'in-debt' arises as the predicate of the 'I am' [*ich bin*]." In the end, it is finally the whole opening of *Dasein* that, through resoluteness, is at play with and in the "I am": "Henceforth, what is attained with resoluteness is the more originary, because authentic, truth of *Dasein*. The opening of the There co-originarily opens the Being-in-the-world that is in each case total, that is, the world, Being-in, and the Oneself that this being is as an 'I am' [*als 'ich bin'*]."[65] Not only does the "I am" not always imply the ontological indetermination of the *sum* in which Descartes founders, but it offers the most visible phenomenon for reaching the Being of *Dasein*, the care that establishes the Oneself. For the unique *I* can be developed phenomenologically in two opposite ways, which are inscribed precisely in the two postures offered to *Dasein*, authenticity and inauthenticity; thus the *I* opens itself to two statures, since "the ontological concept of the subject characterizes *not the ipseity of the I as Self* [*die Selbstheit des Ich qua Selbst*], *but the identity and the constancy* [*Selbigkeit und Beständigkeit*] *of a being that is always already present-at-hand*

29

[*Vorhanden*]." One could not say it more clearly: the *I* can manifest itself either as the identical constancy of substance, and therefore in the mode of a being of the world, and even of a being present-at-hand (persistent and subsistent), or, on the contrary, as and starting from the Self, and therefore from the mineness that puts *Dasein* into play in its Being.

The *I* therefore turns from the status of (subsistent) *res cogitans* to that of the "I am" according to whether it pertains to identity (*Selbigkeit*) or to the Self (*Selbstheit*). The unique *I* sustains resoluteness, in the very sense that *Dasein* does not cease to be at play in it: in order to decide on the way of Being of its Being. How does the *I* indeed reach its non-Cartesian status? By opposing to the ontological indetermination, and therefore also to the existential irresoluteness of inauthentic fallenness, "the ipseity [*Selbstheit*] . . . that is discerned existentially in authentic being-able-to-be, that is, in the authenticity of *Dasein's* Being *as care* [*Sorge*]." Taken starting from care, ipseity could not persist as a *res*; if it offers a "constancy of the Self [*Ständigkeit des Selbst*]," a "self-constancy [*Selbst-Ständigkeit*]," it does so not because the Self "is a constantly present-at-hand ground of care [*ständig vorhandene Grund*]," but because the Self does not cease to resolve itself authentically according to and on the basis of its most proper Being: "Existentially, Self-constancy [*Selbst-Ständigkeit*] signifies nothing other than anticipatory resoluteness."[66] The conclusion becomes unavoidable: the *I* can just as well have to be "destroyed" as to be able to be "confirmed," according to whether it is repeated by one or the other of the possible determinations of *Dasein*; either inauthentically, in the Cartesian way of the persistent and subsistent *res cogitans*; or authentically, in the way of anticipatory resoluteness, of the structure of care, of the mineness of *Dasein*. The "I think" therefore no longer appears as a metaphysical thesis to be refuted, among others, in order to free up the phenomenon of *Dasein*, but as the very terrain that *Dasein* must conquer, since no other terrain will ever be given to *Dasein* in which to become manifest. *Ego cogito, sum* states less a countercase of *Dasein* than a territory to occupy, a statement to reinterpret, a work to redo.

Between the ego and *Dasein*, between Descartes and Heidegger, therefore, it would be a matter, beyond the patent critique, of a struggle for the interpretation of the same phenomenon—"I think," "I am." This placement of the two interlocutors on the same level leads one first to recognize them as interpreters of one another, more essentially than as interpreter and interpreted. But it also leads one to allow a new question to arise. If the *I* is determined ontologically only in the measure of ipseity (*Selbstheit*), such as it is set into operation in care, it becomes legitimate to formulate two questions. (1) Is the *I* of "I am" in fact determined entirely by ipseity? In turn, is the latter defined sufficiently and exclusively by the structure of care? Does that same ipseity reach all beings or only the beings that are on par with *Dasein*? And in that case, what other determination takes over for it for the other beings?[67] These questions are internal to the undertaking of *Sein und Zeit*. (2) There are others that go beyond *Sein und Zeit*, like this one: Even granting that it is attested more essentially as an "I am" than as an "I think," is the *I* that is to be determined exhausted for all that in its status as the *I* of a *sum*? In other words, does the *I* attest to its ultimate ground and does it reach its final phenomenality in its function as an "I am," fulfilled phenomenologically in "*Da-sein*"? Is the putting into play of the self by itself that characterizes the *I* devoted only to Being? Or indeed, in the *I* that I undoubtedly am, is not something also, or even first, at stake other than to be? Is what is put into play in, through, and in spite of the *I* exhausted necessarily, indisputably, and exclusively in terms of Being? Is it Being that is first at issue in the *I*, or, beyond that, is a more original stake at play? Is it permitted, despite the silence of *Sein und Zeit*, to pose this very question?

Can There be an Epistemology of Moods?

STEPHEN MULHALL

By entitling her recent collection of essays on philosophy and literature *Love's Knowledge*,[1] Martha Nussbaum signals her commitment to giving a positive answer to the question posed by the title of this paper. If love can deliver or lay claim to knowledge, then moods (the variety of affective states to which human nature is subject) must be thought of as having a cognitive significance, and so must not only permit but require the attentions of the epistemologist. As Nussbaum points out, such a conclusion runs counter to a central strand of thinking in both ancient and modern philosophy. The rational or cognitive side of human nature is often defined in contrast to its affective or emotional side, the latter being understood as having no role to play in the revelation of reality. On the contrary, where reason and the senses can combine to disclose the way things are, moods typically cloud that cognitive access by projecting a purely subjective colouration onto the world and leading us to attribute properties or qualities to it which have at best a purely personal and internal reality.

Nussbaum contests this understanding of the passions through her reading of Aristotle's moral philosophy. According to that reading, emotions are composites of belief and feeling, shaped by developing thought and highly discriminating in their reactions; they can lead or guide an agent, picking out objects to be pursued or avoided, working in responsive interaction with perception and imagination. Anger, for example, requires and rests upon a belief that one has been wronged or damaged in some significant way by the person towards whom the anger is directed; the discovery that this belief is false can be expected to remove the anger. Furthermore, the acceptance of certain beliefs is not just a necessary condition for emotion but a constituent part of it—even a sufficient condition for it; if one really accepts or takes in a certain belief, one will experience the emotion—experiencing the emotion is necessary for full belief. If a person believes that X is the most important person in her life and that X has just died, she will feel grief; and if she does not, this must be because in some sense she doesn't fully comprehend or has not taken in or is repressing these

[1] Oxford University Press, 1990.

facts. This cognitive dimension to the structure of emotions leads Nussbaum to conclude that the passions are intelligent parts of our ethical agency, responsive to the workings of deliberation and essential to its completion. There are certain contexts in which the pursuit of intellectual reasoning apart from emotion will actually prevent a full rational judgment—by, for example, preventing access to one's grief or love, without which a full understanding of what has taken place is not possible.

Since, however, Nussbaum's main concern is with moral philosophy and literature, she does not develop her general claim about the cognitive dimension of emotions in any detail, and she manages to suggest (however unwittingly) that the knowledge love can provide primarily concerns the person whose passion it is rather than the world that person inhabits, and that it is a primarily ethical species of knowledge. In the essay which gives her collection its title, for example, the knowledge that Proust's Marcel acquires by his love—the knowledge that that love constitutes—is the knowledge that he loves Albertine; it is, in other words, a species of self-knowledge that reveals his capacity for self-deception. In this lecture, I want to explore the question of whether the passions might be considered to have a cognitive function which goes beyond the realm of the ethical, and which is more than reflexive in its focus. My primary guide in this exploration will be the Heidegger of *Being and Time* (BT).[2] In that early, unfinished work, Heidegger argues that moods are one aspect of the way in which human mode of being (what Heidegger refers to as 'Dasein' or 'there-being') discloses or uncovers the world we inhabit; and, perhaps most notoriously, he rests fundamental claims about the nature of both human beings and their world on a highly detailed epistemological analysis of the specific moods of fear and anxiety. I intend to argue that these claims and arguments prefigure and underpin more recent work in the Anglo-American philosophical tradition, reveal important weaknesses in the still highly influential Kantian conception of epistemology, and imply that a radical revision of our conception of the role and nature of philosophical thinking is called for. In so doing, I will deploy and elaborate ideas and arguments developed by Stanley Cavell in his work on Wittgenstein and Emerson.

I. Fear: Subjectivity and Self-Interpretation

Heidegger's analysis of moods in *Being and Time* is embedded in a broader analysis of the ways in which Dasein's relation to its world

[2] Trans. J. Macquarrie and E. Robinson (Blackwell, Oxford, 1962).

Can There be an Epistemology of Moods?

is a comprehending one. He underlines this by claiming that, insofar as we think of our commerce with the world as a relation between subject and objects, then Dasein is the Being of this 'between'. In other words, Dasein is not trapped within a mind or body from which it then attempts to reach out to objects, but is rather always already outside itself, dwelling amidst objects in all their variety. Dasein's thoughts, feelings and actions have entities themselves (not mental representations of them) as their objects, and those entities can appear not merely as environmental obstacles or as objects of desire and aversion, but in the full specificity of their nature, their mode of existence (e.g. as handy, unready-to-hand, occurrent, and so on), and their reality as existent things. This capacity to encounter and disclose entities *as* the entities they are is what Heidegger invokes when he talks of Dasein as the clearing, the being to whom and for whom entities appear as they are. This disclosedness is seen as having two aspects or elements, 'Befindlichkeit' and 'Verstehen' (standardly translated as 'state-of-mind' and 'understanding' respectively); and the former picks out what Heidegger thinks of as the ontological foundation for—that which makes it possible for human beings to experience—moods.

What Heidegger labels 'Befindlichkeit' is an essentially passive or necessitarian aspect of Dasein's disclosure of itself and its world. The standard translation of 'Befindlichkeit' as 'state-of-mind' is seriously misleading, since the latter term has a technical significance in the philosophy of mind which fails to match the range of reference of the German term. Virtually any response to the question 'How are you?' or 'How's it going?' could be denoted by 'Befindlichkeit' but not by 'state-of-mind'; the latter also implies that the relevant phenomena are purely subjective states, thus repressing Heidegger's constant emphasis upon Dasein as Being-in-the-world, as an essentially worldly or environed being. 'Frame of mind' is less inaccurate, but still retains some connotation of the mental as an inner realm; so it seems best to interpret 'Befindlichkeit' as referring to Dasein's capacity to be affected by the world, to find that the entities and situations it faces *matter* to it, and in ways over which it has less than complete control.

The most familiar manifestation of this underlying ontological or existential structure is what Heidegger calls the phenomenon of 'Stimmung' (standardly translated as 'mood'). Depression, boredom and cheerfulness, joy and fear, are affective inflections of Dasein's temperament that are typically experienced as 'given', as states into which one has been thrown—something underlined in the etymology of our language in this region. We talk, for example, of moods and emotions as 'passions', as something passive rather than active, something that we suffer rather than something we inflict—where 'suffering' signifies not pain but submission, as it does when we talk of Christ's Passion or of His suffering little children to come unto Him. More generally, our affections do not just affect others but mark our having been affected by others; we cannot, for example, love and hate where and when we will, but rather think of our affections as captured by their objects, or as making us vulnerable to others, open to suffering.

For human beings, such affections are unavoidable and their impact pervasive; they constitute a fundamental condition of human existence. We can, of course, sometimes overcome or alter our prevailing mood, but only if that mood allows, and only by establishing ourselves in a new one (tranquillity and determination are no less moods than depression or ecstasy); and once in their grip, moods can colour every aspect of our existence. In so doing, according to Heidegger, they determine our grasp upon the world: they inflect Dasein's relation to the objects and possibilities amongst which it finds itself—one and all being grasped in relation to the particular, actualized existential possibility that Dasein presently *is*. In this sense, moods are disclosive: a particular mood discloses something (sometimes everything) in the world as mattering to Dasein in a particular way—as fearful, boring, cheering or hateful; and this reveals in turn that, ontologically speaking, Dasein is open to the world as something that can affect it.

As we have seen, however, it is easier to accept the idea that moods disclose something about Dasein than that they reveal something about the world. Since human beings undergo moods, the claim that someone is bored or fearful might be said to record a simple fact about her; but her mood does not—it might be thought—pick out a simple fact about the world (namely, that it is, or some things within it are, boring or fearsome), for moods do not register objective features of reality but rather subjective responses to a world that is in itself essentially devoid of significance. In short, there can be no such thing as an epistemology of moods. Heidegger wholeheartedly rejects any such conclusion. Since moods are an aspect of Dasein's existence, they must be an aspect of Being-in-the-world—and so must be as revelatory of the world as they are of Dasein. As he puts it:

> A mood is not related to the psychical... and is not itself an *inner condition* which then reaches forth in an enigmatical way and puts its mark on things and persons... It comes neither from 'outside' nor from 'inside', but arises out of Being-in-the-world, as a way of such Being. (BT, 29: 176)

Heidegger reinforces this claim with a more detailed analysis of fear as having three basic elements: that in the face of which we fear, fearing itself and that about which we fear. That in the face of which we fear is the fearful or the fearsome—something in the world which we encounter as detrimental to our well-being or safety; fearing itself is our response to something fearsome; and that about which we fear is of course our well-being or safety—in short, ourselves. Thus, fear has both a subjective and an objective face. On the one hand it is a human response, and one which has the existence of the person who fears as its main concern. This is because Dasein's Being is, as Heidegger puts it, an issue for it—for human beings, the nature and form (and so the continuation) of their existence is a question for them rather than something determined by their biological nature; living is a matter of taking a stand on how to live and of being defined by that stand. The disclosive self-attunement that such moods exemplify confirms Heidegger's earlier claim that Dasein's capacity to encounter objects typically involves grasping them in relation to its own existential possibilities. On the other hand, however, Dasein's Being is put at issue here by something in the world that is genuinely fearsome, that poses a threat to the person who fears; and this reveals not only that the world Dasein inhabits can affect it in the most fundamental ways, that Dasein is open and vulnerable to the world, but also that things in the world are really capable of affecting Dasein. The threat posed by a rabid dog, the sort of threat to which Dasein's capacity to respond to things as fearful is attuned, is not illusory.

Even the relation of moods to those undergoing them—what I have been calling the subjective side of the question of moods—should not be understood in an unduly subjective way. For Heidegger, Dasein's Being is Being-with—its relations with others are internally related to its own individual existence; accordingly, its individual states not only affect but are affected by its relations to others. This has two very important consequences. First, it implies that moods can be social: a given Dasein's membership of a group might, for example, lead to her being thrown into the mood that grips that group, finding herself immersed in its melancholy or hysteria. This point is reinforced by the fact that Dasein's everyday mode of selfhood or individuality is what Heidegger calls the they-self—a mode of existence in which the thoughts and opinions of others determine our sense of who we are, in which our individual answerability for our own existence has been displaced upon or swallowed up by whatever we deem to be the common or agreed-upon way of living one's life. 'Publicness, as the kind of Being that belongs to the "they", not only has in general its own way of having a mood, but needs moods and "makes" them for itself' (BT, 29: 178). A politician determining judicial policy on the back of a wave of moral panic is precisely responding to the public mood.

The socialness of moods also implies that an individual's social world fixes the range of moods into which she can be thrown. Of course, an individual is capable of transcending or resisting the dominant social mood—her own mood need not merely reflect that of the public; but even if it does not, the range of possible moods open to her is itself socially determined. This is because Dasein's moods arise out of Being-in-the-world, and Heidegger understands that world as underpinned by a set of socially-defined roles, categories and concepts; but it means that the underlying structure even of Dasein's seemingly most intimate and personal feelings and responses is socially conditioned.

This Heideggerian idea underpins Charles Taylor's notion of human beings as self-interpreting animals.[3] Taylor follows Heidegger's tripartite analysis of moods, arguing that an emotion such as shame is related in its essence to a certain sort of situation (a 'shameful' or 'humiliating' one), and to a particular self-protective response to it (e.g. hiding or covering up): such feelings thus cannot even be identified independently of the type of situations which give rise to them, and so can be evaluated on any particular occasion in terms of their appropriateness to their context. But the significance of the term we employ to characterize the feeling and its appropriate context is partly determined by the wider field of terms for such emotions and situations of which it forms a part; each such term derives its meaning from the contrasts that exist between it and other terms in that semantic field. For example, describing a situation as 'fearful' will mean something different according to whether or not the available contrasts include such terms as 'terrifying', 'worrying', 'disconcerting', 'threatening', 'disgusting'; the wider the field, the finer the discriminations that can be made by the choice of one term as opposed to another, and the more specific the significance of each term. Thus, the significance of the situations in which an individual finds herself, and the import and nature of her emotions, is determined by the range and structure of the vocabulary available to her for their characterization. She cannot feel shame if she lacks a vocabulary in which the circle of situation, feeling and goal characteristic of shame is available; and the precise significance of that feeling will alter according to the semantic field in which that vocabulary is embedded.

[3] See *Philosophical Papers* (Cambridge University Press, 1985).

Can There be an Epistemology of Moods?

It is not that the relationship between feeling and available vocabulary is a simple one. In particular, thinking or saying does not make it so: not any definition of our feelings can be forced upon us, and some we gladly take up are inauthentic or deluded. But neither do vocabularies simply match or fail to match a pre-existing array of feelings in the individual; for we often experience how access to a more sophisticated vocabulary makes our emotional life more sophisticated. And the term 'vocabulary' here is misleading: it denotes not just an array of signs, but also the complex of concepts and practices within which alone those signs have meaning. When one claims that, for example, no-one in late twentieth-century Britain can experience the pride of a Samurai warrior because the relevant vocabulary is unavailable, 'vocabulary' refers not just to a set of Japanese terms but to their role in a complex web of customs, assumptions and institutions. And because our affective life is conditioned by the culture in which we find ourself, our being immersed in a particular mood or feeling is revelatory of something about our world—is cognitively significant—in a further way. For our feeling horrified (for example) then not only registers the presence of something horrifying in our environment; it also shows that our world is one in which we can encounter the specific complex of feeling, situation and response that constitutes horror—a world in which horror has a place.

This is why both Taylor and Heidegger claim that the relationship between a person's inner life and the vocabulary available to her is an intimate one; and since that vocabulary is itself something the individual inherits from the society and culture within which she happens to find herself, the range of specific feelings or moods into which she may be thrown is itself something into which she is thrown. How things might conceivably matter to her, just as much as how they in fact matter to her at a given moment, is something determined by her society and culture rather than by her own psychic make-up or will-power. It is this double sense of thrownness that is invoked when Heidegger says: 'Existentially, a state-of-mind implies a disclosive submission to the world, out of which we can encounter something that matters to us' (BT, 29: 177).

If we return to the objective side of the question of moods, Heidegger's analysis of fear as potentially revelatory of the way things are in reality—his argument against what might be called a projectivist account of moods—is strongly reminiscent of one developed by John McDowell.[4] In essence, the projectivist is

[4] See J. McDowell, 'Values and Secondary Qualities', in T. Honderich (ed.), *Morality and Objectivity: Essays in Honour of J. L. Mackie* (London: Routledge, 1985).

struck by the fact that when we characterize something as boring or fearful, we do so on the basis of a certain response to it, and concludes that such attributions are simply projections of those responses; but in so doing, she overlooks the fact that those responses are to things and situations in the world, and any adequate explanation of their essential nature must take account of that. So, for example, any adequate account of the fearfulness of certain objects must invoke certain subjective states, certain facts about human beings and their responses. However, it must also invoke the object of fear—some feature of it that prompts our fear-response: in the case of a rabid dog, for example, the dangerous properties of its saliva. Now, of course, that saliva is dangerous only because it interacts in certain ways with human physiology, so invoking the human subject is again essential in spelling out what it is about the dog that makes it fearful: but that does not make its fearfulness any less real—as we would confirm if it bit us.

The point is that there are two senses in which something might be called subjective: it might mean 'illusory' (in contrast with veridical), or 'not comprehensible except by making reference to subjective states, properties or responses' (in contrast with phenomena whose explanation requires no such reference). Primary qualities like length are not subjective in either sense; hallucinations are subjective in both senses; and fearfulness (like secondary qualities and moral qualities, in McDowell's view) is subjective only in the second sense. In other words, whether something is really fearful is in an important sense an objective question—the fact that we can find some things fearful when they do not merit that response (eg house spiders) shows this; and insofar as our capacity to fear things permits us to discriminate the genuinely fearful from the non-fearful, then that affective response reveals something about the world.

II. Heidegger and Kant: Objectivity and Externality

It might be thought that the case so far marshalled against the projectivist has been given more plausibility than it deserves by our exclusive focus on the example of fear. Like love and anger, fear is a response to specific situations or objects, and so can be more easily characterized as responsive to aspects of those situations or objects; but if we shifted our focus from emotions to phenomena that might be more naturally characterized as moods—depression, boredom, despair, cheerfulness, tranquillity—their links to specific circumstances are acknowledged to be far more tenuous and indirect (if indeed they have any such links at all) and so make it more difficult to characterize their colorations of our world as revelatory of reality.

A key point about such moods is, of course, the passive or necessitarian mode of their advent which we mentioned earlier; we experience them as something into which we can be thrown or thrust without warning or control, neither their onset nor their dissolution necessarily triggered by any particular event in either our minds or our world. It seems natural, therefore, to regard them as entirely subjective phenomena—as psychological or affective filters temporarily and arbitrarily imposed on our experience, and to which we must submit without allowing them to deceive us into thinking that they reveal anything other than our own mental state. This same sense of submissiveness is, however, precisely what leads Heidegger to *reject* the projectivist idea that they are purely subjective or inner phenomena. As he puts it: 'A mood assails us. It comes neither from "outside" nor from "inside", but arises out of Being-in-the-world, as a way of such Being' (BT, 29: 176). In other words, insofar as moods do assail us, then they can as legitimately be thought of as coming from outside us as from inside us. This suggests not only that they cannot be regarded as wholly subjective; it also, and more fundamentally, implies that moods put the very distinction between inside and outside, subjectivity and objectivity, in question.

We can best explore the implications of this suggestion by relating Heidegger's conception of moods to Kant's famous and highly influential attempt to explicate and anchor the distinction between subjectivity and objectivity in human experience in the Second Analogy of the *Critique of Pure Reason*.[5] Kant begins by noting that we distinguish in our experience between the order in which our senses represent different states of an object (the subjective temporal order) and the order of those successive states in the object itself (the objective temporal order). For example, when I successively perceive the various parts of a house, I do not judge that my perception of its basement must either succeed or precede my perception of its roof; but when I perceive a ship sailing downriver, I do judge that my perception of it upstream must precede my perception of it further downstream. Since, however, according to transcendental idealism, I never apprehend objects in themselves but only successive representations of objects, I can judge that certain sequences of representations represent changes of state in the object (that is, I can experience an event) only if I can regard their order as irreversible—only, that is, if I subject them to

[5] Trans N. Kemp-Smith (London: MacMillan, 1929).

Stephen Mulhall

an *a priori* temporal rule (the schema of causality). As a condition of the possibility of the experience of an objective succession, this schema is also a condition of the succession itself (as an object of possible experience). In short, the schema has 'objective reality'; its application alone makes possible both the experience of an objective temporal order and (of course) the experience of a merely subjective temporal order. In its absence, the very distinction between inner and outer orders of experience would have no ground.

This line of argument has famously been criticized by Strawson as depending upon a '*non sequitur* of numbing grossness'.[6] On his account, Kant begins from the conceptual truth that in the perception of causal sequence of states A–B, the observer's perceptions must follow the order: perception of A–perception of B; but he then illicitly presumes that this conceptual necessity in the order of perceptions of an event establishes the causal necessity of the relevant event. In other words, Kant can only reach his conclusion about the objectivity of the causal order by distorting both the location and the kind of necessity invoked in his premise. I trust that it is by now equally well-known that Strawson's criticism itself depends upon a profound misunderstanding of Kant's argument. As Allison has demonstrated,[7] Kant is not assuming that the subjective order of our perceptions is a datum or given piece of evidence, from which we must attempt to draw inferences about a putative objective order of events. To do so would be to occupy the position of a transcendental realist, someone who treats objects as things in themselves which exist independently of, although constituting the causal origin of, our experience; but Kant explicitly argues that such a person could not account for the possibility of an objective temporal order, since any such order would by definition be entirely independent of the subjective order of representations to which the transcendental realist thinks we are restricted. Neither is Kant an empirical or dogmatic idealist, someone who thinks that objects are nothing more than constructions from subjective representations or sense data—that only subjective representations are real.

When Kant talks of 'the subjective order' to which the schema of causality is applied, he is rather speaking as a transcendental idealist, and so must be considering it not as something introspected or actually represented, but as the indeterminate preconceptualized material for sensible representation; it is what would remain if

[6] In *The Bounds of Sense* (London: Routledge, 1966), p. 137.

[7] H. Allison, *Kant's Transcendental Idealism* (New Haven: Yale University Press, 1983).

(*per impossibile*) we could remove the determinate structure imposed on the sensibly given (the manifold of inner sense) by the understanding. His claim is that if all we had were this indeterminate subjective order, we would not be able to represent any temporal order at all (whether subjective or objective); since however, we can do so, that manifold must be conceptually ordered by the understanding by subsuming it under a rule. As Kant puts it, 'I render my subjective synthesis of apprehension objective only by reference to a rule in accordance with which the appearances in their succession, that is, as they happen, are determined by the preceding state' (A 195/B 240).

In other words, this subjection of perceptions to a rule is not the means for making the perceptions themselves into objects, but rather the basis for conceiving of a distinct, objective temporal order in and through these perceptions. Kant does not claim that the subjective order of perceptions is itself causally necessary, and that this property is the basis for our inferring that these perceptions reflect a causal necessity in the successive states of the object they represent. Any such property could only be recognized if the order of perceptions is already conceptualized and thereby made into an object for introspection, which in turn presupposes that it is distinguishable from an objective temporal order; but the recognition of this property is supposed to be the condition for the possibility of making such a distinction. The irreversibility to which Kant refers is thus not that of a given perceptual order, which we can inspect and then infer that it is somehow determined by the object; it is the conceptual ordering of the understanding through which the understanding determines the thought of an objective succession. Prior to this conceptual determination there is no thought of an object at all, and so no experience.

Given that Kant's transcendental perspective is not touched by Strawson's criticisms, might the conception of experience which grounds its explication of subjectivity and objectivity be otherwise put in question? We can return to the main thread of my discussion by noting that Heidegger's interpretation of moods as assailing us entails that those aspects of our experience are not tractable by the distinction between the subjective succession of apprehension and the objective succession of appearances that Kant proposes. As Stanley Cavell has put it, discussing a passage of Emerson:[8]

> The fact that we are taken over by this succession, this onwardness, means that you can think of it as at once a succession of

---

[8] Attributed to Emerson by Cavell; cf. 'Thinking of Emerson', in *The Senses of Walden* (SW) (San Francisco: North Point Press, 1981).

> moods (inner matters) and a succession of objects (outer matters). This very evanescence of the world proves its existence to me; it is what vanishes from me. (SW, p. 127)

Kant claims that the possibility of distinguishing an objective from a merely subjective order of experience is anchored in an irreversibility or necessity of succession imposed on the manifold of inner sense by its subsumption under a rule; to judge that we have perceived an event—a change of state in an object of experience—we must judge the order of our perceptions of those states as necessary. But when we experience an alteration of mood—our present cheerfulness assailed by the onset of depression, or fearfulness resolving into boredom—we experience that alteration as something to which we are irreversibly or necessarily subjected; according to Kant's argument, we must therefore regard it as both a subjective succession (something to which we are subjected) and an objective one (something imposed upon us from without). On these terms, we must conclude that the successions of our moods track transformations in the world as well as transformations in our orientation within it. When, for example, our apprehension of the world as a cheerful place is annihilated by a sudden apprehension of it as dreadful, we find ourselves inhabiting a new world as well as a new stance towards that world; as Wittgenstein once put it, the world of the unhappy man is not that of the happy man. The evanescence of our mood—our inability to credit our lost sense of good cheer—is matched by the evanescence of the cheerful or cheering world it revealed; and this mutual exclusion of moods and of worlds itself reveals something about both—that the world and our moods are mutually attuned, and that both can slip from our grasp.

One way of expressing this attunement would be to say that moods must be taken as having at least as sound a role in advising us of reality as sense-experience has—that judging the world to be dreadful or boring may be no less objective (and of course, no less subjective) than judging an apple to be red or green. As Cavell puts it: 'sense-experience is to objects what moods are to the world' (SW, p. 125). The problem with the Kantian attempt to ground the distinction between subjective and objective orders of experience is that it is exclusively geared to sensory experience of objects and not to such experiences as moods; and by relying upon an impoverished conception of experience, it is fated to generate a correspondingly impoverished conception of the reality which that experience reveals. In particular, it accommodates the fact that our experience is of objects whilst failing properly to accommodate the fact that those objects are met with in a world.

Can There be an Epistemology of Moods?

The basic principle of Kant's transcendental idealism is that 'the conditions of the *possibility of experience* in general are likewise conditions of the *possibility of the objects of experience*' (A 158/B 197); and the twelve categories of the understanding give us those conditions. But the implication of Heidegger's and Cavell's accounts of moods is that these categories—functioning as they do to relate our representations of objects to one another—articulate our notion of 'an object (of nature)' without articulating our sense of externality; more precisely, they articulate my sense of each object's externality to every other (making nature a whole, showing it to be spatial), but not my sense of their externality to me (making nature a world, showing it to be habitable). Instead, that idea of objects as being in a world apart from me is registered in Kant's concept of the thing-in-itself; and the problem is that that concept (or the concepts which go into it—the concepts of externality or world) do not receive a transcendental deduction. Kant fails to recognize that these concepts should be seen as internal to the categories of the understanding, as part of our concept of an object in general; and by dropping those concepts into the concept of the thing-in-itself, he makes it impossible to resist the conclusion that he is claiming that there are things, somethings or other, that we cannot know—that our knowledge of reality has limitations rather than limits.

What Heidegger undertakes to provide in *Being and Time* is, of course, something that looks very like a transcendental deduction of the concept of a world, understood as that in which objects are met; he thereby attempts to show that there are more ways of making a habitable world—more layers or aspects to it—than Kant's twelve categories allow. In the next part of this paper, I shall attempt to show how his analysis of moods contributes to this enterprise—how the epistemology of moods casts light on the worldliness of human experience.

III. Anxiety: The Finitude of Self and World

Perhaps the most famous of Heidegger's analyses of mood is his discussion of 'Angst' (anxiety or dread)—a discussion heavily indebted to Kierkegaard. It begins by distinguishing anxiety from fear. Both are responses to the world as unnerving, hostile or threatening, but whereas fear is a response to something specific in the world (a gun, an animal, a gesture) anxiety is in this sense objectless. The distinctive oppressiveness of anxiety lies precisely in its not being elicited by anything specific, or at least in its being entirely disproportionate to the specific circumstances which appear to have triggered it; either way, it cannot be accommodated by responding to those specific circumstances in any concrete way (e.g. by running away). According to Heidegger, what oppresses us is not any specific totality of objects but rather the *possibility* of such a totality: we are oppressed by the world as such—or more precisely, by the worldliness of our existence, our Being-in-the-world. Anxiety confronts Dasein with the knowledge that it is thrown into the world—always already delivered over to situations of choice and action which matter to it but which it does not itself fully choose or determine; it confronts Dasein with the determining and yet sheerly contingent fact of its own worldly existence.

But Being-in-the-world is not just that in the face of which the anxious person is anxious; it is also that *for* which she is anxious. In anxiety, Dasein is anxious about itself—not about some concrete existential possibility, but about the fact that possibilities are the medium of its existence, that its life is necessarily a matter of realizing one or other existential possibility. In effect, then, anxiety plunges Dasein into an anxiety about itself in the face of itself; and since in this state particular objects and persons within the world fade into insignificance and the world as such occupies the foreground, then the specific structures of the they-world must also fade away. Thus, anxiety can rescue Dasein from its fallen state, its lostness in the 'they'; it throws Dasein back upon the fact that it is a being for whom its own Being is an issue, and so a creature capable of individuality.

> [I]n anxiety, there lies the possibility of a disclosure that is quite distinctive; for anxiety individualizes. This individualization brings Dasein back from its falling, and makes manifest to it that authenticity and inauthenticity are possibilities of its Being. These basic possibilities of Dasein ... show themselves in anxiety as they are in themselves—undisguised by entities within the world, to which, proximally and for the most part, Dasein clings. (BT, 40: 235)

What Heidegger claims to identify here is an experience of uncanniness. Anxiety makes unavoidable the realization that human life is always conducted in the midst of objects and events, and that typically we bury ourselves in them—in flight from acknowledging that our existence is always capable of being more or other than its present realizations, and so that we are never fully at home in any particular world. This uncanniness highlights the finitude of Dasein's freedom; Dasein is responsible for choosing its mode of life, but must do so without ever fully controlling the circumstances in which that choice must be exercised, and without ever being able entirely to identify itself with the outcome of any particular choice that it makes. It is always haunted by the choices it didn't make, the choices it couldn't make, and its inability to choose to live without the capacity to choose—the conditions of freedom for a finite creature, a creature that must inhabit a spatio-temporal world.

In other words, the uncanniness of anxiety reveals the world as one component of Dasein's finitude. More precisely, by revealing the conditionedness of human freedom, it demonstrates the externality of the world to its human denizens; for those conditions reflect the fact that human existence is essentially worldly or environed, that the natural world of objects and events is one which we inhabit, and so that the world must be thought of as both intimately related to us and yet separate from us. Furthermore, anxiety elucidates the relative autonomy of the world as a function of its being at once evanescent and permanent. The uncanniness anxiety induces shows that each particular arrangement of objects and events will be succeeded by others, so no such arrangement can be thought of as exhaustive of the significance of the world as such, which exists rather as the horizon of possibilities within which actuality is encountered; and yet, insofar as Dasein is capable of being entirely absorbed in the present arrangements of its world to the point at which it loses its sense of itself as free to live otherwise than it does, anxiety teaches us that the world answers to our conceptions of it—that its successions can be fixed or frozen, and so that the world is such that it constantly and obediently becomes what we make of it. In short, according to Heidegger's epistemology of anxiety, the world's externality must be understood as its inexhaustible capacity to be all the ways our moods tell us it can be—its capacity to be apart from us and yet be a part of us.

IV. Moods and Criteria: The Mutual Attunement of Heidegger and Wittgenstein

Heidegger's claim that moods are revelatory of the world forms part of his more general claim that the passive or necessitarian aspect of human existence—our thrownness, our openness to 'states-of-mind'—forms part of the human capacity to comprehend the world we inhabit. Earlier in *Being and Time*, he argued that the fundamental basis of this comprehension is something he calls 'Rede' (literally 'talk', but standardly translated as 'discourse')—an ontological structure that both is and is not essentially linguistic. According to his analysis, Dasein's encounters with objects are all implicitly structured in terms of 'seeing as': we see a given entity as a table, a door, a carriage, and so on, and thus locate it in a certain field or horizon of significance—one which links the object to other objects and raw materials, to certain goals or outcomes, to other people (customers, fellow-workers) and to a particular existential possibility of our own (a project for which the object might or might not be useful). This socially constituted field of intelligibility is what Heidegger thinks of as the worldhood of the world—that which conditions the possibility of any and all of our encounters with the objects of the world; and the structure of this field of intelligibility—the articulations of this widely ramifying cultural web of concepts, roles, and functional interrelations—he terms 'Rede'. As this term suggests, Heidegger sees a close relation between this field of significance and language. Since any language itself has a worldly existence, our capacity to grasp symbols and sentences must itself be understood in terms of the articulations of the field of significance; but precisely because language is the way in which discourse is expressed, its structure must be seen as internally related to the basic articulations of language—the categories or concepts in terms of which we grasp an entity as a particular kind of thing. Accordingly, insofar as the worldhood of the world is grounded in discourse, it must be understood in terms appropriate to the distinctively human capacity for language; in Heidegger's vocabulary, the ontological structure of the world must be understood in existential terms.

How might such an understanding preserve the world's autonomy from human beings—however relative that autonomy turns out to be? How in other words, can such an account of the world respect its separateness from us as well as our intimacy with it? This difficulty is parallel to one that emerges in Wittgenstein's later philosophy, and I want to suggest that the solution to that difficulty can provide us with a way of seeing how Heidegger might sustain his own balancing-act. I have in mind Wittgenstein's conception of criteria or grammar, and the conception of language that goes with it. For Wittgenstein, criteria govern the use of words; they articulate its grammar, the ways in which it can be combined with other words to formulate propositions that might or might not be true of reality. Assume, for example, that our criterion for a liquid's being water is that it have chemical composition H_2O. That is not itself a claim about reality, something that might be true or false; it doesn't claim that any particular liquid does have that chemical composition, or that any such liquid is to be found anywhere in the world, and so it cannot be falsified if such eventualities occur. It simply licenses us to substitute one form of words ('water') for

Can There be an Epistemology of Moods?

another form of words ('liquid with chemical composition H_2O)'); it determines that whenever the latter is illicitly applied, so is the former. Such articulations of grammar are therefore akin to definitions, and definitions are not descriptions; they are, however, an essential precondition for constructing descriptions since they confer meaning on the terms used in the description.

I suggest that we think of criteria as akin to Heidegger's discourse; the grammatical structures they constitute are articulations of intelligibility, that which makes it possible for us to encounter objects as objects of a particular kind, and so ground the comprehensibility of worldly phenomena—that is, the human capacity to disclose the world. Since any such grammatical structures will individuate phenomena in ways that express human interests and human nature—since the ways in which criteria tell one object from another will reflect the distinctions that matter to their users, their shared sense of what is natural and what outrageous, what useful and what pointless—the worldhood of the world will in this sense be internally related to human culture and forms of life. Since, however, grammatical structures are not in the business of representing reality (since, like rules, criteria cannot coherently be assessed in terms of truth and falsity), then their rootedness in human practices and human nature cannot be said to undercut the world's independence from its human denizens. On the contrary: the world's autonomy finds expression, amongst other things, in reality's capacity to falsify putative descriptions of it; and given that such descriptions could not be constructed without criteria to give meaning to their constituent terms, it could be argued that the disclosedness of the world by grammar is precisely what makes possible the world's independence from human representations of it.

As we saw earlier, however, Heidegger implies that the world's relative autonomy or externality should be understood as a function of its evanescence and permanence—its capacity to answer to and yet transcend our conceptions of it. Does Wittgenstein's idea of the autonomy of grammar help to illuminate that further implication? To see that it does, we need to appreciate the consequences of the autonomy of grammar or discourse for our understanding of scepticism—surely the key point at which modern philosophy has studied the externality of the world. From a Wittgensteinian perspective, scepticism—like any other philosophical dogma—is rooted in confusion concerning the grammar of the terms it employs to give expression to its doubts. In claiming, for example, that although we typically believe that the world exists, we should rather regard it as a highly doubtful hypothesis, the sceptic fails to appreciate that the world's existence—unlike the existence of a given object in the world—is not something in which we 'believe', not an 'opinion' that we hold on the basis of evidence. By the same token, however, it is equally wrong to contradict the sceptic by arguing that we can be certain of the world's existence; if the concepts of belief, doubt and evidence do not apply here, then neither does the concept of certainty. There is, accordingly, a truth in scepticism: the sceptic rightly renders untenable the commonsense view that we can claim to know of the world's existence. Moreover, insofar as the sceptic's scepticism results from a refusal to employ such concepts as 'belief' and 'world' in accordance with our usual criteria—insofar as her scepticism amounts to an attempt to speak outside language games—then it must be acknowledged that our ordinary agreement in the criteria we employ is precisely something that is, and must remain, open to repudiation; anything whose existence requires the continued investment of consent is vulnerable to the withdrawal of that consent.

Of course, on Wittgenstein's view, criteria establish the connection between words and world; so the consequences of their repudiation are grave—the loss of the human capacity to word the world, the fate of finding oneself saying something other than one meant, or unable to say anything meaningful at all. In other words, since criteria disclose the world, their repudiation amounts to making the world vanish from our grasp; in this sense, scepticism makes manifest the evanescence of the world, its capacity to answer to our conceptions—including the conception that it is beyond our grasp. Since, however, a repudiated agreement can always be resuscitated (since it is possible to restore the link between words and world by recalling the sceptic to her criteria) then Wittgenstein's attempts to overcome scepticism amount to an attempted demonstration of the permanence of the world—of its being beyond our capacity for annihilation.

What, however, has this talk of criteria and discourse to do with moods? The connection can be seen at several levels. Most obviously, the sceptical impulse is itself characteristically associated with a specific mood. Insofar as its doubts about the reality of the external world are seriously held or generated (and not viewed as merely a dramatic device for introducing epistemological problems), scepticism is pervaded with anxiety of a kind that precisely matches Heidegger's analysis of it. The sceptic feels an abyss to open up between herself and the world, a sense of its insignificance and nothingness; she experiences a hollow at the heart of reality, and an essential uncanniness in her own existence—a sense of herself as not at home in the world. And of course, given that sceptical anxiety embodies a truth—given that it rightly perceives the inadequacy of cognitive models of our basic relation to reality, and shows that criteria are subject to the withdrawal of consent—then its onset can properly be thought to reveal something fundamental about the world and our inhabitation of it: namely, that our relation to the world is not one of knowing—that the world is not knowable.

However, the connections between criteria and moods run deeper even than this—something that is happily (fortuitously?) registered in the fact that, when Wittgenstein describes the mode of our ordinary agreement in criteria, he uses the term 'Ubereinstimmung'—a word which contains Heidegger's term for moods ('Stimmung') and which invokes exactly the same notion of attunement to the world. For the idea of agreement Wittgenstein wishes to invoke is not that of coming to an agreement on a given occasion (for example, agreeing to a contract), but that of being in agreement throughout (like being in harmony); human beings who agree in the language they use are mutually voiced with respect to it, mutually attuned from top to bottom. This idea of attunement is further specified in the way criteria register the distinctions that matter to their users; if (with Cavell) we think of criteria as in this respect telling what counts or matters to human beings, the multiple connections with Heidegger's understanding of moods should be clear. As we have seen, for Heidegger, moods manifest the human capacity to be affected by the world (to find that we are attuned to it and it to us), they have a social as well as an individual aspect, and they are ultimately grounded in the discourse-based human capacity to disclose or reveal reality. Since criteria make manifest a culture's sense of what matters in the world as well as making knowledge of that world possible, Wittgenstein's sense of our mutual attunement in grammar precisely parallels Heidegger's invocation of our mutual attunement in discourse.

Perhaps most fundamentally, however, both philosophers draw a critical lesson for philosophical method that is itself attuned to a further aspect of moods—their passivity or givenness. Both regard the structures of grammar or discourse as the proper domain of philosophical analysis or description, as the last word in understanding the nature of worldly things and the nature of the being who is alone capable of understanding worldly things; as Wittgenstein puts it, what must be accepted—the given—is the form of human life with language, the ramifying grid of mutual attunements that govern our access to the world. The method of treating philosophical confusions that he advocates is therefore one of recalling us to our criteria, of bringing us to accept them as the fundamental condition of our existence—as a structure that we always already occupy and that we cannot simply choose to reject (on pain of unintelligibility). A final comparison with Kant's philosophical vision may help here. For Kant, experience is a function of combining concepts and intuitions, where concepts are based on the spontaneity of thought, and sensible intuitions on the receptivity of impressions. Thinking is therefore understood as a matter of synthesizing impressions, of the understanding taking up the given manifold of experience and imposing an organization upon it; the intellectual hemisphere is active and the intuitive hemisphere passive. In short, for Kant, there is no intellectual intuition. For Wittgenstein and Heidegger, by contrast, true thinking is passive or receptive; just as one can only overcome scepticism by recognizing that the world is not to be known or grasped in cognition but accepted or acknowledged as the condition for the possibility of knowledge claims, so more generally one can make philosophical progress only by recalling and accepting criteria or the structures of discourse. In short, there is only intellectual intuition; and this receptivity of genuine thinking reflects the fact that human beings are creatures who lead their lives in a world which matters to them, a world which is at once evanescent and permanent, and revealed as such by the mutual attunement of moods and world.

Cristina Lafont, Frankfurt am Main

Die Rolle der Sprache in *Sein und Zeit*

Die Tatsache, daß Heidegger der Sprache in *Sein und Zeit* einen eigenen Paragraphen gewidmet und sie damit abgehandelt zu haben scheint, hat häufig dazu geführt, daß sich Interpretationen ihres Stellenwertes für *Sein und Zeit* mit einem Bezug auf diesen, den § 34, begnügten. Damit hält man sich zwar eng an das Selbstverständnis Heideggers bezüglich dessen, was er ‚Sprache' nennt, übersieht aber zugleich die genauso schillernde wie zentrale Rolle, die die Sprache als im gesamten Verlauf von *Sein und Zeit* stillschweigend in Anspruch genommene Größe spielt.

Die hier eingeschlagene Interpretationsrichtung, die sich – wie oben ersichtlich – *nicht* dem Selbstverständnis des Heidegger von *Sein und Zeit* bezüglich dieses Punktes verpflichtet fühlt, soll es ermöglichen, in zweierlei Hinsicht ein genaueres Bild über das Unternehmen *Sein und Zeit* zu gewinnen: einerseits erlaubt die stillschweigende Inanspruchnahme der Sprache es Heidegger, die von ihm ins Auge gefaßte *hermeneutische* Transformation der Phänomenologie durchzuführen. Andererseits ermöglicht Heideggers eigene Fehleinschätzung der Rolle der Sprache es uns, die internen Gründe für die Sackgasse, in die *Sein und Zeit* gerät, präziser zu fassen – nämlich für genau diese Transformation bei „der transzendentalen Fragestellung" zu verharren. Eine solche Interpretation läßt sich also nur durchführen, wenn man zwischen der von Heidegger in *Sein und Zeit de facto* durchgeführten Analyse der ‚Erschlossenheit' – die dessen eigentliche Neuerung darstellt – und dem *methodologischen Rahmen* unterscheidet, den er für die Durchführung dieser Analyse als einzig geeignet ansieht.

Liest man *Sein und Zeit* auf diese Weise gegen den Strich, läßt sich darüber hinaus die Kontinuität zwischen ‚Heidegger I' und ‚Heidegger II' deutlich erkennen, die im fortschreitenden Auskristallisieren der Problemstellung besteht, die in *Sein und Zeit* anhand der Thematik der ‚Erschlossenheit' angesprochen wird und die von Heidegger nach der ‚Kehre' unter den Stichworten ‚Sprache' und ‚Welterschließung' behandelt wird.

I

Bekanntlich ist für *Sein und Zeit* das Anliegen bestimmend, das Paradigma der Bewußtseinsphilosophie zu überwinden. Dies soll durch eine ‚radikalere' Fragestellung erreicht werden – die den Keim der ‚Erschlossenheitsanalyse' ausmacht –, vor der das zentrale Modell der Bewußtseinsphilosophie, also das Subjekt-Objekt-Schema, kapitulieren muß.

Diese Auseinandersetzung mit der Bewußtseinsphilosophie läuft in zwei Schritten ab: zunächst will Heidegger nachweisen, daß das Subjekt-Objekt-Schema, weil es einzig auf die Zwecke der „Erkenntnistheorie" zugeschnitten ist, abgeleitet ist – was es nicht falsch, sondern schlicht zu beschränkt macht. Zum zweiten ist in der zu diesem Nachweis durchgeführten Radikalisierung der Fragestellung selbst schon eine Erweiterung des Themenkreises der Philosophie enthalten: es soll sich zeigen, daß „Erkennen" ein abgeleiteter Modus von „Verstehen" ist; dieses ‚Verstehen' wiederum konstituiert die Seinsverfassung des Daseins, aus der die verschiedenen Weisen des Welterkennens und damit auch die regionalen Ontologien erst hervorgehen, und die daher unter der Zielsetzung der Philosophie als Grundlegung jeglicher Regionalontologie den zentralen Gegenstand einer durchzuführenden existenzialen Analytik des Daseins als ‚Fundamentalontologie' darstellt.

Heidegger führt daher zur Inangriffnahme der Überwindung der Bewußtseinsphilosophie einen Perspektivenwechsel durch, der den Kern seiner ‚hermeneutischen' Transformation der Phänomenologie ausmacht: hatte die in der Erklärung des „Erkennens" zentrierte Bewußtseinsphilosophie noch das Subjekt-Objekt-Modell, also das eines *beobachtenden* Subjekts gegenüber der Welt als Gesamtheit aller Seienden, vorausgesetzt, so bildet nun die diesem zugrundeliegende Perspektive eines *verstehenden* Daseins *in* einer symbolisch strukturierten *Welt* das für *Sein und Zeit* zentrale Modell.

Der so vollzogene Schritt vom Grundmodell der *Wahrnehmung* zu dem des *Verstehens* läßt sich schon anhand einer immanenten Auseinandersetzung Heideggers mit Husserl erkennen, und zwar genau an der Stelle, an der bereits Husserl auf diesen Wendepunkt stößt, nämlich anhand der Umkehrung dessen, was dieser in Fassung einer nicht-sinnlichen Wahrnehmung als ‚kategoriale Anschauung' bezeichnet hatte. Heidegger bemerkt dazu in der Marburger Vorlesung des Sommersemesters 1925, daß „unsere schlichtesten Wahrnehmungen und Verfassungen schon *ausgedrückte*, mehr noch, in bestimmter Weise *interpretierte* sind. Wir sehen nicht so sehr primär und ursprünglich die Gegenstände und Dinge, sondern zunächst sprechen wir darüber, genauer sprechen wir nicht das aus, was wir sehen, sondern umgekehrt, wir sehen, was man über die Sache spricht. Diese *eigentümliche Bestimmtheit der Welt* und ihre mögliche Auffassung und Erfassung durch die Ausdrücklichkeit, durch das Schon-gesprochen-und-durchgesprochen-sein, ist es, die nun bei der Frage nach der Struktur der kategorialen Anschauung grundsätzlich in den Blick gebracht werden muß." (GA 20, S. 75, Hervorh. von mir)

Die Analyse dieser „eigentümlichen Bestimmtheit der Welt" nun ist es, die in Form der Struktur des In-der-Welt-seins den Kern von *Sein und Zeit* ausmacht, auch wenn es an jener Stelle nicht ganz leicht sein wird, den sich hier schon andeutenden Zusammenhang zwischen ‚Sprache' und ‚In-der-Welt-sein' herauszupräparieren.

Durch diesen Perspektivenwechsel, der ja schon in der Formel *In-der-Welt*-sein besonders hervorsticht, muß sich natürlich auch das Subjekt, das in der Welt ist, verändern: es handelt sich nämlich dann um ein *faktisches* Dasein, das sich diesem Umstand bzw. seiner ‚natürlichen Einstellung' nicht mehr ohne weiteres entziehen kann, ja, eigentlich kann es sich, von dieser Warte aus gesehen, gar nicht mehr – wie bei Husserl noch vorausgesetzt – um eine zuerst verfügbare Einstellung handeln (vgl. GA 20, S. 157).

Diese Prämisse ist es nun, aus der hervorgeht, inwiefern Heidegger gerade durch seinen Perspektivenwechsel keine extramundane Instanz (bzw. kein ‚transzendentales Subjekt') mehr zu Verfügung steht. Daher muß auch die methodologische Unterscheidung, die das Rückgrat der Transzendentalphilosophie darstellt, verzichtbar werden: an die Stelle der Dichotomie empirisch/transzendental wird so die *ontologische Differenz* treten. Nimmt man diese bei einer solchen Konstellation offenkundig notwendige Ersetzung erst einmal hin, kann die von Heidegger mit dem Projekt einer Fundamentalontologie weitergetragene „transzendentale Fragestellung" davon nicht unberührt bleiben.

Aus diesem Blickwinkel läßt sich dann auch absehen, inwiefern das Scheitern des Versuchs von *Sein und Zeit*, die Transzendentalphilosophie unter Verwendung ihrer eigenen Mittel zu überwinden, damit zusammenhängt, daß dieses Unternehmen die Funktionsmöglichkeiten der von Heidegger neu eingeführten Begriffe übersteigt. Damit muß dann aber auch der Vollzug des von Heidegger anvisierten Perspektivenwechsels – eben die Entfaltung der Problematik der „Erschlossenheit" – in *Sein und Zeit* halbherzig bleiben.

Heidegger übersieht nämlich, daß die von ihm benötigte und für dieses ‚kritische' Vorhaben in Anspruch genommene Perspektive gerade auf der *methodologischen* Ebene eine Überforderung der Transzendentalphilosophie darstellt, insofern nämlich, als sie prinzipiell schon den Vollzug einer *Detranszendentalisierung* impliziert, infolge derer die Dichotomie empirisch/transzendental bzw. konstitutiv/konstituiert als solche nicht mehr anwendbar ist.

Am Leitfaden der ontologischen Differenz bringt Heidegger nun die Unterscheidung zwischen formalen, *ontologischen* Strukturen des *Daseins überhaupt* und ihren geschichtlichen, *ontischen* Konkretisierungen in Anschlag und nimmt als selbstverständlich an, daß zwischen beiden ein Fundierungsverhältnis besteht. Die Tatsache, daß der Ausgangspunkt dieser Analyse ein *faktisches* Dasein ist, das immer schon auf eine Welt angewiesen ist, wird jedoch dieses von Heidegger immer wieder (nur) behauptete *Fundierungsverhältnis* zwischen ontologischen Strukturen und ontischen Verkörperungen derselben konterkarieren.

Diese Schwierigkeiten ergeben sich jedoch prinzipiell schon aus der begrifflichen Ersetzung selbst, die Heidegger bei Einführung der ontologischen Differenz implizit vorgenommen hat: Zwar gelingt es ihm mittels der Ersetzung der Dichotomie empirisch/transzendental durch die ontologische Differenz, die – weil sie die obengenannte Detranszendentalisierung voraussetzt – für die Bewußtseinsphilosophie unzugängliche Thematik der ‚Erschlossenheit' zu entfalten, und zwar weil erst in den in dieser Differenz enthaltenen Begriffen der Aufweis einer *ontologischen* Dimension *in den ontischen* Konstrukten *selbst* möglich wird (d.h. weil es nun möglich wird, etwas als ‚ontisch' und *zugleich* ‚ontologisch' zu bestimmen). Diese Möglichkeit erlaubt es Heidegger, die Figur des ‚apriorischen Perfekts' methodisch in Anspruch zu nehmen, ohne daß sein Unternehmen unmittelbar an Plausibilität verliert. Ist dies jedoch erst einmal gelungen, muß auch Heideggers Versuch, Ontisches und Ontologisches in Analogie zur Dichotomie empirisch/transzendental kategorisch zu *trennen*, um so ein Fundierungsverhältnis unaffiziert in Anspruch nehmen zu können, in den Strudel der Detranszendentalisierung geraten. Und in der Tat zeigt sich, daß die von Heidegger angenommene Ersetzbarkeit des transzendentalen Apriori durch das ‚apriorische Perfekt' (vgl. *Sein und Zeit* , S. 441–442 <85b>) im Verlauf der Durchführung der Analysen selbst immer wieder dementiert wird.

Demzufolge wird zunächst zu zeigen sein, wie es Heidegger einerseits gerade dank der Tatsache, daß die ontologische Differenz im Unterschied zur Differenz empirisch/transzendental *per se* noch kein Fundierungsverhältnis impliziert, gelingt, die Problematik der Erschlossenheit zu Tage zu fördern; dabei wird sich andererseits herausstellen, daß er durch sein in der Absicht, eine Fundamentalontologie zu entwerfen, wurzelndes Festhalten an der Methodologie der Transzendentalphilosophie zu einer *hypostasierenden Lesart der ontologischen Differenz* gezwungen wird. Diese wird jedoch gerade durch die von Heidegger selbst vorgeführte Analyse der ‚Erschlossenheit' immer wieder jeglicher Bedeutung entleert.

II

Trotz ihrer Schlüsselposition wird die Einführung der ‚ontologischen Differenz' in *Sein und Zeit* von Heidegger keineswegs mit methodologischen Überlegungen gerechtfertigt. Vielmehr appelliert er an der entsprechenden Stelle an unser intuitives Vorverständnis und erklärt, daß „[uns] der Sinn von Sein schon in gewisser Weise verfügbar sein [muß]" (S. 5)[1] bzw., daß „wir uns immer schon in einem Seinsverständnis [bewegen] (...) *Dieses durchschnittliche und vage Seinsverständnis ist ein Faktum,*" (ibid.) Auf dieses Faktum läßt sich dann die ‚ontologische Differenz', d.h. die Unterscheidung Sein/Seiendes, zurückführen, die Heidegger am Leitfaden der ‚Seinsfrage' folgendermaßen einführt: „*Das Gefragte* (...) ist das Sein, das, was Seiendes als Seiendes bestimmt, das, woraufhin Seiendes (...) je schon verstanden ist. Das *Sein* des Seienden ‚ist' nicht selbst ein Seiendes. (...) *Seiend* ist alles, wovon wir reden, was wir meinen, wozu wir uns so und so verhalten, seiend ist auch, was und wie wir selbst sind." (S. 6/7, Hervorh. von mir)

Diese intuitiv zugängliche *Unterscheidung* Sein/Seiendes wird aber im folgenden unter der Hand mit der *Dichotomie* Dasein/nichtdaseinsmäßiges Seiendes enggeführt, die die „transzendentale Fragestellung" erst ermöglicht; dies geschieht auf der Basis eines Vorrangs dieses Seien-

---

[1] Sofern nicht näher bezeichnet, stammen die Zitate mit Seitenangaben aus *Sein und Zeit*. Die Siglen der verwendeten Werke Heideggers sind folgende:
[SuZ] *Sein und Zeit*, Tübingen [16]1986;
[Brief] Brief an Husserl (1927), in: Husserliana Bd. 9, S. 600–602;
[ZSD] *Zur Sache des Denkens*, Tübingen [3]1988;
[GA 20] *Prolegomena zur Geschichte des Zeitbegriffs*. Marburger Vorlesung Sommersemester 1920, Gesamtausgabe Bd. 20, Frankfurt a.M. [2]1988.

den (Dasein) vor den anderen (nichtdaseinsmäßige Seiende): „Das Dasein selbst ist überdies vor anderen Seienden ausgezeichnet (...) das Dasein ist ein Seiendes, das nicht nur unter anderen Seienden vorkommt. (...) Die ontische Auszeichnung des Daseins liegt darin, daß es ontologisch ist." (S. 11–12)

Den transzendentalphilosophischen Sinn dieser Auszeichnung erklärt Heidegger selbst in einem Brief an Husserl, in dem er die Aufgabe einer Fundamentalontologie folgendermaßen umreißt: „Es gilt zu zeigen, daß die Seinsart des menschlichen Daseins total verschieden ist von der alles anderen Seienden und daß sie als diejenige, die sie ist, gerade in sich die Möglichkeit der transzendentalen Konstitution birgt." (Brief, S. 600)

Im Sinne einer auf diese Weise transzendentalphilosophisch verstandenen Auszeichnung behauptet Heidegger dann, daß das ‚Seinsverständnis', von dem wir ausgegangen waren, nun „selbst eine Seinsbestimmtheit des Daseins [ist]" (S. 12), und damit, daß zugleich mit der Erklärung der ‚a priori notwendigen Seinsverfassung des Daseins' die Bedingung der Möglichkeit jedes möglichen Seinsverständnisses angegeben werden kann; folglich muß eine ‚Fundamentalontologie' die Form einer ‚existenzialen Analytik' des Daseins annehmen.

Mit diesem skizzenhaften Abriß haben wir nun einen Eindruck vom zweiten *Sein und Zeit* bestimmenden Zug gewonnen, nämlich dem Versuch Heideggers, das Band zwischen der Grundlegungsfunktion der Philosophie und ihrer – nunmehr durch ihn erweiterten – Thematik, auf keinen Fall abreißen zu lassen. Nur aus diesem Blickwinkel gewinnt die in ihrer Verwobenheit schwer auszumachende aporetische Struktur von *Sein und Zeit* etwas an Transparenz, deren verschiedene Fäden in der ebenso vielgesichtigen ‚Auszeichnung' des Daseins münden.

Es sind im wesentlichen folgende zwei miteinander zusammenhängende Irrtümer bezüglich dieser ‚Auszeichnung', in denen Heidegger befangen bleibt:

Einerseits identifiziert Heidegger nicht die richtige Instanz, der diese Auszeichnung, nämlich als ontisch und ontologisch zugleich aufzufassen zu sein, primär zugehörig ist: genauso unverzichtbar, wie das Phänomen der Sprache implizit bereits für die Plausibilisierung der ontologischen Differenz gewesen war, wird auch im Kern der Analyse der Struktur des In-der-Welt-seins *eine vom Dasein verschiedene Instanz* werden, nämlich die *Zeichenstruktur*, die insofern in Konkurrenz mit dem Dasein gerät, als auch sie nur aufgrund ihres ontisch-ontologischen Charakters spezifiziert werden kann. (III)

Gerade darin, daß diese – von Heidegger unterschätzte – Instanz der *unverzichtbare Kern* des In-der-Welt-seins ist und bleibt, liegt der Grund für die zweite Verfehlung, denn durch ihren spezifischen Charakter wird andererseits die mit der ‚Auszeichnung' des Daseins ohne jegliche methodologische Rechtfertigung einfach übernommene Begründungsstrategie der Transzendentalphilosophie immer wieder unterlaufen und ihrer methodologischen Rolle beraubt.[2] Das wird sich am deutlichsten im Kern der Erschlossenheitsanalyse bzw. anhand der Trennung von Sprache und Rede zeigen. (IV)

III

Heidegger beginnt die Ausarbeitung dieser neuen von ihm ins Auge gefaßten Perspektive anhand der Frage, worin die ‚Weltlichkeit der Welt' besteht, die die Einführung der Struktur des ‚In-der-Welt-seins' mit sich bringt.
Zu ihrer Beantwortung dient die Zeuganalyse, die ja von Heidegger als „der phänomenologische Aufweis des Seins" des „nächstbegegnenden Seienden" (S. 68) verstanden wird, d.h. der ‚Seinsart' der Seienden, denen das Dasein in seinem ‚alltäglichen Umgang in der Welt' begegnet. Da nun dieser alltägliche Umgang gerade nicht im Erkennen, sondern im ‚hantierenden, gebrauchenden Besorgen' besteht, muß ihm auch eine ‚vorthematische Seinsart des Seienden' zugeordnet werden. Diese bezeichnet Heidegger als ‚Zuhandenheit'. Ein Seiendes dieser Seinsart glaubt Heidegger nun im *Zeug* zu finden, da dieses *als solches* nicht „theoretisch erfaßt" werden kann; dazu heißt es entsprechend in der Erklärung: „*Ein* Zeug ‚ist' strenggenommen nie. Zum Sein von Zeug gehört je immer ein Zeugganzes, darin es dieses Zeug sein kann, das es ist. Zeug ist wesenhaft ‚etwas, um zu...'. Die verschiedenen Weisen des

---

[2] Ironischerweise hat genau diese Bedeutungsentleerung keineswegs den Charakter eines *Sein und Zeit* äußerlichen Urteils, sondern im Gegenteil ist sie dessen fester Bestandteil. Gerade in den Momenten, in denen Heidegger uns die Machbarkeit und Plausibilität einer Durchmischung dessen, was er gerade zuvor noch als durch ein Fundierungsverhältnis *getrennt* erklärt hatte, durch den Rückgriff auf das ‚apriorische Perfekt' (bzw. das ‚In-der-Welt-sein') demonstriert, und dadurch die Möglichkeit einer solchen Trennung für das „faktische Dasein" – die einzige für Heidegger in Frage kommende Instanz – ausschließt, weist er auch selbst auf die Möglichkeit der von ihm ins Auge gefaßten Überwindung der Voraussetzungen der Bewußtseinsphilosophie hin.

,Um-zu' (...) konstituieren eine Zeugganzheit. In der Struktur ,Um-zu' liegt eine *Verweisung* von etwas auf etwas." (S. 68)

Das Besondere an einem ,Zeug' besteht also darin, daß es auf die Präexistenz einer ,Zeugganzheit' verweist. Diese jedoch ist, wie er sehr wohl bemerkt, nicht durch das Zeug selbst konstituiert, und könnte es auch gar nicht sein, denn erst die „verschiedenen Weisen des ,Um-zu'" „konstituieren eine Zeugganzheit". Daher kann man für deren Analyse – bzw. für die Antwort auf die Frage, wie sich einer solchen ,Verweisungszusammenhang' konstituiert – nicht mehr das Zeug in Anspruch nehmen, weil dieses, als durch die Verweisung konstituiert, gerade nicht mehr die Grundlage für die Erläuterung der *Konstitution* selbst abgeben kann.

An diesem Punkt nun geht Heidegger zum nächsten Paragraphen über, um die Analyse des „Phänomens der Verweisung selbst" (S. 77) in Angriff zu nehmen; gewiß nimmt er dort „wieder den Ausgang beim Sein des Zuhandenen" (ibid.), jedoch wird er, wie der Titel des Paragraphen illustriert, dieses Mal ein *besonderes* Zeug behandeln, nämlich *das Zeichen*.

Über die Besonderheit dieses Zeugs gibt uns Heidegger gleich zu Anfang Auskunft, indem er es folgendermaßen beschreibt: „Das Zeichensein für... kann selbst zu einer *universalen Beziehungsart* formalisiert werden, so daß die Zeichenstruktur selbst einen ontologischen Leitfaden abgibt für *eine ,Charakteristik' alles Seienden überhaupt.*" (S. 77, Hervorh. von mir)

Die Zuwendung Heideggers zu genau diesem besonderen Zeug ist deswegen bemerkenswert, weil die Zeichenanalyse, die er nun durchführen wird, darauf hinausläuft zu zeigen, daß „alle Seienden überhaupt" in ihrer „nächstbegegnenden Seinsart", d.h. als Zuhandene, erst dank der Zeichenstruktur zugänglich werden.[3] In diesem Sinne fügt

---

[3] Dies jedoch ist nichts weiter als das notwendige Äquivalent zu der schon in der Einleitung zu findenden These, derzufolge „der ursprüngliche Seinsmodus des Daseins" *Verstehen* ist. Somit stellt sich dieser Konnex als die systematische Erklärung des „Faktums" dar, von dem *Sein und Zeit* ausgegangen war, nämlich daß das Dasein ein Verstehen hat sowohl „seines Seins", als auch von „so etwas wie Welt", sowie „des Seins des Seienden, das innerhalb der Welt zugänglich wird" (S. 13). Auf dieser Basis läßt sich dann die zweite Version dieser Behauptung Heideggers – nämlich daß die ,Auszeichnung' des Daseins darin besteht, daß es ein „Seinsverständnis" hat, das erst seine Unterscheidung von „allen anderen Seienden" ausmacht – in der Weise verstehen, daß das Dasein eine symbolisch vermittelte Beziehung zur Welt hat, bzw. in einer symbolisch strukturierten Welt „ist". Diese Universalität der Zeichenstruktur ist inso-

Die Rolle der Sprache in „Sein und Zeit"

Heidegger im folgenden hinzu: „Zeichen sind aber zunächst selbst Zeuge, deren spezifischer Zeugcharakter im *Zeigen* besteht" (ibid.)

Hier nun endet die Analogie zwischen Zeichen und den anderen „Zeugen", denn: daß die anderen ‚Zeuge' als ‚Um-zu' auf ein ‚Wozu' verweisen, bedeutet, daß ihr spezifischer ‚Zeugcharakter' (also: ihre ‚Seinsart') in diesem ‚Wozu' besteht (‚Hammer-zu-sein' besteht in ‚hämmern'), aber keineswegs im ‚Verweisen selbst'. Dagegen besteht das ‚Zeichen' *als solches* in *nichts anderem* als diesem ‚Verweisen auf'. Deswegen spricht Heidegger zurecht vom *„eigenartigen* Zeugcharakter der Zeichen" (S. 80, Hervorh. von mir). Diese ‚Eigenartigkeit' der Zeichen, die die zentrale Einsicht der Zeichenanalyse Heideggers ausmacht, bringt er dann folgendermaßen auf den Punkt:

„*Das Zeichen ist nicht nur zuhanden mit anderem Zeug*, sondern in seiner Zuhandenheit wird die Umwelt je für die Umsicht ausdrücklich zugänglich. *Zeichen ist ein ontisch Zuhandenes, das als dieses bestimmte Zeug zugleich als etwas fungiert, was die ontologische Struktur der Zuhandenheit, Verweisungsganzheit und Weltlichkeit anzeigt.*" (S. 82, Hervorh. v. mir)

Hier nun findet sich die Stelle, an der deutlich wird, daß der „eigenartige" Charakter dieses Seienden, des Zeichens, mit der Auszeichnung zusammenfällt, die, wie wir schon in der Einleitung gesehen haben, eigentlich das Dasein von allen anderen Seienden unterscheiden sollte.

Diese Erkenntnis, aufgrund derer das Dasein seinen ‚ausgezeichneten Charakter' hätte verlieren müssen, und mit der folglich die Bresche in das festgefügte Subjekt-Objekt-Schema der Bewußtseinsphilosophie tatsächlich hätte geschlagen werden können, wird jedoch in *Sein und Zeit* systematisch verfehlt; vielmehr leitet das Subjekt-Objekt-Schema ganz im Gegenteil in Form der aus methodologischen Gründen für *Sein und Zeit* unverzichtbaren Dichotomie Dasein/nichtdaseinsmäßiges Seiendes weiterhin den Gang der Untersuchung.

Der Grund, warum Heidegger nicht bis zu der Spitze vordringt, den Ursprung der ontologischen Differenz (d.h. des Vollzugs des Unterscheidens von Sein und Seienden oder eben das ‚be-deutens') in der Sprache zu suchen, ist zweifellos, daß er unter einer der *Folgen* des – schon im

---

fern das gesuchte Phänomen, mit dem Heidegger die Bewußtseinsphilosophie konfrontieren wollte, als diese es in ihrem *framework* nicht repräsentieren konnte, oder, wie Heidegger sagt, das die Bewußtseinsphilosophie wegen der Verwendung des starren S-O-Schemas „überspringen" müsse.

Programm der „existenzialen Analyse des Daseins" vorgezeichneten – Verhaftetbleibens im Subjekt-Objekt-Schema leidet, nämlich, daß er immer noch den Sprachbegriff der Bewußtseinsphilosophie, also der Sprache als (‚ontisches') Instrument, teilt.

Das zeigt sich zumal, wenn Heidegger in der auf die oben zitierte folgenden Passage – inkonsequenterweise –, von seinem eigenen Schritt, in dem er das Zeichen als ontisch und zugleich ontologisch bezeichnet hatte, zurückweicht, und so – in Husserlscher Manier – das Untrennbare zu trennen versucht, nämlich das Zeichen und die „Verweisung selbst", die ja das Zeichen als solches – wie Heidegger selbst es gezeigt hatte – irreduziblerweise ausmacht: „Die Verweisung selbst kann daher, soll sie *ontologisch* das *Fundament* für Zeichen sein, nicht selbst als *Zeichen* begriffen werden. Verweisung ist nicht die ontische Bestimmtheit eines Zuhandenen, wo sie doch Zuhandenheit selbst konstituiert." (S. 83, Hervorh. von mir)

So kommt er im folgenden Paragraphen (§ 18), in dem der „Bezugscharakter des Verweisens" (S. 87) als „*be-deuten*" (ibid.) bestimmt wird, dazu, dies einer Abstraktion zuzuweisen, der „Bedeutsamkeit", und zwar als etwas von der Sprache selbst Unterschiedenem: „Sie [die Bedeutsamkeit, C.L.] ist das, was die Struktur der Welt (...) ausmacht" (ibid.) – und sogar darüber hinaus noch das, was die Sprache selbst „fundieren" soll (vgl. S. 87)

Die Inkonsequenz dieses Versuches wird Heidegger später *explizit* erkennen, wie sich in der folgenden auf „fundieren" bezogenen Randbemerkung in seinem Handexemplar von *Sein und Zeit* zeigt:

„Unwahr. Sprache ist nicht aufgestockt, sondern *ist* das ursprüngliche Wesen der Wahrheit als Da." (S. 442 <87c>)[4]

Implizit wird Heidegger jedoch diese unmögliche Trennung rückgängig machen müssen, um die für die Konstitution der ‚Welt' in Spiel gebrachte Instanz (nämlich die Zeichenstruktur) weiterhin unversehrt in Anspruch nehmen zu können. Denn auch wenn die Zugrundelegung der Dichotomie Dasein/nichtdaseinsmäßiges Seiendes dazu führt, daß nur die von allem Ontischen gereinigte Abstraktion der ‚Bedeutsamkeit' zur ‚ontologischen Bedingung der Möglichkeiten' von ‚Welt' erklärt

---

[4] Die explizite Anerkennung dieses Sachverhaltes, d.h. „daß die Sprache nicht nur ontisch, sondern von vornherein ontisch-ontologisch ist" (ZSD, S. 55), findet man in Heideggers Ausführungen über die Sprache, wie sie im „Protokoll zu einem Seminar über den Vortrag ‚Zeit und Sein'" wiedergegeben sind (ZSD, S. 54 ff.).

Die Rolle der Sprache in „Sein und Zeit" 51

werden könnte, hilft Heidegger dieser abstrahierende Schritt genau an dem zentralen Punkt nicht weiter, an dem er versucht, plausibel zu machen, daß das „Dasein sich, sofern es *ist, je schon auf eine begegnende ‚Welt'* angewiesen [hat], zu seinem Sein gehört wesenhaft diese *Angewiesenheit.*" (S. 87, Hervorh. von mir). Um diesem Umstand, der das Hauptmovens der Weltanalyse ausmacht, auch theoretisch Rechnung tragen zu können, ist Heidegger also wiederum zur Rücknahme des vorher vollzogenen Abstraktionsschritts zur ‚Bedeutsamkeit' gezwungen, indem er erklärt: „Die *erschlossene* Bedeutsamkeit ist als *existenziale* Verfassung des Daseins, seines In-der-Welt-seins, die *ontische Bedingung der Möglichkeit* der Entdeckbarkeit einer Bewandtnisganzheit." (S. 87, Hervorh. von mir)

Heidegger kann an dieser Stelle nur deswegen eine schon konstituierte Instanz (die „erschlossene Bedeutsamkeit") als für die „existenziale Verfassung des Daseins" konstitutiv erklären, weil die Rücknahme der vorherigen Trennung des Ontischen vom Ontologischen ohne weiteres durchführbar geblieben ist, bzw. weil er dazu eben noch immer eine ‚ontische' und zugleich ‚ontologische' (bzw. konstitutive und zugleich konstituierte) Instanz zur Verfügung hat. Nur so kann Heidegger mit Plausibilität behaupten und zur Plattform seiner Kritik nehmen, daß das Dasein in einer immer schon erschlossenen Welt ist (bzw. daß die Geworfenheit für das Dasein konstitutiv ist). Damit, daß Heidegger im Zentrum der Analyse der Sorgestruktur die These, daß der Charakter dessen, was für das Dasein konstitutiv ist, schlechthin konstituiert ist, zur zentralen Einsicht bezüglich der Geworfenheit erklärt, ist die Rücknahme des Abstraktionsschrittes dann abgeschlossen. Die These lautet: „Zur Seinsverfassung des Daseins und zwar als Konstitutivum seiner Erschlossenheit gehört die Geworfenheit (...) Die Erschlossenheit ist *wesenhaft faktische.*" (S. 221, Hervorh. von mir)

Dieser einzig durch die ontologische Differenz ermöglichte Standpunkt, der die vorherige Unterscheidung Heideggers zwischen der jeweils „erschlossenen Bedeutsamkeit" und der davon abstrahierten ‚Bedeutsamkeit' überhaupt jeglicher Bedeutung benimmt, wird sich im Verlaufe von Heideggers Analysen in die innere Unmöglichkeit verwandeln, die mittels dieser Abstraktion beanspruchte Begründungsleistung – dergemäß ja die Konstitution von „Welt" auf die „existenziale Verfassung des Daseins" zurückzuführen ist – durch eine ‚existenziale Analytik des Daseins' einzulösen. Damit ist die Sackgasse, in die *Sein und Zeit* gerät, bereits vorgezeichnet. Wir werden im weiteren sehen,

wie sich in der darauffolgenden Erschlossenheitsanalyse das hier sich
schon abzeichnende Problem noch einmal wiederholt.

IV

Die Brisanz der Erschlossenheitsanalyse Heideggers wird erst dann
voll erkennbar, wenn man sie vor dem Hintergrund seiner Auseinandersetzung mit der Bewußtseinsphilosophie situiert.

Gegen sie macht Heidegger nun zwei Einsichten geltend, die den
‚hermeneutischen Kern' von *Sein und Zeit* ausmachen, nämlich: erstens
die *Universalität der Als-Struktur*, die der in der Analyse des In-der-Weltseins herausgearbeiteten Universalität der Zeichenstruktur entspricht[5],
und zweitens die – aus der ersten folgende – Einsicht in den *Vorrang des
Verstehens vor dem Erkennen*, die hier in die These einmündet, daß die
Aussage ein abkünftiger Modus der Auslegung ist.[6]

Das gemeinsame Zentrum, von dem her Heidegger beide Einsichten
entwickelt, bildet diejenige Als-Struktur, die das In-der-Welt-sein charakterisiert, und die sowohl vor jedem ‚schlichten Sehen' als auch entsprechend vor jeder ‚thematischen Aussage' darüber liegt. Um diese vorgängige Als-Struktur zu explizieren, bringt Heidegger in den hier
angesprochenen Paragraphen die „Artikulation der Verständlichkeit" ins
Spiel. Dieses zentrale Argument liest sich bei Heidegger folgendermaßen: „Die *Artikulation des Verstandenen* in der auslegenden Nährung
des Seienden am Leitfaden des ‚Etwas als etwas' liegt *vor der thematischen Aussage* darüber. In dieser taucht das ‚Als' nicht zuerst auf, sondern
wird nur erst ausgesprochen, was allein so möglich ist, daß es als *Aussprechbares vorliegt.*" (S. 149, Hervorh. von mir)

---

[5] Diese These vertritt Heidegger hier mit der Behauptung, daß „alles vorprädikative
schlichte Sehen des Zuhandenen an ihm selbst schon verstehend-auslegend [ist]."
(S. 149) Hiermit wird der wichtigste Schritt innerhalb Heideggers Kritik am Wahrnehmungsmodell der Bewußtseinsphilosophie vollzogen. Damit tritt nun aber zugleich systematisch eine unendliche Vielfalt von Interpretationen an die Stelle der
von der Bewußtseinsphilosophie als gesichert angenommen, interpretationsunabhängigen ‚Außenwelt', die dem ‚schlichten Sehen' unvermittelt zugänglich ist. Um dieser
Einsicht gerecht zu werden, trifft Heidegger die Unterscheidung zwischen Verstehen
und Auslegung (§ 32).

[6] Zu einer ausführlicheren Interpretation der Erschlossenheitsanalyse anhand des Verhältnisses beider Thesen zueinander siehe Lafont, C.: *Sprache und Welterschließung.
Zur linguistischen Wende der Hermeneutik*, Diss. phil., Frankfurt a. M., im Erscheinen.

Die Rolle der Sprache in „Sein und Zeit"

Die Situierung dieser ‚Artikulation der Verständlichkeit' wird Heidegger aber erst im nächsten, „Da-Sein und Rede. Die Sprache" betitelten Paragraphen vornehmen, indem er erklärt: „*Die Rede ist mit Befindlichkeit und Verstehen existenzial gleichursprünglich.* Verständlichkeit ist auch schon vor der zueignenden Auslegung immer schon gegliedert. Rede ist die Artikulation der Verständlichkeit. Sie liegt daher der Auslegung und Aussage schon zugrunde." (S. 161)

In dieser Erläuterung finden wir nun also Heideggers eingangs erwähnte systematische Erweiterung des S-O-Schemas wieder, die ja in der Einsicht in die „eigentümliche Bestimmtheit der Welt (…) durch das Schon-gesprochen-und-durchgesprochen-sein" (GA 20, S. 75) besteht, welche wiederum vor jedem „schlichten Sehen" und jeder „theoretischen Aussage" (bzw. „erkennen") den primären Zugang zum Seienden ermöglicht.

Diese Einsicht in die ‚konstitutive' Rolle der Sprache für die Erschlossenheit des Daseins steht jedoch quer zum methodologischen Vorhaben von *Sein und Zeit*, den Entwurf einer Fundamentalontologie zu leisten, quer also eben zur damit einhergehenden ‚Auszeichnung' des Daseins – dergemäß ja das ‚Ontologische' (bzw. ‚konstitutive') im Unterschied zum ‚Ontischen' der Daseinsverfassung zugeschrieben werden müßte. Um diese ‚Auszeichnung' nun beibehalten zu können, wird Heidegger dieselben Trennungsversuche unternehmen, die schon im Rahmen der Analyse der Bedeutsamkeit erkennbar waren, indem er die Rede zum „existenzial-ontologische[n] Fundament der Sprache" (S. 160) erklärt. So sehr Heidegger sich nämlich dort den impliziten Platonismus in der Trennung zwischen dem Zeichen als innerweltlichem Seienden und der ‚Verweisung selbst' als ‚Bedeutsamkeit' durch sein Festhalten an der transzendentalen Fragestellung selbst aufgezwungen hatte, so sehr bleibt er auch hier letztlich dem Sprachbegriff der Bewußtseinsphilosophie verhaftet.

Statt nämlich eine gegenüber diesem Erbe adäquatere neue Auffassung der Sprache zu entwickeln (wie er es dann nach der ‚Kehre' tat), übernimmt Heidegger hier den Terminus ‚Sprache' im üblichen Sinn als Werkzeug/Zeichensystem – ‚innerweltliches Seiendes'. Da dieses Modell jedoch zugleich zur Situierung seiner bereits erreichten und den Rahmen der Bewußtseinsphilosophie sprengenden Einsicht nicht ausreicht, greift er dann auf die Humboldtsche Unterscheidung zwischen Sprache als System („ergon") und Sprache als Prozeß bzw. Rede („energeia") zurück, um daraufhin die symbolische Strukturierung der ‚Welt' als ‚Verweisungszusammenhang', d.h. die ‚ontologische' Dimension der Sprache, die ja bereits als ‚Bedeutsamkeit' der eigentliche Ertrag der Zeichenanalyse gewesen war, in die ‚Artikulation der Rede' (und damit – wie es Heidegger folgend zunächst scheinen muß – auch in die ‚existenziale Verfassung des Daseins') zu verlegen.

Im Gegensatz zu Humboldt aber meint Heidegger, mittels der Unterscheidung Sprache/Rede, die eigentlich nur die *methodologische* Differenz zweier Perspektiven der Sprachbetrachtung markieren kann, ein *Fundierungs*verhältnis begründen zu können, wenn er nochmals eine Trennung der ‚ontologischen' und der ‚ontischen' Dimension innerhalb dieses Phänomens vornimmt.

Auf diese Weise wird zwar durchaus eine stark an Humboldt orientierte Perspektive der Sprachanalyse erkennbar, in der der *konstitutive* Charakter der Sprache (als ‚Rede') für die „Erschlossenheit des Daseins" in Anschlag gebracht wird[7]; auf der anderen Seite jedoch wird zugleich (wie aus Heideggers Kritik an Humboldt besonders deutlich hervorgeht) dadurch, daß die Rede als ein Existenzial des Daseins aufgefaßt wird, immer noch der Versuch fortgeführt, dieses Phänomen (die ‚Artikulation') als kategorial von der Sprache (als Zeichensystem) unterscheidbar zu betrachten, um die ‚welterschließenden' Leistungen dieser dritten Instanz doch noch auf das Dasein selbst zurückführen zu können.

Aus dem Fundierungsverhältnis zwischen ‚Rede' und ‚Sprache' bzw. aus der von Heidegger anvisierten Trennung zwischen ‚gegliederten Bedeutung' und Worten (derentwegen den Bedeutungen „Worte zuwachsen" (S. 161), die ihrerseits als „Wörterdinge" nicht mit Bedeutungen versehen werden können), resultiert das für diesen Paragraphen charakteristische Verständnis der ‚Sprache' als Instrument: „Die Hinausgesprochenheit der Rede ist die *Sprache*. Diese Wortganzheit, als in welcher die Rede ein eigenes ‚weltliches' Sein hat, wird so *als innerweltlich Seiendes wie ein Zuhandenes vorfindlich.*" (S. 161, Hervorh. von mir)

---

[7] Schon anhand von Heideggers Rechtfertigung der Wahl des Terminus „Rede" zeichnet sich die Linie der Kontinuität ab zwischen dem, was Heidegger in *Sein und Zeit* unter dem Titel ‚Rede' thematisiert, und dem, was er nach der ‚Kehre' als ‚Sprache' fassen wird. Heidegger leitet den Terminus in *Sein und Zeit* ja wie seine Vorgänger aus der Hamann-Herder-Humboldt-Tradition vom griechischen ‚logos'-Begriff her: „Das Dasein hat Sprache. Ist es Zufall, daß die Griechen (...) das Wesen des Menschen bestimmten als *zōon lógon échon?* (...) *Der Mensch zeigt sich als Seiendes, das redet*. Das bedeutet nicht, daß ihm die Möglichkeit der stimmlichen Verlautbarung eignet, sondern daß dieses Seiende ist in der Weise des *Entdeckens der Welt* und des Daseins selbst." (S. 165, Hervorh. v. mir)

Heidegger wird nachträglich in einer Randbemerkung in seinem Handexemplar von *Sein und Zeit* zum obigen Zitat die Unhaltbarkeit dieser Trennung *explizit* benennen, wenn er eingesteht, daß „für Sprache Geworfenheit *wesentlich* [ist]". (S. 443 <161 a>, Hervorh. von mir)

An dieser Bemerkung Heideggers zeigt sich in aller Klarheit, auf welches systematisches Hindernis die in seiner Sprachanalyse angestrebte (aber nur von einem vom Umstand des In-der-Welt-seins unberührten Standpunkt aus durchführbare) Trennung stoßen muß: die ontologische Dimension der Rede, die ‚Artikulation der Verständlichkeit', ist gerade eine Konsequenz der ontischen Beschaffenheit der Sprache als Zuhandenes (weil die Sprache eben wie das Dasein „nicht nur unter anderen Seienden vorkommt"); daher kann die „Artikulation der Verständlichkeit" *nur in der Sprache* „eine spezifisch *weltliche* Seinsart haben" (S. 161.)[8]

Auf diese Weise aber wächst der Sprache hier dieselbe ‚Transferrolle' zwischen ‚ontisch' und ‚ontologisch' zu, die bereits das Zeichen in der Weltanalyse hatte – womit ja gleichzeitig offensichtlich wurde, daß und wovon die ‚Auszeichnung' des Daseins lediglich entliehen war. Gerade weil diese ‚Transferinstanz' für die Erschlossenheitsanalyse nicht verzichtbar ist, wird Heidegger dann auch im weiteren Verlauf der Analyse selbst nicht mehr daran vorbeikommen, die Trennung zwischen Rede und Sprache *implizit* rückgängig zu machen, indem er in Preisgabe aller zuvor getroffenen kategorialen Unterscheidungen sagt: „Die Rede spricht sich zumeist aus und hat sich *schon immer* ausgesprochen. *Sie ist Sprache*. (...) Die Sprache als die Ausgesprochenheit birgt eine Ausgelegtheit des Daseinsverständnisses in sich. *Diese Ausgelegtheit ist so wenig wie die Sprache nur noch vorhanden, sondern ihr Sein ist selbst daseinsmäßiges.* (...) Die Ausgesprochenheit verwahrt im Ganzen ihrer gegliederten Bedeutungszusammenhänge ein *Verstehen der erschlossenen Welt* und gleichursprünglich damit ein Verstehen des *Mitdaseins Anderer* und des *je eigenen* In-Seins. Das so in der Ausgesprochenheit schon hinterlegte Verständnis betrifft sowohl die jeweils erreichte und überkommene Entdecktheit des Seienden als auch das *jeweilige Verständnis von Sein* (...). Über einen bloßen Hinweis auf das Faktum dieser Ausgelegtheit

---

[8] Hierin liegt der Grund für die Schwierigkeiten Heideggers, durch die Unterscheidung Sprache/Rede die Trennschärfe des Fundierungsverhältnisses konstitutiv/konstituiert einzuholen. Heidegger muß immer wieder bemerken: „Weil für das Sein des Da, das heißt Befindlichkeit und Verstehen die Rede konstitutiv ist, Dasein aber besagt: In-der-Welt-sein, hat das Dasein als redendes In-Sein sich *schon* ausgesprochen. Das Dasein hat Sprache" (S. 165)

des Daseins hinaus muß nun aber nach der existenzialen Seinsart der ausgesprochenen und sich aussprechenden Rede gefragt werden. Wenn sie nicht als Vorhandenes begriffen werden kann, welches ist ihr Sein [?]" (S. 167–168, Hervorh. von mir)

Dies nun stellt die Schlüsselstelle für das Verständnis all der Unstimmigkeiten dar, die bislang im Durchgang durch die von Heidegger *de facto* durchgeführten Analysen auf verschiedenen Ebenen aufgetaucht sind.

Die gleiche versteckte Autorschaft des Zeichens, aufgrund deren eigenartiger Funktion des ‚Zeigens' erst der Zusammenhang von Zuhandenem, der die Welt ist, *zugänglich* werden konnte, findet sich hier im Zentrum der Analyse des Daseins selbst in der Form der Rede bzw. Sprache wieder. Im ersten Fall gelang es Heidegger noch, durch sein Entgegenwirken mittels der impliziten Zurückführung des Zeigens des Zeichens auf die „Sorgestruktur" *des Daseins* (vgl. S. 83) die Augen vor dieser versteckten dritten Instanz zu verschließen; da es sich aber bei unserem jetzigen Kontext um den Kern der Analyse der ‚Seinsverfassung' des Daseins selbst handelt, steht ihm diese Verschiebungsstrategie nicht mehr zur Verfügung. Heidegger ist deswegen hier erstmals gezwungen, zuzugeben, daß eine von Dasein unterschiedene Instanz, die Rede bzw. die Sprache, eine Ausgelegtheit in sich birgt, die „sowenig wie die Sprache nur noch vorhanden [ist], sondern [deren] Sein selbst *daseinsmäßig* [ist]." Und dadurch wird die Sprache in ihrem ‚ontischen' und zugleich ‚ontologischen' Status erstmals als verantwortlich für das jeweilige ‚Verstehen von Sein' identifiziert, und d.h. eben für das Faktum, von dem *Sein und Zeit* ausgegangen war.

Hier finden wir deswegen die systematische, wenn auch von Heidegger in *Sein und Zeit* nicht reflektierte Erklärung dafür, daß das Dasein so überzeugend als „In-der-Welt-sein" charakterisiert werden konnte, bzw. dafür, wie es möglich ist, daß dem Dasein so etwas wie „Welt" *vorgegeben* ist (und daher „die Erschlossenheit wesenhaft faktische [ist]"). Somit stellt sich dann der Kern von Heideggers Kritik am Wahrnehmungsmodell der Bewußtseinsphilosophie folgendermaßen dar: „Dieser alltäglichen *Ausgelegtheit*, in die das Dasein zunächst hineinwächst, *vermag es sich nie zu entziehen*. In ihr und aus ihr und gegen sie vollzieht sich alles echte Verstehen, Auslegen und Mitteilen (…). Es ist nicht so, daß je ein Dasein unberührt und unverführt durch diese Ausgelegtheit *vor das freie Land einer ‚Welt' an sich* gestellt würde, um nur zu schauen, was ihm begegnet." (S. 169, Hervorh. von mir)

Vor dem Hintergrund der Ergebnisse der Erschlossenheitsanalyse erscheint nun Heideggers eigenes Vorgehen zu ihrer Durchführung zwar höchst unplausibel, es besitzt aber bei Berücksichtigung des Ganzen des Unternehmens *Sein und Zeit* doch einige Folgerichtigkeit. Heidegger war von der Prämisse eines einheitlichen Sinns von Sein ausgegangen, der aus der Zeitlichkeit der ‚existenzialen Seinsverfassung' des Daseins zu entnehmen wäre. Der Sinn einer solchen Fragestellung (die darauf hinausläuft, das kulturelle Wissen im Ganzen zu ‚begründen') entstammt wiederum der Grundeinstellung, daß es eine Fundamentalontologie geben könne, die die Bedingung der Möglichkeit aller anderen Ontologien wäre, bzw. der Überzeugung, daß „die Bedeutungslehre in der Ontologie des Daseins verwurzelt [ist]" (S. 166). Daher versucht er sich in der Analyse der Sprache die benötigte Einheit zu sichern, indem er die Trennung zwischen den ‚ontischen' gegebenen Sprachen und der mittels seiner eigenen Abstraktion zum Singular geronnenen ‚ontologischen' Artikulation der Verständlichkeit in Angriff nimmt; diese Einheit würde es nun wiederum erlauben, nach dem Erreichen eines „positive[n] Verständnis[ses] der apriorischen Grundstrukturen von Rede überhaupt als Existenzial" (S. 165) „nach den *Grundformen einer möglichen bedeutungsmäßigen Gliederung des Verstehbaren überhaupt* [zu fragen]" (S. 166, Hervorh. von mir). Mit ihr nun ließe sich ohne weiteres die nächste Annahme Heideggers rechtfertigen, daß „aus der Zeitlichkeit *der Rede, das heißt des Daseins überhaupt*, erst die ‚Entstehung' von ‚Bedeutung' aufgeklärt [werden kann]" (S. 349, Hervorh. von mir), und dies sogar ohne den für die „transzendentale Fragestellung" eher unbequemen Umweg einer Betrachtung der verschiedenen ‚ontischen' Sprachen in Kauf nehmen zu müssen, der ja nicht unbedingt für eine solche Einheit bürgen könnte (das macht dann – wie gesehen – auch die Kritik Heideggers an Humboldt in *Sein und Zeit* aus).

Heidegger glaubt nun solange, die ‚Artikulation' der Rede mit dem „Dasein überhaupt" gleichsetzen zu können – und dadurch diese von ihm eingeführte dritte Instanz wieder dem Dasein selbst anzuverwandeln –, wie es ihm gelingt, die ‚ontologische' Dimension der ‚Artikulation der Verständlichkeit' (dank seiner hypostasierenden Lesart der ontologischen Differenz) noch als von den ‚ontischen' Sprachen verschieden zu erklären.[9]

---

[9] Auf diese Weise kann Heidegger also beide o.g. Kunstgriffe gleichzeitig anwenden: einerseits kann er nämlich die ‚Rede' zum konstitutiven Moment der „Erschlossenheit"

Daß Heidegger aus dieser Perspektive heraus Humboldt kritisiert, verwundert dann nicht weiter. Gerade weil Humboldt sich über die ‚konstitutive' Rolle der artikulierten Sprachen als ‚welterschließenden' im klaren war, konnte er es eben nicht mehr als sinnvoll betrachten, die „Grundformen einer möglichen bedeutungsmäßigen Gliederung des *Verstehbaren überhaupt*" aus der „Ontologie des Daseins" entnehmen zu wollen. Gerade aus einer solchen Perspektive tritt die von Heidegger als tragfähig angenommene „*Einheit* der Bedeutsamkeit, das heißt die *ontologische Verfassung der Welt*" (S. 365, Hervorh. von mir) zugunsten der irreduziblen Mannigfaltigkeit der in den natürlichen Sprachen liegenden Weltansicht*en* zurück. Diese sind dann jedoch lediglich einer sprachphilosophischen Behandlung zugänglich. Die Pluralität der Weltansichten kommt erst in dem Moment ans Licht, in dem zwei systematische Aspekte (auf die auch Heidegger in den zwei von uns zitierten Bemerkungen in seinem Handexemplar von *Sein und Zeit* aufmerksam macht) zur Geltung gebracht werden, die den ‚konstitutiven' Charakter der Sprache in verschiedener Hinsicht auf den Punkt bringen, und zwar als ontologischen ‚Ort' der Welterschließung (vgl. *Sein und Zeit*, S. 442 <87c>), und als schlechthin *ontisch-ontologisch* verfaßt – und daher untrennbar von ihrer materiellen Konkretion (vgl. *Sein und Zeit*, S. 443 <161 a>); das hat zur Folge, daß eine hypostasierende Lesart der ontologischen Differenz widersinnig wird, womit sich ferner der Abstraktionsschritt von den gegebenen natürlichen, historischen Sprachen zu so etwas wie ‚den Grundformen einer möglichen bedeutungsmäßigen Gliederung des Verstehbaren überhaupt' verbietet.

Vor diesem Hintergrund versteht man dann besser die internen Schwierigkeiten, auf die Heidegger in *Sein und Zeit* in dem Moment stoßen muß, in dem er unter der Annahme seiner hypostasierenden Interpretation der ontologischen Differenz in der Analyse selbst noch die

---

des Daseins erklären – und damit eine immer schon artikulierte Verständlichkeit als primären Zugang zum Seienden behaupten (statt des „schlichten Sehens" der Bewußtseinsphilosophie). Andererseits vermag er sich der durch die Beibehaltung der transzendentalen Fragestellung erforderlichen Einheit zu versichern, indem er die Hypostasierung einer von den verschiedenen immer schon artikulierten Sprachen abstrahierten „Artikulation der Rede" (überhaupt) vollzieht – und damit die Suche nach „den Grundformen einer möglichen bedeutungsmäßigen *Gliederung des Verstehbaren überhaupt*" (S. 166, Hervorh. v. mir) als sinnvoll betrachten kann; sie stellten dann die hinreichende Bedingung für die Herleitung jeder möglichen Sinnkonstitution dar.

doppelte Seinsart der Sprache endgültig festzumachen versucht, was bedeuten würde, im Rahmen von *Sein und Zeit* eine Antwort auf die Frage zu finden „welche Seinsart der Sprache überhaupt zukommt. Ist sie ein innerweltlich zuhandenes Zeug, oder hat sie die Seinsart des Daseins oder keines von beiden?" (S. 166).

Daß diese Fragestellung *auftauchen mußte*, obwohl es vorher (S. 161) als ausgemacht gelten sollte, daß die Sprache als ‚innerweltliches Seiendes' anzusehen sei, verwundert schließlich nicht weiter, wenn man sich die Aufgabe vor Augen hält, die sich Heidegger vorgenommen hatte, nämlich, „*den ontologischen ‚Ort'* für dieses Phänomen [die Sprache, C.L.] innerhalb der Seinsverfassung des Daseins auf[zu]zeigen." (S. 166) Aber gerade weil es Heidegger gelingt, dieses Phänomen in seiner *ontologischen* (bzw. welterschließenden) Dimension abzuhandeln, müssen ihm solcherlei Zweifel über die „Seinsart der Sprache überhaupt" kommen. Für die einzig mögliche Antwort darauf, bzw. für dieses „keines von beiden" aber gibt es im Rahmen von *Sein und Zeit* keinen Ort.

Hans-Georg Gadamer

2. Destruktion *and* Deconstruction*

Translated by Geoff Waite and Richard Palmer

When Heidegger took the topic of understanding and elevated it from a methodology for the human sciences into an *"Existentiale"* and the foundation for an ontology of Dasein, this meant that the hermeneutical dimension no longer represented merely a higher level of a phenomenological research into intentionality, a research ultimately grounded in processes of bodily perception. Rather, it brought onto European soil and into the whole direction on phenomenology a major breakthrough, a breakthrough which, at almost exactly the same time, was gaining currency in Anglo-Saxon logic as the "linguistic turn." This was of special importance because in the original development of phenomenological research by Husserl and Scheler, language had remained completely overshadowed by other factors, in spite of the strength of the turn to the world of "lived experience."

In phenomenology, then, the same abysmal forgetfulness of language, so characteristic of transcendental idealism, was repeated, thus appearing to confirm, albeit belatedly, Herder's ill-fated criticism of the Kantian transcendental turn. Even in Hegelian dialectic and logic, language occupied no special place of honor. To be sure, Hegel occasionally alluded to the "logical instinct" of language, whose speculative anticipation of the Absolute posed for Hegel the task of his brilliant work on logic. And in fact, after Kant's intricately rococo Germanizing of the terminology of scholastic metaphysics the significance of

---

*This paper was presented in Rome in 1985 and later published in the second volume of Gadamer's collected works under the title "Destruktion und Deconstruktion" (*GW* 2 361-72). Since the essay is in part an effort to show that Heidegger's use of the term *Destruktion* does not mean "destruction" at all but something quite different, we have left the term untranslated in the title and throughout this volume.—Editors' note.

Hegel's contribution to philosophical language is unmistakable. His great linguistic and conceptual energy remind one of Aristotle, and indeed Hegel comes closest to Aristotle's great example to the extent that he was able to recuperate the spirit of his mother tongue in the language of concepts. Of course, just this circumstance set up in front of Hegel's writings a barrier of untranslatability that was simply insurmountable for more than a century, and even to this day remains a most difficult obstacle. Even so, language, as such, was never made a central theme in Hegel's thought.

With Heidegger a similar and even stronger explosion of primal, originary linguistic power occurred in the realm of thinking. But accompanying this breakthrough came Heidegger's conscious reversion to the originality of Greek philosophical discourse. With the sheer palpable power of a vitality rooted in the indigenous soil of the life-world, "language" thus became a force which burst powerfully through the highly refined descriptive art of Husserlian phenomenology. At that point it was inescapable that language itself would become the object of philosophical self-reflection. Already in 1920, as I myself can testify, a young thinker—Heidegger, to be exact—began to lecture from a German university podium on what it might mean to say "*es weltet*": it "worlds." This was an unprecedented break with the solid and dignified, but at the same time scholasticized, language of metaphysics that had become completely alienated from its own origins.

What Heidegger was doing signaled a profound linguistic event in its own right, and at the same time the achievement of a deeper understanding of language in general. At that time, what the tradition of German idealism in von Humboldt, the Grimm brothers, Schleiermacher, the Schlegels, and finally Dilthey, had contributed with regard to the phenomenon of language—and that also had given unexpected impetus to the new linguistic science, above all comparative linguistics—still remained within the conceptual limits of *Identitätsphilosophie*, the philosophy of identity. The identity of the subjective and objective, of thinking and being, of nature and Spirit, were maintained right up into Cassirer's philosophy of symbolic forms, among which language was preeminent. This tradition reached its highest peak, of course, in the synthetic achievement of the Hegelian dialectic: here, throughout all the oppositions and differentiations, identity was reconstructed and the originally Aristotelian conception of *noesis noēseoos* [sic] reached its purest elaboration. The final paragraph of Hegel's *Encyclopedia of the Philosophic Sciences* has given this conception its most challenging formulation. As if the whole long history of the spirit [*Geist*] was really working toward a single goal, which Hegel expressed by borrowing from a famous verse of Virgil: "*Tantae molis erat se ipsam cognoscere mentem*"—"Such was the cost in heavy labor of coming to know one's own mind."[1]

Actually, a perennial challenge to the new postmetaphysical thinking in our century resides in the fact that Hegel's dialectical mediation had already accomplished the overcoming of modern subjectivism. We need look no further than the Hegelian notion of objective spirit for eloquent witness to this. Even the religiously motivated critique that Kierkegaard's "either/or" directed at the "this, but also that" of Hegel's dialectical self-supersession of all propositions could be incorporated by Hegel's dialectic into a totalizing mediation. Indeed, even Heidegger's critique of the concept of consciousness, which, through a radical ontological *Destruktion* showed that idealism of consciousness in its totality was really an alienated form of Greek thinking, and which boldly confronted the overly formal, neo-Kantian element in Husserl's phenomenology, was not a complete breakthrough. For what he called the "fundamental ontology of Dasein" could not—despite all the temporal analyses of how Dasein is constituted as *Sorge* ["Care"]—overcome its own self-reference and hence a fundamental positing of self-consciousness. For this reason, fundamental ontology was not able fully to break away from immanent consciousness of the Husserlian type.

Heidegger himself very soon acknowledged this problem, and so made his own the hazardously radical thought experiments with Nietzsche, without, however, finding any paths other than *Holzwege,* the kind of circuitous dead-ends cut by loggers on wooded hillsides. And these paths, after the *Kehre,* or turn of the way of Heidegger's thinking toward Being, led into impassable regions. Could it be that only the language of metaphysics sustains this paralyzing spell of transcendental idealism? In turning away from the foundationalist thinking of metaphysics, Heidegger drew the extremest possible consequences from his critique of the ontological groundlessness of consciousness and self-consciousness: he turned away altogether from the conceptual attempt of metaphysics to ground itself. Yet, both his "turn" and this "turning away" remained locked in a permanent wrestling match with metaphysics. Not only did Heidegger, in order to prepare for the overcoming of metaphysics, propose to go beyond modern subjectivism through the *Destruktion* or de-structuring of its unproven concepts, but also—on the positive side—to recover the primordial Greek experience of Being by lighting up the idea of Being lying behind the rise and dominance of Western metaphysics. In actuality, though, Heidegger's step back from Aristotle's concept of Being as *physis* to the experience of Being in its Presocratic beginnings remained an adventurous journey into error. Granted, the distant goal, however vague, was always before his eyes: to think anew the beginning, the primal, the originary. But to come closer to the beginning always means to become aware, in retracing the path from whence one came, of other open possibilities.

Whoever stands at the very beginning must choose his path. If one gets back to the beginning, one becomes aware of the fact that from that starting point one could have gone other ways—perhaps just as Eastern thought has taken other ways. Perhaps the direction taken by Eastern thought (like that taken by the West) did not arise from a free choice. Rather, it may be due to the circumstance that no grammatical construction of subject and predicate was present to steer Eastern thought into the metaphysics of substance and accident. So it is not surprising that one can find in Heidegger's journey back to the beginning something of a fascination with Eastern thought, and he even sought to take a few steps down that path with the help of Japanese and Chinese visitors—in vain. Languages—especially the basic structure common to all the languages in one's culture—are not easily circumventable. Indeed, even when tracing one's own ancestry one can never reach back to its beginning. It always slips away into uncertainty, as it does for the wanderer on the coast in the famous depiction of stepping back in time that Thomas Mann gives us in *The Magic Mountain,* where each final promontory of land yields to yet another in an endless progression. Similarly, Heidegger hoped to find in Anaximander, then in Heraclitus, then in Parmenides, then again in Heraclitus, in the originary experience of Being, testimony to the mutual interweaving of concealment and disclosure. In Anaximander he believed he found presence itself and the tarrying of its essence, in Parmenides the untrembling heart of *Aletheia,* or truth as unconcealment, and in Heraclitus the *physis* that loves to conceal itself. But in the end, although all this was valid enough for the kind of indicative linguistic gesture that would point off into timelessness, it was not really valid for the speaking— that is to say, the kind of self-interpretation—one encounters in the early Greek texts. In the name, in the naming power of words and their labyrinthian paths to error, Heidegger found precious veins of gold, in which he could only recognize again and again his own vision of Being: that "Being" is not to be construed as the Being of beings. But, over and over again, each of these texts turned out not to be the final promontory on the way to a free and unobstructed view of Being.

So it was almost predetermined, so to speak, that on this path of mining the primal rock of words Heidegger would finally encounter Nietzsche, whose extremism had already ventured the self-destruction of all metaphysics, all truth, and all knowledge of truth. Of course, Nietzsche's own conceptual artistry could not satisfy Heidegger, however much he welcomed Nietzsche's breaking of the spell of dialectic—"Hegel's veil and those of other veil-makers [*Schleiermacher*]"—and however much he wanted to corroborate Nietzsche's vision of philosophy in the tragic age of Greece, as still something other than the metaphysics of a true world behind our world of appearances. Yet, all these things really only meant for Heidegger becoming a fellow traveller with Nietzsche for a short stretch of his own way. "So many centuries—and no new God"—this was the motto for Heidegger's reception of Nietzsche.

But what did Heidegger know of a new God? Did he dimly imagine God and lack only the language to evoke Him? Was he too bewitched by the language of metaphysics? In spite of all its preconceptual inescapability, language is not simply the Babylonian captivity of the human mind. Nor does the tower of Babel story from our Biblical heritage mean only that human hubris has led to the multiplicity of languages and linguistic families. Rather, this story also encompasses in its meaning the strangeness that arises between one human being and another, always creating new confusion. But precisely in this fact lies the possibility of overcoming confusion. For language is conversation. One must look for the word that can reach another person. And it is possible for one to find it; one can even learn the language of the other person. One can cross over into the language of the other in order to reach the other. All this is possible for language as language.

To be sure, the "binding element" in conversation, in the sense of that which produces itself in the form of the self-generating language of mutual comprehension, is by its very nature necessarily surrounded by *Gerede,* or idle chatter, and thus by the mere appearance of speaking. Jacques Lacan was right when he said that the word not directed to another person is such an empty word. Just this suggests the primacy that must be accorded to the kind of conversation that evolves as question and answer and builds up a common language. A familiar experience among two people who do not speak each other's language yet can halfway understand the language of the other person is that one discovers that one cannot hold a conversation on this basis at all. In effect, a slow motion duel takes place until one of the two languages is spoken by both people, however badly one of the partners may speak it. Anyone can experience this, and it suggests something quite important. For in fact not only do conversational partners speaking different languages experience this, but also partners speaking the same native language, making mutual adjustments as they talk. It is only the answer, actual or potential, that transforms a word into a word.

All rhetoric, too, falls within the scope of this experience. Because it does not permit a constant exchange of question and answer, speaking and responding, rhetoric always contains bursts of empty words that we recognize as fluff or as a mere "manner of speaking." Likewise, the same thing goes on in the actual event of understanding as we listen or are in the process of reading. The fulfillment of meaning in these cases, as Husserl in particular has shown, is interspersed with empty intentions.

At this point we must think further about whether that phrase, "the language of metaphysics," really has a meaning. Certainly what it can mean is not the language in which metaphysics was first developed, namely, the philosopher's language of the Greeks. Rather, what it does mean is that certain conceptual formulations, derived from the original language of metaphysics, have impressed themselves into the living languages of present-day speech communities. In scientific and philosophical discourse we call this the role of terminology. In the mathematics-based natural sciences—above all the experimental sciences—the introduction of terms is purely a matter of convention, serving to designate states of affairs available to all and which do not involve any genuine relation of meaning between these terms introduced into international use and the peculiarities of national language; for instance, in thinking of a "volt," is there anyone who also thinks of Alessandro Volta, the great scientist?

When it comes to philosophy, though, things are quite different. In philosophy there are no generally accessible, that is to say, verifiable realms of experience designated by prearranged terminology. The concept-words coined in the realm of philosophy are, rather, always articulated by means of the spoken language in which they emerge. Of course, here, as in science, concept formation also means that among the many rays of possible meaning a given word has acquired, its definition moves toward a more exactly determined meaning. But in philosophy such concept-words are never completely separable from the semantic field in which they possess their full meaning. Indeed, the complete separation of a word from its context and its enclosure (what Aristotle calls "*horismos*," boundary) within a precise content not only makes it into a concept but also necessarily threatens its use with an emptying out of meaning. Thus, the formation of such a basic metaphysical concept as *ousia*, or substance, is never fully accessible so long as the sense of the Greek word is not present with it in the full breadth of its meaning. In this regard, it enhances our understanding of the Greek concept of Being to know that the primary meaning of the word *ousia* in Greek referred to agricultural property, and that the meaning of this concept as the presence of what is present originates from this.

This example teaches us that there is no "language of metaphysics." There is only a metaphysically thought-out coinage of concepts that have been lifted from living speech. Such coinage of concepts can, as in the case of Aristotelian logic and ontology, establish a fixed conceptual tradition and consequently lead to an alienation from the living language. In the case of *ousia*, such alienation set in early with Hellenistic pedagogy and was continued as this pedagogy was carried over into Latin. Subsequently, with the translating of the Latin into the national languages of the present to form a contemporary pedagogical language, the concept of *ousia* has increasingly lost its original sense as grounded in the experience of being. Thus, the task of a *Destruktion* of the conceptuality of metaphysics was posed. This is the only tenable sense of talk about the "language of metaphysics": this phrase simply refers to the conceptuality that has been built up in the history of metaphysics.

Early on, Heidegger was to put forward as a rallying cry the task of a *Destruktion* of the alienated conceptuality of metaphysics: the ongoing task of contemporary thinking.[2] With unbelievable freshness, he was able to trace in thinking the concepts of the tradition back to the Greek language, back to the natural sense of words and the hidden wisdom of language they contain, and in so doing, to give new life to Greek thought and its power to address us today. Such was Heidegger's genius. He had a penchant for restoring to words their hidden, no longer intended sense, and then from this so-called etymology to draw fundamental consequences for thinking. It is significant in this regard that the later Heidegger speaks of *"Urworten,"* or "primal words," words in which what he regards as the Greek experience of the world is brought to language far more palpably than in the doctrines and propositions of the early Greek texts.

But Heidegger was certainly not the first to realize the scholasticized language of metaphysics had become alienated from its subject-matter. Since Fichte and above all since Hegel, one finds German idealism already striving by means of the dialectical movement of thought to dissolve and melt down the Greek ontology of substance and its conceptuality. Precursors of this striving existed even among those who employed scholastic Latin, especially in cases where, alongside their scholastic treatises, the living word of vernacular preaching marched in parallel, as in Meister Eckart or Nicolaus Cusanus, but also later in the speculations of Jacob Boehme. Admittedly, these were marginal figures in the metaphysical tradition. When Fichte put the word *"Tathandlung"* [action, deed] in place of *"Tatsache"* [fact], he anticipated in a basic way the provocative coinages and definitions of Heidegger, who loved to stand the meaning of a word practically on its head. This shows, for example, in his understanding of *Entfernung,* or distancing, as *Näherung,* or bringing near,[3] or understanding sentences like *"Was heißt Denken?"* ["What does thinking mean?"] as meaning "What commands us to think?" Or, *"Nichts ist ohne Grund"* ["Nothing is without reason"] as asserting that *nothing* itself is groundless. All of these interpretations are clearly acts of violence committed by a swimmer who struggled to swim against the current.

Those who thought within the tradition of German idealism, however, on the whole sought to modify the form of traditional metaphysical conceptuality not so much through recovering words and forcing the meaning of words as rather through the sharpening of propositions to the point of opposition or contradiction. Dialectic has for ages meant the sharpening of immanent oppositions to such a point; and if the defense of two contradictory propositions does not just produce a negative result but instead aims precisely towards a unity of the opposing factors, then the most extreme possibility of metaphysical thinking is reached. Thinking, now moving into primordial Greek concepts, becomes capable of grasping the Absolute. But life is freedom and spirit. The strict, inner consistency of such a dialectic—a dialectic that Hegel saw as fulfilling the ideal of philosophical proof—did in fact enable him to go beyond the subjectivity of the subject and to think mind as objective, as we mentioned earlier. Ontologically, however, this movement culminated, once again, in the absolute presence of spirit present to itself, as the end of the *Encyclopedia* attests. It was for this reason that Heidegger remained in a constant and tense confrontation with the seductive appeal of dialectic, which instead of working towards the *Destruktion* of Greek concepts continued to develop the dialectical concepts of spirit and freedom—while at the same time domesticating its own thinking.

We cannot analyze here how Heidegger in his later thinking actually held to his fundamental project by maintaining, in a sublimated form, the deconstructive [*destruktive*] achievement present in its beginnings. The sibylline style of his later writings testifies to this. He was fully aware of just how "needful" language is—both his and ours. But it seems to me that, along with Heidegger's own efforts to leave behind "the language of metaphysics" with the help of Hölderlin's poetical language, two other paths exist and have in fact been taken in efforts to overcome the ontological self-domestication belonging to dialectic and move into the open. One is the path from dialectic back to dialogue, back to conversation. This the way I myself have attempted to travel in my philosophical hermeneutics. The other is the way shown primarily by Derrida, the path of deconstruction. On this path, the awakening of a meaning hidden in the life and liveliness of conversation is not an issue. Rather, it is in an ontological concept of *écriture*—not idle chatter nor even true conversation but the background network of meaning-relations lying at the basis of all speech—that the very integrity of sense as such is to be dissolved, thereby accomplishing the authentic shattering of metaphysics.

In the space of this tension [between philosophical hermeneutics and deconstruction] a most curious shift of emphasis arises. From the perspective of hermeneutic philosophy, Heidegger's doctrine of the overcoming of metaphysics, with its culmination in the total forgetfulness of Being in our technological era, skips over the continued resistance and persistence of certain flexible unities in the life we all share, unities which perdure in the large and small forms of our fellow-human being-with-each-other. Deconstruction, on the other hand, takes the opposite perspective. To it, Heidegger lacks ultimate radicality in continuing to seek the meaning of Being and thereby clinging to a question which, one can show, can have no meaningful answer corresponding to it. To the question of the meaning of Being Derrida counterposes the notion of "*différance*" and sees in Nietzsche a more radical figure in contrast to the metaphysically tempered claim of Heideggerian thinking. He views Heidegger as still aligned with logocentrism, against which he poses as a counterthesis what he calls "*écriture*": a term signifying a meaning always dispersed and deferred and shattering all totalizing unity. Manifestly, Nietzsche here represents the critical point.

Thus, if one wants to contrast and weigh the outlooks that the two paths leading back from dialectic that we have just described open up, the case of Nietzsche stands out: it allows us to discuss what possibilities there are for a thinking that can no longer continue as a metaphysics.

When I give the name "dialectic" to the point of departure from which

Heidegger seeks his own way back, it is not just for the obvious reason that Hegel created his secular synthesis of the heritage of metaphysics by means of a speculative dialectic that claimed to gather into itself the entire truth of its Greek beginnings. Rather, it is above all because, unlike Marburg Neokantianism and Husserl's Neokantian reshaping of phenomenology, Heidegger himself refused to remain within a tradition of modifying and perpetuating the heritage of metaphysics. What he strove to accomplish in the "overcoming of metaphysics" was not exhausted in a mere gesture of protest, as was the case with the left Hegelians and men like Kierkegaard and Nietzsche. Rather, he attacked his task as being a matter of hard conceptual labor, which one should learn from the study of Aristotle. Thus, the term dialectic, as I am using it here, refers to the whole wide-ranging totality of the Western tradition of metaphysics—just as much to what Hegel called "the logical" as to the "*logos*" in Greek thinking, which had already shaped the first steps in Western philosophy. It is in this sense of the term that Heidegger's quest to ask anew the question of Being, or better, to pose it for the first time in a non-metaphysical sense, the quest he called "the step back," was a way *back from* dialectic.

Likewise, the hermeneutic turn toward "conversation" that I have pursued not only seeks in some sense to go back before the dialectic of German idealism, namely, to Platonic dialectic, but it also aims even farther back before this Socratic-dialogical turn to its presupposition: the *anamnēsis* sought for and awakened in *logoi*. The "recollection" that I have in mind is derived from myth and yet is in the highest degree rational. It is not only that of the individual soul but always that of "the spirit that would like to unite us"—we who are a conversation.[4]

To be in a conversation, however, means to be beyond oneself, to think with the other and to come back to oneself as if to another. When Heidegger thinks the metaphysical concept of *Wesen* or essence no longer as the property of presence in present objects but understands the noun *Wesen* as a verb, he injects it with temporality. *Wesen*, or essence, is now understood as *Anwesen*, as actively being present, in a way grammatically counterposed to the common German expression *Verwesen*, to decay or decompose. This means, however, that Heidegger—in his essay on Anaximander, for example[5]—imputes another meaning to the original Greek experience of time, namely, a sense of dwelling, abiding, or tarrying, such as is captured in the common expression, "a space of time." In this way, he is in fact able to make his way back behind metaphysics and the whole horizon of metaphysics when it is seeking to interrogate Being. Heidegger himself reminds us that when Sartre quotes Heidegger's sentence "*Das Wesen des Daseins ist seine Existenz.*" ["The essence of Dasein is its *Existenz*, or existential possibility"], he is misusing it if he is not aware that the term "*Wesen*" is enclosed in quotation marks.[6] At stake here is decidedly not any concept of "*Essenz*," or "essence," that somehow as essence, is to precede existence or existent things. Nor at stake is some concern with the Sartrean inversion of this relation, so that existence is said to precede essence. In my opinion, when Heidegger inquires about "the meaning of Being," he is not thinking the term "meaning" in the way that metaphysics with its concept of essence does, but rather in the sense of a question that does not await a specific answer, but instead points in a certain direction for inquiry.

As I once said, "Sense is sense of a direction"—"*Sinn ist Richtungssinn.*"[7] One time, Heidegger even introduced an orthographical archaism in spelling the term "*Sein*" as "*Seyn*" in order to underscore its character as a verb. Similarly, my philosophical hermeneutics should be seen as an effort to shake off the burden of an inherited ontology of static substance, in that I started out from conversation and the common language sought and shaped in it, in which the logic of question and answer turns out to be determinative. Such logic opens up a dimension of communicative understanding that goes beyond linguistically fixed assertions, and so also beyond any all-encompassing synthesis, in the sense of in the monologue-like self-understanding of dialectic. Now admittedly, the dialectic of German idealism never completely denied its derivation from the speculative foundational structure of language, as I have explained in the third part of *Truth and Method* (*WM* 432ff./414ff.). But when Hegel put dialectic in the context of science and method, he actually covered up its ancestry, its origin in language.

Thus, philosophical hermeneutics pays particular attention to the relation of the speculative, dual unity playing between the said and the unsaid. This dual unity truly precedes any subsequent dialectical sharpening of a proposition to the point of contradiction and its supersession in a new proposition. It seems very misleading to me for someone to say that just because I emphasize the role of tradition in all our posing of questions and also in the indication of answers, I am asserting a super-subject and thus (as Manfred Frank and Philippe Forget go on to maintain) reducing the hermeneutical experience to an empty word. There is no support in *Truth and Method* for this kind of construction. When I speak there of tradition and of conversation with tradition, I am in no way putting forward a collective subject. Rather, "tradition" is simply the collective name for each individual text (text in the widest sense, which would include a picture, an architectural work, even a natural event). Certainly the platonic form of Socratic dialogue, led by one partner and followed by the other willingly or unwillingly, is a special kind of conversation, but still it remains the pattern for all conversational process insofar as in it not the words but the mind or spirit of the other is refuted. The Socratic dialogue is no spectacular play of dressing up and unmasking for the purpose of knowing better what we already know. Rather, it is the true carrying out of *anamnēsis*. What is accomplished in conversation is a summoning back in thought [*denkende Erinnerung*] that is possible only for the soul fallen into the finitude of bodily existence. This is the very meaning of the speculative unity that is achieved in the "virtuality" of the word:[8] that it is not an individual word nor is it a formulated proposition, but rather it points beyond all possible assertions.

Clearly, the dimension in which our questioning is moving here has nothing to do with a code, and the business of deciphering one. It is certainly correct that a certain decoding process underlies all writing and reading of texts, but this represents merely a precondition for hermeneutic attention to what is said in the words. In this regard, I am fully in agreement with the critique of structuralism. But it seems to me that I go beyond Derrida's deconstruction, since a word exists only in conversation and never exists there as an isolated word but as the totality of a way of accounting by means of speaking and answering.

Obviously the principle of deconstruction involves something quite similar to what I am doing, since in carrying out what he calls *écriture*, Derrida, too, is endeavoring to supersede any metaphysical realm of meaning which governs words and their meanings. Furthermore, the achievement of this *écriture* is not an essential Being but a contour or furrow, a trace that points. So Derrida speaks out against a metaphysical concept of *logos* and against the logocentrism that is inscribed even in Heidegger's question about Being as a question about the *meaning* of Being. But this is an odd Heidegger, a Heidegger interpreted back through Husserl; as if all speaking consisted merely of propositional judgments. In this sense, it is certainly true that the tireless constitution of meaning, to which phenomenological research is dedicated and which operates in the act of thinking as the fulfillment of an intention of consciousness *does* mean "presence." It is the declarative voice (*voix*) assigned to the presence of what is thought in thinking. Even in Husserl's efforts to build a respected philosophy, however, it is precisely the experience of time and time-consciousness that forms the prior basis of all "presence" and even the constitution of supratemporal validity. It is, of course, correct that the problem of time held Husserl's thought in an unbreakable spell because he himself held on firmly to the Greek concept of Being—a spell Augustine had already broken with the riddle he presented to himself about the being of time: that, to put it in Hegelian terms, the "now" both is and at the same time is not.

Like Heidegger, Derrida immerses himself in the mysterious multiplicity lodged in a word and in the diversity of its meanings, in the indeterminate potential of its differentiations of meaning. The fact, though, that Heidegger questions from the proposition and assertion back to the openness of Being that first makes words and propositions possible at all allows him, at the same time, to gain an advantage for understanding the whole dimension of assertions, antitheses and contradictions. In the same way, Derrida appears to be on the track of those traces that are to be found only in the act of reading. He has, in particular, sought to recover the analysis of time in Aristotle: that "time" appears in Being as deferred difference, or what Derrida calls "*la différance.*" But because he reads Heidegger through Husserl, he takes Heidegger's borrowing of Husserlian concepts, which is clearly noticeable in the transcendental self-description present in *Being and Time,* as evidence of Heidegger's logocentrism. Likewise, he deems as "phonocentrism" the fact that I take not only conversation but also the poem and its appearance in the inner ear as the true reality of language. As if voice, or discourse, could ever attain presence simply in the act of its performance, even for the most strenuous reflective consciousness of the speaker, and were not rather itself an act of disappearance. This is no cheap argument about reflection but a reminder of what happens to every speaking and thinking person: precisely because one is "thinking," one is not aware of oneself.

So we may take Derrida's critique of Heidegger's Nietzsche-interpretation—an interpretation of Nietzsche that in fact I find persuasive—as an illustration of the unsettled problematic before which we find ourselves. On the one side stands the bewildering richness of facets and the endless play of masks in which Nietzsche's bold experiments in thinking appear to disperse themselves into an ungraspable multiplicity. On the other side, there is the question one may put to Nietzsche of what all the play in this enterprise might mean. It is not as if Nietzsche himself ever had the unity of this dispersal clearly before him and had a conceptual grasp of the inner connection between the basic principle of will to power and the noontime message of the eternal return of the same. If I understand Heidegger correctly, this is precisely what Nietzsche has not done, so these metaphors of his last visions look like mirroring facets with no underlying unity. In any case, such a unity, Heidegger would say, represents the unified ultimate position in which the question concerning being itself forgets itself and loses itself. This is what the technological era signifies, the era in which nihilism in fact brings about an endless return of the same.

To think this through, to take up Nietzsche in a thoughtful way, does not seem to me to be some kind of falling back into metaphysics and the ontological concept of "essence" in which it culminates. If it were such a relapse, Heidegger's own ways of thinking, in pursuit of an "essence" with a completely different, temporal, structure, would not always lose themselves in impassable regions—let alone be the conversation that may be enriching itself in our own day with great new partners drawn from a heritage extending across our planet. This conversation should seek its partner everywhere, just because this partner is other, and especially if the other is completely different. Whoever wants me to take deconstruction to heart and insists on difference stands at the beginning of a conversation, not at its end.

14 Derridian dispersion and Heideggerian articulation

General tendencies in the practices that govern intelligibility

Charles Spinosa

There are many fruitful questions one can ask about practices. Philosophers typically ask how practices serve as conditions for the possibility of various kinds of complicated human comportments. Philosophers, for instance, who are interested in cognitive acts will show how shared habitual practices are crucial for the application of any rule. Anthropologists and sociologists interested in instituted aspects of human life such as gender or gift-giving tend to focus on showing that neither systems of belief, nor functional analyses, nor systems of structural difference can account for the improvisational character of such instituted forms of life.[1] Others, frequently with some psychological training, are more likely to ask if practices are more like constantly developing skills or more like rigid habits. Are practices more like developing skills when they are actively deployed toward some particular end or more like stable habits when they ground the recognition of something? Historians, like Foucault, reveal how the same ethical maxims or the same social functions produce quite different forms of life as different kinds of practices, say, monarchical or disciplinary, Stoical or Christian, are in place for enacting the maxims or functions. All of these kinds of analysis are important (and I have only surveyed a small number of fruitful kinds of practice analysis). But I want to focus attention on an aspect of the way practices work which I believe is mostly overlooked and which has significant consequences for any ethics founded on practice. I shall spend the first part of this paper fleshing out the aspect of practices that I am interested in exploring. In the second and third parts of the paper, I shall describe how Derrida and Heidegger give two radically different accounts of this aspect of practice. And in a short fourth part I shall conclude by giving a consideration that suggests why I believe Heidegger's account is preferable and how it could be altered to embed Derrida's insights. My main goal, however, is to open consideration of general tendencies in the way practices work and point out the ethical consequences of identifying such tendencies.

The general tendency of elaboration that governs practices

To see what I am getting at when I speak of a tendency in the way practices work, let me take a simple example. Assuming that social practices are generally matters of skill, note that whenever we learn a new practice, even a very simple one such as jogging, we find ourselves constantly sensitive to new things to which we had paid scant attention before. Or we become sensitive to old things in a new way. In jogging, we become sensitive, for instance, to pains in our legs and lungs, to the racing of our hearts, to how much we perspire, to what interests us as we jog, that is, whether we are more interested in having some intellectual problem to try to work through while we jog or having some beautiful trail to look at. Generally, we elaborate our practice according to whatever new sensitivities appear. And we develop these elaborations with awareness or without. So, we might with full awareness experiment to find out if we notice the pain in our legs so much if we jog while trying to solve an intellectual problem. Or we might discover that we had, without any awareness, developed the practice of making the second half of our run with the sea breeze in our faces so that the perspiration would not get in our eyes. In both cases, however, either with awareness or without, we are dealing with some particular issue that arises in the course of jogging simply by engaging in the practice of jogging. As we deal with more and more conditions with more or less awareness, the practice itself will become more elaborated. We will jog, for instance, only when we have thought of a suitable intellectual problem or only in a certain direction. This is only to say that so long as we engage in the practice, we will develop ways of dealing with the wide variety of things that the practice itself opens up to us. There should be little controversial in what I have said so far. I take it that we have all noticed that as we drive or ski or speak in public or teach that we become better at it in ways that go beyond those we explicitly worked at improving. We recognize, for example, that long after we have ceased *trying* to develop our driving skill, we continue improving in smoothing out our ride.

My general point is that practices tend toward their own elaboration. Indeed, that fairly weak and probably uninteresting claim is sufficient for the rest of what I have to say, but I should like to strengthen it because, in its stronger form, its force becomes clearer. I want to say that practices *tend* toward their own elaboration regardless of our explicit intentions. To see that practices have this autonomous tendency, recall that once skills become habitual, they continuously draw us to recognize things relevant to the skill or practice that before we would have passed over. To see that these new recognitions do not depend on the explicit intention to take up the practice, recall that even if I give up jogging, indeed, explicitly and consciously resolve to myself to give up jogging, I will still see this or that trail as looking good for a jog. That is, upon seeing the trail, I will find myself getting my body set to run and wondering where my running shoes are even before realizing that the sight of the trail is enticing me to run. Indeed, I may even realize that the trail enticed me to run at an unaccustomed time, and hence the jogging practice that I sought to curtail was becoming further elaborated despite my intention. Of course, once I catch myself, I will refocus my attention, following whatever practice I have for dealing with irrelevant solicitations to act, and gradually I will become desensitized to attractive running trails. But so long as I have the jogging skill, I will be guided, both with awareness *and without*, by its tendency toward further elaboration of itself.

The question of how to characterize this phenomenon of elaboration has exercised a relatively small number of philosophers. The greatest difference on this point is between Derrida and Heidegger. Derrida argues that the tendency toward elaboration generally involves the production of new ways of deploying a practice that are, in a certain way, discontinuous with the older ways of deploying it. Elaboration is, then, for Derrida, dispersive or disseminating. In contrast, Heidegger argues that this elaboration generally produces a better articulated core practice which we may think of, then, as having a stable (though not a fixed) nature. For Heidegger, then, elaboration is articulative. He sometimes speaks of this articulative nature of practices as gathering and later as *Ereignis*. In developing the Derridian and Heideggerian arguments, we shall see that an account of the nature of elaboration determines whether the stability of things is some sort of imposition that runs against the nature of practice or is the regular tendency of practice. When one considers instituted forms of life such as gender, one can see that arguing for the instability or stability of practices will have large politicoethical consequences.

Dispersion: Derrida on the general tendency of practices

It may seem perverse to connect Derrida to practices. Derrida is associated with deconstructions of structural systems of difference. But, from quite early in his career, Derrida claimed that writing, which for him was a paradigmatic activity for undermining logocentric meaning, and practice were functional equivalents. Practice understood in its ontological structure was the appropriate notion for upsetting the philosophical opposition between theory and practice just as writing understood in its ontological structure was appropriate to upsetting the opposition between speech and writing (Derrida 1981a: 4). More recently, he has claimed that the language system is itself grounded in practices of exchange and that the gift serves the same deconstructive function in social practices generally that writing served in deconstructing metaphysical thinking (Derrida 1992: 80–1).

Since Derrida's claim that practices tend to disperse is less well known than is Heidegger's opposite claim, the argument for it will be deployed in two stages. Leaving out nuances, I will speak of the 'Derridian' argument. First, the Derridian argues for a special sort of externalist decisionism that defeats the Wittgensteinian confidence that habitual practices themselves are sufficient for recognizing stable kinds of things and projecting old meanings into new situations. Second, the Derridian shows that this externalist aspect of practical behavior, which makes practices insufficient for recognizing stable kinds, plays an active role in all of our practical comportments. It is in the second half of this argument that we shall see the Derridian account of practices' dispersive kind of elaboration.

In the first stage of his argument, the Derridian tries to bring out cases where the habitual practices that constitute a context are not sufficient for deciding what some seemingly common kind of thing is. That is to say, habitual practices alone do not determine how we should deal with something familiar. To take a simple case, we may ask if an instance of a door is still an instance of that type when we put it on top of crates and start using it as a desk? Our intuition that the desktop is no longer a door is probably only a little stronger, if it is any stronger at all, than our intuition that it remains a door. To see this, we could change the simple everyday context we start with by weighting more and more details that would strengthen one or the other intuition. We could, for instance, give weight to our sense that the something's origin counts in determining its nature by imagining that we are living in a house full of heirlooms. Or we could add weight to our sense that the function of something determines its nature by imagining that this 'door–desktop' appears in a modern business setting where efficiency is all that counts. The point is to see that we can always give good reasons for giving added weight to considerations that would shift our intuitions concerning this 'door–desktop.'[3]

In these cases where we can give good reasons for seeing something as an instance of either of two incompatible types such as a door or a desktop, we should also see that the way of handling such instances is by an imposition (that could have been directed differently). We run into such impositions in ordinary life when we find that the dissenting opinions of court justices are as compelling as the majority opinions or whenever we, ourselves, must act on very weak intuitions. What determines which type (or law) an instance falls under in such vexed cases is not some determinate detail of the thing or situation. Instead, a determination is made by a speech community (or someone in the authoritative position in the speech community)[4] as to whether the thing will be handled as this or that type of thing.[5] In these kinds of cases, although the context of practices circumscribes the range of the decision, the context of practices alone will not determine under which specific type a given instance falls. To recur to our simple example, in the simple everyday context, no practice will clearly determine whether we have a desktop or a door. But, once the speech community or its representative decides the matter, then we will retrospectively see the situation as a whole in accord with the decision.

So far, though, the Derridian has merely argued that our way of acting *may* include cases where habitual practices do not determine how we deal with something. A decision is then required. To show that the number of such cases is indefinitely large, the Derridian draws on the notion of citationality. *Citationality* is a characteristic of *entities*, namely that they may but need not be taken as instances of the same type in an indefinitely large number of contexts.⁵ This property enables people to ask the question: is this entity, which we recognized as an instance of type X in context A still an instance of type X now that we are in context B?⁷ And citationality allows that entities that are instances of types may be intelligibly imported with appropriate changes into as many contexts as can be imagined. So citationality allows the door to be taken from the context of practices where we normally encounter it – entering a dwelling – and inserted into such contexts of practices as those for dealing with tables, artworks, and philosophers' examples. And, of course, an indefinitely large number of contexts can be imagined.⁸ We only need imagine John Searle asking us about doors inside a whale's stomach to see how far citationality can take us and how unlimited its range is.

But even if there are an indefinitely large number of citationally possible contexts in which practices alone could not tell us how to deal with seemingly common things like doors, one might still argue that Derridian decisionism or imposition is parasitic on situations where habitual practices do succeed in unproblematically determining how to handle something familiar. I take it that a Wittgensteinian would say that if in the cases where imposition occurs, there is a clear choice between two types, then these cases of imposition depend upon the unproblematic cases that determine which types to consider. Consequently, the cases of imposition are logically dependent on the unproblematic, clear cases.⁹ That is, one could not recognize the problematic case requiring an imposition if one did not already have the unproblematic cases.

The Derridian, however, believes that, even if there are moments where habitual practices enable determinations without decisions, his arguments show that we have no grounds for attributing logical priority to them. His account of difficult instances where ways of dealing with things must be imposed is supposed to demonstrate that the habitual ways of dealing with things not only underdetermine possible future applications but also underdetermine all our seemingly stable past ways of dealing with things. To see this, we must look to the retrospective nature of impositions.¹⁰ After the fact of any imposition, previous cases are retroactively transformed so as to appear to determine the present case. The second stage of the Derridian argument takes up *why* this reinterpretation of the past takes place. *That* it takes place we may see by reminding ourselves that this kind of revisioning frequently happens when important laws change. In the United States, for instance, when the judicial determination in *Plessy* v. *Ferguson* was the law of the land, then race relations, civil rights, the constitution, and most social situations were generally taken to support the doctrine of separate but equal. Citizenship at its best was, by and large, just seen as in support of *Plessy*. But when the judicial determination of *Brown* v. *Board of Education* came to rule, then the nature of civil rights, the constitution, most social situations, and even being a good citizen were seen by most as supporting the new *Brown*-type equality. At least one of these judicial decisions must have been an imposition.¹¹ And, with such an example, we see that a present imposition changes the way we deal with the meaning and implications of past cases as well as future ones. We see our past now according to our impositions. Consequently, habitual applications of types are as conceptually dependent on imposed applications as imposed applications are dependent on habitual ones. The nature of both past and future practice depends equally on both habit and imposition. Hence, there is no logical priority for determinations by habitual practices alone.

But so far the Derridian argument has only made claims about the equal logical priority of handling things through habitual practices and handling them by imposing a practice. In the second stage of the Derridian argument, the Derridian shows *why* impositions take place and thereby shows that making impositions is always active in our practical comportment. If we are regularly imposing types, kinds, and so forth, then our dealing with things is always taking into account the discontinuity implicit in making such impositions; consequently, the elaboration of practices would be dispersive not articulative. And so far as we do not recognize this instability in our ethics and elsewhere, we are acting and thinking against our practical natures.

In developing this view, Derrida starts with what he holds to be a basic tendency of all intentional comportment. 'Intention,' he says,

> necessarily can and should *not* attain the plenitude toward which it nonetheless inevitably tends ... Whether it is a question of prediscursive experience or of speech acts, plenitude is at once what *orients and endangers* the intentional movement, whether it is conscious or not. There can be no intention that does not tend toward it, but also no intention that attains it (Derrida 1988c: 136–7).

This is to say, in roughly Searlean terms, that any directed human comportment has conditions of satisfaction that it seeks to satisfy.[12] So, if someone tries to open the door, she will meet the conditions of satisfaction if she brings it about in a standard way that the door is opened. This is what it means for an intentional comportment or practice to seek full plenitude. But the Derridian says that practices never achieve this full plenitude. Surely he cannot be saying simply that conditions of satisfaction are never met. Rather, he is claiming that so far as each situation in which a habitual practice is deployed is different from previous situations of its deployment, the conditions of satisfaction will have to be amended to fit the differences between situations. In short, Derrida is starting by noting that practices must elaborate themselves in different situations. Since the conditions of satisfaction of intentional comportments must be modified to fit the differences between situations, no previously established conditions of satisfaction will be *simply* met. But why not say, as Heidegger does, that these developments of conditions of satisfaction are merely extensions or refined articulations of the general conditions of satisfaction already implicit in the practice? It seems fair to say that, at least, sometimes such amendments of the conditions must be precisely such extensions. But Derrida thinks that this sort of analysis does not take our coping with the differences between situations seriously.

To take these differences seriously, we must note the following things: first, we could not describe what we were doing as engaging in a practice we have engaged in before unless we were able to respond to the current situation as *different* from past situations. Second, this differentiation requires that something about the situation single it out from other past situations. Third, as soon as this difference is recognized with awareness or not, we must assume that the issue of citationality is raised. That is, the issue is opened of whether the conditions of satisfaction for doing X in past situations count as the conditions of satisfaction in this situation. Or must the conditions of satisfaction be amended by an imposition? For Derrida, this constant openness to imposition is enough to claim that the practices tend toward dispersion, which is to say that they tend toward impositions which could not be projected from earlier states of the practices. In short, if we are constantly ready to make impositions, then there are differences enough from situation to situation for us regularly to do so. Here is how Derrida makes this point:

> What . . . I call iterability [here read iterability as citationality] is at once that which tends to attain plenitude and that which bars access to it. Through the possibility of repeating every mark as the same it makes way for an idealization that seems to deliver the full presence of ideal objects . . . but this repeatability itself ensures that the full presence of a singularity thus repeated comports in itself the reference to something else, thus rending the full presence that it nevertheless announces. This is why iteration is not simply repetition (Derrida 1988c: 129).

So for Derrida any stability in the practices, any sense that the practices elaborate themselves by articulating implicit possibilities within themselves is itself based upon citationality and hence on the possibility of imposed practices. Deconstruction is really little more than increasing sensitivity to this instability. As Derrida puts it, the 'norms of minimal intelligibility are . . . by essence mobile' (Derrida 1988c: 147).

The consequences of this position are that all ways of making things intelligible are essentially unstable. To put the matter as Derrida does, "deconstruction' is firstly this destabilization on the move in . . . 'the things themselves" (Derrida 1988c: 147). As an ethical or political matter, it follows that one should become, at least, suspicious of institutions and experiences that tend toward the stability of things. For such institutions and experiences would tend to occlude the way in which our own form of intelligibility works, that is, would tend to occlude the way practices elaborate themselves. Also, those accounts of practice that regard practices as enabling us to have stable if not permanent kinds, according to the Derridian, get it wrong. Stable institutions, like stable practices, are stable because force, which the Derridian usually thinks of as *hegemonic* force, makes them so (Derrida 1988c: 137 and 144). So logocentrism (understanding ourselves as in control of our intentions) repeatedly imposes itself through the violent force of the legal, academic, journalistic, and other ethics-promoting institutions. Since such force goes against the way we make sense of things, it presumably arises out of a warping of practice to further special interests at the expense of intelligibility.

Articulation: Heidegger on the general tendency of practices

As Derrida has noted, the cardinal difference between his view and Heidegger's lies in Heidegger's wholehearted approval of such terms as owning, the proper, and appropriateness in contrast to Derrida's outright rejection of such terms in favor of grafting and dissemination (Derrida 1981b: 54). The simplest way to see the difference in focus would be to start with the example of a craftsperson. For Heidegger, the typical way human intelligibility works is exemplified by the craftsperson's way of making things intelligible. As with the craftsperson learning his craft, for Heidegger, practices tend toward a refinement whose goal is producing a craft product that draws people not only to use it but also to understand better how such products are an important part of their lives. In contrast, in looking at the same craftsperson in order to understand the nature of the intelligibility of things, Derrida would focus on the way the craftsperson has to make her practices clear to materials suppliers, employees, tax assessors, accountants, different kinds of customers, and so forth. Increasing intelligibility does not amount, for Derrida, to refining those practices that will give a product a single, determinate, and cared-for place in the lives of users. Rather, for Derrida, increasing intelligibility amounts to managing all the situations in which the product appears with all the different people who are related to it in various contexts. There is no primordial context of the sort Heidegger would have.

To understand more fully how Heidegger characterizes the way practices tend toward elaboration means seeing more clearly what he meant in the 1950s when he wrote about *Ereignis* as the 'governing force ... [that] brings all ... beings each into its own' (Heidegger 1971a: 127). For this sense of *Ereignis* is what I have so far described with the more general term 'articulation.' Bringing something into its own means bringing it into the context of those practices where the purpose that the thing is recognized as serving comes out most clearly and worthily. What does it mean for something's purpose to be brought out most clearly and most worthily? And what counts as the purpose which a thing is recognized as serving?

Answering the second question is relatively easy. Most of the time, the purpose which something (especially a piece of equipment) is recognized as serving is the purpose for which it was created or the purpose it has come to serve in those social contexts where its loss would be felt as severely constraining. So, for instance, a hammer is for hammering. A car is for driving on roads to get from one place to another in the course of daily activities. But we all know that there are lots of other uses for hammers and cars. Hammers can serve as paper weights and weapons. Cars can serve for off-road races, bedrooms, and so forth. But, for Heidegger, we mostly understand equipment as having a chief role along with other minor roles.[13] The same goes for things other than equipment, but their roles are not so obvious. So, for someone who casually walks through the woods, the deer are for contemplation; for the hunter, however, the deer are for hunting; for the farmer, they are pests, and so forth. It follows that what is generally recognized as the purpose of something changes both with history and with the community of people involved. Bicycles, for young wealthy people, are for maintaining one's fitness and racing from coffee shop to coffee shop. Bicycles, for younger or poorer people, may be for getting around town to do chores, or to get to and from school or work, and so forth. But the changes of purpose are not hidden within each micro act of, say, observing a deer but come out as we cross communities or as we move from the traditional to the vanguard in our own communities.

Purposes, then, are fairly simple. What does it mean for something to exist within a set of practices such that its purpose is brought out most clearly and most worthily? A thing's purpose is brought out most clearly when, first, the thing is in a situation where it solicits those practices which can, in fact, be deployed at the time and which enable one to use the thing effectively and familiarly according to recognized norms. A bottle of wine, for instance, solicits practices for savoring and drinking slowly when we are relaxed and at dinner with friends. It may solicit similar practices when we see it in the shop or while we are driving, but we cannot deploy the appropriate practices on those occasions.[14] Second, a thing will have its purpose come out most worthily when the practices it solicits are ones with which we have a great deal of familiarity. Drinking the wine with friends on many occasions establishes these practices as those that are familiar and indeed embody one of the goods in our lives. This is the kind of familiarity Heidegger has in mind when he is interested in things being brought out in their own.[15] Third, a purpose is brought out clearly and worthily when, for instance, the wine-drinking draws us to express our identities as friends with intensity. That is, we not only feel at home with our fellows but also recognize the vulnerability of our identities as friends as other situations draw us to do things that would make the familiar wine-drinking situation impossible.[16] Fourth, a purpose is brought out clearly and worthily when the thing is able to solicit a general mood that fits with the practices for using it and enables those involved to be attuned to the kinds of distinctions and solicitations that it promotes. The point here is that we may be drinking wine with our friends on a suitable occasion, in the traditional familiar way, and with a sense of the vulnerability of the situation and of our identities to change, but still not feel fully attuned to what is happening. We might be in a sour or nervous mood. The right mood, when it comes, just descends on us.[17] In general, a thing can be said to reveal its purpose most clearly and worthily when the practices that it solicits are important in one's community, make one feel at home in dealing with the thing, enable one to recognize the vulnerability of one's identity, and provoke the right mood for the situation. And a thing's importance to the community, the familiarity with which we engage with the thing, the vulnerability of our identity in the situation of engagement, and the appropriate mood all remain relatively stable.

Heidegger calls *Ereignis* this tendency in the practices to bring things into their own in this way. Thus, the practices for dealing with any thing have a kind of telos; they tend to make the thing connected to the rest of a community's life in such a way that the practices and the personal identities involved are taken as worthy. This telos is relational. It depends upon the rest of the practices in a community, the kinds of identities the community supports, the traditions with which people in the community are familiar, and the kinds of uses that the community holds valuable. Also, this telos is only a tendency, or to put it in Heidegger's terms, it is a gentle law (Heidegger 1971a: 128). The tendency can be constrained by all sorts of contingent circumstances. In times of severe economic stress, for instance, practices for sharing wine with friends, perhaps even practices for having friends just could not get off the ground no matter how the wine bottle and past familiarlization solicited that kind of behavior. But, normally, practices are best understood when they are seen as tending towards the local stability provided by the telos. Such thinking suggests that, as practices elaborate themselves, a stable end is implicit in their elaborations.

Under a Heideggerian view, amendments to conditions of satisfaction that are made in response to differences in situations would be made in the light of a thing's overall telos. This stable telos would govern even if a decision had to be imposed regarding which practices to deploy. Thus, this stable telos shows that the differences between situations are normally *not* what is most important. Of course, significant contingent changes might result in a thing soliciting different practices altogether. But then a new telos would be instituted and the gentle law broken. In general, then, while Derrida treats all differences that occur from situation to situation as always important, Heidegger regards them as mostly, but not always, trivial.

Finally, just as the Derridian calls upon us through deconstruction to come into accord with dispersion, the Heideggerian who sees practices as tending to produce local stabilities calls us, in the name of coming into accord with how human intelligibility works, to preserve those stabilities. And, as Derrida notes, this means defending some notions of property and the proper.

Heidegger's articulation over Derrida's dispersion

There is one important reason for preferring the articulative account to the dispersive account. But to become sensitive to it, we must recall a moment in which we have experienced practices bringing something out in its own. Perhaps we all can recall an experience of a family meal where everyone in the family understood at that moment what it meant to be a family member and that eating the dinner and telling the stories of the day made these identities and the practices of sharing food together at the end of the day clear, important, and worthy. Of course, Derrida, too, can give us an account of how central stabilities – like those involving the nuclear family – could seem valuable to us even if their production ran against the general tendency toward dispersion in the practices. Much of Derrida's discussion of hegemonic forces is meant to explain the seeming value of such stabilities. But the Derridian account suggests that our experience of marginal, non-dominant practices should be dispersive and not articulative. But marginal practices infrequently exhibit a dispersive character. Take, for instance, the marginal example that has already been developed of drinking wine with friends. How could the Derridian account make sense of it being beneficial to the logocentric, phallocentric, carnocentric, or other form of Western centrism still active today that the wine gathers friends together as friends? These meetings of friends over wine seem to do nothing to convince us that our intentions are clearly present to us and fully satisfied. Such meetings sometimes do support the clear bounded identities of phallocentrism, but just as often enable displays of feeling that undermine such identities. Perhaps, in the past, such meetings helped us to dominate animals, but one does not think today that drinking wine with friends involves such domination. If anything, such occasions have more kinship with a kind of nearness that merges intentions and identities so that ownership and dominance are lost rather than anything that fits with one of the hegemonic centrisms Derrida worries about. As a careful reader of Heidegger, Derrida worries about nearness too, but that is because he tends to see it as supporting one of the hegemonies. But though there are no doubt many forms of nearness that do support the various reigning mutually supporting hegemonies, friends gathering to drink wine in no obvious way support this or that current hegemony. Such examples of stabilities that occur when we are engaged in *marginal* practices suggest the superiority of Heidegger's claim that practices usually tend to articulate local stabilities rather than unleash dispersive discontinuities.

On the basis of such marginal situations, a Heideggerian would have us recognize that a telos guides the elaboration of practices around some thing or event. Moreover, the marginality of a practice such as friendship which has never been a central organizing practice in our culture suggests that the telos need not be a trace of some centrism in the general cultural practices that draws us to make impositions of one sort and not another. But, as we noted, Heidegger does not think that the tendency to bring things out in their ownmost is anything more than a tendency. He allows that circumstances override it, but he does not describe such cases. The Derridian analysis can be usefully regarded as an important and fitting addition to Heidegger, one that tells us precisely how such an overriding imposition occurs. A practice engages a new circumstance that cannot be easily accommodated with the considerations of the telos (appropriateness, familiarity, vulnerability, and mood). Hence, an imposition is required, and that imposition is itself retrospectively normalized. Drawing the Derridian account into the Heideggerian account in this way enables the Heideggerian interpreter to account for the development of many new marginal practices and for the discontinuities of change.

The Derridian deconstructionist could reply that all the Heideggerian interpreter has done is uncover the force of a new hegemonic 'centrism' – *Ereignis*, the tendency to bring things out in their ownmost – which has infected Western practice. But to accept this Derridian response requires that we make sense of the revolutionary possibility of dispersive practices giving us the ability to make things and people intelligible without any 'centrism,' telos, or stabilizing practice. While we can conceive of such a Derridian revolutionary possibility, we can ground it only in artistic experiences and in such marginal everyday moments as our experience of shocking moments. For instance, when we find ourselves imposing sense before we can make it in such simple and shocking situations as encountering a fertilized egg or a familiar person in a setting that makes immediate identification difficult. To defend his account, the Derridian would have to go further than allowing that those unusual experiences of change could become a little more usual. The Derridian would have to claim that our common experiences of making sense of the world would be of this sort where imposition is common and stability is rare. For these reasons, it is much more plausible to incorporate the Derridian insights into the Heideggerian interpretation and conceive of stability coming from some aspect of our everyday practices, with breaks in stability arising from the imposed responses to radically unusual contingency to which Derrida draws our attention.

Notes

1 In using the term 'improvisational,' I am recurring to Bourdieu's example of the gift-giving master who is able, in a situation full of unusual contingencies, to act against his habitual training in a completely unusual way and yet be recognized by the community as having done exactly the right thing to preserve both his status and the traditional practice of gift-giving itself. I take it that this improvisation shows that practices are more like skills than habits or habitual dispositions and that they are not in the possession of any individual. For many circumstances – some beyond the master's control – had to line up for the master gift-giver's innovative act to count the giving of a gift. And unless it is recognized as such, the action would not have produced a change in the *gift-giving* practice. See Bourdieu (1990: 98–111, esp. 107).
2 I imagine this on the model of discovering that we have without any awareness developed the distance standing practices typical of our culture.
3 If the example of the 'door–desktop' seems too far-fetched, try considering those cases of 'jokes' that we hesitate to call jokes. I have in mind the case of a public speaker who tells what one imagines he intended as a joke but which not only fails to be funny but is offensive. Is such a humorless offense still a joke? In situations in which such things have occurred – everyday situations – such things have an as undecidable nature as I have tried to claim for the door–desktop. But, if we say that we are going to look at matters strictly in terms of speaker intention, then we can get a clearer intuition of whether the speech act was a joke or not. Also, if we focus on success alone, we can also get a clearer intuition about the speech act. Again, if we focus on listeners' responses, we might be able to get a relatively stronger intuition. But in our simple everyday world, we do not usually give added weight to one of these ways of considering things. If it comes about that we in our

4 Derrida sometimes names those in authoritative positions responsible for fixing contexts and determining meaning 'the police' (Derrida 1988b: 105 and 1988c: 134–7). When he speaks of his own fixing of contexts, Samuel Weber translates Derrida's term by the English 'impose' (Derrida 1988b: 103 and 1988c: 137, 145, 149), but when Derrida speaks of the police in general fixing contexts and meaning, he calls the act, again following Weber, a 'performative operation' (Derrida 1988c: 132).

community come up with a determinate way of handling such 'jokes,' it will be due very likely to an imposition, not to some newly discovered detail of that kind of speech act.

5 See Burge (1979: 73–121) for a well-known analytic form of social externalism which meshes well with Derrida's externalism. Burge argues that the content of concepts such as arthritis is fixed by the authoritative experts in the community.

6 Derrida sometimes speaks as though citationality were another word for iterability as in, 'This citationality, this duplication or duplicity, this iterability of the mark is neither an accident nor an anomaly' (Derrida 1988b: 12 and 1988c: 119). But, more commonly, he thinks of citationality in terms of normal citing – taking the exact words written or spoken in one context and entering them into another context with quotation marks around them – or in terms of grafting, both of which involve dealing with things as simple entities or instances of types, not as types (Derrida 1988a: 12).

7 I think that the distinction between these two characteristics offers a powerful tool for understanding intelligibility. I would claim, following Merleau-Ponty, that if organisms could not recognize *instances of the same type* in many different contexts, they would not have any intelligence at all. If they could not recognize the same *entity* as potentially an instance of a different type in various contexts, they would not have *human* or *higher mammal* intelligence (where the precise line is drawn between human and animal intelligence is a matter for empirical research). See Merleau-Ponty (1983: 175).

8 There are a number of ways to use citationality to defend the claim that one can construct an indefinitely large number of situations. Since citationality enables the grafting of anything into any context and even contexts into contexts, an indefinitely large number of contexts are producible in precisely the same way an indefinitely large number of sentences are producible by recursively using the rules of syntax. Alternatively, so long as human beings go on with individual perspectives – which is to say so long as human intelligibility goes on – then each individual human perspective counts as a new context into which anything may be imaginatively cited.

9 I am using 'logical dependence' in the way Searle used it against Derrida. In explaining the logical dependence of fiction on serious discourse, Searle says, 'One could not have the concept of fiction without the concept of serious discourse.' See Searle (1977: 207).

10 In the controversy that has accompanied Derrida, few have taken the time to point out that Derridian *in*determinacy of meaning (that we cannot completely understand what we mean) follows from the retrospective nature of *under*determination (that we cannot project our meanings into all relevant situations).

11 In his writing on the law, Derrida elaborates the way undecidability occurs and is resolved. See Derrida (1990: 967). Derrida, of course, neither claims that all decisions an actual judge makes are impositions nor that all impositions judges have made can in retrospect be justified. Cases of 'undecidability' occur when the context and types involved imply more than one way of applying the crucial types. Of course, a judge could be so befogged as to follow neither line of implication. But, for Derrida, the cases where we see justice enacted are precisely the ones where a narrowly constrainted imposition occurs.

12 Of course, the conditions of satisfaction of intentionality are not the same as psychological conditions of satisfaction. But so far as intentionality is understood to refer to the way we are directed to things, it refers to a relationship or a comportment to things which can fail in various ways. And that failure cannot just mean that some state of affairs is not in accord with some propositional content, but that a way of relating to the world or of comporting oneself to the world is undermined. Intending, generally, even mere seeing things under an aspect, can always go wrong as a way of being related to the world. For this reason, being directed toward something seeks satisfaction.

13 What I have said here amounts to taking a stand on a rather ambiguous point in *Being and Time* (Heidegger 1962). It may be that Heidegger understands pieces of equipment strictly in terms of their roles. So a hammer used as a paper weight would then be a paper weight. In this way, pieces of equipment are intelligible according to the kind of behavior they afford. In general, I think that the text militates against such an interpretation, but the main points of this paper would remain unchanged regardless of one's stand on this question.

14 This is an interpretation of how a thing thinging gathers what Heidegger calls sky. See Heidegger (1971b: 149 and 1971c: 178).

15 This is an interpretation of how a thing thinging gathers what Heidegger calls earth. See Heidegger (1971b: 149 and 1971c: 178).

16 This is an interpretation of how a thing thinging gathers us as mortals. See Heidegger (1971b: 150 and 1971c: 1978-9).

17 This is an interpretation of how a thing thinging gathers what Heidegger calls divinities or the blessing of divinities. See Heidegger (1971b: 150 and 1971c: 178).

Heidegger on Logic

J. N. MOHANTY

Why should one write on Heidegger's understanding of logic? After all, Heidegger was not a logician, nor did he do philosophy of logic. Indeed, there is no justification for expecting of any great philosopher whatsoever that he should have views, and reasonably plausible views, about the nature of logic or on specific themes belonging to the domain of logic. A moral philosopher may totally bypass any concern with logic, without detriment to his thinking. As an existentialist philosopher, Heidegger could have done that, and much of his *Dasein*-analytic would yet have retained its value. But Heidegger was also an ontologist, and was deeply concerned, all his philosophical career, with metaphysics and with the various questions about the nature of thought and of being. These concerns, to say the least, bring him to the proximity of logic as it had been understood in the tradition going back to Aristotle. And, as a matter of fact, Heidegger's own access to the problems of ontology and metaphysics has been determined by his reflection on logic. Two claims may therefore be advanced. First, it is not unreasonable, and what is more important, not unfair to Heidegger, to enquire into his understanding of logic. Secondly, his reflections on logic may help us to gain a better understanding of his overall philosophical interests than would be possible otherwise. Even if he was not a logician he was concerned with the nature of logic, and with some central problems belonging to the domain of logic. This concern begins with his doctoral work on the problem of psychologism in theory of judgment,[1] continues in the habilitation work on

---

[1] *Die Lehre vom Urteil im Psychologismus. Ein kritisch-positiver Beitrag zur Logik.* Dissertation, Freiburg in Br., 1913. Reprinted in Martin Heidegger, *Gesamtausgabe*, Bd. 1, *Frühe Schriften* (Frankfurt am Main: Klostermann, 1978). Further citations to *Gesamtausgabe* are abbreviated as GA.

The reader is referred to the following secondary literature on this topic: Thomas A. Fay, *Heidegger: The Critique of Logic* (The Hague: Martinus Nijhoff, 1977). Reviewed by the present author in *The Southwestern Journal of Philosophy*, XI, (1980): 174–79; Walter Bröcker, "Heidegger und die Logik," *Philosophisches Rundschau* I (1953-54): 48–56; Albert Borgmann, "Heidegger and Symbolic Logic," in M. Murray, ed., *Heidegger & Modern Philosophy* (New Haven: Yale University Press, 1978), 3–22.

[107]

the semantic categories in Duns Scotus,[2] and reaches its maturity in the Marburg lectures of 1925–28.[3]

In this essay, I will deal with three topics. In the first section, I will try to determine how Heidegger understood the nature of logic. In the second section, I will consider the one problem of logic to which he devoted a great deal of attention: the theory of judgment. In the third section, I will look into how his concern with logic opens up for him several paths to go beyond logic. At the end, I will reflect on this entire account, not so much to find faults with Heidegger's understanding of logic, as to determine its precise nature and limitations.

1. NATURE OF LOGIC

A. A Preliminary Definition.

One commonly held view of the nature of logic, in the traditional accounts, is that logic is a normative science of thought, whose aim is to lay down those *rules* which one *ought* to follow if one aims at truth. This account may be faulted on various grounds. First of all, 'thought' is ambiguous, referring both to the process of thinking and the content of thinking. Of these two, the former belongs to the field of psychology. If the content of thinking is understood in the sense of objective meanings or structures of meaning, propositions or configurations of them, then only logic may be said to be concerned with them. Why then is logic to be still regarded as a normative science? Of course, once there is a logical law to the effect 'If p implies q, and p, then q' (where p and q are propositional variables), then it does follow that if a person believes in a proposition 'A implies B' and also believes that A (where 'A' and 'B' are names of propositions), then he also ought to believe that B. But such a normative demand on the person's rationality is no part of the business of logic. Finally, the term 'truth' is ambiguous, referring both to material truth (the sense in which the statement 'it is raining now in Norman' is true if and only if it in fact is raining in Norman) and formal truth or validity (the sense in which the inference "All men are immortal, all Greeks are men, therefore, all Greeks are immortal" is valid, being a substitution instance of a logical law, even if one of its premises as well as its conclusion are materially false). It may appear as though logic is concerned with validity, rather than with truth understood, as it usually is, in the first of the two senses. If we accept these

---

[2] *Die Kategorien- und Bedeutungslehre des Duns Scotus* (Tübingen: J. C. B. Mohr, 1916). Reprinted in *Gesamtausgabe*, Bd 1.

[3] *Logik. Die Frage Nach der Wahrheit.* Vorlesungen 1925–26, herausgegeben von Walter Biemel. *Gesamtausgabe*, Bd. 21 (Frankfurt am Main: Klostermann, 1976); *Metaphysische Anfangsgründe der Logik*, Vorlesungen, 1928, herausgegeben von Klaus Held, *Gesamtausgabe*, Bd. 26 (Frankfurt am Main: Klostermann, 1978).

three emendations, then we can transform the initial account of logic into some such as this: logic is a science of meaning-structures in so far as they are valid. On this account, the task of logic is to lay down the laws of validity of meaning-structures.

Heidegger, under the influence of Husserl's idea of a pure logic of meaning, concludes his dissertation with a formulation of the task of logic that is very much like the one we have just arrived at. The logician, he concludes, must aim at bringing out the precise meanings of sentences and then proceed to determine the forms of judgments according to objective differences of meanings and their simple or compound structures, and bring such forms into a system.[4] Although the notion of validity does not figure in this account, the way forms of simple meanings and compound meanings can be brought into a system must be by showing the relations of implication amongst them, and the laws of their implication should be able to yield laws of validity of meaning-structures. But Heidegger has no doubt, in those early works, that the proper logical object is neither the mental process of thinking nor the reality (whether physical or metaphysical) about which one thinks, but the *Sinn*, understood both as the meaning of a sentence and as the identical content of judgment.

B. *Critique of Psychologism.*

Such a preliminary account of logic already implies a rejection of psychologism. Heidegger is aware of Frege's rejection of psychologism, but it is Husserl who, he writes, "has systematically and comprehensively laid bare the essence, the relativistic consequences and the theoretical disadvantages of psychologism."[5] Basic to the overcoming of psychologism is the distinction between psychic act and its logical content, the latter alone being the "in itself subsisting sense" ("in sich Bestand habende Sinn"). But can psychologism, which seeks to ground logic in psychology, be logically refuted? Perhaps not, Heidegger concedes in his dissertation, but that does not matter a great deal, he answers us: "the actual ... (also the non-actual) cannot as such be proved (*bewiesen*), but in any case can only be shown (*aufgewiesen*)."[6] While psychologism, according to Heidegger, as it is for Husserl, must be rejected, one needs nevertheless (i) to be clear about the real point of Husserl's critique of psychologism, and (ii) to decide where one should go after the error of psychologism has been discarded. For purposes of (ii), it is necessary (iii) to think about what is to be understood by 'Sinn', a concept which up until now has been used to define the domain of logic.

---

[4] GA, 1: 186.
[5] GA, 1: 20.
[6] GA, 1: 165.

Part of Husserl's critique of psychologism in the *Prolegomena* relies upon a distinction between two modes of being, the real and the ideal. Thinking as a mental process is *real* being; the logical content of thinking has an ideal being. Psychologism confuses the two. The confusion does not lie in mistaking one given thing (the ideal content) for another given thing (the real mental process). It is rather based on the fact that the philosophers concerned were blind to, and prejudiced against, certain modes of being. So far Husserl's point was well taken. But Husserl's concept of 'ideal being' is far from being univocal. In fact, Husserl appears to have brought under this concept things that are very different from each other, such as universals, essences that are not universals, truths as well as the idea of truth. We shall look into some of these equivocations a little later. For the present, what is important in Husserl's critique, according to Heidegger, is not that ontological distinction which, however provisionally useful, could not be the final truth, but rather the implied critique of a naturalistic psychology. Hans Sluga has recently shown that when Frege rejected psychologism, he was, in fact fighting against a more comprehensive philosophical naturalism of which psychologism was a consequence.[7] This reading is corroborated by Heidegger's understanding of Husserl's antipsychologistic critique.

For Heidegger, it is a misunderstanding of Husserl's deeper intentions to read him as though he was improving upon Bolzano's platonism,[8] or even as though his critique was rooted in Lotze's *Geltungs-* and value-logic. These "platonistic" readings of the *Prolegomena* have led to the standard complaint that in the second volume of the *Logical Investigations* Husserl relapsed into psychologism. If we are to make room for the charitable interpretation that Husserl's *Logical Investigations*, even the *Ideas*, constitute a progressive unfolding of the thoughts that were already anticipated in the early works, we have to say with Heidegger that Husserl rejected psychologism because it applied to logical theory a psychology which was not only poor *as a psychology* of the experience of thinking, but which was confused regarding its very project, which, in other words, did not understand its theme, i.e., the logical. The critique of psychologism therefore is a critique of psychology, and an implied plea for an intentional, descriptive, and eidetic psychology to replace the prevailing naturalistic psychology.[9] Such a reading of Husserl's intention makes it possible for Heidegger to go beyond the provisional distinction between the real and the ideal, and to ask how the logical contents or *Sinne* are related to the acts of thinking, and eventually to the thinking being that man is.

---

[7] Hans Sluga, *Gottlob Frege* (London: Routledge and Kegan Paul, 1980).
[8] GA, 1: 87, fn 9.
[9] GA, 1: 98.

It is well known that Lotze's idea of *Geltung* or validity as the mode of being of propositions and truths influenced, in different measures, both Frege and Husserl. In his logic lectures of the twenties, Heidegger concerns himself at some length with Lotze. It is interesting to note that his assessment of Lotze underwent considerable change along the years. In 1912, Heidegger writes that Lotze's logic should be regarded as the basic book of modern logic.[10] In the Marburg lectures of 1925/26 we find him, in the course of a critical examination of Husserl's notion of 'ideal being', tracing Husserl's equivocations to the confusions that characterised Lotze's concept of *Geltung*.[11] I will return to Lotze's concept of *Geltung* when we turn to the theory of truth. For the present it should suffice to note that amongst the entities whose mode of being is characterized by *Geltung*, Lotze includes: propositional contents or sentential meanings (= Frege's Thoughts), truths, the mode of being of a truth and the Essence of Truth. *Geltung* also means: *objective* validity (being true of objects) as well as universality with respect to all knowers. No wonder, then, that Heidegger severely criticizes those who find in this term "a magic band" capable of solving all problems.[12]

Heidegger was no more enthusiastic about Bolzano, the other major influence on Husserl. He cautions against regarding Husserl's *Logical Investigations* as nothing but attempts to improve upon Bolzano. It is, for him, more true to say that both Bolzano and Husserl were influenced by Leibniz. In any case, anti-psychologism does not lead Heidegger to the opposite camp of platonism. The goal is to be able to avoid platonism, without relapsing into psychologism.

C. Remarks on Mathematical Logic.

For one who was so deeply concerned with traditional logic as Heidegger, the rise of mathematical logic could not but be a challenge. We know that Heidegger was enthusiastic about Frege's papers on concept and object, and on sense and reference.[13] Of these he wrote: "G. Freges logisch-mathematische Forschungen sind meines Erachtens in ihrer wahren Bedeutung noch nicht gewürdigt, geschweige denn ausgeschöpft. Was er in seinen Arbeiten ... niedergelegt hat, darf keine Philosophie der Mathematik übersehen; es ist aber auch im gleichen Maße wertvoll für eine allgemeine Theorie des Begriffs."[14] But the appreciation of Frege did not carry over

---

[10] GA, 1: 23 fn.
[11] GA, 21: 62.
[12] GA, 21: 79.
[13] G. Frege, "Begriff und Gegenstand," *Vierteljahreschrift für wissenschaftliche Philosophie*, 16, (1892); "Sinn und Bedeutung," *Zeitschrift für Philosophie und philosophische Kritik*, 100 (1892).
[14] GA, 1: 20.

into an appreciation of mathematical logic. In the same paper of 1912, he argues that logistic—as mathematical logic was alternately called—does not liberate itself from mathematics and so is not able to penetrate into the proper problems of logic. Its chief limitations derive, in Heidegger's view, from an application of mathematical symbols and concepts (above all, of the concept of function) to logic—as a result of which the deeper significance of the logical principles remains in the dark. As a calculus of propositions, it is unaware of the problems of the theory of judgment. Furthermore, the conditions of the possibility of mathematics, as well as of mathematical logic, lie in a domain which those two disciplines cannot reach.[15] In the Dissertation, a new objection is raised against mathematical logic: it is formal, and so is unable to deal with "the living problems of judgmental-meaning, its structure and its cognitive significance."[16] Similar complaints surface in later writings as well. In *Sein und Zeit*, logistic is said to "dissolve" judgment into a system of "Zuordnungen"; judgment becomes an object of "calculation," and so cannot be the theme for ontological interpretation.[17] Since judgment has always a relatedness to objects and a claim to be objectively valid, logistic cannot reach the essence of judgment.

Of what worth are these remarks? There is no doubt that Heidegger's acquaintance with the logic that Frege laid the foundation of, and that by the time Heidegger was writing his dissertation had found its epoch-making systematization in Russell and Whitehead's *Principia*, was superficial and casual. Nevertheless, there may be some substance in his remarks.

That mathematical logic may well be so much of mathematics that it therefore becomes poorer as logic, is already implicit in Frege's criticism of Boole and Schröder. The point of that criticism is that Boole and Schröder used mathematical concepts ('sum', 'product', for example) and often mathematical signs to develop their logics, which is unjustified inasmuch as logic, being more fundamental, cannot and should not borrow its concepts from any other discipline.[18] Consequently, instead of reducing logic to mathematics, Frege reduced arithmetic to logic. He sought to make a fragment of mathematics logical, rather than make logic mathematical. It is true that Frege used at least

---

[15] GA, 1: 42–43.
[16] GA, 1: 174 fn.
[17] Heidegger, *Sein und Zeit*, Seventh edition (Tübingen: Max Niemeyer, 1953), 159.
[18] Cf. Frege: "Anyone demanding the closest possible agreement between the relations of the signs and the relations of the things themselves will always feel it to be back to front when logic, whose concern is also the foundation of arithmetic, borrows its signs from arithmetic. To such a person it will seem more appropriate to develop for logic its own signs, derived from the nature of logic itself." *Posthumous Writings*, ed. by H. Hermes, F. Kambartel and F. Kaulbach (Chicago: University of Chicago Press, 1979), 12.

two important notions in his logic which might be regarded as having been borrowed from mathematics. In fact, however, that is not so. Although the ideas of quantification and function are seemingly mathematical, they are not in reality. The mathematical notion of function Frege found confused and unhelpful. The logical notion that he introduced is that of any entity that is "unsaturated," i.e., has empty places within its structure. Thus a concept is a function inasmuch as its true form, on Frege's theory, is (for example) "——— is wise," and this is an incomplete entity. The same may be said of the quantifiers; they are, for Frege, properly logical notions, and not mathematical ones. Thus we must recognize that Heidegger's anxiety is genuine, but, as against the original Fregean logic, unfounded.

Heidegger's next complaint is that mathematical logic being a calculus of propositions, cannot raise the problems of judgment as discussed in traditional logic and metaphysics. What are these latter problems? As far as I can see, these problems are: (a) the nature of assertion/denial; (b) the nature of the copula and predication; and (c) the problem of truth. Limiting our view for the present only to Frege (and the logic of the *Principia Mathematica*, which is basically Fregean), we may say that Heidegger's critique is not justified if it means that Frege and the *Principia Mathematica* did not know of these problems. The only substance of the critique may be that the solutions offered by these new logicians were hardly satisfactory. Consistently with his critique of psychologism, Frege distinguished between assertion and the thought (or, in the *Begriffsschrift*, the judgable content, *beurteilbare Inhalt*) that is asserted. Thinking is grasping of the thought; judging is recognition of the truth value of the thought so grasped; and asserting is expressing that recognition. There is no doubt that the concept of assertion as a psychological (and linguistic) act and its relation (as well as that of grasping) to the thought (which on Frege's theory has an objective being) remains, in that theory, a "mystery"—no less difficult to clarify than the role Frege assigned to 'assertion' in his logic, despite his anti-psychologism. These difficulties show that Frege's solution to the problem of assertion was not satisfactory, but there is also no doubt that he did concern himself with this aspect of the problem of judgment. As regards the problem of predication, which has been one of the central concerns of traditional logic and philosophy of logic, Frege's answer would run somewhat along the following lines: the problem of predication concerns the internal structure of the thought being asserted, and has nothing to do with judgment. Judging is recognizing the truth value of a total thought; the thought, or the judged content, contains a predicative structure, but even with regard to it one should note that what is the concept (or predicate) depends upon how one analyzes the thought and there is no one way of doing that. What about the copula? The copula as the connecting link between the subject and the predi- cate is no longer needed, for in 'Socrates is wise', the predicate is '——— is wise' and not 'wise'. This new way of analyzing a proposition better explains its unity than the copula does, for if the subject and the predicate were to be linked by a copula one may want to know what links the copula to both the terms, whereas on Frege's theory a thought consists of an "unsaturated" part (with a hole, as it were) and a "saturated" part (which just fits into that hole), each made for the other, and so not in need of a link.

What then is the point of Heidegger's remark that in mathematical logic, judgment is reduced to a system of *Zuordnungen* and not made a theme of ontological interpretation? If he means that modern logic looks upon a proposition as an unanalyzable primitive, then he is wrong. First-order propositional logic does so, but predicate logic precisely analyzes the proposition into its constituents. If he means a proposition is, for modern logic, a mere connection of concepts (or representations), then also he is wrong, for as Frege taught, a thought consists of a concept (or a function) and an object. Further, the concept, for Frege, is not a subjective representation, but an objective entity. What then is the 'ontological interpretation'? It may mean either of four things: (i) interpretation of the fact that a judgment is about something, i.e., about a being; (ii) interpretation of the fact that a judgment is either true or false; (iii) interpretation of the mode of being of the judged content or proposition; and, finally, (iv) an answer to the question *how* something like a judgment is at all possible.

Of these four questions, Fregean logic has an account of (i) in terms of the object constituent of the referent of a thought; and an account of (iii) inasmuch as a sentence which expresses a thought also names a truth-value. Logicians such as Frege and Quine, to take two extreme examples, have ontologized about propositions or thoughts. The spectre of platonism has loomed large before them. It is not clear what is being asked by (iv). In any case, Heidegger's concern goes deeper than these answers. They are not radical enough both in their questioning and in their answers. With regard to (i), the Fregean answer does not succeed in locating the intentionality or object-relatedness of judgment in the more general structure of intentionality, and gets by only with locating an object constituent. As far as (iii) is concerned, considering a sentence as a name of truth-value, in spite of the elegance it succeeds in bringing about in the semantics of first order propositional logic, does not question whether a sentence is after all a name,[19] and it demands an

---

[19] cp. M. Dummett, *The Interpretation of Frege's Philosophy* (London: Duckworth, 1981), 371, 409.

unquestioning acceptance of the very obscure ontology of the true and the false. It also does not, and indeed cannot, raise the deep question, Why is it that a judgment alone is capable of being either true or false? Taken together with a deep understanding of the question (iv), all these foregoing issues constitute what Heidegger calls 'philosophical logic'.

D. *'Philosophical Logic'*.

In his Marburg Lectures, Heidegger develops the notion of a philosophical logic as contrasted with the traditional "school" logic. The latter had its philosophical basis, no doubt, but now is "der veräusserlichte entwurzelte und dabei verhärtete Gehalt" of an original philosophical question. Philosophical logic has been developing through the centuries—its high points are reached in Aristotle, Leibniz, Kant, and Hegel. Amongst his contemporaries, Heidegger appears to have rated Lask most; he is the one who consciously strives toward a philosophical understanding of logic and sought to extend the domain of philosophical logic.[20] Husserl, in spite of the possibilities that phenomenology contained for a philosophical development of logic, did not succeed, in Heidegger's view, in conceiving logic philosophically: "he even intensified the tendency to develop logic into a separate science, as a formal discipline detached from philosophy." Nor did any other amongst the phenomenologists succeed. Pfänder's *Logik*—widely regarded then as *the* phenomenological textbook on the subject—is dismissed as "eine phänomenologisch gesäuberte traditionelle Logik."[21] Without pausing to evaluate these judgments on other philosophers (including those on Kant[22] and Hegel,[23] Bolzano[24] and Lotze), I will proceed to determine the tasks and the problems which Heidegger assigns to philosophical logic.

First of all, philosophical logic, as Heidegger conceives of it, is not a new discipline[25] but rather actualizes a *telos* which has characterized historical logic since its inception. The idea of philosophical logic, Heidegger claims, will first render the history of logic meaningful.[26] Philosophical logic, one may con-

---

[20] M. Heidegger, *The Basic Problems of Phenomenology*. Marburg Lectures of 1927. Ed. and trans. by Albert Hofstadter (Bloomington: Indian University Press, 1982), 178. Henceforth to be cited as BP.

[21] GA, 21: 28.

[22] Kant, according to Heidegger, gave logic a central philosophical function but did not try to rescue academic logic from its "philosophically alienated superficiality and vacuity." (BP, p. 177).

[23] Hegel, Heidegger holds, conceived of logic as philosophy, but did not attempt a radical reformulation of the problem of logic as such. (BP, pp. 177-8).

[24] Bolzano, in Heidegger's view, was overrated by Husserl. (GA, 21, pp. 86-7).

[25] GA, 26: 6.

[26] Ibid, 7.

tend, can be brought about first by determining what philosophy is, and then by applying philosophy to logic. But where and how do we find the idea of philosophy to begin with? Heidegger prefers to follow another route. Let us begin with traditional logic (Aristotle or Leibniz, for example) and develop the central problems in it in such a manner that they will lead us into philosophy. We have no doubt a certain historical understanding of philosophy. With that much in our mind, we can question logic for its philosophical potentialities.

What are the problems that lead us from within traditional logic towards philosophy? These are:

1. Judgment, with which logic has ever been concerned, is characterized by intentionality; it is about an object, an entity. How to understand this intentional structure?[27]
2. What is the relation between the "being" of the copula and the "being" of ontology? How much ontological weight can we assign to the copula?[28]
3. What is predication and what role does it play in judgment?[29]
4. What is 'meaning', and what is its relevance for the possibility of judgment?[30]
5. What is the structure of judgment such that both the possibilities—of truth as well as of falsity—belong to it?[31]
6. How is truth related to judgment? Is it a property of judgment?[32]
7. Why is it that traditional logic has had two concepts of truth: propositional truth, and truth as self-evidence? How are these two concepts related? Are these legitimate concepts? What is their common presupposition, if there is any?[33]
8. There is a theoretical truth, as well as practical truth. Which one of these is the primary sense of 'truth'?[34]
9. How is human thinking related to human existence?[35]
10. What is the metaphysical foundation of logic?[36]

To some of these questions we turn in the next parts of this essay.

---

[27] GA, 26: 158f.
[28] BP, 177, 211f; GA, 26: 26f.
[29] BP, 208ff.
[30] GA, 26: 151f; *Sein und Zeit*, 148f, 216f.
[31] GA, 21: 134–50.
[32] GA, 26: 125–26.
[33] GA, 21: 110–129.
[34] GA, 21: 11–12.
[35] GA, 26: 24.
[36] GA, 26: 170, 128ff.

2. THEORY OF JUDGMENT

A. Rejection of psychologistic theories of judgment.

In his *Dissertation*, Heidegger considers, in considerable detail, four theories of judgment—those of Wundt, Maier, Lipps, and Brentano. Each of these theories is examined with regard to the general definition of judgment it gives; that definition is then tested by how it works in the cases of negative, impersonal, hypothetical, and existential judgments.

Of these four theories, Wundt's theory is concerned with the origin of judgment, Maier's with how a judgment consists of constituent act parts or *Teilakten*, and Lipps' with the completion of the process of judging. Brentano's comes closest to a purely logical theory, but still falls short of it.

(a) Wundt defines judgment as the analysis of a total representation (or thought) into its components. Judgment does not put together concepts, but rather analyses a thought into concepts. Of the latter concepts, the variable component is called the predicate, the relatively constant one is the subject.[37] Heidegger shows that Wundt's theory has no satisfactory account of impersonal judgments (such as "It rains"), existential judgments (the predicate "existence" is not given in the total representation that is analysed), hypothetical judgments (a ground-consequent relation cannot be extracted by analysis) and of negative judgments (Wundt does not in any case regard negation to be of special logical significance.[38]

(b) Maier rejects two common elements of the traditional theories of judgment: (i) the primacy accorded to the declarative sentence (*Aussagesatz*) as a grammatical entity (which, according to Maier, leads to the subject-predicate analysis that takes place under the misleading guidance of grammar), and (ii) the belief that 'true' and 'false' cannot be predicated of representations (*Vorstellungen*) themselves, but only of connections of representations. As against these, and in agreement with Brentano, Maier argues that judgment in its most basic form, is not a connection of representations. In "The sun shines," the subject "The sun" is already a judgment. I assert the sun to be actual on the basis of perception. Even in "This is sun," the "This" is a judgment, a simple "naming-judgment."[39]

---

[37] Contrast Frege who regarded the predicate part or the function as "the stable component" and the sign for the object, i.e., the argument as replaceable by others. Cf. *Begriffsschrift*, §9.

[38] Again compare Frege who regarded the distinction between affirmative and negative judgments as "eine für Logik wenigstens ganz unnötige Unterscheidung, deren Grund außerhalb der Logik zu suchen ist." ("Verneinung," reprinted in Frege, *Logische Untersuchungen*, G. Patzig, ed. (Göttingen: Vandenhöck & Ruprecht, 1966), 61.

[39] Cf. Russell's thesis that "this" is a proper name, together with Husserl's thesis that the naming act may be true or false.

Judgments consist, according to Maier, of acts of presentation, which are then transformed into logical judgments by supervenient acts of objectification. An objectifying act is a positing of actuality, it is a sort of interpretive act. Besides these, there are two other component acts: an identification of the presently apprehended presentation with a reproduced one, and a *Wahrheitsbewusstsein*, which extends over all the three component acts.

Obviously such an account is a psychological, genetic account. The elementary partial acts are generally, according to Maier, involuntary processes.[40] Against it, Heidegger asks: Is the primitive judgment of Maier the same as an elementary judgment in the sense of logic? Above all, Maier is concerned with the *act* of judging, not with the content of judging, the judgment as such. Logic has nothing to do with the processes, be they what they may, that might be "culminating" in the logical judgment. The logical judgment is not the completed final-state of the act; it is rather the objective content.

(c) Brentano, in common with Wundt and Maier, rejects the theory that judgment is a connection of representations. It would not do to say that the content of a judgment is complex, while the content of a representation is simple. The content of a judgment may be as simple as in "A is" (where one is not connecting "A" with "existence"); the content of a representation may be complex (as in the case of a question). This implies that, for Brentano, predication is not an essential component of judgment. What distinguishes a judgment from a mere representation is the presence of either recognition or rejection as a new manner of relatedness of consciousness to its object. Consequently, every judgment is existential, its object is being affirmed as existent or as nonexistent. Thus "Some one person is sick" translates, for Brentano, into "A sick man exists" and "No stone is living" into "a living stone does not exist."

Heidegger's criticisms of Brentano consist in showing in what sense Brentano's theory of judgment is psychologistic. Judgment is, for Brentano, a class of psychic phenomena. The *content* of judgment, that which is recognized or rejected, is of no interest to him. Thus while the distinction between the act and its content could have helped him to overcome psychologism, Brentano's interest remains with the psychic phenomena and he does not succeed in isolating anything specifically logical. It is true that his psychology being "eidetic," Brentano does not deny the universal validity of knowledge. But, as Heidegger insists, it is not a definition of psychologism to say that it denies the universal validity of knowledge.[41] The latter is at most a consequence of psychologism. What is important is that Brentano wants to ground logic in

---

[40] Heidegger does not consider, in his critique of Meier's theory, a possibly transcendental-psychological interpretation of the theory in the sense of Kant's doctrine of three-fold synthesis.
[41] GA, 1: 122.

psychologism. The act of recognition as such is not of interest to logic. The recognition must be justified. And the justification must lie in what is recognized. When one judges a > b (if a=5 and b=3), what is recognized is not the relation "greater than," but that the relation "holds good," its *Gelten*. This *Gelten*, "holding good," subsists independently of anyone's recognition.[42]

(d) Since Lipps' thinking underwent several major changes, he may be said to have held three different accounts of judgment. At first, he defines judgment as the consciousness of actuality (*Wirklichkeitsbewusstsein*), this consciousness being identified with a feeling of constraint (*Zwangsgefühl*). Next, he came to define judgment as consciousness of truth (*Wahrheitsbewusstsein*), where this consciousness is described as being constrained, in one's representation, by the represented objects (*im Vorstellen durch die vorgestellten Objekte genötigt zu sein*).[43] Finally, judgment comes to be defined as consciousness of an object (*Gegenstandsbewusstsein*), where 'object' is distinguished from 'content' in that a content is sensed or represented, while an object is thought or meant and *demands* recognition. This demand or *Förderung* is a logical concept, as distinguished from the constraint or *Nötigung* (of the first two definitions) which is a psychological concept.

In Heidegger's view, Lipps' theory even in its final form remains psychological. Judgment is still an act, "my" response to the experience of *Förderung*. The 'feeling of necessity' even in the alleged logical sense should be kept out of logic.

The dissertation concludes with certain general remarks which point to further reflections. First of all, psychologism cannot perhaps be logically refuted. One can at most exhibit the peculiar nature of logical entities. If a logical entity is a *Sinn*, a *thought* (as distinguished from the act of thinking), then the essence of this entity is to be found not in a *Vorstellung*, but rather in the fact that it *alone* can be *either* true *or* false. It is to this last theme that much of the Marburg lectures of the late twenties are devoted.

Of the other conclusions Heidegger arrives at, some are more viable than others. I have already referred to his insistence that even if the logical entity has to be sharply distinguished from the mental process, the two must be set in some satisfactory relation. This, I think, is important. Both Husserl and Heidegger recognize this need, but pursue it along different paths.

Besides these two general conclusions which suggest further enquiry, Heidegger also proceeds to establish some specific conclusions. He, in a way, reestablishes the subject, predicate and copula analysis, as against its critiques

---

[42] GA, 1: 123f. Compare Frege's view that judgment is the recognition of the truth value of a thought.
[43] Quoted by Heidegger in GA, 1: 135.

by Wundt, Maier, Lipps, and Brentano. A judgment such as "a is equal to b" has to be construed as having 'a' and 'b' as subjects and "being equal" as predicate (as against the grammatical analysis which suggests 'a' as the subject and "is equal to b" as predicate). If the two-membered analysis holds good, then the copula is needed as a third component; it is just the relation between the two.[44] The copula, Heidegger admits, signifies not real existence, but mere validity (*Gelten*). It is in fact characterized as "something eminently logical," the most essential and proper element in a judgment.[45]

Logically more interesting is the next claim that the judgment relation has a certain irreversibility, a directionality, a *Richtungssinn*. Even in "a = b," equality holds good of 'a' and 'b', (and not that 'a' and 'b' of equality). By this, Heidegger rules out the possibility of different analyses of the same proposition.

As to negative judgments, he expresses dissatisfaction with the view that negative judgments are to be understood as judgments with negative predicates and refuses to regard a negative copula as an *Unsinn*.[46] In fact, negation, he adds, belongs originally to the copula,[47] and the two judgments, affirmative and negative, should be logically placed side by side.[48]

What about the impersonal judgment "It rains." The judgment, Heidegger insists, is not a naming judgment. It rather says, something *happens, takes place*, suddenly breaks in. The judgment, then, must be translated to "Raining is actual," "Of the raining, actuality holds good." He adds that this translation is unable to capture what we mean. The true meaning rather is something like this: "Of the raining, it holds good to take place now, the momentary existing."[49]

These are topics which have little influence on his subsequent concerns. So let me turn to his really continuing concern.

B. *Judgment as the locus of truth and falsity.*

(a) Preliminary determination. If judgment is not a representation or a connection of representations, if its logical essence does not lie in its being a mental act, then we have to look for its essence elsewhere. It is generally agreed upon that judgments alone can be true or false. Perhaps it is here that we may be able to discern a clue to the nature of judgment, as also of logic. For logic

---

[44] If only Heidegger had construed the predicate not as "being equal," but as "———— is equal to ————," then he would have realised Frege's point that the names of the so-called subject terms just fill these blanks, and so no third connecting link is needed.

[45] GA, 1: 178–79.
[46] GA, 1: 183.
[47] GA, 1: 184.
[48] GA, 1: 185.
[49] GA, 1: 186.

alone deals with truth in general; the other sciences deal with truths.[50] And logic thinks about 'truth' only in connection with assertive sentences. Heidegger looks for some determination of the nature of such sentences, or of their meanings or propositions, which would account for *both* the possibility of being true *and* the possibility of being false.[51] Contrast Heidegger's problem with Frege's. Frege's problem was such that he could solve it simply by positing two objects which assertive sentences could *name:* i.e., the True and the False. This strategy works for the limited purpose of providing a semantic interpretation of propositional logic, but it leaves the main issue untouched. Are sentences in fact names at all? If they are not,[52] then what sort of structure must they (or their *senses*) have in order to be true *or* false?

The structure that Heidegger identifies is opposition: putting-together (*Zusammensetzen*) and separating (*Auseinandernehmen*). The former is the condition of the possibility of truth and the latter, the condition of the possibility of falsity. But this is only an initial answer, and not quite correct. Not all affirmative sentences—in which elements are put together—are true, just as not all negative sentences—in which elements are separated—are false. The structure that is to be the condition of the possibility of both truth and falsity should consist in both putting-together and separation, in both at once.[53] What we need is a structure that is not merely a thinking together of the two surface structures of synthesis and separation, but which, being a unitary structure, precedes both.[54] We cannot think of this structure—or even of putting-together and separation—as a purely linguistic structure of the sentence. In the false judgment "The board is not black," the *words* are not more separated than in the true judgment "The board is black." Where then are we to look for this structure?

(b) 'Copula'. Perhaps it is in the "is" of the copula. We have seen that Heidegger does not go all the way with many of his contemporary logicians of different persuasions in rejecting the copula from theory of judgment. On the other hand, the precise sense of the "is" of the copula—as distinguished from the "is" of assertion—deeply interests him. In fact, as late as *Sein und Zeit*, Heidegger writes that the ontological significance of the copula has been lost to modern logic.[55] Logic since Aristotle has understood the copula as the sign

---

[50] GA, 21: 7. Compare Frege: "The word 'true' can be used to indicate such a goal for logic . . . of course all the sciences have truth as their goal, but logic is concerned with the predicate 'true' in a quite special way." *Posthumous Writings,* 128.
[51] GA, 21: 135f.
[52] Dummett rejects this part of Frege's semantics.
[53] GA 21: 136f.
[54] GA, 21: 140–41.
[55] *Sein und Zeit,* 159–60. Also see 349.

for a combination of *ideas*, a combination that does not occur among things, but only in thinking. But at the same time, the "is" of the copula also signifies existence, essence (whatness), and truth or validity, in different contexts. (This ambiguity, we are assured,[36] is not a defect, but rather an expression of the intrinsically manifold structure of the being of an entity. This is a suggestion we need not try to understand for our present purpose.) What we need to focus upon is: what unitary structure of synthesis-cum-separation is to be discerned by reflecting upon the nature of the copula?

I do not think Heidegger's logic lectures lead to any definitive answer to this question. But taking up hints from his writings, the following points may be singled out:

(i) In 'S is P', what is asserted is not bare identity, which would make it a tautology; nor is, for that matter, P different from S, which would have rendered the proposition necessarily false. There is thus a relation of identity-cum-difference.[37]

(ii) But what sort of things are S and P? They are not *Vorstellungen*, that was the point of the critique of psychologism. They are not words for obvious reasons. Are they Fregean senses or are they things? (Frege admitted both possiblities, but kept them apart. The sentence 'S is P' expresses a thought that is composed of the senses of 'S' and 'is P'; but the sentence also has a reference that is composed of the referents of the component terms.) I think Heidegger's answer to this is much more complicated, and, if intelligible, profound.[38] *Logos*, in its totality, is a complex structure of words, meanings, the referent (what is thought) and what *is*. It is only when one separates them, that one seeks to tie them together by such relations as that of a sign to the signified. Verbal sound is not a sign for a meaning. Nor is the meaning a pointer to what is thought or to what is. There is an identity between these components,[39] an identity which yet shows the differences.

(iii) This last mentioned relational structure may be described as a structure of identity-cum-difference between thinking and being (where 'thinking' includes speaking, meaning and the meant, and 'being' includes being-as-referred, i.e., object and being as it is in itself). In judgment, thinking and being enter into a relationship. This makes it unacceptable to construe a judgment simply as a mental act directed towards a thought-content. Such a

---

[36] BP, 204–205.
[37] Many Hegelian logicians, such as F. H. Bradley, have used this so-called paradox of predication to imply that judgmental thinking cannot know reality. One may, contrariwise, regard the puzzle as signifying that structure which makes both truth and falsity possible.
[38] BP, 207.
[39] Husserl's sixth logical Investigation has texts which suggest such a view, cf. §§6–7.

construal would set thought (as a timeless, abstract entity) apart from the world, and the act of thinking and expressing (as real, temporal events) from that thought. Thinking is not, as Frege would have it, grasping a thought, but thinking *about* a real being. I think one of the deep concerns Heidegger expresses in the Logic lectures is, how to articulate this *aboutness*, or intentionality of judgment.

With these three points (i)–(iii), we have already gotten some glimpse into the structure of judgment as involving both synthesis (identity, totality, involvement) and separation (difference, distinction). Traditional logic has not seen this interinvolvement of identity and difference, of thought and being, and on the basis of their absolute distinction, distinguishes between verbal and real propositions (Mill) or analytic and synthetic propositions (Kant). This latter sort of distinction has been questioned by many logicians in more recent times: by Quine, because no satisfactory criterion of synonymity is forthcoming, and by F. H. Bradley, earlier than Quine, because every judgment, in so far as it analyzes the totality of immediate experience, is analytic, and, in so far as it seeks to join together what analysis has torn asunder, is synthetic. Heidegger's reason is different from both. The distinction between "the view of beings that makes itself manifest in common meaning and understanding, as it is already laid down in every language," and "the explicit apprehension and investigation of beings, whether in practice or in scientific enquiry" can hardly be maintained; one passes over into the other. In fact, the so-called verbal propositions, Heidegger insists, are but "abbreviations of real propositions."[60]

We still have to understand, how it is possible for a judgment to be about an entity. For Frege, it is so because the component name names an object (and the predicate refers to a concept under which that object falls). Heidegger's question is, how is that possible? Is he asking about the possibility of judgmental intentionality? To that, and some other related questions, we shall turn in the following part.

3. GROUNDING OF LOGIC

(a) Possible Moves. There are various ways philosophers and logicians have sought to provide a "grounding" or foundation for logic. Starting with a logic, the most common move on the part of logicians, is to axiomatize it. This procedure will yield an axiomatic foundation. This is the most you can expect a logician qua logician to do. But in doing so, he is still doing logic, perfecting his logic, not "grounding" it in a sense in which philosophers have understood

---

[60] BP, 197.

that task. Another move is to provide a logic with an ontological interpretation. In this case one starts with an uninterpreted system, and then assigns to symbols of appropriate types suitable entities belonging to appropriate types: such objects as singular entities and concepts, individual concepts, and propositions. One may thus admit various sorts of entities into one's ontology, or if one distrusts abstract entities, then he can use the semantics of possible worlds.

A more radical, and strictly philosophical grounding is called for when one asks about "the conditions of the possibility" of logic. How are logical entities such as judgments possible? How is it that formal logic is able to legislate the formal structure of any object whatsoever? Or, what are the conditions of the possibility of the objective validity and not merely formal validity of logic?

Faced with such questions, one may follow one of three possible paths. One may look for the transcendental foundation of logic in the structure of (human) consciousness; one may look for it in the structure of the world; or, finally, one may want to ground logic in man's intentional relationship with his world. The first is the path of Kant and Husserl, however different their conceptions of transcendental subjectivity, transcendental logic, and formal logic may be; the second is the path of platonistic metaphysics. Heidegger's path is the last one.

(b) *Logic and Intentionality*. In his habilitation work, Heidegger characterizes the nature of the logical thus: "The homogeneity of the domain of logic rests on intentionality, on the character of being-valid-of [*Hingeltungscharakter*]." Also: "Intentionality is the 'regional category' of the logical domain." He proceeds to explicate "intentionality" thus: There can be intentionality only in the case of what has meaning and significance, not in the case of what is just real.[61]

It would appear, then, that we can get at the roots of logic by following the guiding threads of this logical intentionality. This is what Husserl does in *Formal and Transcendental Logic*. But intentionality, for Heidegger, is not self-explanatory. It needs a "metaphysical" grounding, for which Heidegger argues throughout his writings. An intentional grounding of logic will show how the logical entities such as propositions, or the logical principles such as the principle of non-contradiction, are "constituted" in appropriate intentional acts. It will also show, as Husserl does in *Experience and Judgment*, how higher order intentional acts and their objects are built up on more primitive intentionalities and their objects. It should be noted that all this will be carried out within the scope of the transcendental epoché. The classical Kantian way is different, but also shares the same overall orientation. Formal Logic has to be

---

[61] GA, 1: 283.

founded on transcendental logic, and transcendental logic lays bare the synthetic, world-constituting functions of the pure rational subject.

Once psychologism in philosophy of logic was rejected, two alternatives loomed large: the platonic hypostatization of the logical entities, and the Kantian-Husserlian thesis of "constitution" which, for one thing, respects the ideality of those entities, and, for another, sharply distinguishes the transcendental subjectivity from the psychological. Heidegger looked for a third alternative. But, in fact, he tries two different paths, and all his life sought to bring them together. One of these I will call the *metaphysical*, the other may be called the *practical*. They are brought together in a *hermeneutic* thesis.

(c) Logic and Metaphysics. In the Logic lectures of 1928, called "The Metaphysical Foundations (*Anfangsgründe*) of Logic," Heidegger forcefully argues for the thesis that logic must be grounded in metaphysics.[62] Against such a thesis, there is a rather familiar objection which Heidegger considers at length. The objection is that since metaphysics involves thinking and since all thinking must conform to logic, indeed must presuppose logic, metaphysics must presuppose logic rather than the inverse thesis. Indeed, logic must precede all sciences.

According to Heidegger this argument has the advantage that it proceeds from quite general ideas of logic and metaphysics, without considering their specific problem—contents. There is also an ambiguity in the word 'presupposition'. It is true that all thinking—prescientific, scientific as well as metaphysical—must make use of the formal rules of thinking. But *use* of the rules does not require a *science* of those rules, nor does it require a "founded" knowledge of those rules. The fact of their use, as much as the unavoidability of their use for thinking, needs to be accounted for. For such an account, one has to think about the conditions of the possibility of science, about the relation of science to scientific thinking, and of such thinking to human existence; logic itself is a science, historically developed and so determined by a tradition. It therefore cannot be a presupposition of thinking.

The barely formal argument to the effect that every thinking grounding must involve thinking, cannot be formally refuted—Heidegger concedes.[63] But, he adds, it can be refuted only by showing how such an argument is possible and why, under certain presuppositions, it indeed is necessary. At this point Heidegger does not go on to show this. As far as I can see, his point would be something like this: pre-logical thinking which is in direct touch with being, thinking which, according to Heidegger's later writings, is either practi-

---

[62] GA, 26: 128–32.
[63] Ibid., 131.

cal wisdom or poetic, does not follow the rules of logic and so no question arises about logic being its presupposition. It is only propositional thinking that follows the rules of (propositional) logic. A putative metaphysical grounding may remain within the limits of propositional thinking; it then does appear to presuppose logic (allowing for the sort of equivocation of "presupposing" which was hinted at earlier). Such a grounding then does not go to the roots of the matter. A metaphysical grounding which does go to the roots of the matter would think, but think in a different, more originary manner.

What is this more originary manner of thinking, and how could such thinking provide a grounding for logical thinking and for logic as well? To be able to understand Heidegger's answers to these questions, we need to do some more spade work to prepare the ground.

(d) *Logic as Metaphysics of Truth*.[64] Judgments alone can be either true or false. This is because in judgment, thinking and being enter into a peculiar relation of identity-cum-difference. Judgment is "about" a being, and of this being it asserts a true predicate. Let us look closer at this "being about" and also at the copula, the sign of predication.

(i) The "being about" or judgmental intentionality is possible, according to Heidegger, only because a being has already been disclosed prior to the judgment under consideration. A judgment does not first establish the relatedness to the entity-about-which. A judgment is first possible on the basis of an already available disclosure of the entity, and the disclosure of that entity takes place within the context of an already latent relatedness to or *Schon-sein-bei* beings. A judgment is true if its content is in agreement with the already disclosed object-about-which. The metaphysical here is the disclosure of being as a being, a disclosure without which judgment cannot substantiate its truth claim and would not be, qua judgment, possible. Thus judgmental intentionality presupposes a prejudgmental manifestation of being. We need not have to understand this thesis in any weird and mystic sounding sense. The best way to understand Heidegger, at this point, is to take his thesis as exemplified in the familiar case of perceptual judgments. A perceptual judgment "This pen is blue" is possible inasmuch as the object-about-which, this pen, is already disclosed in perceptual experience, as lying there before me. It is important that we do not construe this perceptual disclosure itself as a judgment. What this disclosure is like, I will briefly touch upon later, but only in so far as that is necessary for my present exposition.

(ii) Predication likewise is founded upon display.[65] In predicating, what is

---

[64] GA. 26: 132.
[65] BP, 209f.

disclosed is analyzed into one of its constituent moments, and this separated moment is exhibited as *belonging to* the entity disclosed. Predication determines an entity as being such and such, but the determination is founded on exhibition and separation. This shows why every judgment is both analytic and synthetic at once. The copula signifies the "togetherness," the "belonging-together," that "unifying gathering" which belongs to our very concept of being as the *world*.

(iii) If the foregoing makes sense, then it makes sense to say that although truth in the sense of adequacy or correspondence has its locus in judgment, truth in the sense of disclosedness of being is prior to judgment. If this latter sense of 'truth' be called ontological, then logic is grounded in ontology. Hence Heidegger's enigmatic statement: "Der Satz is nicht das, darin Wahrheit erst möglich wird, sondern umgekehrt, der Satz ist erst in der Wahrheit möglich.... Satz ist nicht der Ort der Wahrheit, sondern Wahrheit der Ort des Satzes."[66]

We thus find that when Heidegger claims to ground logic in metaphysics he should be understood in a sense that takes into account the above mentioned three points. He should not be construed as grounding logic either in the structure of the subject or in the structure of the world.

(d) Logic and Practical Wisdom. Logic, we have seen, deals with meanings. With the rejection of psychologism, one is tempted to look upon meanings as eternally subsistent entities. At no stage of his thinking was Heidegger satisfied with such a hypostatization of meanings. The habilitation work ends with the "metaphysical" suggestion that the opposition between real mental life and ideal meanings, between *Sein* and *Sollen*, be overcome in a more fundamental concept of living *Geist*.[67] The Logic lecture of 1925/26 suggests that although the primacy of theoretical truth in logic is not accidental, it is possible to show that a more radical stance of questioning may lead to a revision of this naive point of departure of logic.[68] In fact, not formal logic but philosophical logic has to settle the question, which truth—theoretical or practical—is primary. Heidegger opts for the primacy of the practical.

To demonstrate this thesis of the primacy of the practical is to argue successfully that the meanings logic is concerned with, propositional meanings and their constituents, are *not* the meanings originally experienced along with that disclosure of being which is presupposed by judgment. The word, as *fixed* and stabilized for purposes of logical thinking, presupposes a pre-logical experience of being as meaningful. This latter sort of meaningfulness is tied to the way

---

[66] GA, 21: 135.
[67] GA, 1: 405.
[68] GA, 21: 11.

we live in our world and concern ourselves—practically and affectively—with things and situations. Things acquire their original significance (*Bedeutung*) from what we have got to do with them, from *Zutunhaben*. A pencil is meant for writing, a hammer for driving nails, and so on and so forth. Original practical judgments express such a significance of things: they do not ascribe properties to a thing. They are about my (actual or possible) relations to a thing.[69]

It may be objected that this sort of practical and affective significance belongs only to tools and artifacts: pens and pencils, houses and automobiles, hammers and clocks, but not to natural objects such as rocks and mountains, rivers and trees, and animals and other persons. I think Heidegger's point is that in so far as these and other natural objects inhabit my *Lebenswelt* and not the world of physics, they fall within the horizon of my interests, passions, and possible actions directed at them. They are not mere objects of cognition. The logic of judgment is founded upon the prelogical disclosure of things as having the sort of practical significance that they have within our *Lebenswelt*. To say this, however, is not to *show* how apophantic judgment arises out of the practical. It would be the task of hermeneutic logic to show that. Heidegger has not himself done hermeneutic logic; some others have, and we need to turn to them. But before doing that we need to be clear about how the practical wisdom which recognizes for each object and situation its practical significance could be characterized as being hermeneutic.

(e) *Logic and Hermeneutics*. It was said earlier that Heidegger tried, all his life, to bring together two different groundings of logic: the metaphysical and the practical, and that they were to be unified under the concept of hermeneutics. We now need to ascertain how this is done. The connecting link is provided by two theses: (i) that action is a mode of understanding the world and involves a certain self-understanding on the part of the agent; and (ii) that the originary disclosure of entities which must precede judgmental "being about" is not disclosure to a cognitive subject, to an objectivating consciousness, but rather to a projecting, caring, and acting being whose mode of being is to be in the world and to-be-already-with-entities. Being-in-the-world is to be interpreted as a certain comprehension or understanding of oneself and one's world. Thus both practice and disclosure of entities involve a certain pre-conceptual understanding of oneself and one's world. To articulate and explicate this understanding is hermeneutics. If logic is grounded in a disclosure of being, and if logical meanings refer back to pre-logical significance, one can as well say that logic is ultimately rooted in a certain understanding of the world as well as of oneself.

---

[69] GA. 21: 150–59.

The same thesis may be supported in a slightly different manner. Judging is an intentional relation to a being. But every intentional relation carries within itself a *specific understanding* of the being of the entity to which the intentionality relates. If judging presupposes a prior disclosure of that entity, it also requires a specific interpretation of it *as* such and such.

With this we are in a position to briefly consider Heidegger's thesis on logic as laid down in §33 of *Sein und Zeit* bearing the title: "Die Aussage als abkünftiger Modus der Auslegung." In this paragraph, Heidegger first distinguishes between three meanings of "Aussage"; all three together constitute the full structure of *Aussage*. First of all, "Aussage" primarily means manifesting an entity as it is. In "The hammer is too heavy," the hammer itself, but not its representation, is manifested in the manner it is at hand. Secondly, *Aussage* also means predication. This sense is grounded in the first. Both the terms of predication, the subject and the predicate, belong to what has been manifested. Predication itself does not uncover anything but rather limits what has been uncovered to the subject, i.e., the hammer. Finally, *Aussage* also means "communication," to let the entity be seen together with an other. What is stated can be shared, can be stated again. Taking these three meanings together, an *Aussage* may be characterized as "communicating and determining, making manifest." But how then is it also a mode of interpretation? The making-manifest that takes place in and through an *Aussage*, is possible only on the basis of what is already disclosed to understanding. It is not a worldless, transcendental ego who performs an *Aussage*. It is rather a *Dasein* who is a being-in-the-world and as such always has a certain pre-understanding of the world, who makes a judgment. The existential fore-structures of understanding, which together constitute its anticipatory structure, form the horizon within which any judgment is possible. In this sense the judgment of logic is founded upon the hermeneutic of *Dasein*.

Heidegger has still to give an account of how the entity with which one is practically concerned (the hammer as a tool for driving a nail here and now) *becomes* an object about which one pronounces a theoretical judgment. Obviously, if Heidegger's thesis is correct, the *Zuhandene Womit des Zutunhabens* has to be transformed into the "*Worüber*" *der aufzeigenden Aussage*. What transpires in this transformation? Something whose mode of being is to-be-ready-at-hand becomes an object that is present-at-hand, merely *vorhanden*. The original "as," which was a hermeneutic "as" (recognizing a hammer as what is just right for my purpose) for practical wisdom, becomes a mere apophantic "as" (*judging* this object over there to be a hammer) which determines the object as possessing a certain property. The logic of *theoretical* judgments is committed to an ontology of objects present at hand.

In an important, but not much commented upon paragraph, Heidegger concedes that between these two extremes, there are many intermediate phases, represented by judgments about happenings in the surrounding world, accounts of situations, depictions of events, etc. These intermediate cases, though expressed in linguistic sentences, cannot be reduced to theoretical statements, but rather refer back to their origin in the pre-conceptual interpretation of the world.

What now has become of the concept of meaning or *Sinn* which was earlier used to define the domain of logic? This concept of *Sinn* is to be traced back to its origin in another, more originary concept of *Sinn* which Heidegger formulates with some precision in §65 of *Sein and Zeit:* "Danach ist Sinn das, worin sich die Verstehbarkeit von etwas hält, ohne daß es selbst ausdrücklich und thematisch in den Blick kommt. Sinn bedeutet das Woraufhin des primären Entwurfs, aus dem her etwas als das, was es ist in seiner Möglichkeit begriffen werden kann." *Sinn* is that towards which the originary project of being-in-the-world is directed. To understand the *Sinn* of a thing (not of a word, in this case) is to grasp, unthematically, the possibility that the thing presents in the context of the prevailing project.

(f) Hermeneutic Logic. It is one thing to claim that formal logic is rooted in a hermeneutic experience of being-in-the-world. It is quite another thing to work out in detail the idea of a hermeneutic logic. Without such a logic, the Heideggerian thesis would remain empty of content, for not only logic but all theoretical cognition, on that thesis, would have the same "origin." With such a logic, the thesis receives specific content, but loses some of its ontological grandeur, for now formal logic will be traced back to another kind of logic, but we would still be within the field of logic, which thereby would receive an extension beyond the formal-theoretical.

Even if Heidegger does not give us sketches of such a logic, luckily we have excellent attempts in that direction. This is not the place to review those attempts, but it surely is appropriate that we briefly recall the more noteworthy amongst them. First of all, Husserl himself, in *Experience and Judgment*, extended the domain of logic to pre-predicative experience, and showed how truth-functional operators such as negation, disjunction and implication have their origin in pre-predicative experience. Husserl's thesis may be regarded as still being cognitive in nature, the pre-predicative experience is construed not as active or affective dealing with entities, but rather as modes of receptivity and various modes of responses to what is received. In this sense, Husserl's pre-predicative logic does not come under the rubric "hermeneutic logic."

The most striking development of hermeneutic logic, developed in close contact with both Husserl and Heidegger, is to be found in the works of Hans

Lipps.[70] If formal logic deals with logical entities which claim to be self-subsistent essences, and appear to have no connection with the living situations of everyday life, what Lipps does is to comprehend precisely the entities and structures of logic as arising out of human life, i.e., to bring out how they originally have the function of accomplishing quite specific roles in quite specific linguistic situations of everyday life. Thus judgment (*Urteil*) in its origin is not a statement, but an action by which a yet-to-be-decided question is finally decided, as in legal judgment. The concepts of traditional logic, according to Lipps, are quite different from the concepts of originary, practical thinking. To comprehend things, in practical life, is to come to terms with things, to know what to do with them, as in overcoming an opposition. Concepts in this sense are not definable, they can only be illustrated by examples. The same sort of distinction is made in the case of inference. In practical life one infers, not from premises, but from circumstances, situations, facts. *Proof* becomes necessary in a situation of conversation, when something has to be demonstrated for the other. An interesting development of the idea of prelogical conception is Lipps' distinction between "practical" and "intuitive" (*sichtenden*) conceptions. Neither needs language, but both may function in a linguistic medium. The practical conception operates in knowing *how;* the intuitive conception operates in one's mastery over a wide range of diverse material without yet subsuming it under a common logical concept.

Meanings of words are, for theoretical logic, precise and fixed entities. In practical life, meanings cannot be fixed with precision. (Lipps elaborates on the Wittgensteinian example: the word "game.") This imprecision is not a deficiency; it is rather a strength. The words derive their meanings not autonomously, but in connection with situations in which they are uttered. This leads Lipps to consider various kinds of words and the great variety of situations that call forth appropriate utterances.

Josef König studied with Husserl, but subsequently attended Heidegger's Marburg lectures, and sought to appropriate their methodologies into a basically Dilthey-oriented position. I would here mention only a few of his important distinctions: (i) In his *Sein und Denken*[71] König distinguishes between the merely present (*vorhanden*) thing and the thing as so-working (*so-Wirkende*). The former is not an original subject of predication, but is rather a transfor-

---

[70] Hans Lipps, *Untersuchungen zur Phänomenologie der Erkenntnis*. Erster Teil, *Das Ding und seine Eigenschaften* (Bonn, 1927). Zweiter Teil, *Aussage und Urteil* (Bonn, 1928). But more specifically, see his *Untersuchungen zu einer hermeneutischen Logik*, Philosophische Abhandlungen, Bd. VII (Frankfurt am Main, 1933).

[71] Halle: Max Niemeyer, 1937.

mation of a judgment of the form "X is present." The true subject of a statement about something present is not this something present, but rather the X of sentences of the sort "X is present." But the latter, i.e., the so-working, or an entity that is not the merely present, is the original entity. The subject of so-working is *nothing but* a so-working being (a pleasing smile is a smile that so works on us; a sublime mountain is one which so works on us). Its being (*Sein*) is to be so-working.

(ii) König also distinguishes between a practical 'this' and a theoretical '*this*'.[72] The theoretical *this* is a *this* of such and such kind: for example, 'under this circumstance' = 'under *such* circumstance'; this man = a man such as this. As contrasted with this, a practical *this* is a pure this. For example, What is *this* that lies there on the table? A practical this is the merely existing reality. The practical this belongs to someone's world; it is hardly compatible with the thought of a closed system or with a world-totality as *Vorhanden*.

(iii) Another of König's related distinctions is that between practical cause and theoretical cause.[73] The former answers a practical "why" question and the latter a theoretical question. A practical "why" question is: "Why does this ball start moving?" A theoretical "why" question is "Why do balls that receive an impact start moving?" The former is answered by giving another event as the efficient cause. The latter requires a ground in a general theoretical implication.

(iv) All these lead him finally to a distinction that is of direct significance for logic: that between practical sentences and theoretical sentences.[74] A theoretical sentence (or proposition) can be rightly seen as built out of a sentential (or, propositional) function 'x is F' either by replacing 'x' by a constant 'A', or by quantifying over x (Some x is F; All x is F). A practical sentence, according to König, cannot be so construed without doing violence to its meaning and its role. The subject of a practical sentence is a practical "this" or "that." The sentence, "That is my friend Karl" cannot be regarded as having been built out of a sentential function "x is my friend Karl."

König's valuable, carefully developed, but incomplete researches shall constitute a necessary part of any satisfactory hermeneutic logic.

Lastly, I should mention the more well known and more recent attempt of

---

[72] Josef König, "Über einen neuen ontologischen Beweis des Satzes von der Notwendigkeit alles Geschehens," *Archiv für Philosophie*, 2 (1948): 5–43. Reprinted in Josef König, *Vorträge und Aufsätze*, ed. G. Patzig (Freiburg/München: Verlag Alber, 1978).

[73] Josef König, "Bemerkungen über den Begriff der Ursache," originally in *Das Problem der Gesetzlichkeit*, Bd. I (Hamburg: F. Meiner, 1949). Reprinted in *Vortäge und Aufsätze*.

[74] König's Göttingen Lectures (1953–54) under the title "Theoretische und praktische Sätze" are still unpublished. They are being edited by G. Patzig for publication.

Paul Lorenzen.[75] Lorenzen develops a systematic constructive procedure for building up formal logical concepts and operations from simple practical situations (such as one in which one person gives an order which the other obeys or does not obey; or one in which two are engaged in a game; or dialogical situations in which there is a proponent and an opponent). Lorenzen, interestingly enough, sees his task as having been made possible only after Dilthey and Frege.[76]

One may want to say that these attempts fulfill the intention implicit in Heidegger's thinking about formal logic, in a more constructive and fruitful manner.

4. CRITICAL REMARKS

But what to say about Heidegger's own foundational thoughts? To recapitulate what has already been pointed out, these thoughts are mainly five:

First, formal logic, *historically*, was possible within a metaphysical system (the Platonic), and can be possible only within a metaphysics.

Secondly, formal logic is committed to an ontology of objects whose mode of being is to be present at hand (*Vorhandensein*).

Thirdly, (in spite of the above) philosophical reflection on the copula yields an insight into the identity-cum-difference, and the togetherness of differentiated elements that belongs to the *meaning* of Being.

Fourthly, judgmental being-about presupposes a prior pre-judgmental disclosure of an entity, which disclosure takes palce within the context of Dasein's already-being-with the others.

Fifthly, judgmental *Sinn*, as also logical-theoretical meaning of words, refers back to a practical understanding of the significance of things in relation to human projects, i.e, in the context of the totality of life situations.

The final evaluation of formal logic would be somewhat as follows: formal logic has its own range of validity, no doubt, but philosophy should replace its naiveté by reflecting on its sense and its "origin." This will require a philosophical logic which is double-pronged: at once ontological and hermeneutic. Modern mathematical logic is degenerate formal logic, for whatever hermeneutic and ontological glimpses the traditional formal logic permitted is, or at least

---

[75] Cf. Paul Lorenzen, *Konstruktive Wissenschaftstheorie* (Frankfurt am Main: Suhrkamp, 1974) and *Methodisches Denken* (Frankfurt am Main: Suhrkamp, 1974).

[76] *Konstruktive Wissenschaftstheorie*, 21. He also writes: "Erst im Anschluß an Dilthey und Husserl haben Misch einerseits und Heidegger andererseits deutlich gemacht, was das heisst, daß Denken vom Leben, von der praktischen Lebensituation des Menschen, auszugehen hat." *Methodisches Denken*, 26.

appears to have been, totally lost to mathematical logic, whose main blunder consists in confusing between a science of quantity and a science of intentionality and which is, historically speaking, possible only in an epoch for which the meaning of Being is understood through technology.[77]

With regard to these thoughts, I would like to submit the following critical and, certainly, tentative reflections.

1. The historical judgment appears to me to be sound, namely, that formal logic arose within the Platonic metaphysics. One needed, to begin with, a doctrine of objective ideas and propositions. But the history of logic shows that logic has tried to free itself from that Platonic origin. Propositions have been replaced by sentences (even if they are 'eternal sentences'), concepts by words (even if they are type words, not tokens), and so on and so forth. To what extent, then, must we say that formal logic unavoidably presupposes a metaphysics (i.e., a theory of Being) and an ontology (a position as to what sorts of entities to admit)? My own view is that although formal logicians have sought to court a nominalistic ontology, that just has not worked. (See how sentences have become eternal sentences.) The logical relations and structures need abstract entities to hold good of, so some sort of Platonism is 'the original sin' of formal logic. But these Platonic entities are of the genre of meanings, Fregean *Sinne* or Husserlian *noemata*. A certain theory of meaning, and its attendant ontology may well be regarded as the minimum commitment of formal logic. No other ontology of *Vorhandensein* is presupposed. Events and happenings, situations and circumstances, tools and gadgets, can all be referents of "objects-about-which" of *propositions* that are subjected to logical operations.

2. It is not clear how much ontological burden can be carried by the copula. Heidegger's multifarious attempts to extract out of it insights into the meaning of 'Being' have been far from successful. By saying that 'Being' involves identity-cum-difference or the togetherness of distincts, is not to say much that could not be divined by simple metaphysical speculation independently of the guidance of the copula.

3. The thesis of the pre-logical, pre-predicative disclosure is important, and its validity recognized. I should add that this thesis derives its strength from the case of perceptual judgments such as "This pencil is blue." But not all judgments are perceptual, and not all disclosure is prior to judgment. In a judgment about electrons, one does not have a pre-theoretical disclosure of the object-about-which: in verifying such a judgment, the disclosure comes *afterwards* as the "fulfillment" of the meaning intention of an originally empty

---

[77] For my present limited purpose, I desist from either expounding or commenting upon this last claim.

judgment. The thesis of *prior* disclosure, then, may be saved by liberalizing the sense of 'disclosure' and at the same time by relativizing it to the context of a judging.

4. With regard to perceptual judgments about persons and material objects, it is true that originary disclosure is not a theoretical-cognitive mode of givenness, but rather practical and affective.[78] This alone justifies Heidegger's basing apophansis on hermeneutics. However, even if one does work out a hermeneutic logic in the manner of Lipps, König, and Lorenzen, one still needs to show how apophantic logic develops out of hermeneutic logic. Lorenzen's is the best attempt to show this, but it works for elementary truth functions, and even there a certain *discontinuity* between the primitive hermeneutic situation and the formal-logical is either slurred over or eliminated by choosing the former at a level that is not originary-practical, but rather primitively theoretical.

5. Heidegger is right, to my mind, in looking upon Husserl's antipsychologism critique as a provisional, though indispensable step. In fact, Husserl himself treated it likewise. The gap between real mental life and ideal meanings has to be bridged. Transcendental philosophy and hermeneutics are two ways of doing this. Their relative strength has to be measured, among other things, by the extent to which each is capable of accounting for the ideality of logical meanings. For hermeneutics, the question is: How do the practical-hermeneutic meanings of things get 'transformed' into the theoretical-logical meanings of words and sentences?

Temple University

---

[78] I have argued for this in my *Phenomenology and Ontology* (The Hague: M. Nijhoff, 1970).

The Conditions of Truth in Heidegger and Davidson*

In this paper I hope to demonstrate that, despite dramatic differences in approach, Analytic and Continental philosophers can be brought into a productive dialogue with one another on topics central to the philosophical agenda of both traditions. Their differences tend to obscure the fact that both traditions have as a fundamental project the critique of past accounts of language, intentionality, and mind. Moreover, writers within the two traditions are frequently in considerable agreement about the failings of past accounts. Where they tend to differ is in the sorts of positive accounts they give. By exploring the important areas of disagreement against the background of agreement, however, it is possible to gain insights unavailable to those rooted in a single tradition.

I would like to illustrate this in the context of a comparison of Heidegger's and Davidson's accounts of the conditions of truth. I begin, however, with a brief discussion of some crucial differences between the Analytic and Continental ways of doing philosophy. An understanding of these differences provides the basis for seeing how Heidegger and Davidson, all appearances to the contrary, in fact follow a parallel course by resisting theoretical attempts at the redefinition or reduction of our pretheoretical notion of truth. Indeed, both writers believe that truth is best illuminated by looking at the conditions of truth—that is, they both try to understand what makes truth as a property of language and thought possible in the first place. Both answer the question by exploring how what we say or think can come to have content. I conclude by suggesting that Heidegger's "ontological foundations" of "the traditional conception of truth" can be seen as an attempt at solving a problem which Davidson recognizes but believes is incapable of solution—namely, the way the existence of language and thought presuppose our sharing a finely articulated structure which only language and thought seem capable of producing.

"The Conditions of Truth in Heidegger and Davidson" by Mark A. Wrathall,
The Monist, vol. 82, no. 2, pp. 304–323. Copyright © 1999, THE MONIST, La Salle, Illinois 61301.

Analytic and Continental Philosophy

If I were to reduce the difference between Analytic and Continental philosophy to a single anecdote, I would refer to two titles: Michael Dummett's *The Logical Basis of Metaphysics*,[1] based on his 1976 William James Lectures, and Martin Heidegger's *Metaphysische Anfangsgründe der Logik*,[2] the published edition of a 1928 lecture course. Here in a nutshell one finds the Analytic's focus on logical analysis as the means toward philosophical questioning, and the Continental suspicion that all knowledge is tinged through and through by hidden metaphysical presuppositions.

As Dummett explains in his introduction, Analytic philosophy's approach to metaphysical issues is premised on the belief that "[p]hilosophy can take us no further than enabling us to command a clear view of the concepts by means of which we think about the world, and, by so doing, to attain a firmer grasp of the way we represent the world in our thoughts."[3] The Analytic philosopher's assault on metaphysical heights, then, will only begin after the exhaustive examination of more pedestrian subjects like language and logic. This is in deliberate contrast to the philosophical tradition, which Dummett views as deeply flawed due to "an underestimation by even the deepest thinkers of the difficulty of the questions they tackle. They consequently take perilous shortcuts in their argumentation and flatter themselves that they have arrived at definitive solutions when much in their reasoning is questionable. I believe that we shall make faster progress only if we go at our task more slowly and methodically, like mountain climbers making sure each foothold is secure before venturing onto the next."[4]

One needs only contrast this position with Heidegger's introduction to see the profound difference in impetus between the Analytical and Continental style. Heidegger argues that we can make no progress at all in philosophical understanding without "a critical dismantling of traditional logic down to its hidden foundations"—"*the metaphysical foundations of logic.*"[5] This is because logic can provide genuine insight into "the way we represent the world in our thoughts" (as Dummett puts it) only if we understand why it is that we human beings are constituted in such a way "as to be able to be thus governed by laws": "How 'is' Dasein [human being] according to its essence so that such an obligation as that of being governed by logical laws can arise in and for Dasein [human being]?"[6] As a result, "[a] basic problem of logic, the law-governedness of thinking, reveals itself to be a problem of human existence in its ground."[7] Consequently, an understanding of logical form would be bootless, for Heidegger, without a prior understanding of the constitution of human existence—an understanding which can only be reached by reflection on the fundamental concepts of metaphysics.

Analytic philosophers, in sum, see themselves as engaged in the painstaking process of clarifying the logical structure of language and mind—a process they believe to be prior to making inroads in metaphysical reflection. Continental philosophers, while also often starting from the structure of language and mind, seek to move from there directly to a reflection on the historical, existential dimension of our language and thoughts. Because Analytics see no evidence of careful and rigorous analysis in the work of Continental thinkers, they consider Continental philosophy to be, at best, "a more or less systematic reflection on the human situation . . . a kind of reflection which can sometimes lead to a new perspective on human life and experience."[8] At its worst, Continental philosophy is viewed as hopelessly muddling about within a "wide-spread ignorance of certain fundamental linguistic principles."[9] Continental philosophers, on the other hand, are intensely suspicious of the Analysts' "fundamental linguistic principles," certain that reliance on them is premised on metaphysical naïvete or even ignorance. So Heidegger argues that "[t]he appearance of a 'philosophy of language' is a striking sign that knowledge of the essence of the word, i.e., the possibility of an experience of the primordial essence of the word, has been lost for a long time. The word no longer preserves the relation of Being to man, but instead the word is a formation and thing of language."[10] And Derrida thinks it typical of the whole Analytic tradition that it conducts its investigations on the basis of "a kind of ideal regulation," which excludes the troublesome cases most in need of examination—troublesome cases which in fact work to deconstruct traditional philosophy[11]

What is often lost in this mutual antipathy is a surprising overlap in views concerning the shared starting point of much of the work in both traditions—language. It strikes me that the best way to overcome the Analytic/Continental divide is therefore to ignore, at least provisionally, the differences in approach and instead explore the areas of agreement.

When left at the level of mutual recrimination, it looks like there is so little in common as to make the two traditions irrelevant to one another, for it seems to both sides as if the other is either incapable of joining issue, or at least willfully refusing to do so. But if one can get beyond the differences and discover a common ground, then the disagreements can be seen to have content and the proponents of the two traditions can be made to engage in productive ways. In the remainder of this paper, I hope to illustrate this by showing how Heidegger's and Davidson's inquiries into truth and the functioning of language, as different as they are, both come to focus on the conditions of the possibility of truth as the means to dissolving traditional philosophical problems. It is true that there are important differences in their accounts of truth conditions. But by seeing their disagreement against the background of an extensive congruence in view, one can highlight in a way not easily available to adherents of one tradition or another the presuppositions and problems which remain for each thinker.

Heidegger and Davidson on Truth Definitions

There are a variety of traditional answers to the question what makes a true sentence (or belief or proposition, etc.) true—answers such as correspondence, coherence, utility, and so on. What all these theories share, as Davidson has pointed out, is a sense that truth is a concept for which we should be able to provide an illuminating definition. From the preceding observations on the difference between Analytic and Continental philosophy, as general as they were, it should come as no surprise that both Davidson and Heidegger are critical of traditional truth theories. The notable similarities between Davidson's and Heidegger's views of truth, on the other hand, are perhaps unexpected. Davidson, after all, has argued for a "correspondence" view, albeit a "correspondence without confrontation."[12] And he pursues the question of truth, in good Analytic fashion, within the context of a semantic analysis of the truth predicate. Heidegger, on the other hand, is widely interpreted as denying a correspondence view in favor of a definition of truth as "unconcealment." And his criticism of correspondence theories is based in a phenomenological, rather than a logical, exploration of our experience of truth.

But, on scrutiny, one discovers that the differences are nowhere near as wide as one might believe. Heidegger, in fact, views propositional truth as a sort of correspondence, and I have argued elsewhere that Heidegger's account of unconcealment is badly misunderstood if taken as a definition of truth.[13] To the contrary, Heidegger's interest in propositional truth is not to redefine it, but to discover what makes propositional entities capable of being true or false. And Davidson, likewise, believes that propositional truth cannot meaningfully be defined in terms of correspondence. More importantly Davidson, like Heidegger, believes that progress cannot be made on the issue of truth by defining it, but only by understanding the conditions of sentences and beliefs being true. The *interesting* disagreement comes, then, not at the level of their respective accounts of propositional truth, but rather in the details of their explanations of the conditions of truth.

In order to get to the point where we can fruitfully compare and contrast Davidson and Heidegger on this topic, however, we must get beyond the seemingly incompatible approaches to propositional truth. By understanding the context provided by their respective traditions for inquiries into truth, we can go a long way toward separating the genuine from the merely apparent disagreement.

Within the Analytic tradition of philosophy, the generally accepted starting point for understanding truth is an analysis of our use of the truth predicate. Many philosophers accept that "just about everything there is to be said about truth" is said by noting that almost all of our uses of 'is true' can be understood in terms of "certain formal features" of the predicate—"notably its disquotation feature."[14] These features allow us to make certain generalizing statements about sentences; "the truth predicate allows any sentence to be reformulated so that its entire content will be expressed by the new subject—a singular term open to normal objectival quantification."[15] In addition, we can account for certain vestigial uses of 'true' (like "That's true!") in terms of its use as an illocutionary device—for instance, to confirm or endorse.[16]

Perhaps the best-known example of a definition of the truth predicate is Tarski's semantic theory of truth. Tarski's Convention T shows how to provide an extensionally adequate description of the truth predicate for each of a number of well-behaved languages. According to Convention T, a satisfactory truth theory for that language must be such as to entail for every sentence of the language a T-sentence of the form

s is true if and only if p

where "*s*" is a description of the sentence, and "*p*" is replaced by that sentence, or a translation of the sentence into the metalanguage.[17]

The problem of restricting analysis to the truth predicate is, as many have noted, that such a definition seems to fall far short of explaining our concept of truth. Dummett, for instance, argues that the failing of a Tarskian truth definition is best seen in the case where we are constructing a T-theory for an object language we do not yet understand. In order to do this, we must know the conditions under which truth can be predicated for each and every sentence of the object-language—something we cannot do unless "we know something about the concept of truth expressed by that predicate which is not embodied in that, or any other truth-definition."[18]

Thus, if all we knew about truth were exhausted by a T-theoretic description of the truth predicate for a language, we would not be able to define truth for a new language. The implications for Analytic philosophers engaged in the Davidsonian project of defining meaning in terms of truth are critical, for if the truth conditions of sentences are to play any role in fixing their meaning, our ability to learn a language depends on having a pre-theoretic understanding of truth. Thus, Dummett explains that

> in order that someone should gain from the explanation that P is true in such-and-such circumstances an understanding of the sense of P, he must already know what it means to say of P that it is true. If when he enquires into this he is told that the only explanation is that to say that P is true is the same as to assert P, it will follow that in order to understand what is meant by saying that P is true, he must already know the sense of asserting P, which was precisely what was supposed to be being explained to him.[19]

So if meaning is to be understood in terms of truth conditions, then understanding language requires an account of truth above and beyond a language-relative characterization of the truth predicate.

But what sense can be given to this pre-T-theoretic concept of truth? The readily available traditional answer, which explains truth as correspondence, is unable to do the work that needs to be done to make truth useful in Davidson's project. According to correspondence theories, we accept that a statement is true if there is some fact to which the statement corresponds. But, in order to do the work we need it to do, the theory must specify the fact to which the sentence corresponds prior to our recognizing the sentence as true. And, as Davidson has shown, a definition of truth in terms of correspondence to facts is unable to do this. For a correspondence theory to be useful, it must be able to generate theorems of the form

(1) the statement that *p* corresponds to the fact that *q*

But if *q* is an extensional description of some fact or state of affairs in the world, *p* will correspond not just to *q*, but to any sentence logically equivalent to *q*, or to any sentence differing from *q* only in the substitution in *q* of a coextensive singular term. Thus, *p* will correspond not just to the fact that *q*, but to any fact at all.[20] And so (1) will fail to assist us in determining whether a sentence is true. Treating the description as less than fully extensional (by, for example, denying the substitutivity of logically equivalent sentences) is no more successful. The very possibility of explaining truth through correspondence is undermined by this move, since nonextensional descriptions rely on the concept of truth in picking out the fact in the first place: "Suppose, to leave the frying-pan of extensionality for the fires of intension, we distinguish facts as finely as statements. Of course, not every statement has its fact; only the true ones do. But then, unless we find another way to pick out facts, we cannot hope to explain truth by appeal to them."[21] Hence, the real objection to correspondence theories is that they "fail to provide entities to which truth vehicles (whether we take these to be statements, sentences or utterances) can be said to correspond."[22]

But, Davidson argues, rather than moving us to look for new definitions of truth, this failure should lead us to question the belief that to make the concept of truth useful we have to be able to specify what makes a true sentence true. Davidson has argued that, in constructing a theory of meaning, what we need beyond a T-theory for a language is not a definition of truth, but an understanding of how we have the concept of truth. It is thus not truth that we should be seeking, but rather a clarification of "the necessary condition[s] of our possession of the concept[] of truth."[23]

To summarize, Davidson's approach to truth has two distinct sides to it. First, as against any attempt to define truth, he takes the notion of truth itself to be "beautifully transparent" and primitive, and thus denies that the general concept of truth is reducible to any other concept or amenable to redefinition in other terms.[24] This leaves intact our pre-theoretic understanding of truth. He accepts a Tarskian T-theory as providing an instructive description of the kind of pattern truth makes in a language.[25] But he resists the urge to believe that such a definition fully captures the concept of truth.

The second part consists in saying enough more about truth to shed light on the other philosophical issues in which truth is implicated: "what we want to know is how to tell when T-sentences (and hence the theory as a whole) describe the language of a group or an individual. This obviously requires specifying at least part of the content of the concept of truth which Tarski's truth predicates fail to capture."[26] Davidson's account of truth consequently turns to the conditions of truth—specifically, the condition that sentences and other propositional entities have content.

Heidegger's inquiry into truth follows a similar strategy. For both Heidegger and Davidson, the problem with correspondence theories is that they presuppose, but cannot explain, the structure of our knowledge of the world. Of course, Heidegger is not motivated by a desire to employ a definition of the truth predicate in a theory of meaning. Instead, his interest in truth stems from the fact that, as Heidegger explains, "the phenomenon of truth is so thoroughly coupled with the problem of Being."[27] By this, Heidegger means that there is a necessary connection between our understanding of truth and the way beings are present to the understanding. But he insists that the relationship between Being and truth cannot be explained by existing correspondence theories because we only recognize the correspondence relation between a statement and things in the world posterior to our relating the statement to the world through our "comportment." Thus, the notion of correspondence cannot help us in knowing how to relate statements to the world.[28]

But Heidegger's criticism of correspondence theories should not be taken to mean that Heidegger intended to redefine the truth of assertions in other terms. Indeed, he accepts that the truth of propositional entities is to be understood as a kind of "correspondence" or agreement with the way the world is; a "proposition is true," he affirms, "insofar as it corresponds to things."[29] Heidegger's objection, then, is not to the notion of correspondence *per se*, but rather to certain types of correspondence *theories* —namely, those which understand correspondence as a relation holding between mental representations and non-mental things. Such theories, Heidegger argues, are unable to instructively explain the notion of a relation of agreement. Thus, rather than seeking to provide a theory of the correspondence relation, Heidegger believes it is enough to note that an assertion is true when what is intended in the assertion "is just as it gets pointed out in the assertion as being."[30] In so doing, he accepts the intuition that the truth of propositional entities consists in agreeing with the way the world is.

In the place of a truth theory, Heidegger proposes examining how it is that beliefs or assertions are the sorts of things which can be true or false. His account of unconcealment is meant not as a definition of truth, but rather as an explanation of what makes it possible for propositions to point to the world in just the way that the world is. And in a manner not unlike Davidson, Heidegger sees the content of propositional states as fixed through our interacting with others and our orientation toward things within a world thereby "erasing," in Davidson's words, "the boundary between knowing a language and knowing our way around in the world generally."[31] It is in the details of their accounts of what fixes the content of our intentional states that the interesting differences are found between Davidson's and Heidegger's views.

Intentional Content as a Condition of Truth

In this section of the paper, I look in more detail at Davidson's and Heidegger's respective accounts of the way intentional content gets fixed. I will first examine Davidson's view, and then show how Heidegger's account of unconcealment can be read in the context of Davidson's approach to the problem.[32]

Davidson begins from the fact that human beings use language and succeed in understanding each other, and asks what makes that use of language possible. Davidson's project of "Radical Interpretation" illuminates the conditions of language by asking what would suffice for an interpreter to interpret the speaker of an alien language. By imagining a radical interpretation—that is, an interpretation which makes no assumptions about the propositional content of the speaker's behavior (linguistic or other)—Davidson focuses us on those properties of languages which allow us to learn them. A radical interpreter faces the problem that we cannot understand what a speaker means by her words without knowing what she believes, and we are deprived of the usual access to her beliefs—her words. Thus, if we can explain how it is possible to interpret her without the benefit of a prior knowledge of her beliefs and meanings, we will learn something important about the way language works—namely, what it takes to give content to the utterances and beliefs of another.

The issue, then, becomes one of understanding how it is that we learn to ascribe meanings and beliefs to each other. Here is where truth is implicated. To give content to the thoughts and assertions of others, Davidson claims, we must be able to ascribe truth conditions to their propositional states. But as we have seen, a Tarskian "definition" of truth is insufficient for this project because it is subsequent to our having a meaningful language and contentful propositional attitudes. Rather, some account of the way in which we come to relate a theory of truth (of the type Tarski has shown us to construct) to other rational agents is required; "If we knew in general what makes a theory of truth correctly apply to a speaker or group of speakers, we could plausibly be said to understand the concept of truth."[33]

Thus, Davidson tries to say something more about truth—not by way of defining truth, but rather by way of understanding the conditions under which we can apply a theory of truth to others. A theory of truth can only apply to a speaker, however, if that speaker's utterances have a content which is about the world. Indeed, from the fact that a language can be learned by one completely unfamiliar with that language, it follows that the content of utterances must be, by and large, about the world. The same holds for beliefs. We have no basis for attributing beliefs to others beyond whatever correlations we can discover between their behavior and the world.[34] We can thus see that a condition of having a concept of truth is having beliefs or utterances which are about objects in the world—objects which exist independently of us.

But Davidson goes beyond simply noting that in order to interpret others, we need to correlate their behavior (verbal and other) with the world. He makes the further argument that we cannot have meaningful beliefs or utterances at all unless we are interpreted by others. This is because, until we enter into relationships of interpretation with others, there can be no way of determinately fixing the cause which gives our beliefs and words their meaning, nor of locating that cause in an independent world.

The problem of locating the cause in the world arises, in the first instance, from the fact that any particular event is implicated in a number of different causal sequences of interaction. These include causes prior to that event (for instance, the event of our seeing a flower is itself caused by whatever made the flower grow), as well as causal intermediaries between us and the world (for instance, reflected light from the flower striking our retinas).

Once we determine which causes are relevant to the content of the belief or utterance, we must determine which features of that cause are included in the belief, and which are excluded. For instance, if we decide that the relevant cause of our belief that there is a flower is the presence of a flower, and subsequently conclude that the content of our belief that there is a flower is fixed by the presence of the flower (rather than the pattern of stimulation of our sensory surfaces), it is still not clear which of the many features of the presence of the flower are included in our belief that there is a flower. It is a feature of beliefs and sentences that they in general are not directed toward every particular of a thing—I can believe that there is a flower without believing that the flower is red. Beliefs also occur under a description—I can believe that there is a flower without also believing that there is a plant's reproductive structure. This second problem, put another way, is that of explaining how the causal interaction, which is extensionally described, becomes an intentional content.

Davidson's way of both locating the cause and determining the content of our propositional attitudes depends on "triangulation"—that is, "two or more creatures simultaneously in interaction with each other and with the world they share."[35] Davidson argues that we go some way toward solving both problems by noting what he calls a primitive or primal triangle. In this triangle, the two creatures observe each other responding to objects in the world. For such a triangle to exist, each creature must respond to a similarity between different objects or different instances of the same object, and also respond to a similarity in the other creature's responses to that object. Once one observer is able to correlate these similarities in this way, the stage is set for locating and determining the cause of the other's response.[36]

This primitive triangle is necessary to solving the problems, but not sufficient, because the "baseline" connecting the two creatures is not complete. The cause of the beliefs cannot be found in an objective world until the creatures have some way of knowing that they both occupy positions in a shared objective world, and this requires that they have some access to the other's perspective.[37] The primitive triangle is also not sufficient for determining the intentional content of propositional entities, for the causal relations which hold between creatures and things are extensionally defined, while intentional content is not. Our beliefs about flowers, for instance, cannot be reduced to an extensional description of flowers, because the contents of our beliefs are determined in part by their relations to other beliefs (beliefs about plants, allergies, romance, etc.), but also because the content of our beliefs, as already noted, generally includes less than all that is true of some object extensionally defined. Without a more fine-grained determination of the other's orientation to the world than that provided by the primal triangle, we cannot adequately fix the content of the other's beliefs.

But how are we to complete the baseline? Davidson argues that what is needed to connect the creatures is language. Linguistic communication contributes several elements missing from the primal triangle. First, language provides a sufficiently rich pattern of behavior to allow an attribution of a determinate intentional content to a person.[38] In addition, communication lets us pick out of this rich pattern of interaction with things some particular cause which determines the content of any given belief or utterance:

> [W]hat makes the particular aspect of the cause of the learner's responses the aspect that gives them the content they have is the fact that this aspect of the cause is shared by the teacher and the learner. Without such sharing, there would be no grounds for selecting one cause rather than another as the content-fixing cause. A non-communicating creature may be seen by us as responding to an objective world; but we are not justified in attributing thoughts about our world (or any other) to it.[39]

Finally, the communication of a particular orientation to objects makes error, and hence objectivity, possible, because by letting us know what the other is responding to, it puts us in a position to expect the other's past pattern of behavior to continue in the future. The failure to satisfy this expectation is, Davidson argues, the only basis for attributing error (and hence truth) to another.

Of course, this does not really provide an explanation of how intentional content gets fixed, because the advanced form of triangulation depends on meaningful utterances—that is, utterances with a content. To complete the account, Davidson claims, one would need to explain a structure of being in the world and of relating to objects in between the primitive account, which simply describes a causal interaction, and the full-blown intentional account, by which point intentional content is already fixed. And Davidson believes we lack a vocabulary for describing this intermediate state: "We have many vocabularies for describing nature when we regard it as mindless, and we have a mentalistic vocabulary for describing thought and intentional action; what we lack is a way of describing what is in between."[40]

In summary, then, Davidson provides an account of the fixing of intentional content which explains how truth is possible. That is, it explains the conditions under which utterances and beliefs become the sorts of things which can be true. Truth requires communication between two or more interlocutors who share a largely similar orientation to the world. As one interlocutor interprets the other—that is, as she fixes the truth conditions of the other's utterances—only then does the utterance of the other come to have a definite content. But Davidson cannot explain how the communication which allows the interlocutors to interpret each other can itself be contentful. For this, he would need some way to account for our ability to focus on some intentionally defined subset of features of the thing—an ability, moreover, which is independent of our propositional attitudes regarding the thing.

If we look at Heidegger's work on the conditions of truth in the context of Davidson's problematic, we find that Heidegger does not recognize the first problem outlined above—the problem of identifying the relevant cause of beliefs. He is satisfied that a phenomenology of perception resolves this issue, for it shows that the object itself, and nothing else, is experienced in perception.[41] But the second problem—the problem of fixing the intentional content—is one to which Heidegger devotes a great deal of attention. We have seen from the discussion of Davidson what sort of explanation would need to be offered to provide an account of this. It would be necessary to show both how our behavior is sufficiently rich and articulated as to be intentionally directed toward things in the world, and how we can be aware of the possibility of error in our directedness toward those things. While Heidegger does not offer a vocabulary for describing our pre-predicative experience of things, he does provide a detailed analysis of the structure of a pre-propositional, but nevertheless intentional, familiarity with the world.

Heidegger's analysis of what makes truth possible—he calls it "unconcealment"—has two parts to it. First, he claims, for the content of an assertion to be fixed by things in the world, those things must be manifest to us. Heidegger's inquiry into *discovery*, the making manifest of entities, aims at exhibiting the structural features of our comportment with things—in particular, those features which fix meaning. The second part of the investigation into unconcealment focuses on *disclosure*—the structural features of human existence that makes possible such uncovering comportment. Although a discussion of disclosure would be essential to completing Heidegger's account—Heidegger argues that the uncovering of what is is possible only on the basis of a "disclosure" of an understanding of Being[42]—I will focus here only on discovery, because it is Heidegger's account of discovery which is most immediately concerned with fixing the content of our intentional comportment toward objects in the world.

Discovery, making things manifest, is analyzed by Heidegger on the basis of those situations in which we have a practical mastery of things, because these are the situations in which our discovery of things is most fully developed. In all such cases, Heidegger claims, one can distinguish several structural features of our relationship to the things we encounter in our everyday comportment in the world. First, Heidegger notes, we recognize things and practices as either belonging to or foreign to the context in which they appear. Things present themselves as belonging together because they are, in Heidegger's terminology, "directionally lined up with each other."[43] Heidegger illustrates this through the example of an office: "Equipment—in accordance with its equipmentality—always is *in terms of* its belonging to other equipment: ink-stand, pen, ink, paper, blotting pad, table, lamp, furniture, windows, doors, room."[44] This belonging is defined only in relation to a "context of equipment"—the totality of other equipment which belongs in the context: "[e]quipmental contexture has the characteristic that the individual kinds and pieces of equipment are correlated among themselves with each other, not only with reference to their inherent character but also in such a way that each piece of equipment has the place belonging to it."[45] Thus, Heidegger claims, our ability to discover an object depends to some degree on our familiarity with the context in which it belongs in virtue of its position *vis-à-vis* other equipmental objects.

In addition to this minimal sense of uncoveredness—i.e., having a place—which things receive from their equipmental context, Heidegger notes that things are uncovered in terms of their functionality, determined by (a) the way they are typically used with other things, and (b) the way they are typically used in certain practices we engage in. Heidegger generally refers to (a) as the "with which" of things (as in "the hammer is used *with* nails and boards"). He refers to (b) as the "in which" of things (as in "the hammer is used *in* hammering"). Together, (a) and (b) comprise what Heidegger calls the context of involvements.

Finally, Heidegger notes that things we use with mastery present themselves as appropriate to certain projects in virtue of which they get their meaning. When viewed from the perspective of the purpose behind use of the thing (as when a blender is used for the purpose of processing food) Heidegger calls this feature of things their "in order to."[46] When viewed from the perspective of the "work to be produced" through use of the thing (as when a blender is used to make a milkshake), Heidegger calls this being-appropriate-for of the thing its "towards which."[47] Any given thing, moreover, is linked into a complex and nested series of "in order tos" and "towards whiches." A hammer, for instance, is used in order to drive nails, in order to fasten pieces of wood together, in order to frame a wall, in order to build a house, etc. Heidegger calls these aspects of things their assignments or references. He calls the network of assignments within which we use things the context of assignments or references.

Taken as a whole, our contexts of equipment, contexts of involvements, and contexts of assignments constitute a "world." Discoveredness, in its fullest sense, consists in having all three contexts well articulated. That is to say, it consists in our articulating a "totality of equipment" or "totality of involvements" within which objects can be understood as having a sense, direction, and purpose. Only within such a context, Heidegger argues, can objects stand out as something with which we can cope and about which we can make assertions. Until it is given at least some minimal foothold in our "world" in this way, Heidegger agues, the object can at best appear in a privative manner—that is, as something which resists our world. In order to uncover anything new, it must first be given at least some minimal directionality within our "world." On the basis of that directionality, it is possible to work with the thing, discovering what involvements and assignments are appropriate to it.

The important thing to note is that we can, in our practices alone, and without the use of predicative language, embody a richly articulated way of dealing with objects within the world. Each of the practical contexts discussed above delineates and orients us to fine-grained features of individual objects. Carpenters, for instance, are able to practically distinguish the appropriateness of this hammer for driving this nail into this board. This will give them a pragmatic sensitivity to things like weight and hardness (as when this hammer is too heavy to drive this nail into that soft wood without marring the surface). They can make very fine distinctions in regard to those features of the totality of involvements relevant to their work—features in fact more fine grained than they may be able to express.

As Davidson points out, the ability to make discriminations is not the same as having a concept. To have something like an intentional relationship to things, what is needed above and beyond the ability to discriminate, is an awareness of the possibility of rightness and wrongness in our way of relating to things. But, as Heidegger's account shows, the practical totality of involvements carries with it just such normativity. In the first place, human practices are never something engaged in alone—we inherit them from others. With the practices, Heidegger claims, we learn public norms for the value and success of our activities.[48] Human activities, Heidegger claims, are marked by a constant concern for how others are acting: "[i]n one's concern with what one has taken hold of . . . there is constant care as to the way one differs from [the others]."[49] In addition, the way practices organize objects gives them a normativity of their own. The world gives a right place for the hammer to be and a right way for it to be used. In addition, we engage in practices with a purpose which itself gives things a normative reference. The carpenter knows, for instance, that this is the right hammer for the job because the purpose of the job is. . . .

Practical expertise thus bestows a normativity on things, a normativity similar to (and Heidegger would say a precursor to) the normative structure discernable in our understanding of truth. The normativity inherent in our engagement with a world is transmitted practically rather than communicatively: "[i]n that with which we concern ourselves environmentally the others are encountered as what they are; they *are* what they do."[50]

It is thus on the basis of our pragmatic discovery of things that language is possible, for it is the structure of equipment and involvements built into our comportment which delineates the features of things which are salient to us—the very features which form the content of our beliefs and utterances. As Heidegger explains, language is based in our "interpreting" the world, by which he means making explicit the "signification" things have as a result of their "involvements": "when something within-the-world is encountered as such, the thing in question already has an involvement which is disclosed in our understanding of the world, and this involvement is one which gets laid out by the interpretation."[51] When we speak of things, the "totality-of-significations of intelligibility is *put into words*. To significations, words accrue."[52]

For Heidegger, then, the truth of assertions finds the conditions of its possibility in discovery. Discovery, by fixing an intentional content to which "words can accrue" makes truth possible by making assertions the kind of things which can be true by giving them a normative content objectively determined. To the extent that we share practical worlds, we can come to "communicate" with another, that is to say, share a determinate and intentionalistic orientation to things, without language. And this practical sharing of a world, in turn, allows Heidegger to explain the puzzle of how to give language content without language.

Let me conclude by noting some consequences of this comparison of Heidegger's and Davidson's accounts. The distinction between Heidegger and Davidson is not simply that of a practical *versus* a cognitive or linguistic account of human experience. Davidson's triangulation recognizes the practical basis of interpretation and hence of thought. Nor is there room in Heidegger's account for human existence without any kind of linguistic interaction (although I have not emphasized this here). Rather, the distinction is found in Heidegger's belief that there is a non-propositional form of intentionality—a form of intentionality, moreover, which makes linguistic interaction possible. This commits Heidegger to the view that propositional content is based in a non-propositional form of intentional content. Davidson, because he starts his analysis of human activity with the radical interpretation of language, ends up reading language's propositional structure back into all forms of human comportment.

Mark A. Wrathall
Brigham Young University

NOTES

*My thanks to Donald Davidson, Hubert Dreyfus, Sean Kelly, Jeffrey Malpas, and Michael McKeon for their helpful criticisms, comments, and suggestions on earlier versions of this paper.

1. Michael Dummett, *The Logical Basis of Metaphysics* (Cambridge: Harvard University Press, 1991).

2. Martin Heidegger, *Metaphysische Anfangsgründe der Logic* (Frankfurt am Main: Vittorio Klostermann, 1978), translated as *The Metaphysical Foundations of Logic*, trans. Michael Heim (Bloomington, IN: Indiana University Press, 1984).
3. *The Logical Basis of Metaphysics* (cited in n. 1, above), p. 1.
4. *Ibid.*, p. 19.
5. *The Metaphysical Foundations of Logic* (cited in n. 2, above), p. 21.
6. *Ibid.*, p. 19.
7. *Ibid.*, p. 20.
8. P. F. Strawson, *Analysis and Metaphysics* (Oxford: Oxford University Press, 1992), p. 2.
9. John R. Searle, "Literary Theory and its Discontents," in *New Literary History* 25 (1994), 639.
10. Martin Heidegger, *Parmenides*, trans. André Schuwer and Richard Rojcewicz (Bloomington, IN: Indiana University Press, 1992), p. 69.
11. Jacques Derrida, "Signature Event Context," in *Limited Inc* (Evanston, IL: Northwestern University Press, 1988), p. 15.
12. Donald Davidson, "Coherence Theory of Truth and Knowledge," in *Truth and Interpretation: Perspectives on the Philosophy of Donald Davidson*, ed. Ernest LePore (Cambridge: Blackwell, 1986). Davidson has since issued a retraction of sorts—not that his view on truth has changed, but he has come to recognize how misleading it is to call his theory a correspondence theory. See Donald Davidson, "Structure and Content of Truth," *Journal of Philosophy* LXXXVII (1990), 302.
13. See my "Heidegger on Truth as Correspondence," *International Journal of Philosophical Studies* 7 (March 1999).
14. Michael Williams, "Epistemological Realism and the Basis of Skepticism," *Mind* XCVII (1988) p. 424.
15. Paul Horwich, *Truth* (Cambridge, MA: Basil Blackwell, 1990) p. 33. See also Scott Soames, "What Is a Theory of Truth?" *Journal of Philosophy* 81 (1984) p. 413.
16. P. F. Strawson, "Truth," in *The Concept of a Person and Other Essays* (London: MacMillan, 1963), p. 147ff.
17. A. Tarski, "The Concept of Truth in Formalized Languages," in *Logic, Semantics, Metamathematics* (Oxford: Oxford University Press, 1956), p. 155ff.
18. Michael Dummett, *Truth and Other Enigmas* (Cambridge, MA: Harvard University Press, 1978), p. xxi.
19. Michael Dummett, "Truth," *Proceedings of the Aristotelian Society* 59 (1959) pp. 148–49.
20. The proof of this is provided by what has been dubbed the "Great Fact" or "Slingshot" argument. The basic argument is that if 'R' and 'S' abbreviate any two sentences alike in truth value, then (1) & (2) and (3) & (4) co-refer (by substitution of logical equivalence), as do (2) & (3) (by substitution of coextensive singular terms):

(1) R
(2) $\hat{x}(x = x.R) = \hat{x}(x = x)$
(3) $\hat{x}(x = x.S) = \hat{x}(x = x)$
(4) S

Thus, if some sentence p corresponds to the fact that R, it also corresponds to the fact that S, and to any other fact, for that matter. Donald Davidson, "Truth and Meaning," in *Inquiries into Truth and Interpretation* (Oxford: Clarendon Press, 1984), p. 19.

21. Donald Davidson, "True to the Facts," in *ibid.*, p. 43.
22. "The Structure and Content of Truth" (cited in n. 12, above), p. 304.
23. "Locating Literary Language," in *Literary Theory After Davidson*, ed. Reed Way Dasenbrock (University Park, PA: Pennsylvania University Press, 1993), p. 303.
24. "A Coherence Theory of Truth and Knowledge" (cited in n. 12, above), p. 308.
25. "The Structure and Content of Truth" (cited in n. 12, above), p. 299.
26. *Ibid.*, p. 297.
27. Martin Heidegger, *Being and Time*, trans. John Macquarrie and Edward Robinson (New York: Harper and Row, 1962), p. 196.
28. "On the Essence of Truth," in *Basic Writings*, trans. David Farrell Krell (New York: HarperCollins, 1993), p. 122.
29. *What Is a Thing?*, trans. W. B. Barton, Jr., and Vera Deutsch (Chicago: Henry Regnery Company, 1967), p. 117. See also Martin Heidegger, "Origin of the Work of Art," in *Basic Writings* (cited in n. 28, above), p. 176: "A proposition is true by conforming to the unconcealed, to what is true. Propositional truth is always, and always exclusively, this correctness."
30. *Being and Time* (cited in n. 27, above), p. 261. See also "On the Essence of Truth" (cited in n. 28, above), p. 122; "What is presents itself along with the presentative assertion so that the latter subordinates itself to the directive that it speak of what is just as it is. In following such a directive the assertion conforms to what is. Speech that directs itself accordingly is correct (true)." For a more complete discussion of this point, see my "Heidegger on Truth as Correspondence" (cited in n. 13, above).
31. "A Nice Derangement of Epitaphs," in *Truth and Interpretation* (cited in n. 12, above), pp. 443–44.
32. I don't address, however, whether Davidson would find Heidegger's account either acceptable or necessary.
33. "The Structure and Content of Truth" (cited in n. 12, above), p. 300.
34. See, e.g., "Empirical Content," in *Truth and Interpretation* (cited in n. 12, above), p. 332.
35. Donald Davidson, "The Emergence of Thought" ("Die Emergenz des Denkens"), in *Die Erfindung des Universums? Neue Überlegungen zur philosophischen Kosmologie*, ed. W. G. Saltzer, P. Eisenhardt, D. Kurth, and R. E. Zimmerman (Frankfurt am Main; Insel Verlag, 1997).
36. Donald Davidson, "The Second Person," *Midwest Studies in Philosophy* 17 (1992), p. 263.
37. Donald Davidson, "Three Varieties of Knowledge," in *A. J. Ayer: Memorial Essays*, ed. A. Phillips Griffiths (Cambridge: Cambridge University Press, 1991), p. 160. See also "The Conditions of Thought," in *The Mind of Donald Davidson*, ed. J. Brandl and W. Gombocz (Amsterdam: Editions Rodopi, 1989), p. 199.
38. "But words, like thoughts, have a familiar meaning, a propositional content, only if they occur in a rich context, for such a context is required to give the words or thoughts a location and a meaningful function." "The Emergence of Thought" (cited in n. 35, above).
39. Donald Davidson, "Epistemology Externalized," *Dialectica* 45 (1991), p. 201.
40. *Ibid.*
41. See, for example, Martin Heidegger, *Basic Problems of Phenomenology* (Bloomington, IN: Indiana University Press, 1982), p. 37, "I see no 'representations' of the chair, register no image of the chair, sense no sensations of the chair. I simply see it—it itself."

42. *Being and Time* (cited in n. 27, above), p. 176. "[T]he world which has already been disclosed beforehand permits what is within-the-world to be encountered."
43. *Ibid.*, p. 136.
44. *Ibid.*, p. 97.
45. *Basic Problems of Phenomenology* (cited in n. 41, above), p. 310.
46. *Being and Time* (cited in n. 27, above), p. 97.
47. *Ibid.*, p. 99.
48. *Ibid.*, p. 165.
49. *Ibid.*, p. 163.
50. *Ibid.*
51. *Ibid.*, p. 191. Heidegger in fact has an "explicit" and an "implicit" form of interpretation. The implicit interpretation seems to be one way of describing the pragmatic articulation of features of things which I have been discussing. Thus he will say, for instance, that "[a]ny mere pre-predicative seeing of the ready-to-hand is, in itself, something which already understands and interprets." *Ibid.*, p. 189. In speaking of things, however, we perform an explicit or "thematic" interpretation of them. See *ibid.*, p. 191.
52. *Ibid.*, p. 204.

HEIDEGGER AND THE INTENTIONALITY OF LANGUAGE

Roderick M. Stewart

RECENTLY, some Anglo-American philosophers have engaged the work of Martin Heidegger by centering on the so-called phenomenon of intentionality[1]. How is it that minds and bits of language come to refer to, or "be about," both real and possible objects, events, and features in the world? These attempts at what Gadamer has called achieving a "fusion of horizons" are made difficult especially because the problem of intentionality for Heidegger quickly raises issues of the very direction and presuppositions of Western metaphysics and epistemology. While ultimately, of course, Heidegger's work must be seen as a "deconstructive" rejection of traditional metaphysics and epistemology (including most work in so-called "analytic" philosophy), it has not always been made clear what positive views (if any) he may be said to have had, at least enroute to his pronouncement of the "end of philosophy." It is the goal of this essay to focus primarily on this latter question of Heidegger's "positive" views on the problem of intentionality. At the very least in his *magnum opus, Sein und Zeit*,[2] Heidegger never seems to deny the human phenomena of intentionality. Rather, the issue that confronts him there is how such phenomena are to be understood philosophically.

The key to Heidegger's elucidation of intentional phenomena (or, we might say, to his philosophy of mind and language) is his famous account of human Dasein. In a clear rejection of Husserlian Cartesianism, Heidegger provides a concrete "existential analysis" of what it means to be a case of Dasein. As cases of Dasein, humans do not come to sight as isolated centers of "intentional consciousness," nor as "transcendental egos" merely capable of representing an external physical world, but bearing only an accidental metaphysical relationship to it. Large portions of SZ are offered by Heidegger as various layers in a positive Existential Analytic (even "descriptive metaphysics") of what it means to be a person[3] embodied and immersed in "worlds of concern." It is within this Existential Analytic that Heidegger describes what it means for Dasein to use language, and it is to this topic which we now turn.

I

A convenient point of departure for our discussion of Heidegger's views on the intentionality of language is Charles Guignon's helpful distinction between an early, "instrumental" approach to language and a later, "constitutive" one.[4]

The "instrumental" approach can be found in SZ when Heidegger takes up the phenomenon of language against the backdrop of his preliminary account of Dasein and non-Dasein in terms of producer-consumers and the "tools" used in their commerce. All non-Dasein "things" (in a sense broad enough to cover skills, capacities, strategies, and so on, in addition to physical objects) are what they are as "tools/equipment" (*Zeug*) which serve the purposes and interests of Dasein. (A social-behaviorist reading notwithstanding, we see a "technical intentionality" pervading human existence. How this intentionality takes on a "practical" character, will be mentioned later).

To the extent that any being, *qua* tool or producer/consumer, can be said to have determinable roles within established concerns and interests, that being can be said to have "significance" (*Bedeutsamkeit*). Such "significance" is grasped by producer/consumers when they understand the explicit or implicit rules for using these "tools." Here is where it is helpful to use the Wittgensteinian language of social practices, "rule-following" behavior, as well as Haugeland's notion of norms, institutions, and herd-behaviors. For, Heidegger is quite clear that most cases of Dasein find themselves "thrown into" a world of well laid out and established practices (ranging from craft guilds to literary critics and scientific schools) with a powerful normative force over each new herd-member.

On this view, Heidegger notes that there may be well developed Heideggerian worlds of such producer-consumers, "tools," and their "significance" without anything like a typical natural language being available. Guignon calls such non-linguistic worlds cases of non-semantic or pre-linguistic significance. "Language" (as ordinarily conceived) is gradually super added to these prior existing fields of non-semantic meaning. When this addition occurs, in effect a new layer of "tools" (and the rules for their use) is acquired by the producer-consumer, Dasein.

One consequence of this "instrumental" view is that so-called problems of "reference" (whether these occur in philosophy of mind, language, or the sciences) become for Heidegger the problem of how the social practices governing referring-"tools" are possible. We shall say some more later why formal semantic approaches, even when augmented by empirical theories of meaning and propositional attitudes, would at best be treated as limiting cases of language-use "existentially" conceived. For the moment, the reader may want to think of an "existential conception" of language as on a par with the emphases of speech act theorists: reference is readily conceived as an action in accordance with the "rule" or conventions governing the uses of different kinds of word-tools,[5] and always within a broader communicative context of making speech acts of assertion, interrogation, requesting, ordering, and so on. If a slogan is in order, then perhaps the emphasis for Heidegger is on the "primacy of pragmatics" over syntactical and formal-semantical inquiries.[6] But even this characterization can be slightly misleading, as we shall see. Let us now turn to Heidegger's "constitutive" view of language.

On the "constitutive" view, language is no longer seen as a "later" acquisition of rarefied tools, skills, and practices by Dasein added onto a prior existing, non-semantic field of meaningful human action and intentionality. Rather, language is now argued to be an essential or "constitutive" part of Dasein in all its dealings.

We should note here, however, that there are several distinct claims (not always clearly distinguished) which appear to comprise this later Heideggerian (and Gadamerian) thesis. First, there is the claim that language (as speech act practices) is (partially) *constitutive of* other specific, often highly conventional, practices within a culture (such as avowals, invocations, and promises). Second, there is the thesis that, when these latter sorts of speech acts are coupled with those of recommending, asserting, rebutting, inquiring, and so on, as well as with acts of *expressing* shame, indignation, a sense of shared responsibilities, there results a specialized "language of morals," which in turn makes possible ("constitutes") the practical intentionality of an agent or person (if not Dasein itself, as the being whose own Being "matters to it").[7]

To see a third, distinct claim, let us note that the first two theses do not rule out (and, in fact, stand in contrast to) what would seem to be the manifold "significant," non-linguistic practices which manifest Dasein's mundane technical intentionality. Think, for example, of all the "rules" governing what counts as carpentry and its component activities, procedures, and materials. With this in mind, a third claim would seem to be that "language" should now cover all forms of rule-following technical and practical intentionality (or, even, Weberian *Sinn*). For Heidegger, the revisionist, what we previously described as significant, non-linguistic practices are only "non-linguistic" in the ordinary (and presumably misleading) sense of the term "language." In this broader sense (as Taylor helpfully notes, reminiscent of Cassirer's use of "symbolic form",) there can be no human care or worldly intentionality without its "expression" in some ongoing social practice. Thus, on the revised view, language is ill-conceived as some extra layer of practices added onto already existing ones. "Language" comprises all human phenomena governed by social practices. And, in this extended sense, it makes sense to say (following Gadamer[8]), that language is the medium of human experience and thereby "constitutive" of it.

Yet, while such an extension of "language" can be meaningfully reconstructed, perhaps its philosophical motivation is not clear, especially to more traditionally-minded philosophers of language more than satisfied with at least the range of phenomena marked out by the first two claims (even if not satisfied with their non-formal, speech act analysis). One motivation behind Heidegger's hermeneutical extension of the term is, on the one hand, wanting to accept some version of the traditional claims that *logos*, *ratio*, and language set Dasein off from what is non-Dasein, while, on the other hand, not wanting to separate in reality or thought our capacity for *logos* from our inherited, rule-following social practices. In a move reminiscent of Hegel's critique of Kantian rationality and *Moralität* and his advocacy of the rationality found in ongoing *Sittlichkeiten*, Heidegger wants to urge the view that Dasein is "by nature" a rational and social animal (but in a non-metaphysical sense of these terms).

A second, and likely more controversial, motivation for putting all social practices on a continuum (called "language") is the sort of anti-metaphysical account of truth and reference it lends itself to: succeeding or failing in referring or making truthful assertions may now quite easily be modelled on how one succeeds or fails in conforming to any social practice. And, with this, we turn to the next section.

II. A. Realism and Anti-Realism

The most far-reaching criticism of traditional concepts of language by Heidegger has to do with his general indictment of modern epistemology and Western "metaphysics of presence."[9] The general "presupposition" to such views, which Heidegger rejects, is that (we can meaningfully say) there is a World in Itself, knowable (in whole or part) or not, in terms of which our "representations" (ideas, propositions, and sentences) are true or false. Following Rorty and Putnam,[10] let us call this the Metaphysical Realist's Presupposition. Heidegger rejects this presupposition, but not because he is a Cartesian or Humean sceptic who denies our knowledge of such Reality. For, such scepticism only makes sense as a special (epistemically deprived) case of Metaphysical Realism. Rather, given his views on truth as disclosedness (*Erschlossenheit*) and the historicity of all understanding,[11] Heidegger finds the view in all its forms to be unintelligible.

Thus, Heidegger can readily be called a general anti-Realist in roughly the sense discussed recently by Putnam and Rorty.[12]

It is important, however, to see that Heidegger's critique of Metaphysical Realism is no mere academic dispute, but forms the core of his negative analysis of Western scientific and technological culture. If Metaphysical Realism is present anywhere, it pervades both the everyday spirit and second-order "rational reconstructions" of modern science and its attendant technological successes. "What else could *best* explain (abductively) the tremendous and spectacular success of recent science in prediction and control than the likelihood that (for the most part) truly scientific theories are in fact "converging" on some ideal of Truth?" For Heidegger, such recent Realist Metascientific Arguments to the Best Explanation[13] would (to use the language of critical theory) be a self-deceiving ideology or *hubris* concealing a dangerous and blind tendency in the culture at large to control and manipulate nature, and squelching any vestiges of reverent attitudes to ourselves and our world.

B. Realist Theories of Reference

It is against this backdrop of Heidegger's anti-Realism that his revisionary views on the character of "language" take on extra point. Most recent theories of language (especially in Anglo-American quarters) presuppose the intelligibility of Metaphysical Realism. This presupposition shows up especially clearly in theories of reference based on (Tarskian) correspondence notions of truth. "Successful reference" for such theories is likely to be defined (for simple sentences) in terms of objects in the World (viewed disinterestedly) "satisfying" or not various names or predicates of some formal or natural language (again, viewed "disinterestedly" as sets of spatio-temporal linguistic tokens or, more problematically, their types). Complex sentences involve more of the same, plus recursive uses of truth-functional connectives.

After this groundwork has been laid, then, depending on what gets counted as a basic linguistic token, (such as lumps of ink, chalk, or vocalized sounds), such theories of "pure" reference can be augmented with some suitable *empirical-*

psychological theory of accompanying "propositional (and other) attitudes"—just in case mental "representations" (suitably construed) have anything to do with the phenomenon of "reference-as-satisfaction" having come about in the first place!

At a third stage of development, this complex of theories may be applied to "natural languages" other than one's own. In the cases made famous by Quine and Davidson,[14] the processes of *understanding* meaning can be seen as a (radical) translation problem. Once the simple "roots of reference" can be discovered for the radical Other, using behavioral evidence, clever tests of the native speakers, and not a few important "analytical hypotheses,"[15] a bit of patience and truth-functionality will do the rest. Or, so it is argued.

Finally, even the "language" used by scientists can be studied, with the issue of how theoretical terms "refer" given a similar formal and empirical treatment. Indeed, the meaning and reference of theoretical terms as theories change, has become an important watershed for many of the metascientific debates over scientific realism: Theory 1 can be said to be better than Theory 2, that is, have more truth and thus show more progress, only if the two talk about the same things to begin with, but the one does it more precisely, with better prediction and control, and so on.[16]

For now, we shall let these past four paragraphs suffice as a summary of how most current theories of reference and their applications are committed to Metaphysical Realism. Let us examine more carefully Heidegger's replacement for them.

C. Towards An Anti-Realist Account of Reference

In a move analogous to one made famous by Kant before him, Heidegger's anti-Realism is not a rejection of the *fact* or phenomenon of reference (in any of its forms), but of certain philosophical elucidations or "justifications" of this phenomenon: to wit, any attempt to construe this concrete, existential phenomenon by presupposing the intelligibility of Metaphysical Realism. Thus, far from rejecting linguistic reference *tout court*, Heidegger should be read as committed to a view of it consistent with his broader views on Dasein's technical and practical intentionality and his anti-Realism.

Let us momentarily focus on Heidegger's instrumental account of language, and act as if the phenomenon of referring can take place even if no "larger" conventional behavior is "constituted" in the process (say, a promise or an avowal). Of course, for a creature like Dasein, all action is always "interested" in some way (in communicating, clarifying, gathering information, showing respect, and so on). A "disinterested" act of reference, then, is (in Heidegger's phrase) understandable only as a "privative" mode of language-use (what others have called a "degenerate" case). On the other hand, if words themselves must be focused on (or "thematized," in Heidegger's phrase), then they are more properly viewed not as inert elements in the domain of some (quasi-) formal calculus, but as word-"tools" ready-at-hand for Dasein's linguistic purposes. Referring, then, as a type of action is to be understood in ways similar to understanding hammering as a type of action. For whatever being in fact functions as the designator- or hammer-"tool," there will have arisen established conventions for that "tool's" use. What the hammer or designator "is" (its Being), is determined exclusively by the (explicit or implicit) rules or conventions for its use. The latter "norms" (borrowing from Haugeland and Brandom) may be conceived, for now, as the conformist patterns of "herd"-intentionality.[17] Thus, "mistakes" in hammering or in designating are determined by failing to conform to the accepted range of uses of the term. (There may, of course, be looser and tighter ranges of use, depending on the degree of conventionality of a given practice).

Furthermore, we may presume that just as there are distinct and identifiable "rules" for distinguishing kinds of hammering from each other and from sawing, chiseling, and so on, there are also distinct and identifiable "rules" or success-conditions for distinguishing kinds of designating from each other and from predicating. Precisely what these rules are for either the "social kinds" of hammering or of designating, or whether they have more or less "open textures," need not concern us here—only that their existence (perhaps only as conformist behavior) must be postulated to clarify the various phenomena of human intentionality as distinct from (say) merely accidental regularities about human behavior.

What is missing in the account so far, however, is why it is anti-Realistic. A Realist could agree that some sort of conformist story is an important part of the socio-psychological explanation of referring, especially of how cases of Dasein come to learn or maintain the "tools" which they use.[18] But, the Realist continues, surely what makes ordinary acts of reference "correct" is not just conformity to established practices, but picking out just the right, "middle-sized" perceptual object which (directly or indirectly) "causes" speakers to have in mind what they are speaking about.[19] After all, surely we must allow that whole cultures and practices can "get it wrong," or fail to refer with their designative-"tools!" Indeed, isn't this precisely what has happened with the rise of modern science and within it? No one really ever "referred" to witches and demons, or perhaps less clearly, to phlogiston, in spite of passing the muster of the available local linguistic and evidential practices. To remove some of the imperial air from such claims, the Realist may even admit that determining whether some form of Dasein "really referred" in its linguistic practices, especially in the natural sciences, is of course always better done in hindsight (and perhaps is never completely done, for any given case of Dasein). But at least we can make sense of some of our theories getting better, progressing, as a "convergence" phenomenon (at least in the natural sciences). To adapt recent Realist metascience, at least when we have noticeable success in prediction and control, we may be confident of the unlikelihood of our only being lucky and only seeming to refer.

In light of this objection from the Realists, we may formulate Heidegger's anti-Realist theory of referring as follows. The Realist seeks to draw a difference between the criteria for correct reference used in the processes of learning and maintaining a group referring-practice and what in fact (from hindsight) either was or was not referred to. This distinction between "real" and "apparent" reference, then, must be thinkable (along sceptical lines) as a difference never in fact or in principle captured in some past or once-and-future set of linguistic practices. Heidegger, the anti-Realist, cannot find intelligible such an alleged difference between apparent and real reference. "Real" versus "apparent" for Heidegger is itself a distinction always indexed to a set of practices chosen as a frame-of-reference (by, if you like, a Principle of Hermeneutic Situatedness), and this frame-of-reference is typically our own (even when we claim to be Romantics).

Finally, even the Realist's Metascientific Induction or Abduction based on an increase in prediction and technological control would be challenged (though not, as far as I can tell, directly by Heidegger in his published writings). We may speculate here that Heidegger's talk of "epochs" of Being, as well as his account of the essence of our technological age,[20] would find him today close to the writings of some critical theorists, on the one hand, and historically-minded metascientists such as Ian Hacking, on the other.[21] Whether this sort of view could accommodate the Realist's Argument from the Best Explanation, is questionable to this author. For, the power of the latter abductive strategy lies in its full admission to the historical connection between scientific activity and a technological interest. The argument then proceeds to point out an apparently unique feature of this "guiding interest"—its success-rate and how this is to be clarified. Perhaps, however, the very concepts of what are probable and improbable, and hence of what counts as a "best explanation," already presuppose the Realist's program. "Circularity" at this level of debate would, of course, not be unusual, as the history of the Problem of Induction would indicate. Whether such "circularity" is devastating intellectually, is another issue.

In sum, for a Heideggerian anti-Realist, "referring" is a human action whose "real" or "apparent" success can only be intelligibly determined "immanently" by locating that (sub-)speech act within some established social practice and its guiding interests. We turn now in the last two sections to an examination of the status for Heidegger of a practice, institution, norm, or convention.

III

In the previous sections, we have seen (1) the sense in which language is viewed as certain practices of Dasein, the producer-consumer, governing the use of certain word—"tools"; (2) the various senses in which language is "constitutive of " other particular practices, and even of Dasein itself as a reflective moral agent (or the being whose Being is always an issue for it); and, finally, (3) how Heidegger's general anti-Realism affects his phenomenological clarification of (sub-)acts of referring. In all of this, we have for the most part left unanalyzed what it means for Dasein to act in accordance with the norms of some practice or institution.

In this section, we shall consider Charles Taylor's self-declared, Heideggerian view that using language (performing speech acts) in accordance with conventions or social practices requires the admission of a kind of social fact called "shared meanings" or "common objects" which resist analysis into such smaller units as individuals and their particular mental states. In particular, we shall be considering Taylor's defense of his position when he seeks to refute what he rightly regards as his most formidable opponent, the "meaning-nominalist" strategy recently articulated by Jonathan Bennett in his masterful study, *Linguistic Behavior*.[22]

In Bennett's own words, meaning-nominalism (as an extension of Paul Grice's work on meaning and intention)[23] is the view "which treats as basic the individual instances of meaning, by one speaker at one time, and gives a derivative status to every kind of general statement about meanings—what the speaker usually means by x, what speakers generally mean by x, what x means in the language . . . " (Bennett, p. 9). Linguistic meaning or intentionality, on this atomistic strategy, comes to be viewed as a "coordination-game" (following David Lewis[24]) based on the well-known "Gricean mechanism" of audiences recognizing not just natural signs for states of mind (that is, sweating, nervous movement) but also speakers' complex intentions that audiences recognize their various intentions.

Taylor's disagreement with this strategy is not with the careful detail with which Bennett sketches behavioral scenarios which serve as the warranted evidence for attributing a purposive mental life of varying degrees of complexity to creatures actively engaged in their environments. Thus, that a creature may be said to have a prelinguistic "technical intentionality" is not an issue between Taylor and Bennett. Taylor's issue is rather with what we must attribute to these creatures' intentionality when they "communicate" (at the very least) their "technical intentionality" to each other.

Taylor's counter-argument to the meaning-nominalist strategy is as follows. (1) Full (linguistic) communication between creatures A & B requires there to be "common objects" or issues for A & B together and not just severally. But (2) to have these "common objects," A & B must already be able to express their shared purposes (or, form of Dasein) in a language. (3) The meaning-nominalist (reductionist) strategy (based on successive applications of the "Gricean mechanism") tries to construct full communication between A & B out of prelinguistic intentional states. Therefore, (4) the meaning-nominalist strategy is doomed from the outset. The moral of the story, then, would seem to be that human intentionality is linguistic "all the way down."

Let us grant the inference from (1), (2), and (3) to (4) and discuss the premises. The meaning-nominalist might accept (1) if it is analysed in a certain way. To discuss (1), consider an example from Taylor and one from Bennett: (i) A & B are from different cultures, but succeed in striking up a rudimentary conversation using exaggerated wipes of their brows on a hot day; (ii) A & B are at the opera and "communicate" their displeasure at the performance not by words, but by holding their noses (or even using "natural signs" in ostentatious ways). The meaning-nominalist would likely analyze these situations as ones with complex intentions on the parts of both A & B. For example, both A & B know that the other knows that the weather is hot or that the performance is lousy. Thus, it is reasonable to assume that each also believes that more is at issue than simple transference of information and thus assumes that some other speech act is being performed. The shared sense of concern expressed in these speech acts, then, would presumably be some sort of causally related "sum" of these speech acts and attendant acts of recognition. For the meaning-nominalist, then, having states of mind "together" (and thus "common objects") rather than "severally" is roughly the difference between this causal writers, or *vice versa*. For, there is likely a major parting of the ways on the issue of anti-Realism and the possibility of traditional metaphysics.[29] Indeed, on such a metaphilosophical issue, most hermeneutical writers under Heidegger's influence would probably find a greater affinity with the works of Wittgenstein, Thomas Kuhn, and Richard Rorty than with Grice, Bennett, and Lewis.[30]

Austin College

Received June 11, 1987

NOTES

1. Hubert Dreyfus, "Holism and Hermeneutics," *Review of Metaphysics*, vol. 34 (1980); Charles Guignon, *Heidegger and the Problem of Knowledge* (Indianapolis: Hackett Publishing Company, 1983); John Haugeland, "Heidegger on Being a Person," *Nous*, (1981), pp. 15-26; Robert Brandom, "Heidegger's Categories in *Being and Time*," *The Monist*, vol. 66 (1983), pp. 387-409; Charles Taylor, "Theories of Meaning," in his: *Human Agency and Language: Philosophical Papers, Vol. I* (Cambridge: Cambridge University Press, 1985), pp. 248-292.

2. Martin Heidegger, *Sein und Zeit* (Tübingen: Max Niemeyer Verlag, 1967), hereafter cited as SZ; English translation by John Macquarrie and Edward Robinson, *Being and Time* (New York: Harper & Row, 1962).

3. Whether or not a case of Dasein is nothing more than a collection of social roles (types of normalized dispositions to behave) at a certain point, and the related question of whether or not "Dasein" ought to be construed as referring primarily to such roles as institutions and practices (which is roughly what Haugeland and Brandom have argued), I discuss briefly in the last section of this paper and more fully in my "Intentionality and the Semantics of 'Dasein'," in *Philosophy and Phenomenological Research*, vol. 48 (1987), pp.93-106.

4. Guignon, *op. cit.*, Ch. 9, pp. 115-132. Guignon also cites passages from SZ which indicate a shift toward the constitutive approach already in portions of SZ.

5. See Wittgenstein's strikingly similar remark about language and "tools" in his *Philosophical Investigations*, (Oxford: Basil Blackwell, 1967) §23, 54, 291, 421, 492, and esp. 569. It is, of course, not clear whether this metaphor is consistent with Wittgenstein's more famous, "language-game" analogy.

6. For a helpful and highly detailed treatment of these issues in recent philosophy of language, see W. G. Lycan, *Logical Form in Natural Language* (Cambridge, MA: Massachusetts Institute of Technology Press, 1984).

7. Charles Taylor has emphasized this aspect of the constitutive function of language for Heidegger and other hermeneuticists. See his "Theories of Meaning," *op. cit.*; also his "What is Human Agency?" and "The Concept of a Person?" in his *Philosophical Papers, Vol. I, op. cit.*, pp. 15-44, 97-114, cited in the first footnote.

8. See his *Truth and Method* (New York: Crossroad Publishing Co., 1975), Part III; and his *Philosophical Hermeneutics* (Berkeley: University of California Press, 1976).

9. See Martin Heidegger, "What Calls for Thinking," in D. F. Krell (ed.), *Basic Writings* (New York: Harper & Row, 1977), pp. 341-368.

10. Richard Rorty, *Philosophy and the Mirror of Nature* (Princeton: Princeton University Press, 1979); and Hilary Putnam, *Meaning and the Moral Sciences* (London: Routledge & Kegan-Paul, 1978).

11. See SZ, §44, 63; see also his essay, "The Essence of Truth," in *Basic Writings, op. cit.*, pp. 113-142.

12. This view should not be confused with materialists and nominalists who are "anti-realists" about minds or numbers, but realists about brains and other physical objects.

13. See Jarrett Leplin, *Scientific Realism* (Berkeley: University of California Press, 1984). Heidegger is not as adept at blocking the abductive inference as, say, Larry Laudan has been. See the latter's, "A confutation of Convergent Realism," *Philosophy of Science*, vol. 48 (1981), pp. 19-49; also the reply by Hardin and Rosenberg, "In Defense of Convergent Realism," *Philosophy of Science*, vol. 49 (1982), pp. 604-615. Laudan confesses, however, to be a form of sceptic about science and not an anti-Realist.

14. W. V. O. Quine, *Word and Object* (Cambridge, Massachusetts: Massachusetts Institute of Technology Press, 1960) and Donald Davidson, "Truth and Meaning," *Synthese*, vol. 17 (1967). In the next section we shall look at one recent attempt by Jonathan Bennett to employ the Quinean and Davidsonian techniques of gathering empirical (especially behavioral) evidence for attributing a

complex intentionality to purposive beings, including the belief and desire packages necessary for a Gricean account of speaker and utterance meaning. At issue will be whether Bennett's "meaning-nominalist" strategy can be helpful in understanding Heidegger's account of linguistic meaning and intentionality. As we shall see, Charles Taylor has argued that the Bennett (-Grice-Lewis) notion of "communication" found here is too impoverished to capture many crucial forms of Dasein's intentionality.

15. Not the least of which is attributing a "core" of rationality to the Other similar to one's own (what we might call a Hermeneutical Postulate of Shared Minimal Technical & Practical Intentionality). For a helpful discussion of these issues, see M. Hollis & S. Lukes, (eds.), *Rationality and Relativism* (Cambridge, MA: Massachusetts Institute of Technology Press, 1984).

16. This is at least how Kuhn and Feyerabend and their followers have conceived the debate over scientific truth and progress.

17. In the next section, we shall return to the issue of the status of institutions, norms, and practices for Heidegger. I shall be arguing, against Haugeland-Brandom's "emergentism" and Taylor's account of "shared meanings," that Heidegger is not committed to the existence of social facts distinct from facts about the "care" of individual cases of Dasein. In effect, we have something like the old debate between holism and individualism in the methodological disputes of the human and social sciences. Also, as mentioned earlier, this can be taken as the issue of the correct "semantics for 'Dasein'."

18. For example, one might accept behavioral learning theory for ontogenetic changes and supplement this with evolutionary biology for phylogenetic causal factors.

19. I am having the Realist here allow for cases of (apparent?) reference within some symbolic practice with no clear physical referent. I am also assuming that, while the symbolic reference (to a sun-god) may have its roots in ordinary perceptual reference, the symbolic practice may come to have a life of its own for more recent users of this "invocative" language. See Taylor's discussion, *op. cit.*. Cases such as these show further the difficulty (impossibility?) of separating reference from other speech acts.

20. See his "The Question Concerning Technology," in *Basic Writings, op. cit.*, pp. 283-318.

21. See Jürgen Habermas, *Knowledge and Human Interests* (Boston: Beacon Press, 1971); and Ian Hacking, "Language, Truth, and Reason," in Hollis & Lukes, *op. cit.*, pp. 48-66.

22. Jonathan Bennett, *Linguistic Behavior* (Cambridge: Cambridge University Press, 1979). Taylor's argument can be found in his review of Bennett's book, *Dialogue*, Vol. 19 (1980), pp. 290-301, and in his "Theories of Meaning," *art. cit.*. An early form of Taylor's position can also be found in his, "Interpretation and the Sciences of Man," *Review of Metaphysics*, vol. 25 (1971), pp. 03-51.

23. Paul Grice, "Meaning," *Philosophical Review* (1957), pp. 377-388; see also his, "Utterer's Meaning, Sentence-Meaning, and Word-Meaning," in: John Searle, ed., *The Philosophy of Language* (London: Oxford University Press, 1971), pp. 54-70.

24. David Lewis, *Convention* (Cambridge, Massachusetts: Harvard University Press, 1969).

25. In fact, see Strawson's argument in "Freedom and Resentment," in P. F. Strawson (ed.), *Studies in the Philosophy of Thought and Action* (London: Oxford University Press, 1968), pp. 71-96. Bennett himself has clarified and expanded upon this position in his "Accountability," in Zak van Straten (ed.), *Philosophical Subjects: Essays Presented to P. F. Strawson* (London: Oxford University Press, 1980), pp. 14-47.

26. Some readers may find it helpful to view this "method" as of a piece with Strawson's "descriptive metaphysics." Cf. his *Individuals: An Essay in Descriptive Metaphysics* (Garden City, N.Y.: Doubleday, 1959), his Kant book, *The Bounds of Sense* (London: Methuen, 1968), and his recent 1983 Woodbridge Lectures, *Skepticism and Naturalism* (New York: Columbia University Press, 1985). Especially in this last work, Strawson takes great pains to distinguish his own "Wittgensteinian" conceptual analysis from any "validitory or revisionary metaphysics." Scepticism (as a form of Metaphysical Realism) is not to be refuted in any of its forms, but simply side-stepped on "practical" grounds, given the kinds of beings we appear to ourselves to be.

27. For a helpful discussion of these themes see Guignon, *op. cit.*, Ch. 10, pp. 132-145.

28. See my "Intentionality and the Semantics of 'Dasein'," cited in note 3 above.

29. Bennett clearly conceives himself to be doing "realist metaphysics" and of a moderate materialist sort. See his "Discussion of Davidson's Anomalous Monism," *op. cit.*, § 23, pp. 80-81. His earlier discussion in § 21 and of "Stable Lake" § 22 also makes it clear that teleological explanations are legitimate and (depending on our interests) may be our best source now for predictions about behavior. However, such teleology is not basic (that is, as found in evolutionary biological accounts of why there are certain mechanisms coexisting under some teleological law).

30. For a helpful discussion of this "fusion of horizons," see Richard Bernstein, *Beyond Objectivism and Relativism* (Philadelphia: University of Pennsylvania Press, 1983).

Michael Friedman

Overcoming Metaphysics: Carnap and Heidegger

It is well known that Rudolf Carnap (in Carnap 1932e) uses examples from Martin Heidegger as illustrations of metaphysical pseudo-sentences — including, most famously, the sentence "Nothingness itself nothings [*Das Nichts selbst nichtet*]" (Heidegger 1929b). It is tempting today for those on both sides — for those who sympathize with Carnap and those who sympathize with Heidegger alike — to view this episode with a more or less tolerant smile. Among those sympathetic to Carnap, Heidegger's sentence now appears as simply unintelligible, but hardly dangerous, nonsense: one is by no means surprised by such obvious absurdities coming from a fuzzy-minded "continental" thinker. Among those sympathetic to Heidegger, Carnap's criticism now appears as a case of simple blindness to Heidegger's point: one cannot expect a narrow-minded "analytic" philosopher even to begin to grasp such profundities. What both sides miss, I believe, is the depth and force this encounter had for Carnap and Heidegger themselves. We thereby miss the meaning and extent of the common context within which both contemporary philosophical traditions — both "continental" and "analytic" traditions — arise and develop.

The first point to notice is that Carnap and Heidegger had earlier met one another: at a celebrated disputation, or *Arbeitsgemeinschaft*, between Heidegger and Ernst Cassirer that took place during the International University Course held at Davos, Switzerland, from 17 March through 6 April 1929.[1] It was on this occasion, two years after the sensational appearance of *Being and Time*, that Heidegger first made public a radical phenomenological-metaphysical interpretation of the *Critique of Pure Reason* developed in explicit opposition to the Marburg school of neo-Kantianism with which Cassirer was closely associated — an interpretation Heidegger then wrote up in a few short weeks following the Davos university course and published as *Kant and the Problem of Metaphysics*.[2] Heidegger thereby presented himself — with extraordinary success, as it turned out — as the author of a fundamentally new kind of philosophy destined to replace the hegemony of the neo-Kantian tradition and to supplant the remaining "rationalist" tendencies in Husserlian phenomenology as well. In July 1929 Heidegger symbolically completed this ascension when he delivered his inaugural address as Edmund Husserl's successor to the chair of philosophy at Freiburg: Heidegger 1929b is the published record of this address. Carnap attended the Davos university course and reported on the occasion in his diary.[3] Like everyone else in attendance he appears to have been especially caught up in the intellectual excitement of the encounter between Heidegger and Cassirer. Moreover, Carnap was clearly impressed by Heidegger and had several philosophical conservations with him (ASP 025-73-03, entries from 18 March, 30 March, and 3 April 1929). When Carnap returned to Vienna he retained this sense of excitement and seems, in fact, to have studied *Being and Time* rather seriously. In particular, he actively participated in a discussion group in the summer of 1930 led by Heinrich Gomperz and Karl Bühler where Heidegger's book was intensively examined.[4] The first draft of Carnap 1932e was then written up in November 1930. Carnap presented it as lectures at Warsaw (November 1930), Zurich (January 1931), and Prague (November 1931) and then (in a revised version) at Berlin (July 1932) and Brünn (December 1932).[5] The published version appeared in *Erkenntnis*, the official journal of the Vienna Circle, in 1932. In §5 of Carnap 1932e, entitled "Metaphysical Pseudo-Sentences," Carnap introduces his consideration of examples from Heidegger 1929b by remarking that, although he "could just as well have selected passages from any other of the numerous metaphysicians of the present or the past," he has here chosen to "select a few sentences from that metaphysical doctrine which at present exerts the strongest influence in Germany."

The second point to notice is that Carnap's analysis and criticism of "Nothingness itself nothings" is more sophisticated and penetrating than one might have antecedently expected. For, on the one hand, Carnap's complaint is not that the sentence in question is unverifiable in terms of sense-data; nor is the most important problem that the sentence coins a bizarre new word and thus violates ordinary usage. The main problem is rather a violation of the logical form of the concept of nothing. Heidegger uses the concept both as a substantive and as a verb, whereas modern logic has shown that it is neither: the logical form of the concept of nothing is constituted solely by existential quantification and negation. On the other hand, however, Carnap also clearly recognizes that this kind of criticism would not affect Heidegger himself in the slightest; for the real issue between the two lies in the circumstance

OVERCOMING METAPHYSICS: CARNAP AND HEIDEGGER

that Heidegger denies while Carnap affirms the philosophical centrality of logic and the exact sciences. Carnap accordingly refers to such Heideggerian passages as the following:

> [N]othingness is the source of negation, not vice versa. If the power of the understanding in the field of questions concerning nothingness and being is thus broken, then the fate of the dominion of "logic" within philosophy is also decided therewith. The idea of "logic" itself dissolves in a vortex of more original questioning.
>
> The supposed soberness and superiority of science becomes ridiculous if it does not take nothingness seriously. Only because nothingness is manifest can science make what exists itself into an object of investigation. Only if science takes its existence from metaphysics can it always reclaim anew its essential task, which does not consist in the accumulation and ordering of objects of acquaintance but in the ever to be newly accomplished disclosure of the entire expanse of truth of nature and history.
>
> Therefore no rigor of a science can attain the seriousness of metaphysics. Philosophy can never be measured by the standard of the idea of science.[6]

Carnap concludes, in his own characteristically sober fashion: "We thus find a good confirmation for our thesis; a metaphysician here arrives himself at the statement that his questions and answers are not consistent with logic and the scientific mode of thinking" (Carnap 1932e, 232 [72]).

Heidegger's "Postscript" to Heidegger 1929b — published in the fourth edition in 1943 — considers three types of criticism that have been directed at the original lecture. Heidegger reserves his most extensive and militant response for the third criticism: namely, that "the lecture decides against 'logic.'" The heart of his response is as follows:

> The suspicion directed against "logic," whose conclusive degeneration may be seen in logistic [that is, modern mathematical logic], arises from the knowledge of that thinking that finds its source in the truth of being, but not in the consideration of the objectivity [*Gegenständlichkeit*] of what exists. Exact thinking is never the most rigorous thinking, if rigor [*Strenge*] receives its essence otherwise from the mode of strenuousness [*Anstrengung*] with which knowledge always maintains the relation to what is essential in what exists. Exact thinking ties itself down solely in calculation with what exists and serves this [end] exclusively. (Heidegger 1943, 104 [356])

It is clear, then, that Heidegger and Carnap are actually in remarkable agreement. "Metaphysical" thought of the type Heidegger is trying to awaken is possible only on the basis of a prior overthrow of the authority and primacy of logic and the exact sciences. The difference is that Heidegger eagerly embraces such an overthrow, whereas Carnap is determined to resist it at all costs.

The above sheds considerable light, I believe, on the context and force of Carnap's antimetaphysical attitude. For, by rejecting "metaphysics" as a field of cognitively meaningless pseudosentences, Carnap is by no means similarly rejecting all forms of traditional philosophy. He makes this perfectly clear, in fact, in his "Remarks by the Author" appended to the English translation of Carnap 1932e in 1957:

> *To section 1, "metaphysics."* This term is used in this paper, as usually in Europe, for the field of alleged knowledge of the essence of things which transcends the realm of empirically founded, inductive science. Metaphysics in this sense includes systems like those of Fichte, Schelling, Hegel, Bergson, Heidegger. But it does not include endeavors toward a synthesis and generalization of the results of the various sciences. (Carnap 1932e, [80])

In Carnap's reply to Paul Henle in Schilpp 1963 the point is made even more explicitly:

> Note that the characterization as pseudo-statements does not refer to all systems or theses in the field of metaphysics. At the time of the Vienna Circle, the characterization was applied mainly to those metaphysical systems which had exerted the greatest influence upon continental philosophy during the last century, viz., the post-Kantian systems of German idealism and, among contemporary ones, those of Bergson and Heidegger. On the basis of later, more cautious analyses, the judgment was not applied to the main theses of those philosophers whose thinking had been in close contact with the science of their times, as in the cases of Aristotle and Kant; the latter's epistemological theses about the synthetic a priori character of certain judgments were regarded by us as false, not as meaningless.[7]

So Carnap is primarily concerned with "overcoming" a very particular kind of "metaphysics": the main target is the post-Kantian German idealism he views as dominating recent European thought, and he views Heidegger, in particular, as the contemporary embodiment of such metaphysical dominance.

When Carnap emigrated to the United States in December 1935, he was therefore especially relieved to have finally left this European metaphysical tradition behind:

> I was not only relieved to escape the stifling political and cultural atmosphere and the danger of war in Europe, but was also very gratified to see that in the United States there was a considerable interest, especially among the younger philosophers, in the scientific method of philosophy, based on modern logic, and that this interest was growing from year to year.
>
> In 1936, when I came to this country, the traditional schools of philosophy did not have nearly the same influence as on the European continent. The movement of German idealism, in particular Hegelianism, which had earlier been quite influential in the United States, had by then almost completely disappeared. Neo-Kantian philosophical conceptions were represented here and there, not in an orthodox form but rather influenced by recent developments in scientific thinking, much like the conceptions of Cassirer in Germany. Phenomenology had a number of adherents mostly in a liberalized form, not in Husserl's orthodox form, and even less in Heidegger's version. (Carnap 1963a, 34, 40)

Carnap's sense of liberation in thus escaping the "stifling" political, cultural, and philosophical atmosphere in Central Europe is palpable.

It is important, then, to understand Carnap's antimetaphysical attitude in its philosophical, cultural, and political context. Carnap's concern for this broader context is characteristic of him and, in fact, formed one of the main bonds uniting him with his more activist friend and colleague Otto Neurath. Neurath himself, as is well known, contributed an extremely engaged, neo-Marxist perspective to the Vienna Circle. Indeed, he had served as economics minister in Ernst Toller's short-lived Bavarian Soviet Republic in 1919 and received an eighteen-month sentence when it was crushed. As is also well known, an especially striking example of Carnap's own attitude toward the relationship between the philosophical work of the Vienna Circle and this wider cultural and political context is the preface to the *Aufbau,* dated May 1928. After calling for a radically new scientific, rational, and anti-individualistic conception of philosophy that is to emulate the slow process of mutual cooperation and collaboration typical of the special sciences, Carnap continues:

> We cannot hide from ourselves the fact that trends from philosophical-metaphysical and from religious spheres, which protect themselves against this kind of orientation, again exert a strong influence precisely

> at the present time. Where do we derive the confidence, in spite of this, that our call for clarity, for a science that is free from metaphysics, will prevail? — From the knowledge, or, to put it more cautiously, from the belief, that these opposing powers belong to the past. We sense an inner kinship between the attitude on which our philosophical work is based and the spiritual attitude that currently manifests itself in entirely different spheres of life. We sense this attitude in trends in art, especially in architecture, and in the movements that concern themselves with a meaningful structuring [*Gestaltung*] of human life: of personal life and the life of the community, of education, of external organization at large. We sense here everywhere the same basic attitude, the same style of thinking and working. It is the orientation that is directed everywhere towards clarity yet recognizes at the same time the never entirely comprehensible interweaving of life, towards care in the individual details and equally towards the greater shape of the whole, towards the bonds between men and equally towards the free development of the individual. The belief that this orientation belongs to the future inspires our work. (Carnap 1928a, x–xi [xvii–xviii])

And, as Carnap explains in his diary, he is here expressing precisely the attitude that he and Neurath share.[8]

Carnap suggests that his and Neurath's orientation has much in common with that of modern architecture and, in particular, with that of the Dessau Bauhaus — a point that is borne out by the recollections of Herbert Feigl:

> Carnap and Neurath also had a great deal in common in that they were somewhat utopian social reformers — Neurath quite actively, Carnap more "philosophically." ... I owe [Neurath] a special debt of gratitude for sending me (I think as the first "emissary" of the Vienna Circle) to Bauhaus Dessau, then, in 1929, a highly progressive school of art and architecture. It was there in a week's sojourn of lectures and discussions that I became acquainted with Kandinsky and Klee. Neurath and Carnap felt that the Circle's philosophy was an expression of the *neue Sachlichkeit* which was part of the ideology of the Bauhaus. (Feigl 1969, 637)

Carnap's basic philosophical-political orientation is thus best expressed by the *neue Sachlichkeit* (the new objectivity, soberness, matter-of-factness): a social, cultural, and artistic movement committed to internationalism, to some form of socialism,[9] and, above all, to a more objective, scientific, and anti-individualistic reorganization of both art and public life inspired equally by the new Russian communism and the new American technology.[10]

Carnap and Heidegger are therefore at opposite ends of the spectrum not only philosophically but also in cultural and political terms.[11] And I think there is no doubt that this cultural and political dimension of their disagreement represents at least part of the explanation for Carnap's choosing Heidegger for his examples of metaphysical pseudosentences in Carnap 1932e. Indeed, particularly when read in the context of such programmatic statements as the preface to the *Aufbau*, this is already suggested by the sentence from §5, quoted above, where Carnap explains that he has here chosen to "select a few sentences from that metaphysical doctrine which at present exerts the strongest influence in Germany." Such a wider cultural and political context is also suggested by a passage in §6, where Carnap explains that the method of logical analysis has both a negative aspect (antimetaphysical) and a positive aspect (constructive analysis of science): "This negative application of method is necessary and important in the present historical situation. But the positive application — even already in contemporary practice — is more fruitful."[12] Carnap expresses this last idea in stronger and more militant terms, however, in the second version of his paper, the one presented at the lectures in Berlin and Brünn in July and December 1932. In this version the lecture closes with a discussion of the positive task of the method of logical analysis (that is, the clarification of the sentences of science) and, in particular, with the following words:

> These indications [are presented] only so that one will *not* think that the *struggle* [*Kampf*] *against metaphysics is our primary task*. On the contrary: in the meaningful realm [there are] many tasks and difficulties, there will always be enough struggle<?>. The struggle against metaphysics is only necessary because of the historical situation, in order to reject hindrances. There will, I hope, come the time when one no longer needs to present lectures against metaphysics. (ASP 110-07-19, p. 4)

One can imagine that this statement, coming at the very end of Carnap's lecture at Berlin in July 1932, had a much more dramatic impact than the more subtle suggestions buried in the published version.[13]

Neurath, for his part, dispenses entirely with all such subtleties. He never tires, for example, of characterizing "metaphysicians" and "school philosophers" — among whom Heidegger is a prominent representative — as enemies of the proletariat:

> Science and art are today above all in the hands of the ruling classes and will also be used as instruments in the class struggle against

52   *Michael Friedman*

> the proletariat. Only a small number of scholars and artists place themselves on the side of the coming order and set themselves up as protection against this form of reactionary thought.
>
> The idealistic school philosophers of our day from Spann to Heidegger want to rule, as the theologians once ruled; but the scholastics could support themselves on the substructure of the feudal order of production, whereas our school philosophers do not notice that their substructure is being pulled out from beneath their feet.[14]

Neurath was particularly ill-disposed toward attempts by such thinkers as Heinrich Rickert, Wilhelm Dilthey, and Heidegger to underwrite a special status for the *Geisteswissenschaften* in relation to the *Naturwissenschaften* (the humanities in relation to the natural sciences) — which attempts, according to Neurath, constitute one of the principal obstacles to rational and scientific social progress.[15]

That Carnap was in fact in basic agreement with Neurath here emerges clearly in a conversation he records after his final lecture presentation of Carnap 1932e at Brünn in December 1932:

> My lecture "Die Überwindung der Metaphysik" (II ... had added: and the world-view of modern philosophy) in the banquet hall. Pretty well attended, lively participation, 1¼ hours. Afterwards various questions. *Erkenntnis* is here completely unknown. Then to a cafe. Prof. B....., chemist, gives philosophical courses at the popular university, will report on my lecture in the socialistic... newspaper. Marxist, is pleased with my Marxist views on how metaphysics will be overcome through reformation [*Umgestaltung*] of the substructure. (ASP 025-73-03, entry for 10 December 1932)

There can be very little doubt, therefore, that Carnap's attack on Heidegger, articulated and presented at an extraordinarily critical moment during the last years of the Weimar Republic, had more than purely philosophical motivations — or, perhaps better: that Carnap, like Neurath, conceived his philosophical work (and the attack on Heidegger in particular) as a necessary piece of a much larger social, political, and cultural struggle.[16]

It is noteworthy, finally, that Heidegger was aware of Carnap's attack and, indeed, explicitly responded to it: in a part of his 1935 lecture course "Introduction to Metaphysics" that does not appear in the published version in 1953.[17] Heidegger explains how, with the collapse of German idealism in the second half of the nineteenth century, the philosophical understanding of Being degenerated into a consideration of the "is" — that is, a logical consideration of the propositional copula. He continues in a memorable paragraph that is worth quoting in full:

> Going further in this direction, which in a certain sense has been marked out since Aristotle, and which determines "Being" from the "is" of the proposition and thus finally destroys it, is a tendency of thought that has been assembled in the journal *Erkenntnis*. Here the traditional logic is to be for the first time grounded with scientific rigor through mathematics and the mathematical calculus, in order to construct a "logically correct" language in which the propositions of metaphysics — which are all pseudo-propositions — are to become impossible in the future. Thus, an article in this journal (2:1931–32, 219ff.) bears the title "Überwindung der Metaphysik durch logische Analyse der Sprache." Here the most extreme flattening out and uprooting of the traditional theory of judgment is accomplished under the semblance of mathematical science. Here the last consequences of a mode of thinking which began with Descartes are brought to a conclusion: a mode of thinking according to which truth is no longer disclosedness of what exists and thus accommodation and grounding of Dasein in the disclosing being, but truth is rather diverted into *certainty* — to the mere securing of thought, and in fact the securing of mathematical thought against all that is not thinkable by it. The conception of truth as the securing of thought led to the definitive profaning [*Entgötterung*] of the world. The supposed "philosophical" tendency of mathematical-physical positivism wishes to supply the grounding of this position. It is no accident that this kind of "philosophy" wishes to supply the foundations of modern physics, in which all relations to nature are in fact destroyed. It is also no accident that this kind of "philosophy" stands in internal and external connection with Russian communism. And it is no accident, moreover, that this kind of thinking celebrates its triumph in America. All of this is only the ultimate consequence of an apparently merely grammatical affair, according to which Being is conceived through the "is," and the "is" is interpreted in accordance with one's conception of the proposition and of thought. (Heidegger 1983, 227–28)[18]

Thus Heidegger, in terms no more subtle than Neurath's, once again expresses a rather remarkable agreement with Carnap concerning the underlying sources of their opposition — which, as is now clear, extend far beyond the purely philosophical issues between them.

165

These philosophical issues, as we have seen, are based in the end on a stark and profound disagreement about the nature and centrality of logic. Thus Carnap criticizes "Nothingness itself nothings" primarily on the grounds of logical form: modern mathematical logic shows that the concept of nothing is to be explained in terms of existential quantification and negation and can therefore by no means function either as a substantive (individual constant) or as a verb (predicate). For Heidegger, by contrast, such a purely logical analysis misses precisely his point: what he calls nothingness is prior to logic and hence prior, in particular, to the concept of negation. In tracing out the roots of this fundamental disagreement over the philosophical centrality of logic, it turns out, we need to appreciate the extent to which the thought of both philosophers arises from the neo-Kantian tradition that dominated the German-speaking world at the end of the nineteenth and beginning of the twentieth century — a tradition within which both men received their philosophical training.

There were in fact two quite distinguishable versions of neo-Kantianism that were dominant at the time: the so-called Marburg school of neo-Kantianism founded by Hermann Cohen and then continued by Paul Natorp and (at least until about 1920) Ernst Cassirer, and the so-called Southwest school of neo-Kantianism founded by Wilhelm Windelband and systematically developed by Heinrich Rickert. The former school emphasized the importance of mathematics and natural science and, in fact, saw the true achievement of the *Critique of Pure Reason* as a laying of the groundwork for Newtonian mathematical physics. The latter school, by contrast, emphasized the distinctive importance of the *Geisteswissenschaften* and, accordingly, devoted considerable philosophical efforts to articulating a sharp methodological distinction between the latter and the *Naturwissenschaften*. Heidegger studied with Rickert at Freiburg (before Rickert succeeded Windelband at Heidelberg) — completing his habilitation under Rickert in 1915. Carnap, for his part, studied Kant at Jena with Bruno Bauch — another student of Rickert's from Freiburg — and, in fact, completed his doctoral dissertation under Bauch in 1921.[19] It is clear, moreover, that Carnap carefully studied both versions of neo-Kantianism and, in particular, the writings of Natorp, Cassirer, and Rickert.[20]

Common to both versions of neo-Kantianism is a certain conception of epistemology and the object of knowledge inherited from Kant.[21] Our knowledge or true judgments should not be construed, according to this conception, as representing or picturing objects or entities that exist independently of our judgments — whether these independent entities are the "transcendent" objects of the metaphysical realist existing somehow "behind" our sense-experience or the naked, unconceptualized sense-experience itself beloved of the empiricist. In the first case ("transcendent" objects), knowledge or true judgment would be impossible for us, since, by hypothesis, we have absolutely no independent access to such entities by which we could verify whether the desired relation of representation or picturing holds. In the second case (naive empiricism), knowledge or true judgment would be equally impossible, however, for the stream of unconceptualized sense-experience is in fact utterly chaotic and intrinsically undifferentiated: comparing the articulated structures of our judgments to this chaos of sensations simply makes no sense. How, then, is knowledge or true judgment possible? What does it mean for our judgments to relate to an object? The answer is given by Kant's "Copernican Revolution": the object of knowledge does not exist independently of our judgments at all: on the contrary, this object is first created or "constituted" when the unconceptualized data of sense are organized or framed within the a priori logical structures of judgment itself. In this way, the initially unconceptualized data of sense are brought under a priori "categories" and thus first become capable of empirical objectivity.

Yet there is a crucially important difference between this neo-Kantian account of the object of knowledge and judgment and Kant's original account. For Kant, we cannot explain, on the basis of the a priori logical structures of judgment alone, how the object of knowledge becomes possible. We need additional a priori structures that mediate between the pure forms of judgment comprising what Kant calls general logic and the unconceptualized manifold of impressions supplied by the senses: these mediating structures are the pure forms of sensible intuition — space and time. Thus the pure logical forms of judgment only become categories when they are "schematized," that is, when they are given a determinate spatio-temporal content in relation to the pure forms of sensible intuition. The pure logical form of a categorical judgment, for example, becomes the category of *substance* when it is schematized in terms of the temporal representation of permanence; the pure logical form of a hypothetical judgment becomes the category of *causality* when it is schematized in terms of the temporal representation of succession; and so on. For Kant, then, pure formal logic (general logic) must, if it is to play an epistemological role, be supplemented by what he calls transcendental logic: with the theory of how logical forms become schematized in terms of pure spatio-temporal representations belonging to the independent faculty of pure intuition. And it is precisely this theory, in fact, that forms the heart of the transcendental analytic of the

Critique of Pure Reason: the so-called metaphysical and transcendental deductions of the categories.

Now both versions of neo-Kantianism entirely reject the idea of an independent faculty of pure intuition. The neo-Kantians here follow the tradition of post-Kantian idealism in vigorously opposing the dualistic conception of mind characteristic of Kant's own position: the dualism, that is, between a logical, conceptual, or discursive faculty of pure understanding and an intuitive, nonconceptual, or receptive faculty of pure sensibility. For the neo-Kantians, the a priori formal structures in virtue of which the object of knowledge becomes possible must therefore derive from the logical faculty of the understanding and from this faculty alone. And, in this way, epistemology or "transcendental logic" becomes the study of purely logical, purely conceptual, *and thus essentially non–spatio-temporal* a priori structures. Space and time, conceived as Kantian pure forms of sensible intuition, can no longer play a role in our explanation of how the object of knowledge and judgment becomes possible.

It is this last feature of their conception of epistemology, moreover, that associates the neo-Kantians (again in both versions) with Husserlian phenomenology and, in particular, with the polemic against psychologism of Husserl's *Logical Investigations*. For the neo-Kantians had also arrived — albeit by a different route — at a conception of pure thought or pure logic whose subject matter is an essentially nontemporal, and therefore certainly not psychological, realm: an "ideal" realm of timeless, formal-logical structures. Indeed, Husserl's conception of "pure logic" — which was generally recognized to have its sources in the earlier work of Bernhard Bolzano, Johann Herbart, Rudolf Lotze, and Alexius Meinong — can be fairly characterized as the dominant idea of the period. Accordingly, it plays a central role not only in the thought of the neo-Kantians of the Marburg and Southwest traditions but also in the early thought of both Carnap and Heidegger.[22]

We shall have to return to the relationship between Husserl and Heidegger shortly. But it is first necessary to appreciate the fundamental problems facing the epistemology of the neo-Kantians (in both versions) — problems that flow directly from their enthusiastic embrace of the idea of "pure logic." For, as we have just seen, the logical forms of judgment, in Kant's original conception, become categories — and thus make the object of knowledge possible — precisely through their prior application to the pure forms of sensible intuition. It is on this basis, and on this basis alone, that we can explain how the purely analytic forms of thought apply to the spatio-temporal world of sense so as to make synthetic knowledge of empirical objects (that is, of appearances) possible. Yet the neo-Kantians entirely reject the idea of such an intermediate faculty of pure intuition and hence the central Kantian conception of the schematism of the pure concepts of the understanding as well. How, then, are the pure forms of thought — now conceived as belonging wholly to an "ideal," essentially non–spatio-temporal realm — supposed to apply to the spatio-temporal world of sense? How do the categories make the object of (empirical) knowledge possible?

It is in attempting to answer these questions that the two schools of neo-Kantian epistemology strikingly diverge from one another. The Marburg school, as indicated above, continues to follow Kant in taking mathematical physics as the paradigm of objective knowledge. That school's most basic move, accordingly, is to "mathematize" the pure forms of thought. Beginning with Cohen's attempt to assimilate the fundamental moment of judgment to the mathematical concept of the differential, this line of thought reaches its culmination in Cassirer's *Substance and Function* — where logic is identified with the pure theory of relations developed especially (building on the work of David Hilbert, Georg Cantor, and Richard Dedekind) in Bertrand Russell's *The Principles of Mathematics*. The timeless realm of "pure thought" is thus identified with the totality of what we now call relational structures — the "objects" thereof being simply abstract "places" within such a relational structure. In empirical knowledge, on the other hand, we develop an essentially nonterminating — but in some sense converging — *sequence* of relational structures, each element of which represents the state of mathematical physics at some particular point in the methodological history of science. (That this sequence does not terminate thus constitutes the essential point of difference between pure and empirical knowledge.) The object of empirical knowledge — the sensible world — is then conceived simply as the ideal limit or infinitely distant X toward which the methodological sequence of science is converging.[23] The Marburg school thereby solves the problem of the categories by a kind of "logicization" of the object of empirical knowledge, and it is with good reason, then, that the school's epistemological conception becomes known as "logical idealism."

Within the Southwest school, on the other hand, logic and the realm of "pure thought" are sharply and explicitly separated from mathematics. And this fundamental divergence between the two schools emerges with particular clarity in a dispute between Natorp and Rickert in the years 1910–11. Natorp argues that the concept of number belongs to "pure thought" and thus neither to pure intuition nor to psychology (Natorp 1919). Rickert directly challenges Natorp's conception — arguing that the concept of one as a number (as the first element of the number series) cannot be derived from the logical concepts of identity and difference and is therefore "alogical" (Rickert 1911). For Rickert, the numerical concept of one (unlike the logical concepts of identity and difference) does not apply to all objects of thought as such but presupposes that we are antecedently given objects arranged in a homogeneous serial order. The numerical concept of quantity can therefore not belong to logic — where logic is here being clearly identified with traditional syllogistic logic.[24] In this approach, since we neither follow Kant in invoking a mediating faculty of pure intuition nor follow the Marburg school in "logicizing" the object of empirical knowledge after the example of mathematical physics, we are therefore left only with the forms of judgment of traditional logic on the one side and the spatio-temporal manifold of given empirical objects on the other. So, as one would expect, particularly vexing problems in attempting to explain the application of the former to the latter arise within the Southwest school.

The underlying tensions expressed in the epistemology of the Southwest school become painfully evident in the work of Emil Lask, a brilliant student of Rickert's who then held an associate professorship at Heidelberg and was killed in the Great War in 1915. The basic argument of Lask 1912 is that whereas the Kantian philosophy has indeed closed the gap between knowledge and its object, we are nonetheless left with a new gap between what Lask calls "transcendental," "epistemological," or "material" logic, on the one side, and "formal" logic, on the other. Formal logic is the subject matter of the theory of judgment — the realm of necessarily valid and timeless "senses," "objective thoughts," or "propositions in themselves" familiar within the tradition of "pure logic."[25] Transcendental or material logic, on the other hand, is the theory of the categories in Kant's sense: the theory of how the concrete object of knowledge and experience is made possible by the activity of thought. But, and here is the central idea of Lask's argument, transcendental or material logic is *not* based on formal logic, and, accordingly, we explicitly reject Kant's metaphysical deduction — the entire point of which, as indicated above, is precisely to derive the categories from the logical forms of judgment.[26] For Lask, what is fundamental is the concrete, already categorized real object of experience: the subject matter of formal logic (comprising the structures of the traditional logical theory of judgment) only arises subsequently in an artificial process of abstraction, by which the originally unitary categorized object is broken down into form and matter, subject and predicate, and so on. Moreover, since this comes about due to a fundamental weakness or peculiarity of our human understanding — our inability to grasp the unitary categorized object *as* a unity — all the structures of "pure logic," despite their undoubtedly timeless and necessary status, are in the end artifacts of subjectivity. Since the pure forms of judgment of traditional logic are now seen as entirely bereft of the capacity even to begin the "constitution" of any real empirical object, the entire realm of "pure logic" appears as nothing but an artificially constructed intermediary possessing no explanatory power whatsoever.[27]

•

Heidegger's earliest philosophical works, as noted above, fall squarely within the antipsychologistic tradition of "pure logic" and receive their primary orientation (not surprisingly) from his teacher Rickert. Accordingly, these early investigations revolve around the central distinctions between psychological act and logical content, between real thought process and ideal atemporal "sense," between being *(Sein)* and validity *(Geltung)*. For, as Lotze in particular has shown, the realm of the logical has a completely different mode of existence (validity or *Geltung*) than that of the realm of actual spatio-temporal entities (being or *Sein*).[28] Moreover, as Rickert has shown, the realm of the logical (the realm of validity) is also distinct from that of the mathematical: for, although the latter is equally atemporal and hence equally ideal, it presupposes a particular object — the existence of "quantity" — and therefore lacks the complete generality characteristic of the logical. It follows that we must sharply distinguish the realm of the logical both from the given heterogeneous qualitative continuum of empirical reality and from the homogeneous quantitative continuum of mathematics.[29] In emphasizing these fundamental distinctions and, above all, in maintaining "*the absolute primacy of valid sense [den absoluten Primat des geltenden Sinnes]*,"[30] Heidegger shows himself to be a faithful follower of Rickert indeed.

Yet, as we have just seen, Rickert's fundamental distinctions lead naturally to fundamental problems — problems that stand out especially vividly in the work of Lask. In particular, once we have delimited the realm of the logical so sharply from all "neighboring" realms, it then becomes radically unclear how the realm of the logical is at all connected with the real world of temporal being *[Sein]*: with either the realm of empirical nature where the objects of our (empirical) cognition reside or the realm of psychological happenings where our acts of judgment reside. The realm of "valid sense," which was intended as an intermediary between these last two realms wherein our cognition of objects is "constituted" and thus made possible, thereby becomes deprived of all explanatory power. Now Heidegger, for his part, was of course most sensitive indeed to the difficult position in which Rickert had become entangled; and, as a consequence, he became increasingly attracted to the more radical position of Lask,[31] which Heidegger also saw as having essential ideas in common with the emerging new phenomenology being developed by Edmund Husserl. After Rickert left Freiburg to take Windelband's chair at Heidelberg and Husserl left Göttingen to take Rickert's chair at Freiburg in 1916, Heidegger became an enthusiastic proponent of the new phenomenology and, in particular, distanced himself further and further from Rickert. This distance from Rickert became quite extreme by 1925–26, when Heidegger was completing the work on *Being and Time*, and it is graphically evident in lectures Heidegger presented at Marburg in the summer semester of 1925 and the winter semester of 1926. Here Heidegger speaks of Rickert with almost undisguised contempt, whereas Husserl appears as the leader of a new "breakthrough" in philosophy — a "breakthrough" that has decisively overcome neo-Kantianism.[32]

The first element of this "breakthrough" is a "direct realist" conception of truth as "identification" — a conception that can be seen as definitively rejecting the idea that formal logic is foundational for truth in general and thus as also overturning the "Copernican Revolution." For, according to the theory of truth articulated in volume 2 of the *Logical Investigations*, truth in general is not even propositional: it consists simply in the circumstance that an intention or meaning (whether propositional or not) is directly "identified" — in immediate intuition — with the very thing that is intended or meant. Thus, truth in general need involve none of the structures (subject and predicate, ground and consequent, and so on) studied in traditional formal logic. On the contrary, such peculiarly logical structures only emerge subsequently in the very special circumstances of "categorial intuition," where specifically propositional intentions or meanings are intuitively grasped in their most abstract — and, as it were, secondary and derivative — formal features. In this sense, then, Husserl's "direct realist" conception of the relationship between logical form and truth in general parallels Lask's view of the artificiality and subjectivity of logical form: in neither case can formal logic be in any way foundational or explanatory for truth as "relation to an object."[33]

The second element of the Husserlian "breakthrough" is just the idea of phenomenology as such — an idea that also emerges in volume 2 of the *Logical Investigations* as that of an "epistemology of the logical." For it is this idea, and this idea alone, that first opens up the possibility of bridging the gulf between the logical and the psychological created by the polemic against psychologism of volume 1. The problem, however, is to explain how such an "epistemology of the logical" —

which is to investigate the *relationship* between psychological act and logical or "essential" content — can itself avoid collapsing into psychologism. The answer is disarmingly simple: phenomenology is not empirical psychology because it aims to elucidate the underlying a priori structures or "essences" of psychological phenomena (the "essences" of perception, recollection, imaginative representation, and so on). Our investigation proceeds by means of "essential analysis [*Wesensanalyse*]" and "essential intuition [*Wesenserschauung*]" — and therefore is, in particular, entirely independent of the actual instances of the psychological structures in question that may or may not exist in the real world.[34] We are interested, that is, only in the purely ideal or "essential" structures of psychological phenomena: in "pure consciousness."[35]

Yet, for this very reason, Husserl's conception of pure phenomenology and "pure consciousness" could not be fully satisfactory from Heidegger's point of view. For Heidegger's problem — arising so painfully and vividly within the neo-Kantian epistemology of the Southwest school — was precisely that of the application of abstract and ideal "valid senses" to concrete and real objects of cognition: the problem of the application of the categories in Kant's sense to actual spatio-temporal objects. And *this* problem, it is clear, cannot be solved within the framework of Husserlian "pure consciousness"; for the latter, as we have just seen, itself belongs to the purely ideal realm of "essences" and is thus entirely independent of the existence of any and all concrete instances (whether of actual states of consciousness or of its empirical objects). It is by no means surprising, therefore, that we already find rumblings in a new and quite un-Husserlian direction in the concluding chapter added to the published version of Heidegger's habilitation in 1916. Heidegger there suggests that a genuine unification of time and eternity — of change and absolute validity — can be effected only through the concept of "living spirit [*der lebendige Geist*]" construed as a concrete and essentially historical subject. The "subjective logic" sought for by Rickert and Husserl requires a more fundamental point of view according to which the subject is no mere "punctiform" cognitive subject but an actual concrete subject comprehending the entire fullness of its temporal-historical involvements. And such an investigation of the concrete historical subject must, according to Heidegger, be a "translogical" or "metaphysical" investigation.[36] Thus, Heidegger is here already beginning to come to terms with the historically oriented *Lebensphilosophie* of Wilhelm Dilthey — an influence that will prove decisive in *Being and Time*.[37]

It is of course in *Being and Time*, completed ten years later, that Heidegger finally works out the desired "subjective logic" with a *con-*

crete subject — the so-called existential analytic of Dasein. Heidegger's concrete subject — Dasein, the concrete living human being — is distinguished from the "pure consciousness" of Husserlian phenomenology in three fundamental respects. First, Dasein necessarily exists in a world: a world of concrete spatio-temporal objects existing independently of it, which it does not create and over which it has only very limited control, and into which — without its consent, as it were — it is "thrown." Indeed, for Heidegger, Dasein essentially *is* such "being-in-the-world." Second, Dasein's relationship to this world is first and foremost practical and pragmatic rather than epistemic and contemplatively intuitive. The items in Dasein's world therefore appear to it originally as practically "ready-to-hand [*Zuhanden*]" — as environmental items to be used in the service of particular concrete projects — rather than as merely "present-to-hand [*Vorhanden*]" for theoretical inspection and consideration. Indeed, for Heidegger, theoretical cognition of the merely "present-to-hand" is a *derivative* mode of Dasein: a particular "modification" of the more basic, essentially practical and pragmatic, mode of involvement with the "ready-to-hand."[38] Finally, Dasein is essentially a historical being — in an important sense it is *the* historical being. For the essence or "being" of Dasein is "care [*Sorge*]" — roughly, the above-described orientation toward its world from the point of view of the totality of its practical involvements and projects — and the "ontological meaning of care" is *temporality*, where temporality in this sense is essentially historical and thus to be sharply and explicitly distinguished from the uniform and featureless "time" of natural science.[39]

There is no doubt, then, that Heidegger's Dasein is much more concrete than Husserl's "pure consciousness" — in the sense that the former has more of the features of a real human being than does the latter. From the point of view of Husserlian phenomenology, however, an obvious dilemma for Heidegger arises at this point. For what can Heidegger's "existential analytic of Dasein" possibly mean from Husserl's perspective? Either Heidegger is trying to describe the concrete reality of empirical human beings in their concrete and empirical character, in which case his enterprise is simply a branch of empirical anthropology having no specifically philosophical interest whatsoever; or Heidegger is trying to elucidate the "essence" or nature of the concrete human being by means of an "essential analysis" of that nature, in which case Heidegger, too, must perform the "eidetic" reduction and abstract from all questions involving the real existence of the entities under consideration. Thus, either Heidegger falls prey to the charge of naturalism and psychologism or his "existential analytic of Dasein" is in the end no closer to actual concrete reality than is Husserl's phenomenology.

It is in response to this dilemma, I believe, that Heidegger's true philosophical radicalism emerges; for it is precisely here — in attempting to construct an a priori analysis of the real concrete subject — that Heidegger fundamentally changes the terms within which the entire tradition of "pure logic" was articulated and, in fact, introduces a fundamentally new existential dimension into this tradition. For Heidegger, the "existential analytic of Dasein" can by no means be assimilated to a description of the "essence" of Dasein in the traditional meaning of this term (where "essence" or "whatness" is contrasted with "existence" or "thatness") precisely because the distinguishing feature of Dasein — as opposed to all other entities encountered within the world — is that Dasein has no "essence" of this kind at all: *What* Dasein is can be determined only by Dasein's own free choice in the face of its fundamental possibility of "being-toward-death" — a choice that can be either "authentic" and "resolute" or "inauthentic" and fallen into the "They" of everyday public existence.[40] In either case, however, since Dasein's "essence" or "whatness" depends in the end on its own free choice — and is thus in no sense simply "given" as in the case of entities encountered within the world — Dasein's "essence" cannot be meaningfully separated from its "existence" at all. Indeed, from this point of view, Dasein's "essence" *is* "existence." The dilemma just raised from the point of view of Husserlian phenomenology therefore has no force whatever from Heidegger's own point of view: by replacing phenomenological "essential analysis" with what he calls "existential-ontological analysis," Heidegger has transcended the traditional distinction between "essence" and "existence" and opened up the paradoxical-sounding possibility of an a priori analysis of concrete existence itself.[41]

At the same time, Heidegger has thereby definitively transcended the problematic of the neo-Kantian tradition as well. This comes out most clearly in §44 of *Being and Time*, entitled "Dasein, Disclosedness, and Truth," where Heidegger explicitly rejects the "Copernican Revolution" and the associated idea that truth is to be understood in terms of "valid judgment" in favor of an apparently "direct realist" account in which truth is conceived as a kind of immediate "disclosedness [*Erschlossenheit*]" or "uncoveredness [*Entdeckt-sein*]" of a being within the world — an account that explicitly invokes Husserl's notion of "identification."[42] Heidegger's "direct realism" is very special, however, for Dasein's most fundamental relation to the world is not a cognitive relation at all. Indeed, Dasein's most fundamental relation to the world is one of either "authentic" or "inauthentic" existence — in which Dasein's own peculiar mode of being (that is, "being-in-the-world") is itself either disclosed or covered over.[43] Moreover, in the moment of an "authentic" decision, Dasein must choose among possibilities already given in the world — possibilities that must themselves be somehow already "present" and available in Dasein's historically given situation. Dasein must thus appropriate its "fate" and, in precisely this way, is essentially historical.[44]

What is therefore central, for Heidegger, is the circumstance that we do not start with a merely cognitive subject together with its "contents of consciousness," but rather with a living practical subject — a subject that is essentially temporally finite and hence necessarily engaged with its historically given environmental situation. Assertion or judgment then appears as a "derivative mode of interpretation" in which the "hermeneutical 'as'" of practical understanding of the "ready-to-hand" (where an item "ready-to-hand" is understood "as" suited for a given end or purpose) is transformed into the "apophantical 'as'" of theoretical understanding of the "present-to-hand" (where an item "present-to-hand" is understood "as" determined by a given predicate). If we forget this derivative character, however, all the misunderstandings prevalent in "the presently dominant theory of 'judgment' oriented around the phenomenon of 'validity [*Geltung*]'" then arise. We end up, in particular, with Lotze's distinction between "being" and "validity." Since we begin, within this latter tradition, with a "Cartesian" subject entirely enclosed within the psychical realm of its own representations, we cannot explain truth as a relation between these representations and an object existing independently of them. Truth can therefore only mean what is constant and unchangeable in the flux of representations and is thus understood as "form" or "essence" in a quasi-Platonic sense standing over and against the realm of flux and change. We thereby arrive at the distinction between "being" and "validity," "real" and "ideal." And this distinction, by the "Copernican" conception of the object of knowledge, is now equated with the distinction between subjective and objective. Finally, since "objectivity" is thus equated with "validity" in the sense of atemporal or eternal "ideal being," "objectivity" is also equated with necessary *intersubjectivity:* with "bindingness" for all subjects.[45]

For Heidegger himself, by contrast, truth is in no way to be equated with "objectivity" in the sense of necessary and universal intersubjectivity. On the contrary, this most basic idea of the Kantian "Copernican Revolution" is definitively rejected in favor of a "direct realist" conception of truth as direct "disclosedness" to Dasein in a particular and irreducibly historical environmental situation: all truth is ultimately both particular and historical.[46] Indeed, to think otherwise is to refuse to acknowledge the essential particularity of an "authentic" decision in the face of "being-toward-death" and to seek refuge instead in the public everydayness of the "They."[47] In the end, therefore, it is Heidegger's radical transformation of the neo-Kantian tradition within which he was trained that underwrites his equally radical rejection of the priority and centrality of logic: his claim that the traditional theory of judgment based on the "is" of predication is itself necessarily derivative from a properly philosophical point of view.

•

We observed above that Carnap also received his philosophical training within the neo-Kantian tradition and, in fact, that he completed his doctoral dissertation in 1921 under Rickert's student Bruno Bauch — a dissertation in which Kantian themes predominate.[48] It was in the years immediately after finishing his dissertation, in 1922–25, that Carnap undertook most of the work on the project that was eventually to issue in *Der logische Aufbau der Welt* (Carnap 1963a, 16–19). And it was on this basis, moreover, that Carnap caught the attention of the "Philosophical Circle" that had gathered around Moritz Schlick at the University of Vienna. Carnap had become acquainted with Schlick in the summer of 1924 and was invited to give lectures to Schlick's circle in the winter of 1925. These lectures on the *Aufbau* project — which was at the time entitled "Entwurf einer Konstitutionstheorie der Erkenntnisgegenstände" (Outline of a constitutional theory of the objects of cognition) — were extremely well received: Carnap returned to Vienna as assistant professor, with his "Entwurf" (then being eagerly read within Schlick's circle) serving as his habilitation.[49] A revised version was finally published in 1928 under the now familiar title.

The aim of the *Aufbau*, as recent scholarship has made increasingly clear, is by no means exclusively to represent the point of view of phenomenalistic or extreme empiricist "positivism." Indeed, Carnap himself explains the relationship between "positivism" and neo-Kantianism as follows:

> Cassirer ([*Substanzbegr.*] 292ff.) has shown that a science having the goal of determining the individual through lawful interconnections [*Gesetzeszusammenhänge*] without its individuality being lost must apply, not class ("species") concepts, but rather *relational concepts;* for the latter can lead to the formation of series and thereby to the establishing of order-systems. It hereby also results that relations are necessary as first posits, since one can in fact easily make the transition from relations to classes, whereas the contrary procedure is only possible in a very limited measure.

> The merit of having discovered the necessary basis of the constitutional system thereby belongs to two entirely different, and often mutually hostile, philosophical tendencies. *Positivism* has stressed that the sole *material* for cognition lies in the undigested [*unverarbeitet*] experiential *given;* here is to be sought the *basic elements* of the constitutional system. *Transcendental idealism,* however, especially the neo-Kantian tendency (Rickert, Cassirer, Bauch), has rightly emphasized that these elements do not suffice: *order-posits* [*Ordnungssetzungen*] must be added, our "basic relations."[50]

Carnap does not intend simply to supplant neo-Kantianism by "positivism" in the *Aufbau:* he hopes, on the contrary, to retain the insights of *both* views.[51]

As Carnap suggests, the influence of Cassirer's *Substance and Function* is especially important to the *Aufbau*. This is not surprising, for the agreement between the two conceptions actually extends far beyond the emphasis on the significance of the modern logical theory of relations stressed here. According to *Substance and Function*, as indicated above, the theory of knowledge consists of two parts. On the one hand, we have the theory of the *concept* (part 1), which, for Cassirer, is given by the totality of pure relational structures provided by the new logic. On the other hand, however, we have the theory of *reality* (part 2), in which pure relational structures are successively applied in the methodological progress of mathematical natural science in such a way that a never completed — but convergent — sequence results. Thus, whereas pure mathematics is given by the collection of all pure or abstract relational structures, applied mathematics (mathematical physics) is given by an infinite methodological series of such structures. And it is this methodological series of abstract structures that, for Cassirer (and for the Marburg school more generally), represents the empirical side of knowledge given by "sensation." The concrete empirical world of sense-perception is not a separate reality existing somehow outside of this methodological series: it is simply the fully determinate and complete "limit theory" toward which this series is converging.

Now Carnap, in the *Aufbau,* also represents empirical knowledge by a serial or stepwise methodological sequence. This sequence is intended to represent, not so much the historical series of mathematical-physical successor theories, but rather the epistemological progress of a single individual or cognitive subject — in which its knowledge extends from the initial subjective sensory data belonging to the *autopsychological* realm, through the world of public external objects constituting the *physical* realm, and finally to the intersubjective and cultural realities belonging to the *heteropsychological* realm. Carnap's methodological series is thus a "rational reconstruction" intended formally to represent the "actual process of cognition."[52] For Carnap, as for Cassirer, we thereby represent the empirical side of knowledge by a methodological sequence of formal structures. For Carnap, however, this is not a sequence of historically given mathematical-physical successor theories but *a sequence of levels or ranks in the hierarchy of logical types* of Russell's and Whitehead's *Principia Mathematica* — a sequence of levels *ordered by type-theoretic definitions*. Objects on any level (other than the first) are thus defined as classes of objects (or relations between objects) from the preceding level.[53]

The construction or "constitution of reality" begins with "elementary experiences" — holistic momentary cross-sections of the stream of experience — ordered by a (holistically conceived) "basic relation" of remembrance-of-part-similarity-in-some-arbitrary-respect. The main formal problem within the autopsychological realm is then to differentiate — on this initially entirely holistic basis — the particular sense qualities and sense modalities from one another. After grouping elementary experiences into classes (and classes of classes ...) thereof via the one given basic relation and a complex procedure of "quasi-analysis," Carnap is in a position to define the *visual field* as the unique sense modality possessing exactly five dimensions (two of spatial location and three of color quality).[54] On this basis we can then define the "visual things" in the physical realm: after embedding the visual fields of our subject in a numerical space-time manifold ($\mathbf{R}^4$), we project colored points of these visual fields along "lines of sight" onto colored surfaces in such a way that principles of constancy and continuity are satisfied. And, in an analogous fashion, we can then define the "physical things" or objects of mathematical physics: we coordinate purely numerical "physical state magnitudes" with sensible qualities in accordance with the laws and methodological principles of the relevant science (e.g., the electro-dynamic theory of light and color).[55] Finally, we can constitute the heteropsychological realm by, first, constructing other subjects of experience analogous to the initial subject (that is, systems of elementary experiences coordinated to "other" human bodies) and, second, constructing an "intersubjective world" common to all such subjects through an abstraction (via an equivalence relation) from the resulting diversity in "points of view."[56]

In this way Carnap's "constitution of reality" achieves a "logicization" of experience or the sensible aspects of reality parallel to that of the Marburg school. For the entire point of Carnap's method of "purely structural definite descriptions" (like that of the visual field sketched above) is to individuate the objects in question in purely formal-logical terms, making no reference whatever to their intrinsic or ostensive phenomenal qualities. The constitutional system thereby demonstrates that objective — that is, intersubjectively communicable — knowledge is possible *despite* its necessary origin in purely subjective experience.[57] Carnap characterizes the resulting kinship between his constitutional system and the "logical idealism" of the Marburg school as follows:

> Constitutional theory and *transcendental idealism* agree in representing the following position: all objects of cognition are constituted (in idealistic language, are "generated in thought"); and, moreover, the constituted objects are only objects of cognition *qua* logical forms constructed in a determinate way. This holds ultimately also for the basic elements of the constitutional system. They are, to be sure, taken as basis as unanalyzed unities, but they are then furnished with various properties and analyzed into (quasi-)constituents (§116): first hereby, and thus also first as constituted objects, do they become objects of cognition properly speaking — and, indeed, objects of psychology.[58]

Indeed, there is one important respect in which Carnap's conception is even more radical than that of the Marburg school. Cassirer's *Substance and Function*, for example, retains an element of dualism between pure thought and empirical reality: the contrast between the pure relational structures of logic and mathematics, on the one hand, and the historical sequence of successor theories representing the methodological progress of empirical natural science, on the other. For Carnap, by contrast, empirical reality simply *is* a particular logical structure: a type-theoretic structure (representing the epistemological progress of an initial cognitive subject) erected on the basis of a single, primitive, nonlogical relation.[59]

The sense in which Carnap has here gone even further than the "logical idealism" of the Marburg school stands out especially clearly in §179 — entitled "The Task of Science." According to the Marburg school, as we have seen, the real individual object of empirical cognition is as a matter of fact never actually present in the methodological progress of science at all: this real empirical object remains always a never completed X toward which the methodological progress of science is converging. But Carnap, in §179, explicitly rejects this "genetic" view of knowledge:

> According to the conception of the Marburg school (cf. Natorp [*Grundlagen*] 18ff.), the object is the eternal X; its determination is an incompleteable task. In opposition to this it is to be noted that

> finitely many determinations suffice for the constitution of the object — and thus for its unambiguous description among the objects in general. Once such a description is set up the object is no longer an X, but rather something unambiguously determined — whose complete description then certainly still remains an incompleteable task.[60]

Carnap thus rejects the idea that the object of empirical knowledge, in contradistinction to the purely formal objects of mathematical knowledge, is to be conceived as a never-ending, necessarily incompleteable progression.[61] For Carnap, all objects whatsoever — whether formal or empirical, ideal or real — are rather to be defined or "constituted" at *definite finite ranks* within the hierarchy of logical types: there are no objects in the constitutional system that remain necessarily incomplete.[62]

In this sense Carnap completes the "logicization" of experience that the Marburg school had begun and, at the same time, arrives at an even more radical transformation of the Marburg tradition. For in the constitutional system of the *Aufbau*, epistemology is transformed into a logical-mathematical constructive project: the purely formal project of actually writing down the required structural definite descriptions within the logic of *Principia Mathematica*. This purely formal exercise is to serve, in particular, as a *replacement* for traditional epistemology in which we represent the "neutral basis" common to all traditional epistemological schools. All such schools are in agreement, according to Carnap, that

> cognition traces back finally to my experiences, which are set in relation, connected, and worked up; thus cognition can attain in a logical progress to the various structures of my consciousness, then to the physical objects, further with their help to the structures of consciousness of other subjects and thus to the heteropsychological, and through the mediation of the heteropsychological to the cultural objects. (Carnap 1928a, §178)

Since the constitutional system precisely represents this common ground of agreement within the neutral and uncontroversial domain of formal logic itself, all "metaphysical" disputes among the competing schools — disputes, for example, among "positivism," "realism," and "idealism" concerning which constituted structures are ultimately "real" — are thereby dissolved.[63] The fruitless disputes of the epistemological tradition are replaced by the seriousness and sobriety of the new mathematical logic, and philosophy (once again) becomes a science: for Carnap, a purely technical subject.[64]

By precisely representing some of the central ideas comprising the "logical idealism" of the Marburg school within the new mathematical logic of *Principia Mathematica*, Carnap has thereby injected the *neue Sachlichkeit* into philosophy itself. Philosophy becomes, in particular, an "objective" discipline capable (like the exact sciences) of cooperative progress and, in principle, of universal agreement as well; indeed, it has now become a branch of mathematical logic — the most "objective" and universal discipline of all. We have thus arrived at a conception of philosophy that, in Carnap's eyes, best serves the socialist, internationalist, and anti-individualistic aims of that cultural and political movement with which he most closely identifies.[65] And this "objectivist" and universalist conception of philosophy (based on the new mathematical logic) of course stands in the most extreme contrast with the particularist, existential-historical conception of philosophy we have seen Heidegger develop (based on an explicit rejection of the centrality of logic) — a conception that, in Heidegger's eyes, best serves the neoconservative and avowedly German nationalist cultural and political stance favored by the latter philosopher.[66] But what is of most interest, from our present point of view, is the extent to which both philosophers develop their radically new conceptions of philosophy by rigorously thinking through the ideas of late nineteenth- and early twentieth-century neo-Kantianism. By pushing these neo-Kantian ideas to their limits in two opposite directions, as it were, Carnap and Heidegger thereby contribute decisively toward defining and shaping the contemporary opposition between "analytic" and "continental" philosophical traditions with which we began.

Notes

I am indebted for helpful discussions and advice to Sandra Bartky, Susan Cunningham, Graciela De Pierris, Lynn Joy, Theodore Kisiel, Alison Laywine, Alan Richardson, Werner Sauer, Thomas Uebel, and Kathleen Wright. All translations from the German are my own.

1. For eyewitness accounts see the report of L. Englert in Schneeberger 1962, 1–6; Pos 1949; and T. Cassirer 1981 — relevant parts of which are reprinted in Schneeberger 1962, 7–9.

2. Heidegger 1929a. This work appears in Heidegger 1991 together with appendices containing Heidegger's notes for his Davos lectures and a protocol of the Cassirer-Heidegger debate prepared by O. Bollnow and J. Ritter. These materials are also found in the English translation of Heidegger 1929a.

3. I am indebted to Thomas Uebel for first calling my attention to the fact that Carnap attended the Cassirer-Heidegger lectures and debate at Davos. Carnap reports on the occasion in ASP 025-73-03, entries from 18 March through 5 April 1929.

4. Heinrich Gomperz, the son of the famous historian of Greek philosophy Theodore Gomperz, was a professor of philosophy at the University of Vienna and the author of *Weltanschauungslehre* (1905). Karl Bühler was an important psychologist and psycholinguist; he founded the Psychological Institute at the University of Vienna in 1922. For Carnap's participation see ASP 025-73-03, entries for 24 May and 14 June 1930.

5. The two versions of these lectures, including reports on the discussions, are ASP 110-07-21 and ASP 110-07-19, respectively. I am indebted to Brigitte Uhlemann of the University of Konstanz for providing me with transcriptions from Carnap's shorthand.

6. Heidegger 1929b, 14, 18 [107, 111–12]. Carnap quotes selections from these passages in Carnap 1932, 231–32 [71–72]. (Pagination of the English translations appears in brackets.)

7. Carnap 1963c, 874–75. On the following page Carnap continues: "I think, however, that our [antimetaphysical] principle excludes not only a great number of assertions in systems like those of Hegel and Heidegger, especially since the latter says explicitly that logic is not applicable to statements in metaphysics, but also in contemporary discussions, for example, those concerning the reality of space or of time." Compare the remarks in Carnap 1963a, 42–43: "It is encouraging to remember that philosophical thinking has made great progress in the course of two thousand years through the work of men like Aristotle, Leibniz, Hume, Kant, Dewey, Russell, and many others, who were basically thinking in a scientific way."

8. See ASP 025-73-03, entry for 26 May 1928: "In the evening with Waismann at Neurath's, I read the Preface to the 'Logischen Aufbau' aloud: Neurath is astonished and overjoyed at my open confession. He believes that it will affect young people very sympathetically. I say that I still want to ask Schlick whether it is too radical." (Schlick did indeed think it was too radical: see entry for 31 May.)

9. Carnap became attracted to the antimilitarist internationalism of the "socialist worker's movement" already during the Great War (Carnap 1963a, 9–10).

10. For a general cultural and political history of this orientation see Willett 1978. For a specific discussion of the relationship between the Vienna Circle and the Dessau Bauhaus see Galison 1990. Not all members of the Vienna Circle shared in this orientation, however. Schlick, in particular, was attracted neither to Marxism nor to anti-individualism more generally. Thus, for example, Feigl poignantly describes Schlick's reaction when he was presented with the manifesto (Hahn, Neurath, and Carnap 1929) — which calls for a new internationalist and collaborative form of philosophy and, in keeping with this spirit, is not even signed by its authors — on his return from Stanford in 1929: "Schlick was moved by our amicable intentions; but as I could tell from his facial expression, and from what he told me later, he was actually appalled and dismayed by the thought that we were propagating our views as a 'system' or 'movement.' He was deeply committed to an individualistic conception of philosophizing, and while he considered group discussion and mutual criticism to be greatly helpful and intellectually profitable, he believed that everyone should think creatively for himself. A 'movement,' like large scale meetings or conferences, was something he loathed" (Feigl 1969, 646).

11. The literature on Heidegger's own political involvement is now enormous. See, in particular, Ott 1988; Farias 1987; and Schneeberger 1962. Wolin 1991 is a very useful selection — including a translation of Heidegger's notorious *Die Selbstbehauptung der deutschen Universität*, delivered in celebration of the new Nazi regime when he assumed the rectorate at Freiburg in May 1933. A particularly interesting contribution, locating Heidegger's involvement in the context of that of the other German philosophers of the time, is Sluga 1993.

12. Carnap 1932e, 238 [77]. Compare also the preface to *Logical Syntax of Language*, dated May 1934: "In our 'Vienna Circle' and in many similarly oriented groups (in Poland, France, England, USA and *in isolated cases even in Germany*) the view has currently grown stronger and stronger that traditional metaphysical philosophy can make no claim to scientific status" (Carnap 1934b, iii [xiii]; emphasis added). For Carnap's view (from Prague) of the situation in Germany and Central Europe in 1934 see Carnap 1963a, 34: "With the beginning of the Hitler regime in Germany in 1933, the political atmosphere, even in Austria and Czechoslovakia, became more and more intolerable.... [T]he Nazi ideology spread more and more among the German-speaking population of the Sudeten region and therewith among the students of our university and even among some of the professors."

13. In ASP 025-73-03, entry for 5 July 1932, Carnap triumphantly records the fact that there were 250 people in the audience at Berlin.

14. Neurath 1932a (reprinted in Neurath 1981, 572–73). Orthmar Spann was an especially virulent Austrian-Catholic right-wing ideologue of the time.

15. See, e.g., Neurath's remarks (made in 1933) in Neurath 1981, 597n: "Here [in Austria] there is not an exclusive dominance by metaphysics as it is practiced by Rickert, Heidegger, and others — through which those of a new generation become well-known through *geisteswissenschaftlicher Psychologie, geisteswissenschaftlicher Soziologie* and similar things." Compare Carnap's remarks on Neurath's commitment to physicalism, unified science, and Marxism in Carnap 1963a, 22–24.

16. Compare also the following retrospective remarks of Neurath's (made in 1936): "The strong metaphysical trends in Central Europe are probably the reason that within the Vienna Circle the antimetaphysical attitude became of central significance and was purposefully practiced — much more, for example, than would have been the case with the adherents of similar tendencies in the United States, among whom a particular, more neutral common-sense empiricism is very widespread and where metaphysics could not exert the influence that it did in Germany, say.... It is entirely understandable that a Frenchman is at first surprised when he hears how the adherents of the Vienna Circle distance themselves in sharp terms from 'philosophers' — he thinks perhaps of Descartes and Comte in this connection, the others however of Fichte and Heidegger" (Neurath 1981, 743).

17. As is well known, *Introduction to Metaphysics* depicts Germany as Europe's last hope for salvation from Russian communism, on the one side, and American technological democracy, on the other, and contains Heidegger's notorious remark about the "inner truth and greatness" of the National Socialist movement (Heidegger 1953, 152 [166]).

18. I am indebted to Kathleen Wright for first calling my attention to this passage. As Wright also first pointed out to me, the noted Heidegger scholar Otto Pöggeler comments on *Introduction to Metaphysics* as follows: "Heidegger had sufficient taste not to deliver a previous version of his lecture in which Carnap's emigration to America was put forth as confirmation of the convergence between Russian communism and the 'type of thinking in America'" (quoted from Wolin 1991, 218–19). Given that Carnap did not emigrate until December 1935, however, whereas Heidegger's lectures were held in the summer of that year, Heidegger cannot be here referring to Carnap's emigration. It is more likely, for example, that he is referring to Schlick's trip to Stanford in 1929, which is prominently mentioned in the foreword to Hahn, Neurath, and Carnap 1929. The remark about Russian communism, on the other hand, almost certainly refers to Neurath's activities.

19. The dissertation appeared as Carnap 1922. Carnap defends a modified version of the Kantian synthetic a priori according to which the topological — but not the metrical — properties of space are due to the form of our spatial intuition. Bauch was influenced not only by his teacher Rickert but also by the more scientifically oriented neo-Kantianism

of the Marburg school — as well as by his colleague at Jena, the logician Gottlob Frege (who also greatly influenced Carnap, of course). Some discussion of Bauch in relation to both Frege and Carnap can be found in Sluga 1980. Sluga (1993) explains the depth and centrality of Bauch's involvement with Nazism — in comparison with which Heidegger's own engagement somewhat pales. Curiously, Carnap himself never mentions Bauch's political involvement.

20. Carnap explains his neo-Kantian philosophical training in Carnap 1963a, 4, 11–12. Writings of Cassirer, Natorp, and Rickert (as well as Bauch) play an important role in the *Aufbau:* see Carnap 1928a, §§5, 12, 64, 65, 75, 162, 163, 179.

21. Some of the most important epistemological works of the two traditions are Cohen 1902; Natorp 1910; E. Cassirer 1910; and Rickert 1892. Rickert 1909 and Natorp 1912 are very useful summary presentations of the two traditions.

22. See Husserl 1900–1901. For Husserl and the neo-Kantians see, for example, Natorp 1912, 198; and Rickert 1909, 227. Husserl's notion of *Wesenserschauung* plays a central role in Carnap's conception of "intuitive space" in Carnap 1922. All of Heidegger's earliest works fall squarely within the antipsychologistic tradition of "pure logic" and, accordingly, are dominated by the thought of Rickert and Husserl: these include "Neure Forschungen über Logik" (1912), his doctoral dissertation *Die Lehre vom Urteil im Psychologismus* (1913–14), and his habilitation *Die Kategorien- und Bedeutungslehre des Duns Scotus* (1915–16) — all of which are reprinted in Heidegger 1978. There is, of course, a close relationship between this "pure logic" tradition and the work of Frege: indeed, as is well known, it was Frege's review of Husserl's earlier *Philosophie der Arithmetik* that inspired the antipsychologistic polemic of the *Logical Investigations*. It is interesting to note also that Heidegger comments very favorably on Frege's work in his "Neure Forschungen über Logik" (Heidegger 1978, 20).

23. This "genetic" view of the object of empirical knowledge is common to Cohen, Natorp, and Cassirer. It is articulated with particular force by Natorp (in the works cited in note 21 above). Cassirer's achievement, in *Substance and Function*, is to make the view precise by finally articulating a coherent conception of logic (as the theory of arbitrary relational structures) — something that had eluded both Cohen and Natorp. Thus, for example, whereas Cohen and Natorp self-consciously attempt to align logic more closely with mathematics, they still continue to make essential use of the traditional classification of the forms of judgment.

24. Natorp (1912) then replies to Rickert's criticism. E. Cassirer (1929, 406 [348]) brings out the issue between Rickert and the Marburg school here with particular clarity: "Rickert's proof-procedure, in so far as it is simply supposed to verify this proposition [that number is not derivable from identity and difference], could have been essentially simplified and sharpened if he had availed himself of the tools of the modern logical calculus, especially the calculus of relations. For *identity* and *difference* are, expressed in the language of this calculus, *symmetrical* relations; whereas for the construction of the number series, as for the concept of an ordered sequence in general, an *asymmetrical* relation is indispensable."

25. Here Lask cites, among others, the theories of Herbart, Bolzano, Husserl, Rickert, Meinong, and (Heinrich) Gomperz (see Lask 1912, 23–24). Note that what Lask calls "formal logic" coincides with what Rickert calls "transcendental logic."

26. Lask (1912, 55) writes: "The 'form' of judgment, concept, inference, etc. is a completely different thing from form in the sense of the category. One best distinguishes these two kinds of form as structural form and contentful form." Kant's metaphysical deduction, by contrast, rests entirely on the idea that "the same understanding, through precisely

the same action whereby it brought about the logical form of a judgment by means of analytic unity, also brings about, by means of synthetic unity, a transcendental content in its representations in virtue of which they are called pure concepts of the understanding" (A79/B195).

27. For a discussion of Lask's argument from the point of view of the Marburg school see E. Cassirer 1913, 6–14. I am indebted to Werner Sauer for first calling my attention to this essay and for emphasizing to me, in this connection especially, the crucially important differences between Cassirer and the Southwest school.

28. The reference is to Lotze 1874, §§316–20. See, for example, Heidegger 1978, 170.

29. See Heidegger 1978, 214–89. As Heidegger notes, his discussion here is based on Rickert 1911.

30. Heidegger 1978, 273. The realm of valid sense enjoys this primacy because *all* realms of existence as such (the natural, the metaphysical-theological, the mathematical, and the logical itself) become objects of our cognition only through the mediation of the logical (Heidegger 1978, 287).

31. Heidegger's judgment of the superiority of Lask over Rickert emerges already in his dissertation of 1913–14 (Heidegger 1978, 176–77n).

32. Heidegger spent the years 1923–28 as associate professor at Marburg, after serving as Husserl's assistant at Freiburg from 1916 through 1922. It was at Marburg, through his lectures, that Heidegger established a reputation as one of the most brilliant and exciting young philosophers in Germany even before the appearance of *Being and Time*. The Marburg lectures in question appear as Heidegger 1979 and Heidegger 1976, respectively. To be sure, Husserl's own overcoming of neo-Kantianism is by no means complete from Heidegger's point of view — a point to which we shall return below.

33. Husserl's discussion of truth as "identification" occurs in Husserl 1900–1901, vol. 2, §§36–39. The discussion of "categorial intuition" then follows in §§40–58. For Heidegger's assessment of the relationship between these ideas and the work of Lask — which Heidegger sees as together destroying once and for all the Kantian "mythology" of a synthesis of understanding and sensibility, form and matter — see Heidegger 1979, 63–90.

34. When Husserl speaks of the realm of the logical and asks after an "epistemology of the logical" he has in mind the entire realm of a priori "essences" accessible to *Wesensanalyse* and *Wesenserschauung* (which include, for example, the a priori "essences" of spatial phenomena studied by geometry, of color phenomena studied by the a priori "eidetic science" of color, and so on). The very special structures studied by formal logic properly so-called (subject and predicate, and so on) represent, as we have just seen, only a tiny fraction — the most abstract part — of this "essential" realm.

35. This idea of phenomenology as a pure or "transcendental" psychology becomes fully explicit only in Husserl 1911; it is developed in elaborate detail in Husserl 1913. In the first edition of volume 2 of the *Logical Investigations* Husserl had misleadingly characterized phenomenology as "descriptive psychology" — which, as he himself immediately recognized, concealed precisely the "transcendental" relation in which he intended phenomenology to stand to (empirical) psychology. See Husserl 1911, 318n [115–16n].

36. See Heidegger 1978, 341–411. Heidegger there links his conception of "subjective logic" with the problem of the application of the categories on p. 407: "If anywhere, then precisely in connection with the problem of the *application* of the categories — insofar as one admits this in general as a *possible* problem — the *merely* objective-logical treatment of the problem of the categories must be recognized as one-sided." The attached footnote then emphasizes the importance of Lask 1912. For Husserl himself, on the other hand, since he developed the idea of phenomenology entirely independent of the Kantian and

neo-Kantian traditions, this problem of the application of the categories was never a problem. Husserl's own problem was always rather the relationship between the logical and the psychological — a problem that need not involve the relationship in general between the abstract and the concrete.

37. For Heidegger's assessment of Dilthey's conception of the subject as "living person with an understanding of active history" in contrast to Husserl's more formal conception of the subject, see Heidegger 1979, 161–71. The influence of Dilthey is further exhibited in 1916 in Heidegger's preface to his habilitation, with its call for philosophy to become *weltanschaulich* — that is, engaged in the concrete historical events of the time (Heidegger 1978, 191; and cf. 205 n. 10). This call contrasts sharply with Husserl's own arguments (in Husserl 1911, 323–41 [122–47]) — contra Dilthey — that philosophy *as a science* must be eternally valid and thus essentially unhistorical. It seems clear, moreover, from the remarks on Emil Lask's "distant soldier's grave," that Heidegger's call for a *weltanschaulich* philosophy here is directly connected with his attitude toward the Great War.

38. The idea of "being-in-the-world," together with the idea that the theoretical orientation toward the "present-at-hand" is founded on the more basic practical orientation toward the "ready-to-hand," is presented in Heidegger 1927, §§12–13 and is then developed in detail in the remainder of division 1.

39. For "Care as the Being of Dasein," see Heidegger 1927, §§39–44; for "Temporality as the Ontological Meaning of Care," see §§61–66; for "Temporality and Historicality" see §§72–77. In developing this conception of the essential "historicality [*Geschichtlichkeit*] of Dasein," Heidegger is, as emphasized in note 36 above, self-consciously following the work of Dilthey — work that he explicitly opposes to the "superficial" and "merely methodological" attempt to distinguish the *Geisteswissenschaften* from the *Naturwissenschaften* (based on the distinction between "generalizing" and "individuating" modes of concept formation) developed within the school of Windelband and Rickert. See the comments on Rickert in Heidegger 1927, §72, and compare the polemic called "Die Trivialisierung der Diltheyschen Fragestellung durch Windelband und Rickert" presented in Heidegger 1979, 20–21.

40. The analysis of "being-toward-death" and the ensuing possibility of "authentic" existence are presented in Heidegger 1927, §§46–60 — an analysis that is intended to present the "being of Dasein" (which was presented only fragmentarily, as it were, in the preceding sections) for the first time as a unitary and unified whole.

41. For the priority of "existence" over "essence" in the analytic of Dasein, see Heidegger 1927, §9. For Heidegger's diagnosis of the failure of Husserlian phenomenology as resting on a neglect of the question of the *existence* of "pure consciousness," see Heidegger 1979, 148–57, in particular 152: "Above all, however, this conception of ideation [that is, *Wesenserschauung*] as abstraction from real individuation rests on the belief that the What of any being is to be determined in abstraction from its existence. If, however, there were beings *whose What is precisely to exist and nothing but to exist*, then this ideational mode of consideration with respect to such a being would be the most fundamental misunderstanding."

42. The footnote to Heidegger 1927, §44 (p. 218), refers us to the sections on truth and "categorial intuition" in volume 2 of the *Logical Investigations* discussed above, along with the work of Lask. Heidegger warns us against relying exclusively on the first volume of the *Logical Investigations*, which appears merely to represent the traditional theory of the proposition (in itself) derived from Bolzano.

43. See Heidegger 1927, §44 (p. 221): "Dasein *can* understand *itself* as understanding from the side of the 'world' and the other or from the side of its ownmost

possibility-for-being [*aus seinem eigensten Seinkönnen*]. The last-mentioned possibility means: Dasein discloses itself to itself in and as its ownmost possibility-for-being. This *authentic* disclosedness shows the phenomenon of the most original truth in the mode of its authenticity. The most original and authentic disclosedness in which Dasein as possibility-for-being can be, is the *truth of existence*."

44. The temporality of "authentic" existence is articulated in Heidegger 1927, §§61–66, the temporality of everyday "inauthentic" existence in §§67–71, the temporality of "historicality" in §§72–77. How the temporality of Dasein is actually the prior ground of the "ordinary conception of time" (namely, the all-embracing public time within which events are dated and ordered) is explained in §§78–81.

45. See Heidegger 1927, §33, "Die Aussage als abkünftiger Modus der Auslegung," and compare the discussion of Lotze's theory of "validity" in Heidegger's lecture course on logic from 1925–26 (Heidegger 1976, 62–68). This discussion clarifies the relationship Heidegger perceives between the "Cartesian" predicament of the world-less subject enclosed within its own contents of consciousness and the "Husserlian" predicament of the ideal subject isolated from all questions of real existence. In Husserlian terminology, it clarifies the relationship between the "phenomenological" reduction that withdraws our attention from the external world and focuses on the contents of consciousness themselves and the more radical "eidetic" reduction that then focuses only on the "essence" or formal structure of these conscious phenomena — arriving, in the end, at "pure" or "absolute" consciousness. Heidegger's idea is that if we once start with the "Cartesian" predicament, but nonetheless demand a kind of objectivity, then all we have left, as it were, is the contrast between change and constancy, the real and the ideal. We thus arrive at a conception of truth or objectivity on which truth is fundamentally necessary, "essential," or eternal truth; and, in this way, the denial of "naive realism" leads to "essentialism." And it is this last form of "essentialism" that is Heidegger's ultimate target.

46. Thus Heidegger 1927, §44 contains such provocative assertions as, "Before Newton's laws were uncovered they were not 'true' "; and "[these] laws became true through Newton, with him a being became accessible in itself for Dasein" (226–27). Given Heidegger's fundamentally historical conception of truth, together with his "existential conception of science" (§69, pp. 362–64), the meaning of these assertions is relatively straightforward: Newton arrived at the laws of motion by means of an "authentic projection" of a particular scientific framework in a given historical situation — the context of the scientific revolution of the sixteenth and seventeenth centuries (cf. §3, pp. 9–10, on "scientific revolutions"). Outside of this historical context, on the other hand, Newton's "discovery" and accompanying "assertion" of the laws of motion simply make no sense. For Heidegger, there is then no "valid sense" or "proposition in itself" beyond Newton's (and our) actual historical "assertions" capable of serving as a "vehicle" of "eternal truth." Nevertheless, *what* Newton discovered of course existed before Newton: "With the uncoveredness the being showed itself precisely as that being that was already there before. So to uncover is the mode of being of 'truth' " (p. 227).

47. See the remarks on the "objectivity [*Objektivität*]" of authentically historical truth in Heidegger 1927, §76, p. 395: "In no science are the 'universal validity' of standards and the pretensions to 'universality' that the They and its common sense require *less* possible criteria of 'truth' than in authentic history."

48. See n. 19 above.

49. Carnap 1963a, 20–22. An outline of Carnap's lecture to the Circle on 21 January 1925, bearing the title "Gedanken zum Kategorien Problem: Prolegomena zu einer Konstitutionstheorie," appears as ASP 081-05-03. The "Entwurf" manuscript has not yet been

found. A table of contents, bearing the dates 17 December 1924 and 28 January 1925 (a revision after the lecture in Vienna), appears as ASP 081-05-02.

50. Carnap 1928a, §75. The passage from Cassirer's *Substance and Function* to which Carnap is here referring (E. Cassirer 1910, chap. 4, §9) is a criticism of Rickert's well-known argument that concepts in the *Naturwissenschaften* cannot individuate (cf. note 39 above). Cassirer diagnoses Rickert's error here as stemming from a neglect of the essentially relational mode of concept formation of modern mathematics and logic. Carnap (1928a, §12) points out, again referring to this discussion of Cassirer's (and also to Rickert, Windelband, and Dilthey), that the "logic of individuality" desired in the *Geisteswissenschaften* can be attained precisely in the modern theory of relations.

51. For recent work on Kantian and neo-Kantian aspects of the *Aufbau*, see, for example Haack 1977; Moulines 1985; and Sauer 1985, 1989 (which particularly stress the importance of Cassirer and the passage from Carnap 1928a, §75); Friedman 1987, 1992b, and Richardson 1992b (which also emphasizes the importance of Cassirer and the Marburg school); and Webb 1992. Two recent extended treatments of the development of logical positivism, Coffa 1991 and Proust 1986, are also worth consulting in this connection.

52. See Carnap 1928a, §§100, 143. Cf. the remarks in Carnap 1963a, 18: "The system [of the *Aufbau*] was intended to give, though not a description, still a rational reconstruction of the actual process of the formation of concepts."

53. See especially the discussion of "ascension forms [*Stufenformen*]" in Carnap 1928a, pt. 3.B. There are exactly two such "ascension forms", namely, class and relation extensions (§40). As Carnap (1963a, 11) explains, he first studied *Principia Mathematica* — whose type-theoretic conception of logic pervades the *Aufbau* — in 1919.

54. See Carnap 1928a, pt. 4.A. and cf. §§67–94. The procedure of "quasi-analysis" is a generalization (to nontransitive relations) of the "principle of abstraction" employed by Frege and Russell in the definition of a cardinal number (see §73).

55. See Carnap 1928a, pt. 4.B. for the constitution of the physical realm — including the qualitative realm of ordinary sense-perception (§§125–35) and then the quantitative realm of mathematical physics (§136). As Carnap makes clear in §136, the constitution of the latter realm is based on his earlier methodological studies (Carnap 1923, 1924).

56. See Carnap 1928a, pt. 4.C. According to Carnap, *only* the purely abstract world of physics — and not the qualitative world of commonsense perceptual experience — "provides the possibility of a unique, consistent intersubjectivization" (§136; cf. §133).

57. For the independence of the definition of the visual field, in particular, from all phenomenal qualities, see Carnap 1928a, §86. For the importance of purely structural definite descriptions, see pt. 2.A. especially §16: "*[E]very scientific statement can in principle be so transformed that it is only a structural statement.* But this transformation is not only possible, but required. For science wants to speak about the objective; however, everything that does not belong to structure but to the material, everything that is ostended concretely, is in the end subjective." "From the point of view of constitutional theory this state of affairs is to be expressed in the following way. The series of experiences is different for each subject. If we aim, in spite of this, at agreement in the names given for the objects [*Gebilde*] constituted on the basis of the experiences, then this cannot occur through reference to the completely diverging material but only through the formal indicators of the object-structures [*Gebildestrukturen*]." For a fuller discussion, as well as detailed arguments against an empiricist-phenomenalist interpretation of Carnap's motivations, see my articles cited in note 51 above.

58. Carnap 1928a, §177. Section 116 presents the actual constitution of *sensations* —

78   *Michael Friedman*

defined via a purely structural definite description containing only the basic relation as a nonlogical primitive.

59. Carnap's type-theoretic sequential construction therefore takes the place of the "general serial form" Cassirer sees as expressing the essence of empirical knowledge. Carnap agrees with Cassirer, however, that this kind of methodological sequence is the ultimate "datum" for epistemology and, in particular, that the contrast between "being" and "validity" — which, as we have seen, generates fundamental problems for the Southwest school — therefore has only a *relativized* meaning in the context of such a sequence (see Carnap 1928a, §42; and cf. E. Cassirer 1910, 412–13 [311]). In Friedman 1992b, §3, I mistakenly read §42 as a *criticism* of the Marburg school and, in general, failed to draw the crucial distinction between the Marburg view of this question and that of the Southwest school. I am indebted to Alan Richardson and Werner Sauer for rightly protesting against this assimilation (cf. nn. 27 and 51 above).

60. The reference is to Natorp 1910, chap. 1, §§4–6; cf. E. Cassirer 1910, chap 7, especially 418–19 [315]. I am indebted to Alison Laywine for emphasizing to me the importance of this aspect of Natorp's view in the present connection.

61. Cf. E. Cassirer 1910, 337 [254]: "In contrast to the mathematical concept, however, [in empirical science] the characteristic difference emerges that the construction [*Aufbau*], which within mathematics arrives at a fixed end, remains in principle *incompleteable* within experience."

62. It is worth noting, in this connection, that the well-known technical problems afflicting the constitution of the physical or external world in the *Aufbau* appear in fact to undermine Carnap's attempt to distinguish himself from the Marburg school here. It appears, in particular, that Carnap's rules for assigning colors to points of space-time ($\mathbf{R}^+$) never close off at a definite set (that is, a definite relation between space-time points and colors) located at a definite rank in the hierarchy of logical types: for this assignment is to be continually revised as we progress to higher and higher ranks (Carnap 1928a, §§135, 136, 144). And this means, from the point of view of Carnap's own constitutional system, that the Marburg doctrine of the never completed X appears after all to be fully correct — at least so far as physical (and hence all higher-level) objects are concerned.

63. See again Carnap 1928a, §178: "*[T]he so-called epistemological tendencies of realism, idealism, and phenomenalism agree within the domain of epistemology. Constitutional theory presents the neutral basis* [neutrale Fundament] *common to all. They first diverge in the domain of metaphysics and thus (if they are to be epistemological tendencies) only as the result of a transgression of their boundaries.*" All other properly philosophical disputes are similarly dissolved. Thus, for example, both sides in the debate over the relationship between the *Geisteswissenschaften* and the *Naturwissenschaft* are correct: cultural objects are constructed out of heteropsychological objects and the latter, in turn, out of physical objects; in this sense the theses of physicalism and the unity of science are correct. On the other hand, however, cultural objects nonetheless belong to a distinct "object sphere" in the type-theoretic hierarchy; in this sense the thesis of the autonomy and independence of the cultural realm is equally correct. See §56 and also §§25, 29, 41, 151. Cf. nn. 15, 39, and 50 above.

64. See the (first edition) preface to Carnap 1928a: "The new type of philosophy has arisen in close contact with work in the special sciences, especially in mathematics and physics. This has the consequence that we strive to make the rigorous and responsible basic attitude of scientific researchers also the basic attitude of workers in philosophy, whereas the attitude of the old type of philosophers is more similar to a poetic [attitude].... [T]he individual no longer undertakes to arrive at an entire structure of philosophy by a [single] bold stroke. Instead, each works in his specific place within

the *single* total science." Cf. also the discussion in Carnap 1963a, 13, on the impact of reading Bertrand Russell's *Our Knowledge of the External World* in 1921: Carnap is most impressed by Russell's description of "the logical-analytic method of philosophy" — together with its accompanying call for a new "scientific" philosophical practice.

65. In this respect, Carnap's identification with the *neue Sachlichkeit* is even more radical than Neurath's. For Neurath, unlike Carnap, makes no attempt to turn philosophy itself into an "objective" — purely technical — discipline. See the remarks on Neurath in Carnap 1963a, 22–24, 51–52, and cf. Uebel 1996 for an illuminating discussion of the relationship between Neurath's philosophy and his politics. This significant difference between Carnap and Neurath seems to be missed in the otherwise quite useful discussion of the relationship between the Vienna Circle and the *neue Sachlichkeit* in Galison 1990, which generally ignores the important areas of disagreement between the two philosophers.

66. Heidegger himself is perfectly explicit about the connection between his political engagement and his philosophical conception of the necessary "historicality of Dasein" in a well-known conversation (in 1936) reported by Karl Löwith (Wolin 1991, 142). Curiously, this crucial connection seems to be missed in Bourdieu 1988, an otherwise very interesting study of the relationship between Heidegger's philosophy and German neoconservatism.

Logic and the Inexpressible in Frege and Heidegger

EDWARD WITHERSPOON*

FREGE AND HEIDEGGER LIE SO FAR APART on the philosophical spectrum that any suggestion that we might profitably discuss them together is apt to seem implausible. Frege's philosophical project is to clarify the foundations of mathematics; this leads him to a logical investigation in the course of which he invents most of the apparatus of modern symbolic logic. Heidegger embarks on a more general project, the elucidation of Being itself, which he approaches via an investigation of human life (and, famously, death). The projects and methods of the two philosophers are so different that there is no obvious arena for a fruitful dialogue between them. Indeed, it is fairly safe to suppose that each would have regarded the other's work as alien to his own: Frege would likely have regarded Heidegger's "existential analytic of Dasein" as a work of anthropology and social psychology that is of dubious relevance to philosophical questions, while Heidegger seems to have regarded the introduction of symbolic logic into philosophy as an attempt to reduce all thought to mere "calculation" and to avoid what Heidegger calls "essential thinking."[1]

The differences between Heidegger and Frege can seem to be crystallized in their attitudes toward logic. For Frege, logic is the most general science—a science whose task is to articulate the principles that govern any investigation whatsoever. By contrast, it appears that Heidegger wants to displace and dismantle logic in favor of a more fundamental kind of investigation:

---

[1] Martin Heidegger, "Postscript" to "What is Metaphysics?", Joan Stambaugh, trans., in Walter Kaufmann, ed., *Existentialism from Doestoevsky to Sartre*, rev. ed. (New York: Meridian, 1989), 262. In this context it should be noted that Heidegger has nothing against symbolic logic so long as it remains in what he regards as its proper place. An indication of this is the admiration for Frege's "On Concept and Object" and "On Sense and Meaning" that Heidegger expresses in his early "Neuere Forschungen über Logik," in his *Gesamtausgabe*, vol. 1, *Frühe Schriften* (Frankfurt a. M.: Klostermann, 1978), 20.

---

* **Edward Witherspoon** is Assistant Professor of Philosophy and Religion at Colgate University.

Journal of the History of Philosophy vol. 40, no. 1 (2002) 89–113

[T]he destiny of the reign of "logic" (i.e., the *traditional* interpretation of thinking) in philosophy is . . . decided. The idea of "logic" itself disintegrates in the turbulence of a more originary questioning.[1]

Heidegger seems to believe that this more fundamental investigation, which he calls "metaphysics," will be hampered by a rigid adherence to logical principles. Frege surely would have rejected Heidegger's idea of an investigation that is more fundamental than logic, and he would have regarded any attempt to pursue "metaphysics" (or any other investigation) without respecting the laws of logic as deeply confused.

Given the differences between Frege and Heidegger, how could the thought of one possibly throw light on that of the other? I will argue that despite their seemingly stark differences on the status of logic in philosophy, they both find that, in the course of analyzing thought and thinking, they are forced to engage in reflection that lies outside the bounds of logic. For each philosopher finds himself in possession of an insight that by his own lights cannot properly be stated. Moreover, this inexpressibility is in each case a consequence of the insight itself; in grasping the insight one sees why it cannot be expressed. Each philosopher considers it crucial to somehow convey his insight to his audience, despite its inexpressibility. Both Frege and Heidegger recognize the difficulty of conveying what is inexpressible, and they attempt to resolve this difficulty in ways that turn out to be deeply similar. By considering them together and recognizing these similarities, we can come to notice and understand aspects of their respective positions that have been missed by those who look at them separately.

My paper falls into three major parts, whose respective topics are Heidegger, Frege, and the parallels between them. My discussion of Heidegger emphasizes his treatment of "the Nothing" in *Being and Time* and in the lecture "What is Metaphysics?". A central concern of these works is to show that an understanding of the world as a whole is a condition for the possibility of making assertions or having thoughts about objects; I argue that when Heidegger makes remarks about "the Nothing"—remarks that have been criticized as illogical by many analytic philosophers—he is attempting to draw our attention to the logical difficulties inherent in his discussion of the world as a whole. Although he himself recognizes that his utterances are logically defective, he thinks that they can nevertheless convey his metaphysical insights to his readers.

My discussion of Frege focuses on his explication of the elements of a judgment whose content is a simple predication. He argues that in reflecting on the structure of such a thought it is absolutely essential to distinguish the thought-components that he calls "concepts" from those he calls "objects." In "On Concept and Object" and related writings, he comes to recognize that the sentences in which he attempts to express this distinction are, by his own standards, logically

---

[1] "What is Metaphysics?", David Farrell Krell, trans., in Martin Heidegger, *Pathmarks*, William NcNeill, ed. (Cambridge: Cambridge University Press, 1998), 92. This is a translation of Heidegger's inaugural lecture at Freiburg, delivered and first published in 1929, now included in *Gesamtausgabe*, vol. 9, *Wegmarken* (Frankfurt a. M.: Klostermann, 1976). Hereafter I cite Krell's translation (sometimes with slight emendations) as "WIM."

The parenthetical remark appeared in the original version of "Was ist Metaphysik?" but not in later ones.

ill-formed. Yet he thinks that these logically defective utterances can nevertheless convey his essential insights to his readers.

In the conclusion, I make the parallels between Heidegger and Frege explicit, and thereby show that despite their different conceptions of logic's relation to philosophy they share a commitment to conveying the inexpressible. In closing I mention the difficulties inherent in this commitment and sketch the lines that a criticism of Heidegger and Frege might take.

1. DASEIN'S UNDERSTANDING OF BEING

Heidegger's principal concern in the works I will be discussing is the "question of being." For our purposes the important thing is not this question itself, but rather the groundwork Heidegger lays for posing it. To be in a position to pose the question of being, Heidegger thinks we must recognize what is sometimes called the "ontological difference." This is the difference between Being (*das Sein*) and entities (*das Seiende*), which Heidegger expresses in formulations like the following:

The Being of entities 'is' not itself an entity.[3]

Heidegger uses "*das Seiende*" to refer to what there is, to all the particular things that we are able to encounter—that is, to think about or do something with. (This usage can be captured by the English "everything," although I will use the more conventional translation "entities.") While *das Seiende* is what there is, *das Sein* (Being) is what it is to be an entity. It is the answer to the question of what makes an entity an entity. Heidegger says that Being is "that which determines entities as entities, that on the basis of which entities are already understood, however we may discuss them in detail" (*Being and Time*, 25–6).

Heidegger approaches the task of articulating Being via an investigation of a particular kind of entity, namely, human beings, or Dasein. He takes this approach because he thinks that Dasein always has an understanding of Being, though this understanding is typically inexplicit and confused. It is an understanding exhibited in Dasein's comportment toward entities, but is not typically articulated. Heidegger sees his task as clarifying and rendering explicit the understanding of

---

[3] Heidegger, *Being and Time*, John Macquarrie and Edward Robinson, trans. (New York: Harper and Row, 1962), 26.

The terms "*das Sein*" and "*das Seiende*" pose special problems for the translator. Both terms are substantives derived from the verb *sein* (to be). Either could be translated naturally as "being." But since Heidegger makes an absolutely crucial distinction between *das Seiende* and *das Sein*, we need to mark the different terms in English.

Macquarrie and Robinson and most other translators use "Being" for *das Sein*. Some translators use the lower-case "being," in an effort to demystify the *Seinsfrage*. I see no advantage in this: Heidegger himself insists that what is being investigated when we investigate *das Sein* will not be obvious, and using the lower-case can make it hard to keep track of the ontological difference.

Translators differ in their renderings of "*das Seiende*": some use "beings," some "entities," some "what is." None of these is perfect: "beings" makes it hard to keep track of the Being/beings distinction; "entities" loses the etymological connection between *das Sein* and *das Seiende*; "what is" is grammatically awkward. Because I want to avoid both the risk of conflating *das Sein* with *das Seiende* and grammatical awkwardness, I will use "entities," except where I resort to the expedient of bringing the German into the text.

I will alter quotations from translations as necessary to consistently render "*das Sein*" as "Being" and "*das Seiende*" as "entities."

Being that Dasein already possesses prior to its pursuit of explicitly philosophical inquiry.

Heidegger starts with the idea that Dasein's understanding of Being is exhibited in its knowing what things are. There are at least two ways Dasein can exhibit a knowledge of what something is: it can take up and use the thing in the course of its practical pursuits, or it can say what the thing is and say something about what characteristics it has. Heidegger thinks that the ability to grasp a particular entity either practically or theoretically—to know what it is—presupposes a grasp of the totality to which it belongs. In using an entity in one's practical activities or in making statements about an entity, one grasps the entity as an instance of a certain type within a structured range of possible types; one grasps it as possessing certain features out of a range of possible features of which one has a prior understanding. To give a simple example: in order for me to be able to say that the table is brown, I must be able to identify things as tables (as opposed to chairs, desks, bureaus, etc.) and to recognize the color brown (as opposed to red, orange, etc.).

Heidegger believes that Dasein, as part of its understanding of Being, has an understanding of the most comprehensive totality—the totality that allows us to recognize any entity as an entity. This is the totality of entities as a whole. In *The Essence of Reasons*, Heidegger describes Dasein's understanding of this totality as follows:

> Human Dasein, an entity situated *in the midst of entities* and relating itself *to* [behaving toward] entities, exists in such a way that entities as a whole are always manifest, and manifest as a totality. But this totality must not be conceived in any explicit fashion; its range is variable, and the fact that it belongs to Dasein can be concealed. We understand this totality without grasping, or "completely" investigating, the whole of manifest entities in all their particular connections, realms, and strata.[4]

Entities as a whole [*das Seiende im Ganzen*] are manifest to Dasein, even though Dasein does not grasp every individual entity. Dasein understands the totality. And it is Dasein's understanding of this totality—the manifestness of the totality to Dasein—that makes it possible for Dasein to grasp (in either a practical or an articulate manner) any entity at all, including Dasein itself. To encounter an entity—to recognize something as what it is—is to locate it within the totality of entities.

Heidegger uses the term "world" for the totality within which Dasein locates itself and encounters other entities. So we can say that Dasein's understanding of the world makes it possible for Dasein to encounter any particular entity. Because Dasein understands the totality of entities [*das Seiende im Ganzen*], Dasein can perceive, think about, and talk about particular entities. As Heidegger puts it:

> As a totality, world "is" no particular entity but rather that by means of and in terms of which Dasein *gives itself to understand* [*signify*] what entities it *can* behave toward and how it *can* behave toward them. (*The Essence of Reasons*, 85)

My topic is a problem that arises from Heidegger's reflections on this doctrine. He comes to see a logical problem in his attempts to describe the relationship

---

[4] Heidegger, *The Essence of Reasons*, Terrence Malick, trans. (Evanston, IL: Northwestern University Press, 1969), 83–5.

between Dasein's grasp of the world, or of entities as a whole, and Dasein's ability to encounter particular things. I now turn to the way this problem emerges in "What is Metaphysics?".

2. THE GUIDING QUESTION OF "WHAT IS METAPHYSICS?"

The ostensible topic of Heidegger's lecture "What is Metaphysics?" is the character of inquiry in the sciences (the *Wissenschaften*).[5] But since the way researchers encounter the objects of their studies is a special case of the way Dasein encounters entities, Heidegger promptly turns to the general issue of what makes it possible for Dasein to make assertions about, or think about, *das Seiende*. He says:

> In this "pursuit" [of science] nothing less transpires than the irruption by one entity called "the human being" into the whole of entities [*das Seiende im Ganzen*], indeed in such a way that in and through this irruption entities [*das Seiende*] break open and show what they are and how they are. (WIM, 83)

The main point of the lecture is to explicate Dasein's relation to *das Seiende im Ganzen*—the relation that allows entities to show what they are and how they are.

Heidegger attempts to clarify Dasein's relation to *das Seiende im Ganzen* by way of contrast with what it is not. He writes:

> As surely as we can never comprehend absolutely the whole of entities in itself, we certainly do find ourselves stationed in the midst of entities that are unveiled somehow as a whole. In the end an essential distinction prevails between comprehending the whole of entities in itself and finding oneself in the midst of entities as a whole. The former is impossible in principle. The latter happens all the time in our Dasein.... No matter how fragmented our everyday existence may appear to be, however, it always deals with entities in a unity of the "whole," if only in a shadowy way. (WIM, 87)

Heidegger distinguishes finding ourselves in the midst of entities as a whole — which is the characteristic of Dasein that he seeks to clarify — from something that is "impossible in principle." It is impossible to "comprehend absolutely the whole of entities in itself."

What exactly is said to be impossible? There are two ways in which someone might think she could comprehend the whole of entities. One way would be to run over every entity in thought, to think about everything in turn. But even if this were humanly possible, it would not bring entities "as a whole" into view. The whole of entities is an organized totality; you would fail to grasp this totality as a totality if you simply thought about each entity one at a time.

The second way in which it might seem that one could comprehend the whole of entities is, not to think about every entity in turn, but to grasp the *whole* to which all entities belong. This is what Heidegger declares to be impossible. He thinks it is confused to suppose that one could, as it were, get outside the whole of entities in thought, and from this perspective conceive the whole. To try to turn the whole of entities into an object of thought in this way would be to treat the whole of entities as an entity. But the world is not an entity; it is instead that to which we are related in such a way that we are able to encounter entities. Accord-

---

[5] I will occasionally use the German word as a reminder that Heidegger's investigation is not concerned exclusively with the natural sciences, but expressly includes all fields of knowledge.

ing to Heidegger, whatever our relation to the whole of entities is, it is fundamentally different from our relation to a particular entity that we comprehend.

Heidegger's claim that Dasein can never grasp or comprehend the whole of entities seems to contradict Heidegger's doctrine concerning Dasein's relation to the world. According to that doctrine, Dasein always has an understanding of entities as a whole, and this understanding is what makes it possible for Dasein to encounter any particular entity. But now Heidegger has said that it is impossible for Dasein to grasp the whole of entities. Heidegger finds himself committed both to the view that Dasein *must* understand entities as a whole and to the view that Dasein *cannot* grasp or comprehend entities as a whole.

The tension between these views is an expression of the predicament in which Heidegger finds himself when he investigates the conditions for the possibility of encountering (using in a competent manner, thinking about, talking about) entities. I will suggest that "What is Metaphysics?" is Heidegger's attempt to extricate himself from these seemingly incompatible commitments. But in order to read "What is Metaphysics?" this way, we first have to figure out what is going on when Heidegger introduces what appears to be a bizarre, if not absurd, change of topic — namely, the Nothing.

3. ENTITIES AND THE NOTHING

Heidegger has claimed that entities as a whole [*das Seiende im Ganzen*] are not themselves an entity; they are not an external object nor a potential object of thought. We may see Heidegger as moving from this claim to a discussion of "the Nothing" in three steps. First, he says that the totality of entities is *no thing*. Second, he says that when entities as a whole are revealed to us what is revealed is *nothing*. Third, he poses the following question: what is the character of this Nothing that is revealed?[6]

In these three steps we may identify two distinct verbal transitions involving Heidegger's use of the word "nothing": (i) a transition from saying that the totality of entities is not any thing to saying that the totality of entities is nothing; (ii) a transition from using the word "nothing" in expressions like "Nothing is revealed to Dasein" to using it as a substantive in statements and questions about the Nothing that is said to be revealed. Each of these two transformations invites the objection that Heidegger is twisting words and deforming language to such an extent that what he is saying is at best highly misleading and at worst meaningless. I think an examination of this objection will clarify what Heidegger takes himself to be doing when he discusses "the Nothing" in *Being and Time* and "What is Metaphysics?".

The first transformation is most explicit in Heidegger's discussion of anxiety in *Being and Time*. In both *Being and Time* and "What is Metaphysics?", anxiety figures as a fundamental mood of Dasein in which Dasein's relation to entities as a whole ("Being-in-the-world") is revealed.[7] Heidegger first says that what is revealed

---

[6] I will capitalize "Nothing" when it is used to translate Heidegger's "*das Nichts.*" The capitalization marks that Heidegger is using the grapheme "Nichts" in a nonstandard way, and that his word may turn out to be a neologism.

[7] Although I will not say much about anxiety in this paper, my argument ought to clarify the logical status of Heidegger's talk about anxiety.

in anxiety (that in the face of which Dasein is anxious) is not an entity: "That in the face of which one has anxiety is not an entity within-the-world " (*Being and Time*, 231). It then comes naturally to say: "Nothing which is ready-to-hand or present-at-hand within the world functions as that in the face of which anxiety is anxious" (*ibid.*). This is expressed, Heidegger thinks, when, after anxiety has subsided, we say that "'it was really nothing'" (*ibid.*; cf. WIM, 89).

But Heidegger also says, "as a phenomenon . . . *the world as such is that in the face of which one has anxiety*" (*Being and Time*, 231). Again, "Being-anxious discloses, primordially and directly, the world as world " (*ibid.*, 232). If we combine these two ways of describing that in the face of which one is anxious, we may conclude that the world is nothing. This is, at best, a highly misleading formulation. Even if it is right to say that the world as a whole is not an entity, or that it is no thing, it is perverse to express this by saying that the world is nothing. For this latter expression suggests that the world is nonexistent, or perhaps (on a more idiomatic reading) that the world is insignificant. And neither of these suggestions can possibly capture what Heidegger means.

Heidegger in effect concedes that it is misleading to say that the world is nothing, but the way he expresses this concession hardly clears matters up. Heidegger explicitly acknowledges the equivalence between the world and nothing that I just inferred when he writes "the Nothing—that is, the world as such—is that in the face of which anxiety is anxious " (*ibid.*). The concession comes when Heidegger describes that in the face of which Dasein is anxious:

> But this Nothing ready-to-hand . . . is not totally nothing. The Nothing ready-to-hand is grounded in the most primordial 'something'—in the *world*. (*ibid.*)

The world, Heidegger says, is not really nothing; it is the "most primordial 'something.'" This means that Heidegger is not in earnest when he says or implies that the world is nothing. We can understand him as using a form of words that, though literally false, is supposed to remind us that the world is not itself a thing, but is rather that totality within which particular things can manifest themselves.

But now the way Heidegger has framed his rejection of the idea that the world is nothing involves the second transition I mentioned above. Heidegger moves from the claim that that in the face of which Dasein is anxious is nothing within-the-world to the claim that that in the face of which Dasein is anxious is *the Nothing* (which he then glosses as "the world as such"). That is, he takes the word "nothing," which has been functioning as a logical particle in expressions like "nothing ready-to-hand," and turns it into a substantive, viz., "the Nothing."

This is the move that has drawn the critical fire of Rudolf Carnap and, following him, of many analytic philosophers.[8] Carnap cites several of Heidegger's sentences about the Nothing as examples of metaphysical nonsense. According to Carnap, Heidegger is trying to use a logical particle as a substantive; that attempt violates the rules governing the logical structure of sentences, and consequently Heidegger's sentences about the Nothing are nonsense.

---

[8] Carnap's critique is contained in "The Elimination of Metaphysics through the Logical Analysis of Language," A. Pap, trans., in A. J. Ayer, ed., *Logical Positivism* (Glencoe, IL: Free Press, 1959). Philosophers who have followed Carnap's lead in criticizing Heidegger include A. J. Ayer, W. V. O. Quine, and George Pitcher.

To understand what Heidegger is up to, it will be helpful to consider whether this criticism is successful. The first thing to note is that Carnap's criticism wouldn't apply if Heidegger were simply introducing a new use of the string of letters "nothing." If Heidegger were clear about when he is using the string "nothing" as a logical particle and when he is using it as a substantive, and if we could figure out what the words "the Nothing" referred to, then Carnap would have no grounds for saying that Heidegger is producing nonsensical utterances. (Carnap might still regard Heidegger's coinage as a confusing or unhelpful piece of terminology; but such a criticism would fall far short of the charge of nonsensicality that Carnap actually levels.)

But Heidegger deprives himself of this kind of defense against Carnap's criticism. In the way Heidegger introduces his talk of the Nothing, he appears to deliberately blur the two uses of the string "nothing" that a defense against Carnap would require him to hold firmly distinct. He seems to insist that the substantive use of the string (in the expression "the Nothing") is the same as—or is implicit in—the use of "nothing" as a logical particle. In the passages I quoted above, after saying that that in the face of which Dasein is anxious is nothing ready-to-hand, Heidegger refers to "this Nothing ready-to-hand," as though the former use of "nothing" implied that there is something he can refer to as "this Nothing." This seems to be exactly the sort of attempt to turn a logical particle ("nothing ready-to-hand") into a substantive ("this Nothing ready-to-hand") that Carnap criticizes.

The passages we have examined so far come from *Being and Time*, but the same verbal transitions occur also in "What is Metaphysics?", and they occur there in a setting that seems especially calculated to raise the ire of philosophers like Carnap. Such philosophers take their inspiration and their topics of investigation from the sciences. And in "What is Metaphysics?" Heidegger purports to direct his investigation to the status of the sciences; in particular, he says he is concerned to characterize the proper domain of the *Wissenschaften* in the spirit of a "scientific man." And he begins his investigation of the domain of the sciences with a thought that ought to be congenial to scientifically minded philosophers. To characterize the domain of the *Wissenschaften*, to say what it is they study, it is quite natural to say that they study *everything*: any entity can be a topic of scientific investigation. Heidegger expresses this idea when he writes:

What should be examined is *das Seiende* only, and besides that—nothing; *das Seiende* alone, and further—nothing; solely *das Seiende*, and beyond that—nothing. (WIM, 84)

Now we might wonder whether this formulation is likely to spring naturally to the lips of a scientifically minded philosopher. Such a philosopher might well say, "The sciences study everything there is." But he would likely find it strange to add "and beyond that nothing." We could perhaps imagine a scientifically minded philosopher saying, "The sciences study everything there is—and nothing there isn't," where the appended phrase is meant to say that the sciences do not study pseudo-objects like witches and astrological influences. If the "and beyond that—nothing" that Heidegger puts in the mouth of his "scientific man" is meant in some such way, then perhaps there will be no reason for a scientifically minded philosopher to object to Heidegger's formulation.

But regardless of whether the phrase "and beyond that—nothing" can be made to seem part of a natural characterization of the domain of the *Wissenschaften*, Heidegger is sure to elicit the Carnapian objection when he says the following about the scientific man's statement of the domain of the *Wissenschaften*: "[W]hat is remarkable is that, precisely in the way scientific man secures to himself what is most properly his, he speaks, whether explicitly or not, of something different " (WIM, 84). According to Heidegger, when the scientific man tries to express what the sciences concern themselves with (namely, what there is, *das Seiende*), he mentions—in addition to what there is—nothing. And Heidegger then turns his attention to the Nothing that the scientific man allegedly refers to; he asks, "How is it with this Nothing?" Heidegger seems to be assuming that the statement "The sciences study *das Seiende*, and further—nothing" involves a reference to "the Nothing." Heidegger even seems to think that a study of the Nothing is particularly urgent because it is the one thing the sciences ignore. He writes:

The Nothing is rejected precisely by science, given up as a nullity. . . . If science is right, then only one thing is sure: science wishes to know nothing of the Nothing. (WIM, 84)

If Heidegger is in fact assuming that when one says "The sciences study *das Seiende*, and further—nothing" one is referring to something called "the Nothing," if he is in fact assuming that "nothing" is the name of "something different" from *das Seiende*, then it seems that Carnap's criticism is justified. To unmask the fallacy that Heidegger seems to be committing, we need only a passing acquaintance with modern logic.[9] Logical reflection shows that the word "nothing" as it appears in the scientific man's statement is not the name of something; rather it is a logical particle which is used to form a negated existential statement. To make the example more tractable, let's reformulate the scientific man's statement so as to bring its use of "nothing" to the fore: "Nothing falls outside the scope of the *Wissenschaften*."[10] Using the standard tools of modern logic, we may symbolize this as: $\sim(\exists x)Ox$, where Ox = "x falls outside the scope of the *Wissenschaften*." This shows that the word "nothing" disappears into the logical analysis; there is no symbol corresponding to it; it is not a name. We seem forced to conclude —as Carnap does—that if only Heidegger would take cognizance of this insight, he would give up the idea that there is some mysterious nonexistent thing called "nothing" that calls for metaphysical investigation.

I think that Carnap is right that one would have to be confused to claim that the scientific man, in saying that the sciences study *das Seiende* and nothing else, is referring to something called "the Nothing."[11] But I want to challenge the assumption

---

[9] Actually, we do not need any instruction in logic at all. Even children can appreciate the silliness of an adult answering their complaint "There is nothing to play with around here" with "Grab that nothing and start playing with it." We must presume that Heidegger too is aware of the manifest silliness of supposing that the use of "nothing" as a logical particle involves a referential use; we need an interpretation of him that can accommodate such an awareness.

[10] I am assuming that this sentence captures the meaning of "The *Wissenschaften* study *das Seiende* and nothing else"; but in any case "Nothing falls outside the scope of the *Wissenschaften*" is in the spirit of the scientific man's statement.

[11] I here credit Carnap with a valid criticism of what he takes Heidegger to be doing in the passage at issue. But I actually think that, even if we grant that Heidegger really is confused in the way that Carnap takes him to be, Carnap's criticism still misses its mark. In making his criticism, Carnap

of Heidegger's critics that we have to attribute this claim to Heidegger. I have granted that it can easily look as though Heidegger is trying to conflate the use of "nothing" as a logical particle with his idiosyncratic use of "the Nothing" as a substantive. But a closer examination shows that this is not in fact what Heidegger is trying to do. Carnap's criticism assumes that Heidegger is using "the Nothing" as a referring expression, and that Heidegger attributes such a referential use of "nothing" to the scientific man as well. But immediately after he introduces the phrase "the Nothing," Heidegger raises the question of whether it even makes sense to regard "the Nothing" as a referring expression; later he concludes that the Nothing is not an entity of any kind, and so it is not something that can be referred to in the straightforward way in which we refer to entities.

These features of Heidegger's use of "the Nothing" are quite difficult to understand, and in the next section I will try to come to terms with some of the difficulties they entail. But they are already sufficient to show that Carnap's criticism—based as it is on the assumption that Heidegger is using "the Nothing" to refer to some thing—misses its mark. Still, an interpretative puzzle remains: why does Heidegger *seem* to attribute a reference to the Nothing to the scientific man? That is, why does Heidegger say that "when science tries to express its own proper essence it calls upon the Nothing for help" (WIM, 84)? Why does he say that the scientific man, in saying that the sciences study *das Seiende* and nothing else, "speaks, whether explicitly or not, of something different" (WIM, 84)? I would suggest that in making this particular transition from the scientific man's statement to his own investigation of the Nothing, Heidegger is speaking tongue-in-cheek. He knows full well that the scientific man isn't referring to something he calls "the Nothing"; as we've seen, according to Heidegger the Nothing isn't even something one can refer to in the usual way. Heidegger is trying to make the point that the scientific man, whether he realizes it or not, presupposes an understanding of *das Seiende* of the sort that Heidegger's metaphysical investigation aims to elucidate.

This presupposition won't be obvious to the scientific man, and so Heidegger uses a slightly high-handed, even cheeky, formulation to draw attention to it. We can bring out the way the scientific man implicitly presupposes an understanding of *das Seiende* by reconsidering the attempt to provide a logical analysis of the scientific man's statement. Its logical symbolization is $\sim(\exists x)Ox$. Heidegger is concerned with that which has to be in place in order for us to understand such a symbolization. One salient feature of the symbolization is the use of the quantifier. Our grasp of the quantifier involves a grasp of the role that quantified statements play in inferences; for example, my grasp of the quantifier "all" in "All whales are mammals" must involve my understanding of its role in the inference from "Moby Dick is a whale" to "Moby Dick is a mammal." My ability to grasp quantified statements is inseparable from my ability to grasp statements about particulars. Heidegger's investigation is supposed to explain the ability to grasp statements about particulars and thereby to explicate what makes it possible for us to understand the symbolizations of formal logic.

---

has to say that Heidegger is actually using the logical particle as a substantive. But I think there is no such thing as using a logical particle in that way. I argue for this claim in my "Conceptions of Nonsense in Carnap and Wittgenstein," in Alice Crary and Rupert Read, eds., *The New Wittgenstein* (New York: Routledge, 2000).

The other noteworthy feature of the symbolization $\sim(\exists x)Ox$ is the presence of a negation symbol. In order to understand this symbolization, we must know what it is to negate an existential statement; understanding this kind of negation requires understanding how negation works in general. This is a second aspect of our thinking that Heidegger wants to elucidate. He holds that negation is partly constitutive of thinking: every thought is negatable, and a thought is what it is partly by virtue of its being the negation of another thought. His account of the Nothing is an attempt to elucidate negation. He notoriously claims that negation arises out of the Nothing: "the Nothing is the origin of negation, not vice versa " (WIM, 92). Without pausing to try to explicate this claim, we may take the general point that Heidegger's discussion of the Nothing is meant at least in part as an account of the possibility of negation.

On my interpretation, when Heidegger suggests that the scientific man is referring to the Nothing, he is trying to draw attention to the need for a metaphysical investigation of whatever it is that underlies the investigation of particular entities that is the business of the *Wissenschaften*. He may or may not succeed in bringing about such reflection on the part of scientifically minded philosophers — the reception of Heidegger by the analytic tradition provides little occasion for optimism in this regard—but he is not falling into the plain logical confusion that Carnap attributes to him.

I would maintain further that Carnap and other analytic critics haven't addressed the metaphysical issues Heidegger is concerned with. Carnap considers it a sufficient refutation of Heidegger's discussion of the Nothing to produce logical symbolizations that show that the word "nothing" is used to form negated existential statements. Heidegger could respond that the use of the word "nothing" in negated existential statements is exactly the sort of thing that he wants to clarify. While Carnap seems to think that providing a logical analysis of a sentence like "Nothing lies outside the scope of the *Wissenschaften*" is the end of philosophical inquiry, Heidegger thinks it is just the beginning. His aim is to explicate that which makes it possible for us to understand quantification and negation. When Heidegger asks, "How is it with this Nothing?", part of what he is concerned with can be expressed by such questions as: "How does the logical particle do its work?" and "How is Dasein able to understand the negation and quantification in terms of which sentences like the scientific man's are analyzed?". The logical analysis of sentences presupposes answers to these questions; it does not provide them. In sum, Carnap and other critics do not see that Heidegger is engaged in a metaphysical inquiry into the understanding of entities that is presupposed by logical analysis. Heidegger's inquiry may or may not actually shed any light on the character of this understanding, but we should credit him with a genuine interest in the metaphysical underpinnings of the uses of language that symbolic logic seeks to represent.

Heidegger's investigation of the possibility of encountering particular entities impels him to discuss entities as a whole. In this section, I have considered the way Heidegger turns his talk about entities as a whole into talk about the Nothing, and I have suggested that Heidegger would maintain that modern logic's analysis of the role of the word "nothing" actually presupposes the understanding of the Nothing that he aims to elucidate. But now we have to confront the apparent illogicality of referring to the Nothing.

4. HEIDEGGER'S VIOLATION OF LOGICAL CONSTRAINTS

We have seen that Heidegger's talk of the Nothing belongs to his attempt to articulate that which makes it possible for us to encounter (to manipulate in a competent manner, to think about, to talk about) entities at all. Our encountering any particular entity presupposes that entities as a whole have been revealed to us. But this revelation is difficult to describe, for entities as a whole (*das Seiende im Ganzen*) are not another entity. As we have seen, Heidegger is led to say that the revelation of *das Seiende im Ganzen* is the revelation of *the Nothing*. He then frames his question about the conditions for the possibility of encountering entities as "What is the Nothing?".

The first thing Heidegger notes about his question is that it is logically peculiar. He formulates the paradox involved in asking about the Nothing as forcefully as his harshest critics:

> What is the Nothing? Our very first approach to this question has something unusual about it. In our asking we posit the Nothing in advance as something that "is" such and such; we posit it as an entity. But that is exactly what it is distinguished from. Interrogating the Nothing—asking what and how it, the Nothing, is—turns what is interrogated into its opposite. The question deprives itself of its own object.
>
> *Accordingly, every answer to this question is also impossible from the start. For it necessarily assumes the form: the Nothing "is" this or that. With regard to the Nothing, question and answer alike are inherently absurd.* (WIM, 85)[12]

The question "What is the Nothing?" appears to be directed toward an object, viz., the referent of the expression "the Nothing." Asking a question or making an assertion presupposes an object about which we ask or assert something. Questioning and asserting are ways in which Dasein encounters entities: questions and assertions direct our attention to the entities they are about. If the sentences involving the words "the Nothing" are questions and assertions, then the Nothing must be the sort of thing that can be the topic of questions, assertions, or judgments—that is, it must be an entity.[13]

But Heidegger's point in using the words "the Nothing" for the topic of his inquiry is to emphasize that what he is investigating is *different* from entities. The Nothing is not an entity but is instead that which makes all thought about entities possible. Heidegger declares that the Nothing is distinct from entities, from any possible object of thought; but he wants to think and talk about the Nothing, and thought and talk always have an object. Thus it seems that Heidegger is committed both to the claim that the Nothing is not an object of thought and to the claim that the Nothing is an object of thought. Hence Heidegger concludes that "[w]ith regard to the Nothing, question and answer alike are inherently absurd."

---

[12] Heidegger makes essentially the same argument in the lectures published as *An Introduction to Metaphysics*, Gregory Fried and Richard Polt, trans. (New Haven: Yale University Press, 2000), 25ff. In general, the treatment of the Nothing in these lectures follows the lines laid down in "What is Metaphysics?".

[13] This argument is based on Heidegger's discussion of assertion in *Being and Time* (Section 32, "Assertion as a derivative mode of interpretation"). He is thinking principally of simple predications (e.g., "The hammer is too heavy"), but his argument concerning the way assertions point out and direct our attention to entities also applies to more complicated assertions (e.g., "Mammals are warm-blooded").

The contradiction inherent in talk about the Nothing is essentially a reprise of the tension between Heidegger's commitments both to the idea that Dasein must understand entities as a whole and to the idea that Dasein cannot comprehend entities as a whole. This problem is not an artifact of his idiosyncratic expression "the Nothing"; even if he eschewed the words "the Nothing" and only talked about entities as a whole the same problem would arise. Entities as a whole are not an entity; one cannot make entities as a whole an object of thought. But then how can we think about entities as a whole? How is it that Dasein can (indeed, must) have a grasp of entities as a whole? The problem of talking about the Nothing just is the problem of talking about entities as a whole, and this problem is in turn the problem of talking about the world: in each of these cases we appear to have an assertion about something, but there is no object to which it is directed.

In having incompatible commitments, in saying things that are "inherently absurd," Heidegger violates a principle that he takes to belong to logic, namely, the principle of non-contradiction. In discussing the question "What is the Nothing?", Heidegger acknowledges as much:

> The commonly cited ground rule of all thinking, the proposition that contradiction is to be avoided, universal "logic" itself, lays low this question. For thinking, which is always essentially thinking about something, must act in a way contrary to its own essence when it thinks of the Nothing. (WIM, 85)

To understand how this raises an internal problem within Heidegger's work, we need to consider Heidegger's views about logic. Many readers of Heidegger—both hostile and friendly—assume that Heidegger wants somehow to do away with logical constraints. They think that Heidegger wants to engage in an inquiry that need not respect the fundamental principles of logic, e.g., the principle of non-contradiction. But such readings are difficult to reconcile with views about logic that Heidegger expressed just one year before he delivered "What is Metaphysics?". These can be found in the transcription of a lecture course published as *The Metaphysical Foundations of Logic*. In these lectures, Heidegger embraces a thesis that most analytic philosophers would find congenial, namely, the thesis that thinking requires following the rules of thought. Heidegger singles out four traditional rules of thought: the principle of identity, the principle of non-contradiction, the principle of excluded middle, and the principle of sufficient reason. He characterizes the relation between such principles and thought as follows:

> These basic principles [*Grund-Sätze*] are not rules alongside a thinking that would be determined from elsewhere, but they are the grounds for statements [*Sätze*] in general, grounds which make thinking possible.[14]

According to Heidegger, the basic principles of thought make thinking possible. Thinkers owe allegiance to the principles of logic; there is no such thing as thinking that ignores them. This applies even to metaphysical thinking:

> Every science, including metaphysics, and every form of prescientific thinking uses, as thinking, the formal rules of thought. Using the rules of thought in the thinking process is uncircumventable.[15]

---

[14] Heidegger, *The Metaphysical Foundations of Logic*, Michael Heim, trans. (Bloomington, IN: Indiana University Press, 1984), 19. In subsequent quotations I will occasionally modify Heim's translation.

[15] Heidegger, *The Metaphysical Foundations of Logic*, 104.

Heidegger's commitment to the uncircumventability of logic means that it cannot be right to say that he wants to pursue an inquiry in the absence of logical constraints. But then "What is Metaphysics?" presents a formidable interpretative problem. To say that the principles of logic make thinking possible means, at a minimum, that when a thinker recognizes that she is in violation of the laws of logic, she is obliged to bring herself into conformity with them. If she refuses to modify her cognitive position as regards the violation, Heidegger's conception of logic entails that she does not then have a thought, even though she may mistakenly take herself to have one. Since Heidegger recognizes that his talk of the Nothing is incompatible with the principle of non-contradiction, his conception of logic would seem to require that he modify or withdraw this talk. But Heidegger does no such thing. He concedes "the ostensible absurdity of question and answer with respect to the Nothing" and "the formal impossibility of the question of the Nothing" (WIM, 86). He says that "the objections of the intellect would call a halt to our search" (WIM, 87). But he persists in his search nonetheless; he says that this "formal impossibility" and "the objections of the intellect" should not be allowed to derail his metaphysical investigation.

Heidegger is in a difficult predicament. Some of his most fundamental commitments are in conflict. On the one hand, his conception of logic implies that there is no such thing as a thought about the Nothing. But, on the other hand, when he attempts to elucidate how the revelation of *das Seiende im Ganzen* makes possible our thoughts about entities, he finds himself compelled to think about the Nothing in just the way ruled out by his own conception of logic. In the face of this conflict, Heidegger perseveres with his investigation of the Nothing. What does this signify? Does it mean that he is giving up his conception of logic, or that he is denying that logic applies to metaphysics? Does he have some way of bringing his commitments into harmony?

5. HEIDEGGER'S ATTEMPT TO OVERCOME HIS PREDICAMENT

Any attempt to understand the status of Heidegger's talk of the Nothing must take into account Heidegger's openness about the problematic character of assertions and questions about the Nothing. Heidegger has scarcely introduced his question "What is the Nothing?" when he makes the point that, since "thinking ... is always essentially thinking about something" (WIM, 85), the very question itself involves a logical incoherence. Furthermore, Heidegger alludes to his view that all thinking owes allegiance to the laws of logic, or, in other words, that there can be no such thing as illogical thought. He writes:

Since it remains wholly impossible for us to make the Nothing into an object, have we not already come to the end of our inquiry into the Nothing—assuming that in this question "logic" (i.e., logic in the usual sense in which one takes this term)[16] is of supreme importance, that the intellect is the means, and thought the way, to conceive the Nothing originally and to decide about its possible unveiling. (WIM, 85)

---

[16] This parenthetical remark appeared in the original 1929 version but was later deleted.

LOGIC AND THE INEXPRESSIBLE IN FREGE AND HEIDEGGER

Here Heidegger implies that using thought in answering a question is to assign "logic" supreme importance.[17] This is a restatement of his basic commitment in *The Metaphysical Foundations of Logic*. But he has departed from his earlier position in one crucial respect. In *The Metaphysical Foundations of Logic* Heidegger regards any sort of inquiry (even metaphysics) as thinking and as therefore owing allegiance to the laws of logic. But now in "What is Metaphysics?" he says that the notion that the metaphysical question of the Nothing is to be addressed by thinking is merely an assumption. He thereby suggests that there is some alternative mode of inquiry, different from thinking and not beholden to logic, to pursue the question about the Nothing. We are now in a position to see how this inquiry is supposed to proceed.

What lesson does Heidegger want us to take from his arguments that his inquiry into the Nothing is formally impossible, that every question or statement about the Nothing is ostensibly absurd? I suggest that what Heidegger wants us to conclude from the incompatibility between his conception of logic and his sentences involving "the Nothing" is the following: the sentences that purport to be about the Nothing are not assertions or questions. If the sentences are not assertions or questions, then they will not be subject to the logical strictures that questions and assertions are, and they will not have to be about some entity. If the sentences are not assertions or questions, then we need not think that "the Nothing" refers to an entity.

It might well seem that this interpretative option (taking Heidegger's sentences involving "the Nothing" to be neither assertions nor questions) is no favor to Heidegger. On my reading, Heidegger wants us to realize that his sentences do not express thoughts. His sentences appear to have cognitive content, but Heidegger, on my reading, wants us to regard this appearance as deceptive. It would thus seem that I am reading Heidegger precisely as Carnap does when he declares that Heidegger's metaphysical writings do not even get as far as expressing thoughts.

To see how Heidegger, on my reading, differs from his critics, we need to consider what happens when Heidegger puts forward sentences that appear to be assertions, even while he emphasizes their logical defects. The sentence "The Nothing makes it possible for us to encounter entities," for example, *appears* to tell us something about the Nothing; "the Nothing" seems to be functioning as a referring expression. When Heidegger reminds us of the peculiar character of the Nothing, we are supposed to recognize that "the Nothing" is not a referring expression. But then the meaning that we thought we could hear in "The Nothing makes it possible for us to encounter entities" is not available. The sentence

---

[17] I believe that Heidegger uses scare-quotes around "logic" in order to refer to the usual philosophical articulation of the basic principles of logic, or what he also calls the "*traditional* interpretation of thinking" (WIM, 92, note c). (In *The Metaphysical Foundations of Logic* he lists these traditional principles as the principles of noncontradiction, of excluded middle, of identity, and of sufficient reason.) Heidegger does not want to commit himself to the claim that these traditional principles do in fact capture that to which any thinking owes allegiance. But his purpose in "What is Metaphysics?" is not to challenge whether some particular set of logical principles adequately captures that to which any thinking owes allegiance, but rather to challenge the idea that metaphysical thinking owes allegiance to *any* set of logical principles.

misfires; it fails to express anything. But in seeing the precise way in which the sentence misfires, we come to see (Heidegger thinks) what it is that makes it possible for Dasein to encounter entities. When we see exactly why "the Nothing" and "*das Seiende im Ganzen*" do not refer to anything, we come to see how our relation to the whole of entities underlies our encounters with particular entities.

It is tempting to try to give a positive formulation of the insight into the necessary conditions for encountering entities that Heidegger seeks to convey; I have just yielded to this temptation by writing the phrase "our relation to the whole of entities underlies our encounters with particular entities. " But any such positive formulation will use an expression (e.g., "the whole of entities") that purports to refer, and so will fail to capture the inexpressible insight that Heidegger seeks to convey. At best, such a sentence can evoke the insight in a reader. Heidegger's sentences about the Nothing and entities as a whole do not *say* anything; nevertheless, according to Heidegger, they *show* something through their breakdown. Moreover, it is the very thing that these sentences show—the very insight they provide—that precludes them from saying anything. For when we grasp the insight we will understand that "the Nothing" (like "entities as a whole" and "the world") is not a referring expression, and that sentences that purport to use these words as referring expressions do not say anything. Precisely by not saying anything, Heidegger's sentences can show this insight to the discerning reader; and this is why he stresses that his sentences do not say anything.

6. FREGE'S PREDICAMENT AND HIS ATTEMPT TO OVERCOME IT

The predicament that we have been examining bears important similarities to one that Frege finds himself in when he tries to explain his logical vocabulary in "On Concept and Object."[18] By considering how Frege attempts to extricate himself from his predicament we will gain a new perspective on Heidegger's project. From this perspective, we will be able to see that Heidegger's metaphysical investigation of the conditions for the possibility of thought is a project of the same general type as Frege's logical investigations of the structure of thought. And we will be able to see that the resort to logically suspect locutions is not simply a consequence of Heidegger's idiosyncratic project or supposed antipathy to logic, but is instead a move that is quite compelling when one reflects on the fundamental structure of thought.

In laying out the logical symbolism he calls "Begriffsschrift,"[19] Frege distinguishes various kinds of propositional components. He distinguishes, for example, between objects and concepts, which are represented by different kinds of expressions when sentences are symbolized in Begriffsschrift. A sentence expressing a simple predication is represented by a well-formed combination of an object-expression and a concept-expression.

One of Frege's fundamental ideas is that the meaning of a sub-sentential expression is the contribution that it makes to the meaning of the sentence in which

---

[18] P. T. Geach, trans., in *Translations from the Philosophical Writings of Gottlob Frege*, P. T. Geach and M. Black, eds., 3rd ed. (Oxford: Blackwell, 1980). Hereafter cited as "CO."

[19] I use the German word without italics to refer to Frege's system of logical notation.

it appears. Different kinds of sentence components are distinguished by the different functional roles they play in making up meaningful sentences. For an expression to be a concept-expression, for example, is for it to play a predicative role in the sentences in which it appears; for an expression to be an object-expression is for it to stand for that which is said to fall under a concept in the sentences in which it appears. One way Frege explains the functional role of a concept-expression is by saying that it stands in need of supplementation; a concept-expression is *unsaturated*, or, in other words, its sign in Begriffsschrift has blanks which have to be filled in, in order to yield a sentence. We can represent a concept by writing, e.g., "___ is a horse" (CO, 47n). Object-expressions, by contrast, are *saturated*; they fill the blanks in concept expressions so as to yield sentences. According to Frege, a sentence that expresses a simple predication, e.g., "Black Beauty is a horse," can be analyzed as consisting of a predicative part ("___ is a horse"), which stands for (*bedeutet*) a concept, and a subject part ("Black Beauty"), which stands for an object.

Since object-expressions and concept-expressions play distinct functional roles in making up a complete sentence—since object-expressions are saturated while concept-expressions are unsaturated—an expression cannot at one and the same time stand for both a concept and an object. Frege stresses this point when, at the outset of *The Foundations of Arithmetic*, he lays down his guiding principles, one of which is "never to lose sight of the distinction between concept and object."[20] In a discussion of Frege's views, a philosopher named Benno Kerry claimed that in certain cases this distinction does not hold. In these cases, Kerry claimed, a single expression is serving simultaneously as a concept-expression and an object-expression. Frege's response to Kerry's examples will bring out the predicament in which he finds himself.

Kerry thinks that an expression is serving as both a concept-expression and an object-expression in sentences like the following:

The concept *horse* is a concept easily attained.

The expression "the concept *horse*" would certainly seem to be the name of a concept, namely, the concept *horse*. Indeed, the sentence says that the concept *horse* is a concept; if the sentence is true (as it surely seems to be), then the expression "the concept *horse*" means a concept. Yet when one applies Frege's methods of analysis to Kerry's example it turns out that the words "the concept *horse*" are functioning as an object-expression: "the concept *horse*" names a saturated item that is combined with the concept expressed by "___ is a concept easily attained." Thus Kerry concludes that the expression "the concept *horse*" stands for both a concept and an object.

In his response to Kerry, Frege says that this argument involves a misunderstanding of what it is to be a concept and what it is to be an object. To use Frege's techniques of analysis properly, we cannot assume that "the concept *horse*" stands for a concept. To determine what this expression stands for, we must consider *only* its role in the sentence. Since its role is to serve as the subject of predication (and

---

[20] Gottlob Frege, *The Foundations of Arithmetic*, J. L. Austin, trans., 2nd rev. ed. (Evanston, IL: Northwestern University Press, 1980), x.

it is not itself predicative), this expression names an object, not a concept. In Kerry's example, "the concept *horse*" is not a concept-expression. Frege expresses this conclusion when he says, "the concept *horse* is not a concept."

There is something peculiar about this conclusion, as Frege acknowledges:

> It must indeed be recognized that here we are confronted by an awkwardness of language, which I admit cannot be avoided, if we say that the concept *horse* is not a concept, whereas, e.g., the city of Berlin is a city, and the volcano Vesuvius is a volcano. (CO, 46)

This "awkwardness of language" is not confined to isolated or contrived examples. It appears whenever one tries to identify a concept as such. And such attempts occur whenever one tries to explain Frege's logical system. One of his basic tenets is that the "fundamental logical relation is that of an object's falling under a concept."[11] If we then describe a particular thought-content in these terms, we will say, for example, that the sentence "Black Beauty is a horse" says that the object named by Black Beauty falls under the concept *horse*. But now "the concept *horse*" is functioning as the name of one item in relation to another (the object named by "Black Beauty"), and so, by Frege's criterion of what it is to be a concept, these words do not express a concept. So we fail to properly express the fundamental logical relationship that the sentence instantiates.

Here is Frege's description of this predicament and of a way to address it:

> In logical discussions one quite often needs to say something about a concept, and to express this in the form usual for such predications—viz. to make what is said about the concept into the content of the grammatical predicate. Consequently, one would expect that what is meant by the grammatical subject would be the concept; but the concept as such cannot play this part, in view of its predicative nature; it must first be converted into an object, or, more precisely, an object must go proxy for it. We designate this object by prefixing the words 'the concept'; e.g.:
> *'The concept man is not empty.'*
> Here the first three words are to be regarded as a proper name, which can no more be used predicatively than 'Berlin' or 'Vesuvius.' (CO, 46–7)

According to Frege, an object "goes proxy" for the concept. But this means that what we appear to say about the concept (e.g., that it is easily attained, or that it is not empty) is not said about the concept at all, but about this proxy object. Indeed, even when Frege says, "An object must go proxy for the concept," the words "the concept" do not name a concept; they already name one of these proxy objects that he means to be explaining to us. Frege wants to pin down a concept and to make it a subject of predication, but the concept always slips away.

The problem with Frege's sentences is not simply that they fail to capture his thought. They suffer from a logical defect as well. Consider an example of the sort of sentence that unavoidably arises in logical discussions:

> The concept *horse* is a component of the judgment expressed by "Black Beauty is a horse."

This statement is, we now see, false: "the concept *horse*" is the name of an object, but the only object referred to in "Black Beauty is a horse" is Black Beauty. But the sentence is supposed to convey an insight to the reader, and it is supposed to be

---

[11] Frege, *Posthumous Writings*, H. Hermes, F. Kambartel, and F. Kaulbach, eds., P. Long and R. White, trans. (Chicago: University of Chicago Press, 1979), 118.

able to do this because the object designated by "the concept *horse*" is going proxy for the concept. The special form of representation that Frege calls "going proxy for" must be the proxy object's playing a saturated role on behalf of a thought-component that is essentially predicative, or unsaturated. And in order for the proxy to be of any use in getting around the awkwardness of expression, it must be capable of allowing us to "say something [true] about a concept." If there are any truths in this area at all, surely one of them is "The concept *horse* is a component of the judgment expressed by 'Black Beauty is a horse.'" Thus Frege is led to treat such sentences as strictly speaking false but as somehow also true. And this puts him in a logically untenable position. He cannot consistently regard the sentences he uses to convey his thought either as false or as true; but the distinctive characteristic of indicative sentences is that they are either true or false. Frege concludes that the sentences that he must use in order to lead the reader to his intended thought are not expressions of possible contents of judgments, but are misfiring expressions that are strictly speaking nonsensical. The problem with them is not that they are awkward or obscure or even false, but rather that they are not even sentences in the sense proper to logic. They lie outside logic's purview.

One might wonder whether Frege has to concern himself with such elusive things as concepts and objects. Couldn't he just forego all talk about such (apparent) items? To see why the answer is no, we have to recall Frege's purpose in developing the Begriffsschrift. The Begriffsschrift is a symbolic language that is to assist us in analyzing our thoughts and expressions so as to clarify their cognitive content. Analysis in terms of the Begriffsschrift requires distinguishing concepts and objects, and so when Frege describes his method of logical analysis or tries to instruct someone in its use, he comes out with sentences that are problematic in the way we have been discussing. Frege comes out with sentences that necessarily fail to say what he needs them to say.

Moreover, Frege argues that any investigation of the logical structure of thought will encounter difficulties analogous to those he finds himself in. Thinkable contents have components, and logic's business is to decompose complete thoughts into these components in such a way that the inferential relations between thinkable contents become clear. No matter what components a logician takes as the basic units of her particular brand of logical analysis, in describing these basic units she will find herself in a version of Frege's predicament.[22]

---

[22] Many philosophers believe that Frege is wrong to claim that a version of his predicament will arise in any system of logical analysis whatsoever, for they think that there is (or must be) a technical solution of his paradoxes. There are at least two candidates for such a solution: one is a theory of types that would ban the formation of the paradoxical sentences that so exercise Frege; the other, offered by Michael Dummett, is a recipe for replacing the problematic Fregean sentences with supposedly unproblematic ones. For example, Dummett would replace the illegitimate sentence "The concept *horse* is a concept" with "'A horse is something which everything either is or is not' (i.e., 'For every α either α is a horse or α is not a horse')" (Michael Dummett, *Frege: Philosophy of Language*, 2nd ed. [Cambridge, MA: Harvard University Press, 1981], 216–7).

It is beyond the scope of this essay to evaluate whether either of these proposals succeeds in circumventing the difficulty Frege sees in making an assertion about a concept. But I am inclined to think that they do not. In the case of a theory of types, it appears that the statement of the theory itself will involve statements of the kind Frege was suspicious of. Any theory of types will somehow have to

Frege expresses this conclusion when he writes:

> [O]ver the question what it is that is called a function in Analysis, we come up against the same obstacle; and on thorough investigation it will be found that the obstacle is essential, and founded on the nature of our language; that we cannot avoid a certain inappropriateness of linguistic expression; and that there is nothing for it but to realize this and always take it into account. (CO, 55)

This passage expresses Frege's conviction that any attempt to describe the logical components of sentences will necessarily misfire. It also expresses Frege's conviction that the misfiring can be overcome: he thinks that if both he and his reader always take into account the fact that "a certain inappropriateness of linguistic expression" is unavoidable, then they can reach an understanding that will convey the crucial insights. The possibility of achieving this understanding is described as follows:

> I do not at all dispute Kerry's right to use the words 'concept' and 'object' in his own way, if only he would respect my equal right, and admit that with my use of terms I have got hold of a distinction of the highest importance. I admit that there is a quite peculiar obstacle in the way of an understanding with my reader. By a kind of necessity of language, my expressions, taken literally, sometimes miss my thought; I mention an object, when what I intend is a concept. I fully realize that in such cases I was relying upon a reader who would be ready to meet me halfway—who does not begrudge a pinch of salt. (CO, 54)

If a reader will take his words with a pinch of salt, the misfiring of his sentences can be overcome, and Frege and his reader can come to an understanding —can come to grasp the same (inexpressible) thought.

What exactly does Frege think is involved in this communicative transaction? We might elaborate Frege's brief remarks along the following lines. In laying out the Begriffsschrift, Frege has been seeking to impart an understanding of what concepts and objects are and how to represent them in his symbolic notation. To this end, he has formulated sentences like "The concept *man* is not empty." At an early stage of our introduction to logical analysis, we hear this sentence as referring to the concept *man*, an item that is the very thing we predicate of individual

---

specify which linguistic expressions belong to which types; this will entail specifying predicative expressions without using them predicatively. But this is to violate Frege's doctrine that an expression belongs to a certain logical type only insofar as it is being used in the way characteristic of that type. The result of the attempt to specify logical types will be sentences like "The expression '___ is a horse' is a first-order predicate," which are just as problematic as sentences like "The concept *horse* is a concept."

And it is not clear to me that Dummett's suggestion fares any better in avoiding paradox. For example, Dummett would recast "In that sentence, the concept *horse* is predicated of Black Beauty" as follows: "In that sentence, what 'ξ is a horse' stands for is predicated of Black Beauty." Here the expression "what 'ξ is a horse' stands for" is, according to Dummett, "not a proper name but a predicative expression" (Dummett, 214). But is the expression "what 'ξ is a horse' stands for" really predicative? In this example it is not functioning predicatively in a proposition, so by Frege's principle we will have to conclude that it is *not* a predicate, and if it is not after all a predicate, a version of the paradox will arise for Dummett's reformulation too.

These remarks obviously do not settle the issue of whether there is a technical solution of the paradox. (For further, provocative discussion, see Anthony Palmer, *Concept and Object* [New York: Routledge, 1988].) But for the purposes of my comparison of Frege and Heidegger the most important thing is to note that Frege himself (rightly or wrongly) thought that the paradox is inevitable because it is inherent in language itself.

men. But when we reflect more deeply on the character of objects and concepts (as Kerry's objection forces us to do), we are to recognize that such sentences misfire. At the earlier stage, when we hear such sentences as being about a concept, we have but an imperfect grasp of the distinction between concept and object. We do not fully appreciate this essential distinction until we see what is wrong with such sentences, for part of having a full understanding of the distinction between concepts and objects is seeing why any sentence that purports to say what concepts or objects *are*—i.e., any attempt to express the full understanding—is bound to misfire. If we fully understand the distinction between concept and object, we will see why that distinction cannot be properly stated. And how do we come to a full understanding of Frege's point? As I read Frege, we come to this understanding by recognizing what the misfiring sentences are, as it were, *trying* to say and why they fail to say it. Frege's sentences do not *say* what the distinction is, but they *show* what it is.

7. Conclusion

Now we are in a position to bring out the resemblances between Frege's predicament and Heidegger's. Heidegger wants to explicate what it is to have a thought about a particular entity. To encounter a particular entity in this way presupposes an understanding of entities as a whole, *das Seiende im Ganzen*. But the sentences in which Heidegger discusses *das Seiende im Ganzen* prove to be logically problematic. They appear to be about some entity; but this appearance is deceptive, because *das Seiende im Ganzen* is to be distinguished from any particular entity. Yet if the sentences are not about some thing, then, by Heidegger's own lights, they are not assertions, and they do not communicate any statable content. Nevertheless, Heidegger thinks that, by drawing attention to their absurdity, he can bring his audience to grasp his crucial but unstatable doctrine concerning the relation between having a thought about a particular entity and having an understanding of entities as a whole. To grasp his doctrine is to see why the statements that initially purport to express it in fact fail to say anything.

Frege wants to explicate the logical structure of propositions (or, in his idiom, thoughts). This explication requires him to distinguish concepts and objects. But the sentences in which he expresses this distinction prove to be logically problematic. He forms sentences that appear to have a concept as their logical subject; but this appearance is deceptive, because concepts are to be distinguished from logical subjects. His sentences are in a certain sense ill-formed; they necessarily fail to express the distinction that he wants to draw between concepts and objects. Nevertheless, he thinks that his sentences can serve as hints, which, if his readers meet him halfway, can lead them to grasp his crucial but unstatable insight —the insight that we try but fail to express in such misfiring formulations as "A simple predication is to be analyzed as bringing an object under a concept." To grasp his insight is to see why the sentences that initially purport to express it in fact cannot do so; when he considers these sentences in the strictest, most literal way, he regards them as nonsense.

In drawing attention to this parallel, I don't mean to elide the differences between Frege and Heidegger. They come to what they regard as their inexpressible insights by very different paths. Frege is searching for a perspicuous way to represent possible contents of judgment, a system of formal logic that adequately captures the logical relations among propositions. Heidegger is trying to articulate that which enables human beings to make judgments about entities; he aims thereby to take a preliminary step toward articulating Dasein's understanding of Being. Frege is unconcerned with how we come to grasp the thoughts (the contents of possible judgments) that he analyzes, whereas Heidegger, in his existential analytic of Dasein, aims in part to explain the human ability to think. For Heidegger, Frege's project can have at best a secondary importance, since it presupposes the sort of understanding Heidegger wants to analyze.[23] This difference in their projects can in turn explain the differences in their reactions to their respective employments of logically defective expressions. Frege purports to be operating on thought with thought; he is making (and trying to express) judgments about the nature of judgment. Consequently, the "inappropriateness of linguistic expression" that inevitably arises in logical discussion is a problem, something to be worked around by readers and authors meeting halfway, by readers' readiness to take an author's misfiring words with a pinch of salt. On the other hand, because Heidegger is trying to get to a level of Dasein's kind of existence that lies below thinking, that lies below the making of moves within the realm of logic, he can at least initially be untroubled by the discovery that what goes on at that level is not subject to the laws of logic. He can be prepared to embrace, indeed almost to celebrate, the illogicality of attempts to describe this pre-logical aspect of Dasein's existence.

But these differences do not diminish the parallel I have drawn. What Heidegger's rejection of the sovereignty of logic comes to is, as we have seen, the notion that there is a way of conducting an inquiry and of imparting insights that does not involve asking questions or making assertions and so lies outside logic's purview. It now appears that Frege too is (implicitly) rejecting the sovereignty of logic when he seems to make assertions about concepts. An indication of the parallel is the resemblance between Heidegger's remark, "With regard to the Nothing, question and answer alike are inherently absurd" (WIM, 85), and the following statement of Frege's:

> The word 'concept' itself is, taken strictly, already defective, since the phrase 'is a concept' requires a proper name as grammatical subject and so, strictly speaking, it requires something contradictory, since no proper name can designate a concept; or perhaps better still [would be to say that it requires] something nonsensical.[24]

In making the statements that serve to bring their audiences to grasp what it is to be a thought about an object (respectively, to be a judgment about some particu-

---

[23] Michael Friedman's interpretation of Heidegger suggests a further respect in which Heidegger would have regarded Frege's inquiry as of secondary importance. Friedman portrays Heidegger in *Being and Time* as coming to terms with a problem he inherited from the neo-Kantian tradition (especially as embodied in Heinrich Rickert), namely, the problem of explaining how laws from the atemporal, ideal realm of logic can apply to actual, temporal thinking about concrete objects. Frege (whom Freidman does not discuss in connection with Heidegger) was comparatively unmoved by the neo-Kantian problem of explaining logic's connection with thinking. See Michael Friedman, *A Parting of the Ways: Carnap, Cassirer, and Heidegger* (Chicago: Open Court, 2000).

[24] Frege, *Posthumous Writings*, 177–8 (my interpolation).

lar entity which has been identified against a background of entities understood as a whole, to be the bringing of an object under a concept), Frege and Heidegger come into tension with the conception of logic that they both inherit from Kant, and which Kant expresses as follows:

> If, now, we set aside all cognition that we must borrow from *objects* and reflect solely upon the use of the understanding in itself, we discover those of its rules which are necessary throughout, in every respect and regardless of any special objects, because without them we would not think at all.[15]

Kant conceives the laws of logic as rules without which "we would not think at all." This is the conception of the laws of logic that Heidegger embraces in *The Metaphysical Foundations of Logic* when he says that "Using the rules of thought in the thinking process is uncircumventable " (104). Frege likewise endorses Kant's conception when he says the following about the laws of logic:

> [T]hey are the most general laws, which prescribe universally the way in which one ought to think if one is to think at all.[16]

Thus each philosopher finds that he has a conception of what it is to be a thought that rules out the possibility of making that conception of thought a possible content of thought. And each philosopher responds to this paradox by self-consciously using sentences that fail to express his insight (because they are "absurd" or "nonsensical"), but that are supposed to elicit the insight in the audience in some other way, to *show* it to them.

My purpose in this essay has been to explain why both Heidegger and Frege find themselves caught in a tension between their own conception of the laws of logic as governing all thinking and their need to convey insights that lie outside the purview of those laws. I have argued that they try to resolve this tension by saying that their logically ill-formed sentences bring their readers to grasp these extra-logical insights. I have so far refrained from critically evaluating Heidegger's and Frege's resolutions of the tensions that they confront, and I do not propose to render a final judgment on them here. Nevertheless, I will conclude with some remarks about what I think would be involved in criticizing the positions I have attributed to Frege and Heidegger.

The line of criticism I envision would challenge the idea that Frege and Heidegger are in possession of *insights*. I would argue that they have only the *illusion* of insights: they think that they have grasped a determinate cognitive content, when in fact there is no content there to be grasped. In suggesting that Frege and Heidegger are under an illusion, I do not mean to diminish their respective achievements. Their illusions of insights (if indeed this proves to be the right way to describe their results) are responses to genuine philosophical needs. Frege and Heidegger recognize that certain philosophical positions are fundamentally misguided, and they seek to expose these confusions by laying out an account of the nature of thought. I have been trying to bring out how, in giving

---

[15] Immanuel Kant, *Logic*, Robert S. Hartmann and Wolfgang Schwarz, trans. (New York: Dover, 1974), 14.
[16] Frege, *The Basic Laws of Arithmetic*, Montgomery Furth, trans. and ed. (Berkeley: University of California Press, 1964), 12.

such an account, they seem forced to think of what they are offering as insights that are extra-logical. In suggesting that what Frege and Heidegger have achieved are merely the illusions of insights, I am suggesting that there is no intelligible content to them. But I have been trying to show that it is quite intelligible that they find themselves under the illusion that they possess extra-logical insights, even if there is no intelligible content to the supposed insights themselves.

This is not the place for a full discussion of the confused positions that Frege and Heidegger seek to untangle, but I will try to indicate them in a few words. The importance Frege initially attaches to the distinction between concept and object is that observing the distinction will show a formalist theory of fractional, negative, etc., numbers to be untenable.[17] I think the ultimate importance of his conception of concepts and objects is that it provides for a critique of itemizing accounts of judgment (accounts, that is, which fail to recognize the characteristic unity of a judgment).

Heidegger has grander aspirations. He aims to recover a relationship to Being that has been distorted or covered up by all Western philosophy since the ancient Greeks. One aspect of this project requires combating a conception of the relation between thought and its object according to which thoughts are representations that have their content quite apart from any relations between the thinker and the entities represented. On this (broadly Cartesian) conception of thought, the content of a thought is not affected by whether the entities that the thought represents actually exist; it does not even matter to the content of a thought whether any entities at all exist. Heidegger's claim that a pre-theoretical grasp of *das Seiende* provides the ground for thought (judgment, assertion) is meant, at least in part, to correct the distortions inherent in the conception of thought advanced, in different ways, by Descartes and Husserl.

I would argue that Frege and Heidegger are right to criticize these targets. But their respective methods of criticism require them to erect what appear to be systems of positive claims standing in opposition to the views they criticize but lying outside the purview of logic. This is an inherently unstable position, in that Heidegger and Frege are compelled to claim both that they are in possession of thoughts (insights, graspings which have cognitive content) and that the thoughts in question are not subject to the laws that are at least partially constitutive of thinking. In order to argue that Frege and Heidegger ought never to have deviated from their official conception of logic —in order, that is, to argue that we ought to regard what they say about concepts and objects and about the world as a whole as expressing merely illusions of insight —it would be necessary to find some other way of satisfying the genuine needs to which they are responding when they come out with their problematic utterances. It would be necessary to find another way of combating philosophical error, another mode of criticism.

The aim of such a mode of criticism would be to expose the target of criticism as confused rather than false. A critic in this mode would not regard herself as setting up a position in opposition to the target position, but as revealing the target to be only the illusion of a position. In the course of bringing out the confusion of

---

[17] Frege, *The Foundations of Arithmetic*, x.

the target "position," this critic would no doubt have to come out with sentences that, like Frege's and Heidegger's problematic utterances, seem to promulgate extra-logical insights. But this critic herself would recognize that these supposed insights are *merely* supposed, and she would try to bring her readers to recognize this also. At the end of the day, the critic I am envisioning would not be trying to advance any positive theory; she would seek to impart to her readers only an understanding of how the targets of her criticism are confused, together with a certain self-consciousness about the means by which the confusion has been exposed. [28]

The criticism I am imagining is really quite similar to that offered by Frege and Heidegger. The crucial difference is that Frege and Heidegger unwittingly purvey mere illusions of positive insight, whereas the critic I envision would recognize that she is trafficking in illusions. If such a mode of criticism proves to be available, we can address the genuine needs that elicit Frege's and Heidegger's problematic utterances without having to advance alleged insights that are supposed to lie beyond the purview of logic. And only if we can succeed in this will we be entitled to find fault with Frege's and Heidegger's convictions that they are in possession of extra-logical insights. [29]

---

[28] The critic I am envisioning is the early Wittgenstein portrayed in James Conant, "The Search for Logically Alien Thought," *Philosophical Topics* 20 (1991): 115–80, and his "Frege and Early Wittgenstein," in Alice Crary and Rupert Read, eds., *The New Wittgenstein* (New York: Routledge, 2000), and in Cora Diamond's essays "What Nonsense Might Be" and "Throwing Away the Ladder: How to Read the *Tractatus*" in her *The Realistic Spirit* (Cambridge, MA: MIT Press, 1991). I will not enter upon the question whether Conant and Diamond are right about Wittgenstein; for my purposes it is enough that a mode of criticism such as they claim to find in Wittgenstein is possible.

[29] I would like to thank John Haugeland, who guided me into Heidegger's work; Jim Conant, who pointed to important source material and helped me untangle numerous intellectual knots; David Finkelstein, who dispensed invaluable editorial and philosophical advice at crucial moments; and especially John McDowell, who encouraged my speculations with a steady stream of incisive comments.

The Other Minds Problem In Early Heidegger*

HARRISON HALL
Department of Philosophy
University of Delaware

In *Being and Time,* Heidegger seems to have gotten the other minds problem backwards—taking it as obvious that we are in the midst of an intersubjective or "public" world and struggling with the question of how (in some sense) we come to know ourselves (given intersubjectivity, how to find an "I" or individuate myself). In what follows, I will try to make sense of Heidegger's backwardness here; to piece together the somewhat sketchy treatment of the traditional problem which prepares the way for his move in the opposite direction.

Heidegger's discussion of our knowledge of others in *Being and Time* consists largely of brief and scattered remarks which look like conclusions without argument.[1] One is tempted to join Sartre in his charge that Heidegger has "solved" the philosophical problem by simply defining human existence as coexistence and awarding, without justification, privileged status to our ordinary beliefs.[2]

I will argue that Heidegger cannot be dismissed so easily. By placing his remarks about our encountering of others into the context of the theory of the nature of things and the world which emerges from earlier sections of *Being and Time,* I will try to show that Heidegger offers a substantial criticism of, and a plausible alternative to, the traditional account of the relation of self to others which leads to the other minds problem.

Being and Time represents, at least in part, Heidegger's response to Husserl's suggestion that a complete characterization of the "natural standpoint" (or attitude) would be a task of great importance—though one which Husserl could not take time to pursue, the more pressing task being the

---

*Work on this paper was supported by a grant from the University of Delaware. Earlier versions were read at the meeting of the American Philosophical Association, Western Division, 1976, and at a number of universities in the United States and Canada. I am grateful for many helpful suggestions made on these occasions. I am particularly indebted to Hector-Neri Castaneda, Hubert Dreyfus, and Samuel Todes.

[1] M. Heidegger, *Being and Time,* 1962—hereafter referred to as *B&T.* pp.153-163.
[2] J.-P. Sartre, *Being and Nothingness,* 1966. pp. 333-336.

study of the "transcendental standpoint" from which strictly philosophical problems could be raised and solved. Reaching the transcendental standpoint required, according to Husserl, only brief attention to the most general features of the world of the natural attitude.[3] He saw the task of further analysis of the mundane world as an important *application* of phenomenology, but not as potentially productive of major methodological insights.

In his attempt to employ phenomenology in a careful examination of the world of the natural attitude ("everydayness"), however, Heidegger made discoveries which led to his rejection of much of Husserl's transcendental method and which he took to undermine traditional metaphysics. One of these discoveries is that our most fundamental sense of things is not a sense of "mere things" whose basic properties are independent of us ("present-at-hand"), but a sense of things which matter to us, things as they fit into our actions and concerns ("ready-to-hand"), equipment in the broadest sense of the term. The important feature which distinguishes equipmental things from "mere thngs" is their essential embeddedness in a context of purposive human activity. An "item" of equipment is not understandable as a separate, independent particular. A thing (a hammer, for example) is what it is only insofar as it fits in a certain way into an equipmental totality (perhaps the tools and workshop of the carpenter) which in turn draws its significance from its place in a hierarchy of purposes and projects (such as hammering, house building, family sheltering). The total network of purposes and projects is what Heidegger calls the "world"—the broadest pragmatic context in which things are encounterable. The relations holding between items in this context, along the sequence of purposes or between "pieces" of equipmental complexes Heidegger calls "reference" or "assignment." Things encountered in ordinary practical activity carry a reference in this sense to other things with which they are bound up and to the human purposes and projects in which they figure. Heidegger's claim is that these references are essential to a thing's being what it is.[4] He takes it to follow that an appropriate ontology must fly in the face of traditional accounts by taking the equipmentality ("readiness-to-hand") of things rather than "mere thinghood" as basic and purposive practical involvment with things ("being-in") rather than disinterested spectating as the fundamental relation between man and the world. Much of the argument for the correctness on this ontological approach

---

[3]At least at the time of *Ideas;* see pp. 95ff.

[4]There is not space here to reproduce Heidegger's argument for the correctness of this claim. The argument occupies most of Chs. 2 and 3, Div. I of *B&T;* and in a sense, all of *B&T* can be viewed as defending this claim by showing that the account which results from it best fits the whole of our experience. One of Heidegger's more specific grounds for the claim is summarized below.

comes to something like this. If we take the equipmentality of things as basic, we can understand both the world of practical involvement and the world of "mere things" which traditional ontology describes; the latter being understandable in terms of the non-equipmentality or non-usability of things ("unreadiness-to-hand") which results from the breakdown or abandonment of ordinary practical activity. On the other hand, if we take "mere thinghood" as ontologically basic, we will not be able to build up the purposive referential context ("world") of practical activity which makes the equipmentality (or the value) of things intelligible.[5]

Against the background of this ontological account, Heidegger's remarks about our experience of others suggest two criticisms of the traditional treatment of the other minds problem. The first of these is a specification of the general claim that the traditional ontological approach[6] produces a picture of the world and our interaction with it which does not fit our experience. Heidegger has in mind any theory which takes immediate presence as the principal criterion of the real or the knowable and leads to the following descending ontological/epistemological scale: my own inner mental life and its contents, the external world of material objects, other subjects of experience like myself with inner mental lives of their own. Such a theory suggests that our experience of others ought to be divisible into the experience of their bodies as mere things and our less direct experience of them as complete persons via an inference[7] which "adds" minds to bodies. Heidegger wants to say that our experience presents a very different picture. We do not actually encounter that mythical realm[8] in which we would experience ourselves as isolated subjects (Heidegger, 1962):

> ...we have shown that a bare subject without a world never 'is' proximally, nor is it ever given. And so in the end an isolated 'I' without others is just as far from being proximally given. [p. 152][9]

And the others we do encounter are not experienced as a composite of bodily thing and "tacked on" mental properties (Heidegger, 1962):

> The Others who are thus 'encountered' in a ready-to-hand, environmental context of equipment, are not somehow added on in thought to some Thing which is proximally just present-at-hand.[10]

---

[5] See *B&T*, pp. 131-133.

[6] The target here is Descartes; and Heidegger attempts to show that later historical figures (Kant, for example) may be viewed as working within the relevant Cartesian assumptions. See *B&T*, pp. 122-127.

[7] Some form of the "argument from analogy."

[8] Husserl's "sphere of ownness" in the *Cartesian Meditations*.

[9] *B&T*, p. 152. Heidegger cites Scheler's *Wesen und Formen der Sympathie* to support his reading of these "facts" about the content of our experience.

[10] *B&T*, p. 154.

This is not to suggest that such descriptive inadequacy is sufficient to undermine the traditional treatment of the other minds problem. Nor does Heidegger intend to offer a simple description of our ordinary experience as a solution to the standard epistemological puzzle. What he wants to do is draw attention to the ontology which underlies the other minds problem. Heidegger is looking, not for one more solution to the traditional problem, but for an ontological alternative to the theory which makes our experience of others so problematic in the first place.

The gist of Heidegger's initial criticism of the traditional treatment of the other minds problem, then, is that we have reason to suspect that something is wrong with its ontological underpinnings. His second criticism attempts to put the finger on exactly what goes wrong ontologically when we try to explain our experience of others in the traditional way. Briefly put, Heidegger's charge is that traditional ontology cannot account for those general structures (or categories, if we can translate the point into very non-Heideggerian language) which make possible (or make sense of) our experience of others. One of the things needed to make this charge "stick" is an understanding of what happens when we change the subject from epistemology to ontology—a sense of what Heidegger is and isn't up to here. He is *not* primarily concerned with the separation of our experience of others into real and apparent, or with the validation of certain of our claims to know that or what another is thinking or feeling. The issue he wants to raise concerns something more like the "conditions for the possibility of" our experience of others, real or apparent. Heidegger wants to know how our experience, regardless of its epistemic credentials, is able to have "of otherness" about it—how our world comes to be structured in such a way that certain of its contents can be experienced *as* other subjects of experience. And the answer to this question will presumably bear on how we should describe and assess the particular experiences involved. It is in this sense that the ontological issue is prior to the epistemological one.

Heidegger attributes to the tradition a stand on the ontological issue which includes the following. Starting from a point at which my ontology has room only for myself and things, I am motivated by the behavior of certain of these "things" to add to my world the ontological machinery for dealing with others. Heidegger's criticism is that this provides no explanation of the relevant ontological structures at all. We want to account for the ontological machinery which makes it possible to experience certain contents of the world as more than (or other than) things—and the traditional explanation seems to be that the experiencing of them as things and something more gives rise to the appropriate ontological machinery. To use Heidegger's terminology, this inverts the relationship between the "ontic" and the ontological, between actual experiences of others and the general structures which make such experiences possible. The actual (ontic) recognition of others which is supposed to expand the world (ontologically) from private to intersubjective is unintelligible prior to the expansion (Heidegger, 1962):

> ...Dasein, as Being-in-the-world, already is (ontologically) with Others. 'Empathy' (or any other kind of actual relating to others) does not first constitute Being-with; only on the basis of Being-with does 'empathy' become possible...[p. 162]"[11]

If we do experience "others" as "more than" things, it is because our *ontological* resources, from the start, exceed those of the solipsist's world and cannot possibly be explained in terms of the features of that world. At rock bottom, the world must be intersubjective in ontological structure, if not in fact (a "with world" in Heidegger's terminology), and my most fundamental sense of myself must include some sense of my being, at least in principle, just one of an indefinite number of subjects (in Heidegger's terminology, my "being" is essentially a "being-with"). Or, to put the point a bit differently, the most elementary ontologial account of subject and world must have a place for the possible experience of other subjects.

Following this line of reasoning, Heidegger returns to his earlier treatment of the world of practical activity[12] to show that the ontological theory which emerged from that discussion has the resources for making sense of intersubjectivity. The relevant points of this theory are: (1) the equipmentality or instrumentality ("readiness-to-hand") of things is ontologically basic; (2) the essential nature of human being ("Dasein") is purposive, practical involvement with things as items of equipment or instruments; and (3) the world is the referential [13] context generated by purposive human activity. Heidegger wants to show that this context (the "world") is necessarily intersubjective in ontological structure (a "with world") and that human being ("Being-in-the-world") is essentially "public" or intersubjective (a "Being-with") independent of any actual experience of "others" (Heidegger, 1962):

> Being-with...(is) an existential attribute which Dasein, of its own accord, has coming to it from its own kind of Being...(and not) by reason of the occurrence of Others [p. 156][14]

Heidegger's story is as follows. Things in their equipmentality or instrumentality already carry an implicit reference to an open and indefinite intersubjectivity. Equipment is always encounterd in practial activity as having a certain generality or "publicness" attached to its usability. It is experienced as "usable by *one*," "what *one* uses to hammer," and so on.[15] We do not experience and could not understand any item of equipment whose

---

[11] *B&T*, parenthetical material added.
[12] *B&T*, Div. I, Chs. 2 and 3, summarized on pp. 248–249 above.
[13] In Heidegger's sense of "reference"—see p. 248 above.
[14] *B&T*, parenthetical material added.
[15] *B&T*, pp. 153–154.

usability would be private, not simply in fact but in principle. Correlatively, human activity—the practical utilization of equipment—takes on a certain general or public aspect. Every purposive enterprise ("project") is something "*one* can do"—*one* hammers," "*one* builds houses," and so on.[16] My sense of myself as practical subject is not one of privacy or uniqueness, but rather a sense of filling anonymously a set of essentially public roles which are indifferently or equivalently fillable by anyone. As a result, the context generated by practical activity is necessarily intersubjective in ontological structure; has, independent of any particular encountering of them, places for other practical subjects. And the human way of being, purposive, practical involement in the world, is a way of being related to possible others—as filling the same roles, engaged in the same or similar projects, using the same items of equipment, and so on. In Heidegger's (1962) words:

> The world of Dasein is a with-world. Being-in is *Being-with* Others.[17]
> So far as Dasein *is* at all, it has Being-with-one another as its kind of Being.[18]

This ontological understanding leads to a description of our actual experience of others which differs markedly from the traditional one.[19] "...Others...show themselves...in terms of what is ready-to-hand..."[20]. For example, "...along with the equipment to be found when one is at work, those Others for whom the 'work' is destined are 'encountered too'."[21] Our most basic experience of others is not as objects of passive observation or theoretical cognition, but as coparticipants in the everyday world of practical activity.

The strength of Heidegger's position seems to depend on its being taken as a response to *metaphysical* (or ontological) views—solipsism as a metaphysical thesis or any theory which takes the solipsist's world as the legitimate metaphysical/ontological starting point. The Heideggerian reply is clear. The world cannot be limited to a solitary subject and his "private" experience. The practical activity of even a single human subject is sufficient to make the world of his experience "public" or intersubjective in ontological structure. What is not so clear is the way in which Heidegger's ontological story might be used to address the standard *epistemological* problems associated with our knowledge of others. What is at issue when epistemological problems are raised is not the "in principle" (ontological) intersubjectivity of the world, but its actual (ontic) intersubjectivity. And the "publicness" or intersubjectivity for which Heidegger argues seems to be compatible with my being, for all I

---

[16] *B&T*, p. 164.
[17] *B&T*, p. 155.
[18] *B&T*, p. 163.
[19] See p. 249 above.
[20] *B&T*, p. 160.
[21] *B&T*, p. 153.

can *know, in fact* the only subject around. Let me suggest briefly both why Heidegger did not address, and how he might nevertheless have addressed, this issue.

Heidegger's investigation of "everydayness" revealed that the natural attitude and the practical activity constitutive of it enjoy an ontological priority over the traditional philosophic attitude and its theoretical activity which is removed as far as possible from the natural world of human concerns and purposes.[22] This means, for Heidegger, that any adequate philosophic account of human experience will have to be, at bottom, an account of the practical world on its own terms, from within the perspective of purposive involvement rather than from a theoretical standpoint divorced from the world it attempts to understand. Heidegger's hermeneutic method and revised version of Husserl's phenomenology[23] purport to make philosophy possible within this constraint. What is important to our discussion is that within the context of this restriction solipsism as an epistemological problem cannot arise. Behind Heidegger's apparently factual account of the everyday world in which an "isolated I without others"[24] *is* never given, lurks the much stronger Husserlian claim that a radical (i.e. philosophical) questioning of the givenness of others *cannot* occur within natural experience. Within the natural attitude specific experiences of others may be questioned, but only when these questions are concretely or practically motivated, and only against a background in which our ability to have had and to continue to have veridical experiences of other is presupposed—that is, only within a context which rules out in principle any radical or general doubt as to my ability to know that I am not the only subject in the world.[25] So Heidegger's successful restriction of philosophy to the natural attitude (a consequence of his ontological theory) precludes his taking epistemological solipsism seriously.[26] Heidegger's ontological story accounts for the *possibility* of our experiencing others and prescribes the following general explanation of our *actual*

---

[22]See pp. 2-4 above, and *B&T*, p. 99.

[23]See *B&T*, pp. 37-38, 49-63.

[24]See p. 5 above, and *B&T*, p. 152.

[25]See E. Husserl, *Ideas*, 1962, pp. 92-96; and Cartesian Meditations, pp. 83-85. See also my "Criteria, Perception, and Other Minds," *Canadian Journal of Philosophy*, VI, 2, June 1976, especially pp. 268-274, for a fleshing out of this claim which is free of phenomenological jargon.

[26]Husserl avoids serious confrontation with this issue by making the opposite move. Husserl's radical separation of the natural and philosophic attitudes and his understanding of the consequent "unnaturalness" of philosophy (transcedental phenomenology) take the bite out of the other minds problem. Questions which seem initially to concern the referents of those conscious acts which are (at least apparently) of others, turn out really to concern only the meaning (in a very broad sense) of those acts. See D. Føllesdal, "Huserl's Theory of Perception," Ch. 21 in *Handbook of Perception*, Vol. I, E. C. Carterette & M. P. Friedman ed. (New York: Academic Press, 1974); and my "Idealism and Solipsism in Husserl's *Cartesian Meditations*," *Journal of the British Society for Phenomenology*, VII, 1, January 1976, pp. 53-55.

experiencing of them. I experience others whenever I experience beings involved in the practical world of useful things and uses for them in a manner similar to that which is definitive of my own being. If the fabric of everydayness or the natural world is so tightly woven as to prohibit the usual *philosophical* questions, and if the general theory of the nature of things and the world in *Being and time* is roughly correct, then that is the whole story. The other minds problem is a pseudo-problem, its source a "backward" metaphysical/ontological view.

Finally, even if the world of ordinary experience is not as restrictive epistemologically as Husserl and Heidegger believe it to be, there is still a way to bring Heidegger's ontological theory to bear on epistemological solipsism. The ontology of *Being and Time* provides a global theory of what there is and how it fits together, supported as a whole by its intuitive fit with our pretheoretical experience and by its explanatory power. This theory carves out correlative places for certain complexes of equipment and practical subjects with purposive roles which involve the utilization of that equipment. There are, in fact, actual items of equipment (surgical instruments, for example) which refer to purposive roles which I do not, and in some cases could not, fill.[27] And there seem to be other practical subjects filling these roles who would, if actual, explain the existence and apparent utilization of such equipment. Heidegger's ontological theory commits us to the actual existence of these others at least to this extent—any philosophical (non-practical or non-concrete in motivation) questioning of their actual existence, being strictly theoretical in origin, will in effect put in question the entire ontology of *Being and Time*. This means that any radical or general questioning of our knowledge of others—the kind which has traditionally made epistemological solipsism attractive—will have to be embedded in a global ontological theory preferable to Heidegger's on grounds normally relevant for the comparison of theories. This restriction would make it extremely difficult to raise seriously the problem of other minds.

REFERENCES

Heidegger, M. *Being and Time.* New York: Harper & Row, 1962.
Husserl, E. *Cartesian Meditations.* The Hague: Martinus Nijoff, 1960.
Husserl, E. *Ideas.* New York: Collier Books, 1962.
Sartre, J. P. *Being and Nothingness.* New York: Washington Square Press, 1966.

---

[27] *B&T* pp. 153-154.

Philosophy after Wittgenstein and Heidegger

CHARLES GUIGNON
University of Vermont

1. Philosophy's "Legitimate Heir"

Richard Rorty began a series of lectures in the early seventies by saying, "Just as no one in the nineteenth century could go on doing philosophy without coming to terms with Kant, so no one in our century can go on doing philosophy without coming to terms with Wittgenstein and Heidegger." Though not everyone would agree with this judgment, it does pose an interesting question about what it is we are supposed to come to terms *with* in the writings of these two figures. How are we to understand the upshot of their thought for philosophy? Rorty himself seems to hold that Wittgenstein and Heidegger are master diagnosticians of the tradition whose "therapies" and "de-structions" have enabled us to stop doing philosophy. In contrast, Charles Taylor claims that their writings open the way to a new type of inquiry into the conditions for the possibility of intentionality. In his view, what they offer is a "critique of epistemology in which we discover something deeper and more valid about ourselves [as agents], . . . something of our deep or authentic nature as selves."[1] Rorty replies that Taylor has gone only halfway in grasping the consequences of Wittgenstein's and Heidegger's thought. For if human beings are truly "self-interpreting animals," if they are "interpretation all the way down" (in the phrase Taylor borrows from H. L. Dreyfus), then "there are lots of ways to describe, and thus to study, human beings," and hence "there is no metaphysical privilege attached to [the] way of describing them" as agents that Taylor advocates.[2] Taylor, for his part, thinks Rorty is too precipitous in taking the collapse of foundationalism to mean the end of philosophy. What Wittgenstein and Heidegger show us is not how to shut

---

[1] "Overcoming Epistemology," in K. Baynes, J. Bohman, and T. McCarthy, eds., *After Philosophy: End or Transformation?* (Cambridge: The MIT Press, 1987), pp. 482-83 (henceforth "OE").

[2] "Absolutely Non-Absolute," *Times Literary Supplement*, December 6, 1985, p. 1379.

philosophy down, but how to open up a new, nonfoundationalist kind of inquiry that can shore up our views on politics and society.

Behind this debate is the shared assumption that Wittgenstein and Heidegger have undermined what Rorty calls "epistemology-centered philosophy," and so have permanently shifted the ground on which philosophy moves. In what follows, I want to examine some of the convergences in the writings of Wittgenstein and Heidegger that justify this assumption, focusing especially on their descriptions of our everyday predicament as agents in the world and on their visions of the role of language in our lives. But there is a deeper question I want to address, and that is the question: What direction does their thought point for the future of philosophy? Is it purely negative, undermining traditional philosophical questions and putting nothing new in their place? Or is it positive in the sense of paving the way to a refurbished and transformed philosophy? Wittgenstein once spoke of the "legitimate heir" of the subject which used to be called "philosophy."[3] The question, then, is: What, if anything, is philosophy's legitimate heir? Although it will be impossible to argue for it here, my hunch is that Taylor's positive vision of the future of philosophy is more defensible.

At first sight it might seem bizarre to think that Wittgenstein and Heidegger can be compared at all. Heidegger's *Being and Time* announces itself as a work of "fundamental ontology" whose aim is to lay a foundation for the regional sciences by posing "the question of the meaning of Being." Its turgid prose and heavy-handed architectonic mark it as a work in the grand tradition of metaphysics. The writings of the later Wittgenstein, in contrast, consist of sprightly aphorisms, piecemeal therapies for "what we are tempted to say," and often inconclusive exchanges with an unidentified interlocutor. Where Heidegger is steeped in the history of philosophy and wants to "de-structure the history of ontology," Wittgen-

---

[3] Wittgenstein, *The Blue and Brown Books* (New York: Harper Torchbooks, 1958), pp. 28, 62 (hereafter cited as BB). In the text I also use the following abbreviations: from works by Wittgenstein, *Philosophical Investigations*, trans. G. E. M. Anscombe (New York: Macmillan, 1967) = PI; *On Certainty*, trans. D. Paul and G. E. M. Anscombe (New York: Harper Torchbooks, 1969) = OC; *Philosophical Remarks*, trans. R. Hargreaves and R. White (Oxford: Basil Blackwell, 1975) = PR; *Remarks on the Foundations of Mathematics*, trans. G. E. M. Anscombe (Cambridge: MIT Press, 1983) = RFM; *Zettel*, trans. G. E. M. Anscombe (Berkeley: University of California Press, 1967) = Z; by Heidegger, *Sein und Zeit* (Tübingen: Max Niemeyer, 1972) = SZ, with translations from *Being and Time*, trans. J. Macquarrie and E. Robinson (New York: Harper & Row, 1962), which contains the German pagination in the margins. Unless otherwise noted, quotes from Wittgenstein's works refer to sections rather than page numbers.

stein concentrates on natural assumptions that arise when doing philosophy and generally ignores the history of philosophy.

Yet despite these important differences, there are also some striking affinities in their thought. Both writers focus on our practical lives and criticize attempts to justify those practices by appeal to timeless truths about the nature of reason or to facts about the world. Both challenge representationalist accounts of our relation to the world — Wittgenstein by criticizing traditional theories of meaning and designation, Heidegger by questioning the primacy accorded "mere seeing" in the tradition. Both are "contextualists" in the sense of holding that, since we have no clear access to forms and categories of pure reason or to intuitions of essences, our starting point must be a description of our everyday situations in the world, or a "phenomenology of everydayness."[4]

The source of these similarities, I believe, is to be found in the "philosophies of life" that dominated so much of German thought at the turn of the century.[5] With the collapse of Idealism, and with the growing sense of a "loss of meaning" accompanying the ascendancy of positivist science, a natural response was to interpret the role of philosophy as trying to articulate what is contained in the contingent and temporal flow of life itself. So we find Schopenhauer's demand that philosophy begin with a "hermeneutic" of concrete life-forms, Herder's and Humboldt's treatment of language as an expression of life, Lotze's "teleological idealism" which defines the "real" in terms of what is valuable for life, Marx's emphasis on the basic needs of life, Nietzsche's call for life-affirmation, and the Neo-Kantians' definition of truth in terms of its value for life ("truth-values"). The vitalisms, energisms and biologisms of the turn of the century, together with the immensely influential *Lebensphilosophie* movement, which evolved in the twenties into the "philosophy of existence" and later into "existentialism," all testify to the appeal of this concern with rooting philosophy in life.[6]

---

[4] The expression is Heidegger's, but see T. R. Schatzki's valuable discussion of Wittgenstein's method as a "phenomenology of the everyday" in "The Prescription is Description: Wittgenstein's View of the Human Sciences," in S. Mitchell and M. Rosen, eds., *The Need for Interpretation* (Atlantic Highlands, New Jersey: Humanities, 1983).

[5] Nicholas F. Gier has made a convincing case for Wittgenstein's affinities with life-philosophy in *Wittgenstein and Phenomenology* (Albany: SUNY University Press, 1981), Chapter 3. I discuss Heidegger's debt to life-philosophy in *Heidegger and the Problem of Knowledge* (Indianapolis: Hackett, 1983), section 4.

[6] See Herbert Schnädelbach's *Philosophy in Germany: 1831-1933* (Cambridge: Cambridge University Press, 1984) for a discussion of the crucial concept of "life" in German thought.

Although Heidegger came to feel that "philosophy of life . . . says about as much as 'the botany of plants'" (SZ p. 46) and needs a deeper grounding, his early interest in examining *Leben-in-der-Welt* and the meaning "inherent in factical life"[7] still shows through in his project of discovering the "roots," "origins," "wellsprings," and "soil" from which our concepts originate. If it is to avoid *Bodenlosigkeit* (groundlessness), philosophy must start from our own personal or "existentiell" grasp of what life is all about in our ordinary being-in-the-world. In order to find the "existentials" or essential structures of human being (Dasein) in general, we must begin from our own concrete lives: "the roots of the existential analytic, for its part, are ultimately existentiell" (SZ p. 13). When Heidegger says that the question of Being is "nothing other than the radicalization of an essential tendency-of-being which belongs to Dasein itself — the pre-ontological understanding of Being" (SZ p. 14), he means that ontology starts from the everyday, pretheoretical grasp of life embodied in our practical agency. Similarly, Wittgenstein tells us to get out of the *Luftgebäude* (castles floating in the air) of theorizing, and to get "back to the rough ground" (PI 118, 107) of our concrete, ordinary grasp of language in use. Our words have meaning only in "the stream of life" (PR p. 81), in the whole "tapestry of life" (PI, p. 174), not in a "sublime" logic beyond life. When we look for justifications for our practices, we find that what we simply *do* in living is "bedrock" (PI 217); there is nothing deeper than life which could explain or justify it.

The affinities with life-philosophy help to clarify the similarities in Wittgenstein's and Heidegger's procedures in dealing with philosophical problems. Both suggest that these problems arise from a stance of disengaged, theoretical reflection, and both try to dissolve these problems by providing descriptions of how things show up for us in the course of our ordinary, prereflective lives. Heidegger begins with a description of "average everydayness" where one is caught up in a "nonthematic absorption" in ordinary affairs and "loses oneself" in what one encounters in the world (SZ p. 76). His goal is to capture the way we encounter things "in the concern which makes use of them without noticing them explicitly" (SZ p. 74). Wittgenstein's method is also descriptive: "We must do away with all *explanation*, and description alone must take its place" (PI 109). The aim is to bring out the "aspects of things that are most important for us [which] are hidden because of their simplicity and familiarity," those things one is "unable to notice . . . because [they are] always before one's eyes" (PI 129). His frequent references to the "prim-

---

[7] See *Heidegger and the Problem of Knowledge*, p. 59.

itive" (*ursprünglich* or *primitiv*) serve as reminders of the unnoticed features of ordinary life that make our practices intelligible.

The description of everydayness serves as a basis for articulating features of our agency that are generally hidden and only implicit in everyday life. From his phenomenology of everydayness, Heidegger arrives at "transcendental generalizations" about the conditions for the possibility of agency in general: those "fundamental existentials" which are the "basis on which *every* interpretation of Dasein which is ontical [that is, particular and concrete] and belongs to a world-view must move . . ." (SZ p. 200). Such structures of being-in-the-world as involvement in practical concerns, future-directedness, and situatedness are said to be "more primordial" (*ursprünglich*) than theoretical reflection in the sense that, whereas theory can be seen as a derivative or founded mode of being-in-the-world, practical activities cannot be accounted for solely in terms of the representationalist picture assumed by the theoretical attitude. Although Wittgenstein officially eschews any "craving for generality" (BB p. 18), his procedure has often been compared to a transcendental argument[8] in the way it moves from plain features of our lives to the background conditions that make those activities possible. The notions of language-games, grammar, and forms of life may be seen as identifying those general (if not exactly "essential") characteristics of our lives which make our activities possible.

Both Wittgenstein and Heidegger reject argument in the familiar sense. In struggling to convey a sense of our human situation that provides an alternative to the traditional, "commonsense" picture of representationalism, they concentrate on description and claims about the conditions for the possibility of our daily activities. Since the traditional representationalist picture is so deeply ingrained in our thinking and language, both also deploy detailed therapies and de-structurings, often loaded with metaphors and neologisms, to help us bypass the assumptions that arise when language is "idling" or when we adopt a theoretical stance toward life. What emerges in their writings is an understanding of human existence as finite, contingent, and contextualized, a picture which undermines the

---

[8] For instance, by Rorty in "Verificationism and Transcendental Arguments," Noûs 5 (1971): 3-14; by Taylor in "The Opening Arguments of Hegel's *Phenomenology*" in A. MacIntyre, ed., *Hegel: A Collection of Essays* (Garden City, New York: Anchor, 1972); and more recently by Lynn Rudder Baker in "On the Very Idea of a Form of Life," *Inquiry* 27 (1984): 277-89. To note this similarity to the procedure of transcendental arguments is not to suggest that Wittgenstein is developing a "transcendental philosophy." The differences between Wittgenstein and transcendental philosophy are clarified in Susanne Thiele's excellent book, *Die Verwicklungen im Denken Wittgensteins* (Freiburg: Karl Alber, 1983).

assumptions of traditional philosophy and paves the way for the recent thought of such figures as Rorty and Taylor.

2. Everydayness, Understanding, and Meaning

The representationalist picture of our human situation we have inherited from Descartes fixes in advance how things can appear to us "like a pair of glasses on our nose through which we see whatever we look at" (PI 103). When we are doing philosophy, we tend to think of ourselves as essentially minds set over against a collection of independent physical objects which our ideas represent and our words designate. The goal of philosophy, then, is to show how our ordinary competence in interacting with the world is possible and justified. In other words, philosophy tries to account for the familiar intelligibility of things as they show up in our day-to-day lives. The intractable puzzles of traditional epistemology-centered philosophy arise precisely because of the assumptions of the representationalist model. For it seems that what is "given" in ordinary experience on this model (sensory input and possibly some inbuilt rules) is too limited to ground or make sense of our full-blown understanding of ourselves and our world. Our grasp of things appears to be underdetermined by the "data" and capacities available to us.

The way Wittgenstein and Heidegger handle these traditional philosophical problems is to suggest that they arise in part because of the representationalist portrayal of the self as a "subject" set over against an objective external reality. By describing everydayness in detail, they lead us away from the tendency to think of ourselves as subjects or minds distinct from a world of brute objects, and they thereby suggest a new way of grasping the sources of intelligibility that are already present in our lives as agents.

Heidegger's phenomenology of human agency starts out from a description of life as a "happening" caught up in "dealings" with equipment in ordinary contexts. In our prereflective activities, he suggests, we find ourselves absorbed in handling things, and in coping with situations we encounter as "significant" in the sense that things *matter* or *count* for us in specific ways. What shows up for us in such contexts is not a collection of brute objects to be represented, but a totality of equipment organized into a web of means/ends relations by our projects. Heidegger's well-known example of the workshop shows how, when everything is running smoothly, the hammer appears *in* hammering, *in order to* fasten boards together, which is *for* building a bookcase. Such familiar contexts of activity are encountered as holistic fields of involvements — the "ready-to-hand" — organized around our undertakings ("what it's for"), and ultimately around our self-interpretations as agents in the world (the "for the sake of which" of our concerns). Given this picture of everydayness, there is simply no way to drive in a wedge between the representing subject on the one hand, and mere objects to be represented on the other. The equipmental context gains its significance and structure from my sense of what I am doing in that setting. Yet, at the same time, who I *am* as an agent there is defined by the context in which I am engaged: in the workshop, for instance, I can *be* a craftsman or an amateur, but not a linebacker or an ayatollah. The ability to see things as mere objects on hand to be represented — as "present-at-hand" — requires a "change-over" in our stance toward things which Heidegger calls "the disworlding of the world."

The description of everydayness also brings out the way in which our lives are always nested in the wider context of a historical culture. Our possibilities of self-interpretation and our concrete ways of acting are generally guided in advance by the public roles, standards, and conventions we all absorb in growing up into a communal life-world. For the most part we are not so much unique individuals as we are participants and placeholders in what Heidegger calls the "They" (*das Man*): "We take pleasure and enjoy ourselves as *they* take pleasure; we read, see, and judge about literature and art as *they* see and judge. . . . The 'They' . . . which [we] all are, though not as the sum, prescribes the kind of Being of everydayness" (SZ pp. 126-27). This attunement to public ways of acting — the ingrained tendency to respond according to social standards, to fall into step with the crowd, to enact standardized roles — defines our identity in everydayness without residue. For this reason Heidegger says that being the They is a "primordial phenomenon" which "belongs to Dasein's positive constitution" (SZ p. 129). What I am doing at any time, as well as my thoughts and feelings, has a point and makes sense only against the background of practices and institutions of my community — as, for example, talking to a group of people counts as an academic lecture only given the background of the university system. Heidegger's description of everydayness leads us to see the world as a field of significance laid out by communal practices: "the They itself articulates the referential context of significance" (SZ p. 129). In this sense we exist as a shared "clearing" in which things can show up as relevant in relation to our lives.

The description of human existence as bound up with a public world provides the basis for identifying three fundamental structures of human agency. First, we find ourselves "thrown" or situated within a familiar world where things "matter" to us because of our prior attunement (*Stimmung*) (SZ p. 137). Because things always show up as mattering to us in some way or other, there is no horizonless vantage point for the apprehension of brute "facts." Second, as agents we are "outside of ourselves" in addressing the concerns of daily life according to our culture's sense of what is important. In dealing with equipment, according to Heidegger, "Dasein addresses itself to the objects of its concern," and thereby "expresses itself too; that is to say, it expresses its *being at home with* the ready-to-hand" (SZ pp. 407-8). As we shall see, the way in which Dasein "expresses itself [*spricht sich aus*] as a being toward entities" (SZ pp. 223-24) is focused by the possibilities of interpretation articulated by a public language. Finally, we are always "ahead of ourselves," organizing and interpreting current situations in the light of future possibilities. Understood as "projection," human life is teleological, a purposive thrust toward the future which Heidegger calls "Being-toward-the-end." This futurity unfolds not so much in conscious goal-setting or planning as in simply drifting along into the routines and undertakings defined by socially approved tasks and obligations. Our being toward the future is the source of the "forestructure of understanding" which preshapes the ways things can show up for us in our everyday lives together.

Heidegger's claim, then, is that explicit awareness of mere objects is possible only for beings who have some prior competence in coping with what he calls an "as structure" of practical involvements. This prereflective mastery of the "hermeneutic as" of equipment — the ability to handle things in familiar ways in meaningful situations — is made possible by our participation in the public life-world opened up by the They. It follows that we are always caught up in a "hermeneutic circle": our dealings with what we find around us are preshaped by our culturally-defined overview of how things can count for our community, while that background understanding is itself constantly revised in the light of our encounters with what shows up in our activities. And so there can be no access to raw facts independent of our pre-understanding: if one is engaged in interpretation and one wants to appeal to what just "stands there," Heidegger says, "then one finds that what 'stands there' in the first instance is nothing other than the obvious undiscussed assumption of the person who does the interpreting" (SZ p. 150). In other words, what can *count as* a relevant "fact" is always preshaped by the background of intelligibility embodied in our skilled practices. For this reason Heidegger points out that fundamental ontology — the inquiry into what makes things the things they are — asks "about Being itself insofar as Being enters into the intelligibility of Dasein. The meaning of Being can never be contrasted with entities, or with Being as the 'ground' which gives entities support; for a 'ground' becomes accessible only as meaning, even if it is itself the abyss [*Abgrund*] of meaninglessness" (SZ p. 152). The Being of things is therefore constituted by our shared background of attuned intelligibility, a background which itself has no deeper ground than the contingent practices that have emerged in our historical culture.

Where Heidegger's phenomenology focuses on our involvements with equipment, Wittgenstein's *Philosophical Investigations* begins by inquiring into how we refer to things with words. But Wittgenstein's concerns may be seen as congruent with Heidegger's to the extent that the basic question for both is how we are able to understand the world, or how intentionality is possible. A commonsense way of accounting for our understanding of the world presupposes "the model of 'object and designation'" (PI 293). According to this model, we start out in life finding ourselves surrounded by objects; we then learn the names for those objects through "ostensive training" (someone points to a piece of paper and says "paper"); and thereafter we know what objects of that type are. Our understanding of the world is built up from such instances of learning the significations of words. This traditional account of language presupposes the representationalist picture of ourselves as minds related to objects, and then tries to explain our understanding in terms of mental processes linking words to things, that is, knowing the *meanings* of words.

Wittgenstein challenges every aspect of this account of the basis for our understanding. How, he asks, would a preverbal child know what pointing is, or that the teacher is pointing to the paper and not to its color, size or shape? How does the child learn the *use* of the word (as a mass term, say, rather than as a count noun)? Does the child start out with *our* understanding of objects in the world, so that the only issue is grasping what conventional sounds we associate with those objects? Or isn't it the case that the child first finds out how we articulate the world into "objects" by learning our language? Ostensive training seems to explain how we come to understand things because it is seen on the model of "ostensive *definition*," i.e., cases where someone *already* knows our language — can ask, for instance, "What color is that?" — and so understands the reply — "That's called 'sepia'" (PI 30). But ostensive definitions succeed because the learner already knows "what place in language, in grammar, we assign to the word," "the post at which we station the word" (PI 29). In other words, some understanding of language is necessary before this kind of ostension can succeed: "One has already to know (or be able to do) something in order to be capable of asking a thing's name," just as one must already have mastered the game of chess to some extent in order to understand the words, "This is the king," when shown a particular piece (PI 31). The traditional account of how we come to understand words therefore presupposes the very understanding it was supposed to explain.

"We may say: only someone who already knows how to do something with it can significantly ask a name" (PI 31).

Wittgenstein's reflections here lead to an inversion of the traditional order of explanation. The question asked was, "How can we explain our ordinary competence in dealing with things and grasping the world?" and the philosophical response was to show how understanding could be built up from particular cases of grasping the meanings of words. What Wittgenstein suggests, however, is that we can learn words (and, hence, grasp what objects are) only if we *already* have an understanding of the world, an understanding itself rooted in a prior mastery of language. What is basic is the "preunderstanding" embodied in our know-how: our "ability to do" things, our "mastery" of standard patterns of discrimination and articulation as competent agents in a familiar life-world. Items in the world can stand out as counting for us in certain ways only because we have some mastery of what Wittgenstein calls the "significance" or "importance" of the ordinary situations in which we find ourselves: "What is happening now has significance in these surroundings. The surroundings give it its importance" (PI 583). Words have meanings and can be understood only within "intelligible situations" (Z 17). But in that case the intelligibility of things cannot be explained atomistically in terms of isolated identifications. Rather, "[l]ight dawns gradually over the whole" (OC 141).

It follows from the priority of this holistic background of understanding that we can pick out or identify "facts" only against the backdrop of a prior sense of how things can count as significant in our lives. Wittgenstein asks, "But what things are 'facts'? Do you believe you can show what fact is meant by, e.g., pointing to it with your finger? Does that of itself clarify the part played by 'establishing' a fact?" Suppose it takes a grasp of the practices constitutive of some region of our life-world "to define the *character* of what you are calling a 'fact'" (RFM p. 381). The world in which we find ourselves is always already organized into intelligible, meaningful contexts which determine what facts there can be, and so, as for Heidegger, there is no way to see our understanding of the world as built up from discriminations of originally meaningless, isolated facts. When Wittgenstein asks, "What are the simple constituents of a chair? — The bits of wood of which it is made? Or the molecules, or the atoms?" (PI 47), he makes it clear that the simple component parts of things are specifiable only by reference to our interests and purposes in dealing with them.

Wittgenstein's undermining of the traditional conception of grounding is summed up in the familiar slogan, "What has to be accepted, the given, is — so one could say — *forms of life*" (PI p. 226). The full meaning of this can be brought out by considering what Wittgenstein says about following rules. The tradition tries to explain the orderliness and regularity in our activities in terms of underlying "mental" rules. Without the mental, it seems, there would be not "action" but mere physical movement. Wittgenstein criticizes the assumption that there must be inner mental rules guiding our actions by, among other things, showing that rules have to be interpreted, that every interpretation of a rule relies on another rule, and consequently that the appeal to rules leads to an endless regress. Generally, wherever we might feel that the mental would explain our actions, Wittgenstein undercuts that notion by showing that appeal to the mental is pointless.

If meaningful human agency can be accounted for neither in terms of mental processes nor solely in terms of physical movement, how is it possible? Here Wittgenstein's description of our everyday activities gives us a new way of looking at our agency and, indeed, at our own identity as humans. "To obey a rule," he says, "to make a report, to give an order, to play a game of chess, are *customs* (uses, institutions). . . . To understand a language means to be master of a technique" (PI 199). What comes across here is that action gains its meaning not from "inner" accompaniments, but from its place within the background of regular practices, techniques and customs of a community. As we are initiated into a communal life-world, we become tuned in to those ways of responding that make up the background of intelligibility embodied in the "common ways of acting" (*Handlungsweise*) of our culture. Consider, for example, how bowing is learned in Japan. From an early age Japanese infants are tapped on the back of the head when someone enters the room. Through this conditioning they begin to "duck" in the appropriate circumstances, and this ducking evolves into the formal Japanese bow. It would be a mistake, however, to think that bowing is *nothing other than* the conditioned reflex of ducking, for a bow is a profoundly meaningful gesture in Japanese society. Yet the meaning of the bow does not depend on something "mental" behind the movement; anything, or nothing, might be "going through one's mind" when one bows. Rather, the gesture gains its meaning from its *place* within the background of practices, customs and institutions of the entire culture. Generally, then, what is "given" as the source of intelligibility of our actions is the attunement — the "agreement in judgments" (*Übereinstimmung*, PI 242) — we pick up by becoming participants in a public world. As Wittgenstein says, what "determines our judgment, our concepts and reactions, is not what one man is doing now, an individual action, but the whole hurly-burly of human actions, the background against which we see any action" (Z 567). Our actions are "rule-governed," coherent and meaningful because of their position in the entire fabric of social practices that make up our form of life.

This conception of shared forms of life as the basis for our practices points to a way of envisioning the self which provides an alternative to the representationalist model. According to this viewpoint, what defines our identity as human agents is not our capacity for conscious representation, but rather our mode of "presentation" — our ways of *expressing* ourselves in the mesh of a public world.[9] Wittgenstein advises us to think of the language of the mental not as designating something "inner," but as an expression of natural life-processes: for example, the word "pain" as connected with a "primitive, natural expression" (PI 244); the words "We mourn . . ." at a funeral as "an expression of mourning" (PI p. 189); the exclamation, "Now I know how to go on!" as "an instinctive sound, a glad start" (PI 323); the utterance "I hope he'll come" not as a "*report* about [one's] state of mind," but as "an *expression* [Äusserung] of [one's] hope" (PI 585); and the sentence "I am in pain" as like moaning — an "expression" of pain, not a report on a mental state (BB pp. 68-69). The force of these suggestions is to lead us to shift from thinking of the mental as something "inner" represented by our words to thinking of it as what is presented or expressed in our communal lives. It is something we embody, something we "body forth" in making manifest our attuned being-in-the-world together. Seen from this perspective, we exist as "meaningful expressions" in a shared life-world rather than as minds representing objects.

Wittgenstein's description of our everyday lives overlaps the picture we find in Heidegger. The self, regarded as agency, appears as an ongoing "happening" embedded in a public life-world whose actions and self-understanding draw their significance from their location in the practices and customs of the "They." Given this portrayal of our human situation, the picture of the self as a mind representing objects simply has no role to play. For both thinkers, to grasp the situatedness of our lives within a background of life-expressions of a community is to see that the mental can be made intelligible without recourse to a "yet uncomprehended process in the yet unexplored medium" (PI 308). As Wittgenstein says, "Only surrounded by certain normal expressions of life *[Lebensäusserungen]* is there such a thing as an expression of pain. Only surrounded by an even more far-reaching expression of life, such a thing as the expression of sorrow or affection" (Z 534). And, for both thinkers, the contextualization

---

[9] This account draws on James C. Edwards' *Ethics Without Philosophy* (Tampa: University of Florida, 1982), pp. 183ff.

of our lives in a communal world — our existence as, so to speak, commentaries on the text of our culture's ways of interpreting things — implies that there can be no access to brute, uninterpreted "facts" about independently existing objects to be used in justifying or explaining our practices. At the same time, however, the description of everydayness lets us see that our lives and the world are *already* intelligible, and therefore do not need any philosophical explanation or grounding.

3. Language and Truth

In the writings of both Wittgenstein and Heidegger, language plays a crucial role in articulating our shared sense of ourselves and the world around us. We saw that, for Heidegger, Dasein "expresses itself" in its everyday dealings with equipment. These ordinary ways of articulating our surroundings into a field of significance are focused and organized in advance by a background of intelligibility opened by discourse: "Intelligibility has always been articulated, even before there is any appropriative interpretation of it. Discourse [*Rede*] is the articulation of intelligibility. Therefore it underlies both interpretation and assertion" (SZ p. 161).

To understand what Heidegger means by discourse here, we must keep in mind that the term "Dasein" does not simply designate isolated individual human beings. Dasein, as we have seen, is essentially "Being-with," a communal being whose sense of reality is initially preshaped by the way the "They" articulates significance. Accordingly, language is the medium in which a community's "clearing" (its understanding of itself and its world) is opened up and maintained. "In language, as a way in which things have been spoken out, there is hidden a way in which the understanding of Dasein has been interpreted. . . . Proximally, and with certain limits, Dasein is constantly delivered over to this interpretedness, which controls and distributes the possibilities of average understanding and of the situatedness belonging to it" (SZ pp. 167-8). Seen from this standpoint, Dasein as a clearing is made possible by the articulations built into a public language. "For the most part, discourse is expressed by being spoken out, and has already been so expressed; it is language. But in that case understanding and interpretation already lie in what has thus been expressed" (SZ p. 167). Heidegger elsewhere calls this linguistic background the "projective saying" of a people, the linguistically attuned goal-directedness in which "the concepts of a historical people's essence, i.e., of its belonging to world history, are preformed for that people."[10]

---

[10] "The Origin of the Work of Art," in Heidegger, *Basic Writings*, ed. D. Krell (New York: Harper, 1977), p. 185.

Our everyday talk contributes to sustaining this shared background of intelligibility. In talking, Heidegger says, our "Being-with becomes 'explicitly' *shared*"; through talk "the articulation of being with one another understandingly is constituted" (SZ p. 162). In other words, the central role of language use is to "express" or "make manifest" our shared attunement to a public world: "In talking, Dasein *expresses* itself not because it has, in the first instance, been encapsulated as something 'internal' over against something outside when it understands. What is expressed is precisely this being-outside. . ." (SZ p. 162). Charles Taylor has discussed the role of language in expressing or making manifest our shared "being-outside" with one another.[11] As Taylor points out, the tradition generally regarded language as a tool at our disposal for designating and communicating information about objects. In contrast to this kind of "designative" view of language, Taylor proposes we see language as primarily a medium in which a "public space" is opened up. To take his example, if I get onto a crowded bus on a hot day and say to a fellow-passenger, "Hot, isn't it?" my utterance neither conveys information nor asks a question. Instead, its role is to make manifest our shared predicament, to "get something out into the open between us," to fine tune our sense of the existential space in which we stand.

Similarly, for Heidegger, "[c]ommunication is never anything like a conveying of experiences, such as opinions or wishes, from the interior of one subject into the interior of another. Dasein-with is already essentially manifest in a co-situatedness and a co-understanding" (SZ p. 162). It follows that language is not primarily a tool for relaying ideas from one subject to another, but is instead the *medium* in which our shared understanding of ourselves and our world is deposited and maintained. This is why Heidegger says that it is not humans who speak, but rather "language speaks" — "Humans speak only insofar as they corespond to language."[12] Because our shared sense of reality and the public space of our practical life-world are constituted by language, "essence and Being express themselves in language."[13] Language is the "dwelling" in which our sense of who we are emerges, and so "we human beings remain committed to and within the essence of language, and can never step outside of it in order to look at it from somewhere else."[14]

---

[11] "Language and Human Nature" and "Theories of Meaning," reprinted in his *Human Agency and Language, Philosophical Papers*, Vol. I (Cambridge: Cambridge University Press, 1985).

[12] *The Piety of Thinking*, trans. J. G. Hart and J. C. Maraldo (Bloomington: Indiana University Press, 1976), p. 25.

[13] *Introduction to Metaphysics*, trans. R. Manheim (Garden City: Doubleday, 1961), p. 44.

Correlated with Heidegger's description of the self as a place-holder in the public life-world, and of language as making manifest a shared background of intelligibility, is a transformed way of looking at "truth." According to this outlook, "primordial" truth is the "disclosedness" which makes it possible for things to emerge-into-presence, and truth as "correspondence" or "correct representation" is derivative from this more primordial truth. The notion of primordial truth is clarified in Heidegger's attempt to show that what usually is assumed to be the primary locus of truth, the subject/predicate assertion, is derivative from a more basic involvement in practical affairs (SZ sec. 33). In our normal transactions with equipment, we lay out and appropriate equipment according to our aims and needs. Language, when it has a role to play, usually speaks *into* these concerns, lighting up aspects of the "hermeneutic as" of taking something *as* something in our concernful dealings. For example, calling out "Too heavy! Hand me the other hammer!" in the midst of hammering makes manifest how things stand in the workshop: it shows how the work is going, and lets things become manifest as they are in our clearing. Through this expression, the entire context of significance relations is lit up.

When we shift from using language in order to express our absorption in a field of significance to using it to make "apophantic assertions," there is a change-over in our mode of comportment to the world. In a subject/predicate assertion such as "The hammer weighs four pounds," we focus on the hammer as a present-at-hand object with a property, supposedly severed from any particular context of practical significance. "In its function of appropriating what is understood," Heidegger says, "the 'as' no longer reaches out into a totality of involvements. . . . [I]t has been cut off from that significance which, as such, constitutes environmentality" (SZ p. 158). The bare subject/predicate assertion is disengaged from its role in disclosing how things stand with our activities, and is regarded as merely representing a "fact" about a meaningless, present-at-hand thing. Only when there has been this kind of change-over to decontextualized assertions can questions about "correctness" or "correspondence to the facts" arise, and now standard sorts of checking and confirmation get under way. What this account of assertion shows, however, is that encountering things as mere objects represented by subject/predicate assertions is parasitic on the "clearing" opened in advance by those practical concerns and involvements through which things are discovered as meaningful in our lives.

---

[14] *On the Way to Language*, trans. P. D. Hartz (New York: Harper & Row, 1971), p. 134.

Heidegger's derivation of the traditional concept of truth as correspondence from a "more primordial" experience of truth as disclosedness (SZ sec. 44) follows the same pattern. The claim is that only because the world and the things in it are already opened up by our discursive preunderstanding is it possible for a conception of things as mere objects to arise. Our practical activities disclose the arena in which questions about the correctness of beliefs or the truth of statements get off the ground. And within this clearing, "things stand in different truths"[15] depending on our interests and our concerns — for example, a crucifix would play a different role within the "truths" of science, aesthetics, or religious experience. But it is only because Dasein in general *"is 'in the truth,'"* and because disclosedness "belongs to its existential constitution" (SZ p. 221), that these "different truths" and the standard types of regional inquiry correlated with them are possible.

Wittgenstein also sees our language and practices as opening a field of intelligibility in which the issue of truth as correspondence can arise (though, to be sure, he would not call this background itself "truth"). As the medium in which our understanding of ourselves and our world is maintained, language articulates and shapes our attunement to shared forms of life and defines our own being as meaningful expressions. Our ordinary language-games make manifest our attuned participation in the customs and practices of our public world. But language-games do not merely formulate an understanding we could just as well have without language. For language *constitutes* our ways of encountering things and interpreting ourselves. When Wittgenstein says that a dog can "feel fear but not remorse," and that this is so because it "can't talk" (Z 518), he means that, although a dog can react to physical danger, it lacks the capacity to grasp public standards of conduct, to recognize the significance of the situation in relation to those standards, to contrast remorse with shame or regret, to revise its self-evaluation in the light of redescriptions of the situation — all those language-dependent capacities that constitute *our* ability to feel remorse. We are able to have certain sorts of feelings and to identify things in our environment as significant, then, because of the mastery of what Wittgenstein calls the "grammar" — the background articulation of our possibilities of understanding — that prestructures the language-games we learn in growing up into a linguistic community. For this reason he says, "*Essence* is expressed [*ausgesprochen*] by grammar," and "grammar tells us what kind of object anything is" (PI 371, 373).

---

[15] *What Is a Thing?*, trans. W. B. Barton, Jr. and Vera Deutsch (Chicago: Henry Regnery, 1967), p. 14.

I take Wittgenstein's concept of "grammar" as referring to what he sometimes calls the "system" of standard connections and relations organizing our language use which is embodied in the regular practices and contexts of communal life. Thus, it seems to be part of the grammar of obtaining and reporting results of measuring that there is "a certain constancy in the results of measuring" (PI 242). Similarly, it is part of the grammatical *"framework* on which the working of language is based" that "[d]isputes do not break out (among mathematicians, say) over the question of whether a rule has been obeyed or not" (PI 240, my emphasis). The "framework" or "scaffolding" that makes the activity of mathematics possible is found not by conceptual analysis, but by describing the familiar life-expressions of mathematicians. This context of familiar practices is referred to (perhaps misleadingly) as "agreement in judgments": "If language is to be a means of communication there must be agreement not only in definitions but also . . . in judgments" (PI 242). The attunement to regular, orderly practices makes up the "grammatical multiplicity" of our language, but it cannot be thought of as justifying or explaining our language-games: "I have not said *why* mathematicians do not quarrel, but only *that* they do not" (PI p. 226). Nevertheless, our attunement constitutes the concepts we have: "If there were not complete agreement [in the calculations made by mathematicians], then neither would human beings be learning the technique which we learn" (PI p. 226).

If this way of reading Wittgenstein's notion of "grammar" is right, then grammar might be thought of as a web of practices which, like a grid or template, guides our ways of speaking and taking things in ordinary language-games. Wittgenstein compares this background of understanding to a "world-picture" or a "mythology" that makes up the tacit, "inherited background against which I distinguish true and false" (OC 94-95), and to "a system, a structure" of taken-for-granted convictions (OC 102) that makes identifications and discriminations possible. But this background of understanding is not a "web of beliefs" (as the term "judgments" suggests); it is something that is embodied in those shared practices we come to express as we become initiated into the forms of life of our culture. For this reason, Wittgenstein says that giving grounds does not come to an end in a proposition that one just *sees* as true: "it is not a kind of *seeing* on our part; it is our *acting* which lies at the ground of the language-game" (OC 204). The ground of our beliefs and practices "is not an ungrounded presupposition: it is an ungrounded *way of acting*" (OC 210; my emphasis).

For Wittgenstein, then, language embodies a grammar which constitutes our sense of reality and grounds our beliefs and ways of doing things. But, as is true of Heidegger's background of intelligibility, grammar cannot itself be grounded by appeal to any extra-linguistic facts. According to Wittgenstein's well-known "autonomy of grammar" argument, "I cannot use language to get outside of language" (PR p. 54). That is, to put it roughly, since every attempt to justify grammar by appeal to "facts" about reality only succeeds in making use of some *description* of reality which itself presupposes the correctness of the grammar in question, any such attempted justification begs the question. Insofar as our grammar *constitutes* what can count as reality for us, there is no exit from language to non-linguistic "facts" about ourselves or our world which could ground the grammar we have. But neither is it correct to think we *create* our language-games or their grammar: "a language-game does not have its origin in *consideration* [or reflection]. Consideration [or reflection] is part of a language-game" (Z 391). Hence, though language may look "arbitrary" to the extent that "the use of language is in a certain sense autonomous" (Z 320), in another sense it is not something we cook up ourselves (it is "not as if we *chose* this game" [OC 317]). A language-game "is not based on grounds. It is not reasonable (or unreasonable). It is there — like our life" (OC 559).

In the picture of our situation that emerges from Wittgenstein's reflections, we come to see ourselves as participants in public language-games which are not grounded on anything outside our lives, and yet, insofar as they constitute our lives, they are not something we create or can fully master. The background of intelligibility opened by our grammar is neither true nor false ("If the true is what is grounded, then the ground is not *true*, nor yet false" [OC 205]). Yet, as the "scaffolding of our thoughts" (OC 211), it is what makes it possible to believe and say things that count as either true or false. For language as a whole, "we see that the idea of 'agreement with reality' does not have any clear application" (OC 215). Thus, although Wittgenstein would eschew Heidegger's talk of "primordial truth," the view he presents parallels Heidegger's notion of a linguistically constituted "clearing" or "disclosedness" as the backdrop which makes possible our everyday assertions and denials, testing and disconfirming, explanations and justifications.

4. The Legacy of Wittgenstein and Heidegger

The question posed at the outset was: What is the impact of Wittgenstein's and Heidegger's thought for traditional philosophy? In this concluding section I want to summarize the results of the comparisons I have made, and sketch out some of the issues in the debate between Rorty and Taylor. We might sum up the outcome of the thought of Wittgenstein and Heidegger by saying that it is holistic, anti-dualist, and nonfoundationalist. The holism appears in their convergent pictures of our transactions with the world as constituted by a background of understanding embodied in our practices and shaped by our language. For Heidegger, our dealings with equipment make it possible for the world to show up for us as an interrelated web of "significance" where what anything *is* is "ontologically defined" by its relation to our goals and practices. The relations of "in order to," "for which," and "for the sake of which" that define our life-world are not properties tacked onto pre-existent objects. As "relationships in which concernful know-how as such already dwells" (SZ p. 88), they define not only the "worldhood of the world" but our own identity as agents in the world as well. Similarly, for Wittgenstein, the "essence" of anything — what makes it the object it is — is defined by the "grammatical multiplicity" of our language-games. What things *are* is inseparable from their place in the contexts of significance opened up by the linguistic customs, conventions, and practices of our life-world.

One consequence of this holism is that understanding always operates within a hermeneutic circle. Our ways of encountering things in the world are sketched out in advance by what Heidegger calls a "blueprint" or "groundplan" of preunderstanding, while that understanding is constantly redefined as a result of our ongoing transactions with the world. There is consequently no way to gain access to brute facts or raw data independent of some framework of understanding. In Wittgenstein's example, a chemist's investigations are made possible by the fact that he "has got hold of a definite world-picture — not of course one that he invented: he learned it as a child." This world-picture "is the matter-of-course foundation for his research and as such also goes unmentioned" (OC 167). Yet, since a world-picture or mythology "may change back into a state of flux, the river-bed of thoughts may shift" (OC 97), there is no unchanging foundation that underwrites the grammar we have.

A second affinity between Wittgenstein and Heidegger is found in the way they undercut traditional dualisms. It should be evident, first of all, that their thought subverts the Cartesian oppositions of subject and object or mind and matter. If our actions are understood as expressions interwoven into a public "tapestry of life," then the notions of mind and consciousness have no necessary role to play in describing and grasping our everydayness. One can "divide through" by the mental; "it cancels out, whatever it is" (PI 293). Yet, at the same time, neither Wittgenstein nor Heidegger feels that displacing the mental thereby commits us to physicalism or behaviorism. In their picture of our lives as bound up with a life-world where things show up as significant in relation to our purposes and needs, there is no place in the description of everydayness for the notion of brute, meaningless physical objects or "mere" physical movement. In fact, since both thinkers suggest that the natural sciences are derivative from and parasitic on a "more primordial" way of understanding ourselves and our world as participants in the meaningful contexts of everyday life, there is no reason to assume that the conception of reality we get from physics has any privileged status in telling us what the world is "really" like.

Deflating the opposition between subject and object should also undermine the traditional distinction between idealism and realism. This distinction has always been parasitic for its sense on the representationalist picture of our situation, according to which reality is either "out there," independent of us, or "in here," within the mind. But if the representationalist model is discarded, so is the dilemma: *either* realism *or* idealism. Thus, it seems misleading to suggest that, since *"our* language . . . shows us everything as it appears to our interests, our concerns, our activities," and since these are "things which are expressions of mind," this "provides grounds . . . for calling such a view a kind of *idealism.* . . ."[16] For the very notion that our interests, concerns and activities are "expressions of *mind"* is exactly what Wittgenstein and Heidegger have blocked. We cannot explain our activities by recourse to extra-linguistic facts, but neither can we consider the possibility that all there is is language or mind *as opposed to* getting in touch with the facts. It also seems wrong to say, "Horses and giraffes, colors and shapes — the existence of these is not [a product of human linguistic practice]. . . . But the metaphysical necessities belonging to the nature of such things — these *seem* to be regarded by [Wittgenstein] as 'grammatical rules.'"[17] For, on the one hand, since what we *mean* when we try to affirm the existence of horses and giraffes is always constituted by the linguistic articulations made possible by the background of our "grammar," there is no way to get out of language in order to assert the existence of these types of things as they are in themselves independent of any grammar. And, on the other hand, since the "metaphysical necessities" of such things are indistinguishable from the concrete ways those things show up for us in our language and actions, talk about metaphysical necessity seems to be a wheel in a machine that turns when nothing else is moving.

Finally, Wittgenstein's and Heidegger's vision of our situation is nonfoundationalist to the extent that it undermines the prospects of finding a final explanation or justification for our lives. For Heidegger, our exis-

---

[16] Bernard Williams, "Wittgenstein and Idealism," in his *Moral Luck* (Cambridge: Cambridge University Press, 1981), p. 153.

[17] G. E. M. Anscombe, "The Question of Linguistic Idealism," in her *From Parmenides to Wittgenstein* (Minneapolis: University of Minnesota Press, 1981), p. 121.

tence as a "happening," as a "thrown projection," is finite, contingent and historical in the sense of being an ongoing dialogue with the past for the purposes of the future. As the source of all intelligibility, the clearing that we are is itself suspended over "the abyss of meaninglessness" (SZ p. 152). And Wittgenstein constantly reminds us of "the groundlessness of our believing" (OC 166), the transience of even our most central "mythology" (OC 96-99), and the seemingly "arbitrary" nature of our core beliefs.

But for both thinkers this groundlessness does not lead to skeptical resignation or perpetual uncertainty. As Wittgenstein says, "The difficult thing here is not to dig down to the ground; no, it is to recognize the ground that lies before us as the ground" (RFM p. 333). Recognizing the rootedness of our beliefs and activities in our shared forms of life and in the "common behavior of mankind" (PI 206) can throw us back onto the grounds we *do* have — our patterns of upbringing, natural "primitive" responses, capacities for picking up skills, and so on — with a deeper respect for their dependability and bindingness. To acknowledge, with Seabright, that "[m]eanings are not in the head but in the world"[18] would be to see our practices as guided by the steady and regular "expressions of life" of our cultural world, and to realize that, since our shared forms of life *constitute* our identity, there is no way to regard them as arbitrary impositions or as mere excess baggage with no real connection to who we really are. In a related way, Heidegger thinks that facing up to our own finitude can throw us back onto our lives in a fuller way. In his view, to clear-sightedly acknowledge that we are caught in the hermeneutic circle is also to realize that this circularity is an enabling condition which first gives us access to our lives, with the result that our aim should be "not to get out of the circle but to come into it in the right way" (SZ p. 153). And his discussion of "authentic historicity" (SZ secs. 74-77) proposes that once we fully recognize the finitude and temporality of our possibilities of self-interpretation, we will take over the "happening" of our community's history with deeper commitment and respect, appropriating the past as a "heritage" and orienting our goals for the future as part of a shared "destiny." What this nonfoundationalism does imply is that there is no *final* explanation for our forms of life that would put an end to inquiry, and consequently that attempts to understand ourselves and our world are an open-ended, ongoing project.

---

[18] Paul Seabright, "Explaining Cultural Divergence: A Wittgensteinian Paradox," *Journal of Philosophy* 84 (1987): 11-27, p. 22.

The divergent readings of the significance of the writings of Wittgenstein and Heidegger found in Rorty and Taylor might be seen as resulting from emphasizing different strands of these thinkers' work. Rorty focuses on the anti-foundationalism and contextualism of their writings and draws the conclusion that they have put an end to traditional epistemology-centered philosophy as a search for final truths about ourselves and our world. On Rorty's reading, the writings of Wittgenstein are primarily therapeutic and negative, clearing away the presuppositions of traditional philosophy and offering nothing new in their place: "When Wittgenstein is at his best, he resolutely avoids . . . constructive criticism and sticks to pure satire. He just shows, by examples, how hopeless the traditional problems are; . . . he just makes fun of the whole idea that there is something here to be explained."[19] And the legacy of the later Heidegger (who threw off the vestiges of "fundamental ontology" still found in his early work) is not a new picture of humans, but "the endless, repetitive, literary-historical 'deconstruction' of the Western metaphysics of presence" (CP p. xxii).

The outcome of Wittgenstein and Heidegger, according to Rorty, is "epistemological behaviorism," the pragmatist attitude that is content with explaining rationality and epistemic authority "by reference to what society lets us say"[20] rather than by privileged representations or by criteria dictated by pure reason. And "behaviorism which dispenses with foundations is in a fair way towards dispensing with philosophy."[21] To see a human being as a self-interpreting animal is to see "man as a self-changing being, *capable of remaking himself by remaking his speech.*"[22] The lesson to be drawn from the insight into "the ubiquity of language" is that "one cannot see language-as-a-whole in relation to something else to which it applies, or for which it is a means to an end" (CP p. xix). Wittgenstein and Heidegger, then, are "making only *negative* points" that there is nothing behind language which could ground it (CP p. xx). Grasping the outcome of the development of thought in the twentieth century should lead us to a new attitude of irony and playfulness: to "abjure the notion of 'the truly human'" and to "become increasingly

---

[19] *Consequences of Pragmatism* (Minneapolis: University of Minnesota Press, 1982), p. 34 (henceforth "CP").

[20] *Philosophy and the Mirror of Nature* (Princeton: Princeton University Press, 1979), p. 174.

[21] "Epistemological Behaviorism and the De-transcendentalization of Analytic Philosophy," in R. Hollinger, ed., *Hermeneutics and Practice* (Notre Dame: Notre Dame University Press, 1985), p. 102.

[22] Ibid., p. 104.

ironic, playful, free, and inventive in our choice of self-descriptions."[23] A certain "ethnocentrism," which acknowledges we can never "step outside our skins" or escape from "the 'merely conventional' and contingent aspects of one's life" (CP p. xix), is combined with the ability to "see every human life as a poem"[24] created by individuals through imaginative self-descriptions.

Taylor, in contrast, emphasizes the way in which the phenomenology of everydayness provides us with an alternative way of understanding who we are. For Taylor, the fact that we are self-interpreting animals insures that we have what he calls "agent's knowledge" (OE p. 475), that is, insight into what we are doing insofar as our own self-descriptions constitute our movements *as actions*. Although a person's own self-understanding may be shot through with self-deception, it provides the explanandum from which any account of the agent must begin, and it therefore has a privileged status in grasping his or her action. Taylor's hope is that our agent's knowledge will also provide a basis for uncovering deeper insights into the underlying structures of agency in general. Rorty, in contrast, thinks this belief in something "deep" or "more authentic" about ourselves is just a remnant of the "craving for metaphysical comfort" that Wittgenstein and Heidegger have undermined. The faith that we have "privileged access" to ourselves — that we can "read our own program" (CP p. 165) — presupposes a now untenable essentialism.

Though it is impossible to adjudicate this dispute here, I want to suggest that Taylor's reading of the "legitimate heir" of philosophy is more in line with the overall direction of Wittgenstein's and Heidegger's thought. Taylor correctly criticizes Rorty's view that all language-games are optional and up for grabs. Both Wittgenstein and Heidegger have shown us that, although our self-descriptions are ungrounded, they are nevertheless constitutive of who we are, and so cannot be taken up or abandoned at will. As Taylor says, Rorty's picture of all vocabularies as optional makes sense only if we can think of ourselves as "in fact at home nowhere," and this assumption seems to rely on a "notion of the subject as disengaged" which is itself "generated by the epistemological tradition" Rorty seeks to overcome.[25] If we recognize that, as agents, we are always enmeshed in a concrete cultural context, we will see that there is no vantage point for the stance of global irony and playfulness Rorty recommends.

---

[23] "Freud and Moral Reflection," in J. H. Smith and W. Kerrigan, eds., *Pragmatism's Freud: The Moral Disposition of Psychoanalysis* (Baltimore: Johns Hopkins, 1986), p. 12.

[24] "The Contingency of Selfhood," *London Review of Books*, May 8, 1986, p. 14.

[25] "Philosophy and Its History," in Rorty, Schneewind, and Skinner, eds., *Philosophy in History: Essays on the Historiography of Philosophy* (Cambridge: Cambridge University Press, 1984), p. 30.

Within our own background of understanding, then, we can try to formulate the types of "transcendental generalization" about the conditions for agency Heidegger sought — such pervasive features as situatedness, future directedness, involvement in significant situations, and linguisticality — while holding onto Wittgenstein's distrust of totalization and his insistence on detailed, case-by-case description. The results of such a quasi-transcendental inquiry will be defeasible given our embeddedness in an ongoing historical culture, and they can be defended only by local skirmishes with specific objections rather than by knock-down arguments starting from indubitable premises. But, to the extent that this search for a deeper self-understanding through the critique of representationalism points to a transformed outlook on pressing puzzles about our human situation, it reveals the potential of a post-Wittgensteinian/Heideggerian philosophy.[26]

---

[26] Research for this paper was supported by a University Research Grant from the University of Vermont and an NEH Summer Seminar grant. I am grateful to Kathleen Emmett, Mark Bickhard, and Lynn Rudder Baker for comments on an earlier draft of this essay.

5

Meaning constitution and justification of validity: has Heidegger overcome transcendental philosophy by history of being?

The problem as a consequence of the present impact of Heidegger's philosophy

Let me start out with a question: what explains the fascination of Heidegger's philosophy in the present era? Certainly, this fascination no longer emanates from the so-called philosophy of 'existence', which was, no doubt, formulated in *Being and Time* in an expressive and appealing way. Nor is it, I suppose, the concern of a 'fundamental ontology', that is the response to the question as to the 'meaning of being', which Heidegger himself opposed to what he called the 'existentialist misunderstanding' of his main work. The source of fascination in our day is rather, it seems to me, his venture of a 'destruction' of occidental metaphysics which was postulated already in *Being and Time* but later, after the so-called 'turn' (*Kehre*), was directed against the conception of fundamental ontology as well. In other words: at present, the following programme of Heidegger's seems to stand in the foreground of interest: his attempt at thinking back – by critical reconstruction and destruction of all current conceptual schemes, metaphysics and science – beyond the beginnings of classical Greek philosophy, in order possibly to regain the 'free space' (*Spielraum*) of an 'initial thinking' that might have existed in the time of myth or even of the pre-Socratic philosophers. This free space, on Heidegger's account, might eventually open up the preconditions for a post-metaphysical and post-technological thought to the extent that such a possibility may be actualized by the 'happening of being', that is through a 'clearance' of the meaning of being.

It is especially the last suggestion of a post-metaphysical, nay even post-philosophical and post-rational (although not – according to Heidegger – 'irrational'),[1] thinking that within the last decade has aroused the greatest fascination – for example in the sphere of

French and Italian postmodernism,[2] but even beyond this in a special version of American neo-pragmatism which thinks it possible – although with certain political reservations – to bring into line the thought of Dewey, Wittgenstein and Heidegger.[3]

However, beyond this vague outline of the history of Heidegger's impact, let us ask more closely: which forms or schemes of Heidegger's thought lend support to these aspects of its reception history in the present era? I will try to sum up the answer to this question in a thesis that allows me to introduce the topic that I indicated in the title of this chapter.

The fascination of the later Heidegger and the far-reaching implications of the reception of his thought by the postmodernists and the post-Wittgensteinian neo-pragmatists derive primarily from the fact that in Heidegger's late philosophy (of the history of being) the initially transcendental-phenomenological problem of the constitution of meaning is subject to a detranscendentalization and historicization. In Heidegger's philosophy this is a consequence of his conception of truth as *aletheia*, a conception that was already implied in *Being and Time* in the existential-hermeneutical analysis of the 'pre-structure' of all world-understanding, conceived as 'disclosedness' of being-in-the-world and later terminated in the conception of the *clearing* (*Lichtung*) of (the meaning) of being. The latter, as a happening of disclosure and simultaneously concealment, precedes the possibility of true and false judgements. Within the context of French post-structuralism – for example in the work of Derrida – the structure of the 'ontic-ontological difference', which in Heidegger's philosophy was connected with the 'happening' of 'clearance' as a condition of the possibility of linguistic meaning constitution, came to be fused with Saussure's notion of a semiotical constitution of difference and Derrida's conception of *différance* as the happening of simultaneously opening up and shifting of meaning.

But why or in what respect may one say that by Heidegger's analysis of 'disclosedness' in *Being and Time* a transcendental or quasi-transcendental problem is raised and at the same time is tendentially subject to a detranscendentalization?

To address this question I will first distinguish and elucidate two pertinent dimensions of Heidegger's so called 'pre-structure' of existential world-understanding and self-understanding. For this pre-structure of what is 'always already pre-understood' has a quasi-transcendental function in *Being and Time*.

The 'pre-structure' of the 'disclosedness' of being-in-the-world as an answer to the transcendental question as to the conditions of the possibility of the world's meaning constitution

Heidegger's analysis shows that the subject–object relation of scientific knowledge is always already embedded in the contextual structure of being-in-the-world as understanding the coherent significance of the world. The beings encountered within the world are not primarily understood as existing or present (*vorhandene*) objects of theoretical observation and predicative determination but (rather) as equipment to hand (*zuhandenes Zeug*), looked upon from the viewpoint of care, and pre-understood from this point of view 'as something' (i.e. as significant). Therefore, the world itself is not primarily an aggregate of present objects or – as for Kant and natural science – the 'existence of things in as far as they make up a coherence according to laws'; but, for Heidegger, the world is 'the situational context of understanding according to reference-marks as a (teleological) horizon of possible encounterings of beings that have a specific significance'. (In German: 'Das Worin des sich-verweisenden Verstehens als Woraufhin des Begegnenlassens von Seiendem in der Seinsart der Bewandtnis.')[4]

On the presupposition of this Heideggerian concept of the world, those critical-epistemological (*erkenntniskritische*) questions that are suggested by the traditional reflection upon the pure objectivity of beings prove to be pseudo-problems: for instance, the question whether perhaps all objects (and that means: even all human subjects of action and knowledge qua objects) might be only within human consciousness. This must be a pseudo-problem, since those modes of being-in-the-world that are supposed in the critical question – namely 'being with' mere representations or sense data or being solitary in principle – can be understood by us only as 'deficient modes' of being-in-the-world as 'being with the beings themselves' and 'being-together-with' other people.[5]

This Heideggerian analysis, which is phenomenological and existential-hermeneutical, is almost exactly confirmed by a

Wittgensteinian analysis of language games – namely of the interwovenness of language games, world interpretations and activities as parts of life forms. For this analysis reveals that the idealistic and solipsistic paradigms of the philosophy of consciousness are parasitic upon non-idealist and non-solipist everyday language games, that is on language games that even Descartes (and Husserl) must make use of in order to articulate their problems linguistically. Thus with regard to the Cartesian dream argument, one may prove that the meaning of the phrase 'all that is considered to be real, might possibly be merely my dream' is parasitic upon a language game, according to which there must be a difference in principle between a real world outside my consciousness and that which might be 'merely my dream'. Thereby one may justify also Heidegger's objection to Kant that the 'scandal of philosophy' does not lie in the lack of a proof for the existence of an outer world but rather in demanding such a proof.[6] To put it briefly: the hermeneutic-phenomenological reflection on the 'being-always-already-in-the-world' proves its priority with regard to the post-Cartesian reflection on the 'object-consciousness' in the same sense as the pragmatically oriented analysis of language games can prove that those language games of ordinary language that are interwoven with the *praxis* of life are presupposed by the philosophical language games – and also by the constructive languages of the logic of science.

Thus far we have already shed light on the point of Heidegger's interpretation of what the late Husserl called *Lebenswelt* and of the fundamental relation of this lifeworld to the abstractive and idealizing world-thematization of the sciences. And the point of Heidegger's analysis of the lifeworld appears to me to be more radical and more illuminating than that which can be found in the remaining part of Husserl's last writings on the *Krisis*.[7] This holds especially with regard to the quasi-transcendental function of our pre-understanding of the lifeworld as a precondition of the subject–object relation of scientific knowledge. For, on Heidegger's account, it becomes clear that a pure transcendental consciousness of objects does not suffice as a basis for the constitution of a world of significance – and this for at least two reasons. On the one hand, there is a lack of the horizon of practical engagement and hence of cognitive interests that could guide our searching and asking for something 'as something'. On the other hand, there is also a lack with regard to the medium of language by which the interpretation of something as something must be mediated in order to be intersubjectively valid.

However, given the features of the lifeworld that we have elucidated thus far, we have not yet revealed the whole significance of what Heidegger always characterizes as the 'pre-structure' of 'being-in-the-world' by using the phrase 'always already' (*immer schon* or *je schon*). Our explanation of this by pointing to the lifeworld as a presupposed embedding of the object-consciousness could still be understood in the abstract sense of claiming only necessary preconditions of knowledge as Kant does in his transcendental logic. And already on the ground of this understanding, one could speak of a heightening of the transcendental problematic of the conditions of meaning constitution beyond the special problematic of the constitution of 'objectivity' in the Kantian sense. But in this case the dimension of existential temporality, which is also indicated by Heidegger's using the terms 'always already', would not yet be taken into consideration. In fact the world- and self-understanding of human *Dasein* according to Heidegger is dependent on its 'pre-structure' not only in an abstractive transcendental-logical sense but also in the temporal sense of being 'always already ahead of itself' (*sich vorweg*). The *Dasein* cannot pull up, so to speak, its 'thrownness' into a historically conditioned situation-world (and its having always already become addicted to this world in a specific way).

Now, if one carries through the analysis of the temporality structure of being-always-already-in-the-world, then the inescapable insight into the 'historicity' of the finite *Dasein* and its possible understanding of meaning must be the result. It is in this respect, I suggest, that the most radical effects of Heidegger's philosophy on the rest of contemporary philosophy have been exerted: those effects that, as being quasi-transcendental conditions of the world-meaning constitution, have contributed most effectively to the detranscendentalization of contemporary philosophy – in Rorty's sense, for example.

Thus the following Heideggerian insight, which was further elaborated by Gadamer, has presumably found a world-wide acceptance: there is a temporally and historically determined (conditioned) pre-understanding of the world that belongs to the pre-structure of all cognition – that of every day as well as that of the sciences. This pre-understanding is always already linguistically articulated in the sense of the 'public interpretation' of the lifeworld. This is what Heidegger elucidated in *Being and Time* as follows:

> The *Dasein* is never able to escape this everyday world-interpretation to which it has been familiarized from the beginning. Within, from, and against it, all genuine understanding, interpreting and communicating, all appropriation afresh is performed. It is not the case that a *Dasein* should ever be posed before or confronted with the open space of a world in itself, i.e., untouched by the pre-interpretation, just to gaze upon what is presented to it.[8]

Here is an elucidation of that dimension of the pre-structure of being-in-the-world by which Heidegger's hermeneutical phenomenology is definitely distinguished from Husserl's optical and pre-linguistic type of 'evidence-phenomenology'. And it is this dimension that made possible the convergence of the hermeneutic phenomenology with the post-Wittgensteinian development of linguistic philosophy.

But, in what respect may those insights into the temporality and historicity still be considered as dimensions of a possible reconstruction and transformation of transcendental philosophy? Does this question really expose the problematic and intriguing aspect of our topic?

First it has to be pointed out that it is Heidegger himself who, in his early work, established an internal relationship between his analysis of the pre-structure of the disclosedness of being-in-the-world and the problematic of transcendental philosophy.

Heidegger's attempt at understanding his 'fundamental ontology' as a radicalization of Kant's project of a transcendental philosophy

In *Being and Time* Heidegger emphasized that his programme of a 'fundamental ontology', which placed the question as to the 'meaning of being' before the question of traditional ontology and tried to answer this question by recourse to that 'understanding of being' that belongs to human *Dasein*, may by no means take its orientation toward a pre-Kantian understanding of cognition as an innerwordly relation between a subject and an object. Thus far Heidegger dissociated himself from Max Scheler's and furthermore from Nicolai Hartmann's conception of 'ontology' or of cognition as an ontological relationship between beings. He wrote: 'Scheler as well as Hartmann, notwithstanding their different phenomenological point of departure, overlook the fact that ontology in its traditional basic orientation fails with regard to (human) *Dasein* and that precisely that "relationship of being" that is implied in cognition enforces a revision and not only a critical repair of ontology.'[9] The 'relation of being' that is at stake here cannot, on Heidegger's account, be regarded as a relation between two beings in the world but has to be thought of as 'transcendental' in so far as, along with *Dasein*'s understanding of being, the horizon of a world, which transcends every possible object as well as every possible subject, is projected and, so to speak, extended in a primordial way.

Thus far in *Being and Time* Heidegger can still maintain (in connection to Husserl's ideas): 'compared with realism, idealism, however opposed and untenable it is in effect, has a priority in principle, if it does not misunderstand itself as "psychological" idealism'.[10] And he explains: 'if the term "idealism" means as much as understanding that being [*Sein*] can never be explained by beings, since it is always already the transcendental with regard to each being, then idealism implies the only and right possibility of a philosophical problematic'. But he adds: 'if idealism means reducing all being to a subject or consciousness that is distinguished only by the fact that it remains undetermined in its being and at best is negatively characterized as "non-substantial" (*undinglich*), then idealism is no less naive than the crudest realism'.[11] Here Heidegger seems to make explicit the need for a fundamental-ontological transformation of Kant's transcendental philosophy.

But Heidegger clarified the relationship between his programme of fundamental ontology and transcendental philosophy much more precisely and thoroughly in his first book on Kant, *Kant and the Problem of Metaphysics.*[12] There he also had to pose the most difficult question with regard to the relation of his own approach to classical transcendental philosophy: the question regarding the relation of 'pure reason' to human *Dasein*, which precisely in (or on the ground of) its temporality and historicity is presupposed as condition of the possibility of the understanding of being. A transcendental philosopher might ask immediately: how is it possible to compare the pre-structure of the temporal-historical being-in-the-world – characterized by Heidegger as that of a 'thrown project' (*geworfener*

Entwurf) – with the transcendental basic structure of pure reason, which is presupposed by Kant?

In his first book on Kant Heidegger tried to solve this problem by interpreting Kant's 'pure reason' primarily as 'finite reason'. In this sense he tried to lay open the root of the transcendental synthesis of apperception as that of 'understanding being' in Kant's faculty of imagination (*Einbildungskraft*) and to understand this faculty as 'original temporality' of the transcendental projection of the world. For Heidegger the transcendental faculty of imagination is the capacity of 'pure synthesis' and thereby of projecting by which the finite reason of human beings must display the horizon of all understanding of being in advance of all possible affect by beings. As a projecting of 'pure intuition' in the Kantian sense, the transcendental faculty of imagination must generate (*bilden*) the horizon of time in such a way that it simultaneously engenders the ecstatic dimensions of the present, the past and the future and thereby opens up the conditions of the possibility of the 'pure succession of the nows' as providing a 'schema-image' (*Schemabild*) for the possible givenness of object representations.[13]

Thereby Heidegger reconstructed Kant's transcendental faculty of imagination as a testimony and illustration for what he himself had claimed in *Being and Time* to be the threefold ecstatic temporalizing function of the 'original time'. And Heidegger left no doubt about the fact that the original function of ecstatic temporalization, which corresponds to Kant's 'faculty of imagination' as 'original synthesis', constitutes the essence of understanding – that is of the 'synthesis of apperception' and moreover the essence of theoretical and practical reason.

However, already in Heidegger's first book on Kant there is some evidence for the fact that Heidegger's separation of empirical intratemporality (*Innerzeitlichkeit*), that is of the succession of the nows within the horizon of time, from the original time as ecstatic temporalization or 'pure synthesis' is counter-intuitive and cannot be sustained. It does not seem to be possible for Heidegger simply to draw a parallel between his distinction of original and vulgar time and Kant's transcendental distinction of reason as synthesis and *Innerzeitlichkeit* as empirical succession of moments. For at the end of his first book on Kant, where he summarizes his interpretation of the *Critique of Pure Reason* along the lines of a fundamental ontology, Heidegger is compelled to abandon the analogy between Kant's and his own 'architectonics'. This happens, I think, as a result of his discussion — apparently only in passing — of the occurrence of the finiteness of the understanding in *Dasein* and the 'transcendental subject'. According to Heidegger, this occurrence is to constitute after all 'the transcendental subjectivity' of the subject, the finiteness of reason.

The failure of the Heideggerian quasi-transcendental interpretation of 'original time' and the abandonment of transcendental philosophy after the turn of his philosophy

In what sense may one say that the use of the word 'occurrence' or 'happening' (*Ereignis* or *Geschehen*) amounts to an overthrowing of the Kantian 'architectonics' of transcendental philosophy? I think that the word 'happening', which, as is well known, is characteristic of Heidegger's later philosophy and has also a central significance in Gadamer's *Truth and Method*, points to a difficulty of Heidegger's analysis of time already in *Being and Time*. It is a difficulty that must become visible, if (or, rather, when) one parallels Heidegger's 'ontic-ontological difference' with Kant's 'empirico-transcendental difference', as Heidegger himself in his first book on Kant still endeavours to do.

Heidegger asserts time and again that the 'original time', which constitutes the essence of the transcendental synthesis, is radically different from the vulgar conception of time in the sense of a succession of moments within the horizon of time because the original ecstatic time precedes the 'intratemporality' as a condition that generates the horizon for the succession of moments. This appears quite *transcendental* — even in the Kantian sense. But the question is whether in this case Heidegger is right to talk meaningfully about a 'happening' of 'transcendence', or of the 'transcendental synthesis' generating the horizon? Is it possible to speak in a meaningful way of a 'happening' without already making use of the traditional concept of time as a succession of moments, that is to say, of intratemporality?

One may easily grant Heidegger that the traditional concept of time does not heed the moment of (quasi-transcendental) 'temporalization' (*Zeitigung*), that is of generating the three ecstatic dimensions of the present, the past and the future, and that this ecstatic structure of temporalization (which may be paralleled to the triadic structure of the 'apprehensive', 'reproductive' and 'recognitive' faculty of imagination) is always already presupposed in our talk of 'now' (in contradistinction to 'a minute ago' and 'soon'). At the same time, however, one has nevertheless to insist that, by referring to a 'happening', the factual 'one after another' of a succession of moments and thus far empirical 'intratemporality' in the Kantian sense is presupposed too. If one abstracts completely from 'intratemporality' – as Heidegger seems to suggest in *Being and Time* and still in his first book on Kant – that is if one tries to conceive of an 'original time' only in the sense of the simultaneous originating of the three 'ecstasies', then one can no longer understand the moving of the time. (It is not accidental that most philosophers, for example Kant, James and Husserl, used the metaphor of a stream in talking about the time or the consciousness of time. But a stream – being a continuous happening – is something that in Kant's sense is also 'intratemporal'. It can be experienced within the frame of Kant's temporal form of intuition, and that means: it must be empirically ascertainable, e.g. by the distinction between the simultaneity and the succession of two events.)

Thus far the suspicion arises that Heidegger's reconstruction of Kant's conception of transcendental synthesis in terms of 'original time' may be doomed to failure. And this suspicion, I think, is fully confirmed by the changes in philosophical 'architectonics' that are connected with Heidegger's *Kehre*. The quasi-transcendental understanding of the ('original') time, and thereby also the quasi-Kantian distinction between ecstatic 'temporalization' and 'intratemporality', is now tacitly given up together with the whole philosophy of subjectivity which now has to be overcome.

Heidegger now speaks quite openly of a 'happening' of 'clearing' and simultaneously 'concealing' of being and thus far of a 'history of being'. Still it may not be overlooked that Heidegger, by the 'happening' (*Ereignis*) of the mission (*Schickung*) of being, still means 'temporalization' (and 'spacing' or 'spacialization') as primordial constitution of meaning horizons of a lifeworld rather than 'occurrence' within the world that has been already constituted. The quasi-transcendental notion of 'temporalization' qua meaning constitution by *Dasein*'s project is transformed into the notion of a world- and meaning constitution by the mission (*Schickung*) of being. But it must not be overlooked also that Heidegger now talks of 'epochal' happenings of the 'history of being', that is of happenings that followed each

CONSTITUTING MEANING AND JUSTIFYING VALIDITY 113

other and may be considered as corresponding to the well-known intratemporal and intra-historical epochs of the history of philosophy, as for instance the foundation of metaphysics by the Greeks, the transformation of this foundation by the Romans and Christianity, and finally the instauration of modern science and technology as the frame (*Gestell*).

It is precisely this intratemporality and intra-historicity of 'happenings' (*Ereignisse*), which at the same time are considered to have opened up and thus originated the meaning of being, that precedes the possibility of true and false judgements. And it is this intertwining of quasi-transcendental temporalization and intratemporality that makes up the challenge of Heidegger's later philosophy to a transcendental philosophy that is oriented toward Kant's conception of a universally valid constitution of the world's objectivity by the synthetical functions of understanding or reason. This challenge culminates in Heidegger's claims that the whole philosophy of the transcendental subject – and, moreover, the whole philosophy in general as an enterprise of the *logos*, or reason (*Vernunft*), as a faculty of demanding and providing reasons – is now to be understood with regard to its validity as a finite result of an originating event of the history of being.

Here a question might arise: how can this Heideggerian thesis itself still be thought or stated with a claim to universal validity? Does it not turn out, after all, that time in the traditional sense, which was already considered by Parmenides and Plato as the most serious endangering of the possibility of thought's validity – that time in this sense in Heidegger's late philosophy holds sway over reason which according to the earlier Heidegger was to be identical with 'orignal time'?[14] (With Gadamer the same problematic reappears – the only difference being here that Gadamer does not take pains to deny the intratemporal character of what he calls *Sinngeschehen* or even *Wahrheitsgeschehen*. He still wishes to respond in a sense to the transcendental question as to the 'conditions of the possibility of understanding',[15] but he no longer sees any difficulty in answering this question exclusively in terms of historical happenings or even processes – finally in terms of ontological or cosmological processes of playing that seem to be conceived in a pre-Kantian sense of ontology.)[16]

Nevertheless, after this reconstruction of Heidegger's 'time' philosophy which finally amounts to a destruction of transcendental philosophy, we must again ask the question whether Heidegger's approach is justified as an answer to the question about the conditions of the possibility of the meaning constitution for the lifeworld. With regard to this question we have suggested that it points to the need for a transformation of transcendental philosophy, since a pure transcendental consciousness cannot explain the constitution of the concrete pre-understanding of the significance of the lifeworld that is presupposed by all cognition. To this extent Heidegger's transformation of Kant's transcendental philosophy seems to be plausible to me.

But our reconstruction of this transformation has also led us to make the following point: Heidegger's presupposition of a meaning-constitutive temporality and historicity of world-understanding, which finally leads to the meaning-constitutive happenings of the history of being, turns out to be incompatible with the possibility of answering Kant's question as to the conditions of the possibility of the universal objectivity and hence inter-subjective validity of our understanding. Which consequence may be drawn from this dilemma? Do we perhaps – following Heidegger – have to consider the possibility that all objective validity of knowledge and thus far the possible truth and falsehood of judgements is dependent, in a unilateral way, on the preceding happenings of a world disclosure that articulates and delivers itself in the historical languages?

The spirit of our time appears to be prepared to accept this principled subordination of the question of the validity of knowledge (and, by the way, also of norms) under the question of historical world disclosure qua meaning constitution. Thus the truth and falsehood of scientific discoveries – according to Thomas Kuhn – may be understood as dependent upon the preceding constitution of the 'paradigms' of 'normal science' which themselves may be compared with the historical 'clearings' or 'concealings' of the 'history of being'. In accordance with this conception also the rightness or wrongness of moral norms seems be dependent on a particular, contingent 'consensus-basis', as Rorty suggests. In brief: the validity of the *logos* (reason) and its modes, which serve universality and identity, seems to be subordinated to a meaning-constitutive happening of temporal-historical generation of differences (what Derrida terms 'la différance').

However, there is a transcendental-reflexive argument that we could oppose to this tendency: the universal validity claim of the detranscendentalization arguments themselves is not compatible with the propositional content of these arguments: arguments that relativize their own validity claim to temporal-historical happenings cannot state at least this relativization itself with a corresponding validity claim. Apart from this central paradox, the question arises whether there is in fact a unilateral relation of dependence between the truth and falsehood of (empirical) judgements and the preceding clearing-concealing world disclosures as suggested by Heidegger's theory of truth. Could it not be that there is rather a relation of reciprocal dependence between both sides – such that also the linguistic disclosure of meaning on its part is dependent on its being tested in those processes of experience and learning that itself has made them possible? In *Being and Time* Heidegger himself had suggested the possibility of such a relation of mutual correction by introducing his notion of the 'hermeneutic circle'.

However, even if one defends the latter strategy, as I would, one is blatantly supposing – in contradistinction to classical transcendental philosophy – that the question as to the conditions of the possibility of meaning constitution is not the same as the question as to the conditions of the possibility of justifying the validity of knowledge (or of norms). This distinction, which, on its part, makes possible a new relating of both dimensions of the transcendental problem, appears to me to turn out as an interim result of our reconstruction of Heidegger's transformation of transcendental philosophy.

In my opinion this interim result may serve as a vantage point for another strategy which is an alternative to the fashionable strategy of detranscendentalization: this alternative should do justice, on the one hand, to the historicity of the world's meaning constitution and its being the precondition for true and false judgements, but also to the conditions of the universal and timeless validity of these judgements, on the other. (This holds not only for the empirical judgements that have been made possible by the meaning constitution but also for the philosophical judgements about the relationship between meaning constitution and the validity of judgments.)

To corroborate this thesis I must discuss in a detour the internal relation and the difference between the problematic of meaning constitution and of the justification of validity within the history of transcendental philosophy.

The relationship of meaning constitution and justification of validity in the frame of a transcendental pragmatics of language

The relation between the question of meaning constitution and the question of validity within the history of transcendental philosophy

Let me first state that for Kant the question as to the conditions of the possibility of the objective validity of scientific knowledge coincides with the question as to the transcendental conditions of the constitution of the *a priori* meaning of objectivity (i.e. *Gegenständlichkeit*). More specifically, Kant does answer the first question by reducing it to the second. This constitutes the point of the 'Copernican turn' which is inspired by the basic *topos* of modern philosophy, according to which we can understand *a priori* only what we ourselves have made or in a certain sense can make.[17] But Kant could make plausible this solution of the transcendental problem only by confining his entire problematic to the question of the constitution of the *a priori* valid form of objective experience and hence of the objectivity of the world to be experienced.

This situation was changed however in a fundamental way by Husserl's expanding of the Kantian problematic of 'transcendental constitution', that is by Husserl's transcending Kant's question in order to account for the constitution of the concrete manifoldness of the meaning contents of experience of the lifeworld – such as it expresses itself in language. Such an expansion implied as its immediate consequence, I believe, that the Kantian identification of the formal *a priori* conditions of meaning constitution with the conditions of the justification of the validity of knowledge could no longer be redeemed. For the presuppositions of meaning constitution in the sense of the concrete manifoldness of world disclosure refer indeed to those temporal-historical conditions that were assumed by Heidegger.

Be that as it may, the peculiarity and the deficiency of Husserl's transformation of transcendental philosophy are due to the fact that he preserved the solution strategy of Kant's philosophy of the transcendental subject even with regard to his expanded problematic of meaning constitution. For although he had extended the question in the way I pointed out, he nevertheless wished to give the answer – in a certain analogy to Kant – by reducing the meaning constitutions

CONSTITUTING MEANING AND JUSTIFYING VALIDITY 117

of the lifeworld to the intentional achievements of a transcendental consciousness, without taking into account the language mediation of the vast variety of the meaning contents of the lifeworld. Thus he was able, as it appeared, to escape Heidegger's problematic of a temporal-historical world-meaning constitution and thereby adapt his newly detected problematics of the pre-scientific meaning constitution of the lifeworld to that of a Kantian transcendental philosophy. But this restoration of the programme of classical transcendental philosophy was evidently doomed to failure because Husserl totally overlooked the role of linguistic mediation and thus of the dependence on history of concrete meaning constitution.

Does this rejection of Husserl's project of transcendental philosophy allows for an alternative to Heidegger's transformation and destruction of transcendental philosophy? Must the alternative to Husserl's strategy of reducing the justification of the validity of experience to meaning constitution by the transcendental subject be – necessarily – the reduction of all validity to the meaning constitution by the history of being, as suggested by Heidegger?

A transcendental-pragmatic renegotiation of the analysis of the 'pre-structure' of understanding in *Being and Time*

In my opinion there is an alternative to the Heideggerian suggestion. It is opened by the same reflection that – as a first step – enforced the assumption of a temporal-historical meaning constitution: namely by the reflection on the language mediation of our understanding of the lifeworld. For this reflection points not only to the undeniable historicity of meaning constitution but also to the fact that, already on the level of communicative understanding of the meaning of our utterances, a claim to universal validity of meaning is presupposed: a claim to the validity of meaning which can be definitively redeemed – if at all – only by the possible consensus of an indefinite, ideal community of communication and interpretation (as understood by Peirce and Royce).[18] In a semiotically transformed transcendental philosophy this 'regulative idea' has to take the place (so to speak) of the transcendental subject of meaning constitution (which on Husserl's account was to warrant the universal inter-subjective validity of meaning by its solitary intentional achievements).

If the definite consensus of the ideal community of interpretation may be presupposed – which of course can never be supposed empirically – then the universally valid redemption of all justifiable meaning claims would be identical with the historical meaning constitution (i.e. everybody would at least understand anybody else).[19] And therefore, under this ideal presupposition and the additional supposition of an exhaustion of all truth criteria that are available to an indefinite community of researchers – for example of all possible criteria of evidence and coherence – the redemption of all discursively justifiable truth claims would also be possible.[20]

I argue that this counterfactual supposition of the ideal of a consensual justification of validity claims (which was first envisaged by Peirce) represents the alternative, or, so to speak, 'counterinstance' of reason, to Heidegger's conception of the history of being, and to the transcendental subject of classical transcendental philosophy. Being a counterfactual supposition and a regulative idea of what consensual justification of validity would be, it obviously does not contradict the factual dependence of our understanding, for example of our capability of asking questions and hence also of the truth or falsehood of possible answers, on the temporal-historical meaning constitution of the lifeworld, as it is articulated in the language as medium of understanding. Nevertheless, we have to insist that from this dependence – which was explored by Heidegger – it does not follow that the possible justification of validity – of meaning and truth – is conditioned in a unilateral way by the preceding historical meaning constitution.

In light of the variety and diversity of languages or language games, the postulate of consensual justification of validity firstly functions as a regulative idea of translatability and hence for a progressive translation and hermeneutic interpretation of meaning; furthermore it functions as a regulative idea for the progressive research qua searching for the truth under the restrictive conditions of abstractive meaning constitutions. Even these restrictive conditions however do not constitute themselves merely in dependence on the background conditions of the lifeworld as they are always already opened up by the history of being. For they are also always already constituted in dependence on learning processes in the sense of 'trial and error', and this means, in the age of science, on methodically controlled processes of discursive redemption or refutation on the basis of criteria.

It has to be conceded that we shall always remain under the sway of the historical and socio-cultural 'background' assumptions of the lifeworld. Up to this point, a view that, along with Heidegger and

Wittgenstein, focuses only on the factual conditions of understanding may appear as if it finally considers only the historical happening of meaning and truth. However, such a position would be blind to the actual, performative validity claims that are brought forward in the situation of communication, and it is finally the validity claims of the philosophers themselves who argue for the historicist position that have to be put under scrutiny.

As I see it, Heidegger himself, who discovered the idea of the temporality of being (which is not to be confused with the abstract beingness of traditional ontology), could never bring to bear, as against the generative power of time, a counter-instance of reason, for example such a thing as Kant's 'regulative ideas'. This fundamental deficiency seems to be caused, in the last resort, by the fact that Heidegger, already in *Being and Time*, in his analysis of the pre-structure of being-in-the-world or of understanding being, did not account – by strict transcendental reflection – for the claim to universal validity and the presuppositions of his own analysis of the (existential-ontological) structures of being-in-the-world. Instead, his analysis, so to speak, fell upon the contingent, historically conditioned structures of 'facticity' (*geworfener-Entwurf*). Hereby he indeed discovered for the first time those structures that today are called 'background' presuppositions of the lifeworld. Thus in *Being and Time* the later turn of his philosophy in the sense of deriving the 'thrown project' from the 'happening' of the 'mission of being' had already been grounded – at least in the sense that there was no *logos* of the philosophical thought itself that could be counterposed to the history of being. The way to 'detranscendentalization' which today seems so plausible for many people was paved then.

But this whole surrender of the *logos* to the superiority of time – at least in Heidegger – rests on the fact that one part of the pre-structure of world understanding was overleapt, so to speak: namely that part which contains the specific validity claims and presuppositions of the philosophical analysis of being-in-the-world. In short: a deficiency of reflection came about that – by contrasting it with Heidegger's talk of 'oblivion of being' (*Seinsvergessenheit*) – we may call it 'oblivion of the *logos*' (*Logosvergessenheit*). And it should be noted that by '*logos*' I would not understand the *logos* of the *Gestell*, that is of making available by objectifying or making present in Heidegger's and Derrida's sense, but a much wider *logos*, which is presupposed by a communicative understanding and – finally in a form that cannot be reflectively denied without self-contradiction – by the philosophical discourse itself.[21]

At this point the task of a reiteration of Heidegger's analysis of the pre-structure of world-understanding arises, if we desire a transformation of transcendental philosophy that would be oriented toward a pragmatics of language communication. Such a transformation should avoid Heidegger's reflection deficit of the *Logosvergessenheit* without losing sight of his discovery of the temporal-historical background presuppositions of the lifeworld – especially of the clearing–concealing structure of the meaning constitution by the linguistic world disclosure. It seems clear that this task cannot be carried through to the end by a return to a transcendental philosophy of the transcendental subject or consciousness, that is neither by a restriction of the problematic of meaning constitution to the constitution of objectivity in Kant's sense nor by recourse to a meaning constitution that – along Husserlian lines – could be conceived as an intentional achievement of a self-sufficient subject in the wake of 'transcendental solipsism'. Instead I suggest that, at the beginning of the philosophical venture, we reflect on those transcendental-pragmatic presuppositions of arguing, that is of the argumentative discourse, that must be acknowledged – in order to avoid a performative self-contradiction – by each interlocutor, in other words, even by each subject of empirically solitary thinking. And I do insist on this suggestion, even if, at present, this appears to be very unfashionable with regard to the opening move of the philosophical language game.

Notes

First published in E. Agazzi (ed.), *Entretiens sur philosophie et histoire*, Actes du Congrès de Santa Margherita Ligure et Genes 1989 (Genoa: Academia Ligure di Science e Lettere, 1990), 127–46.

1 M. Heidegger, 'Das Ende der Philosophie und die Aufgabe des Denkens', in *Zur Sache des Denkens* (Tübingen: Mohr, 1969), 79.
2 K.O. Apel, 'Le défit de la critique totale de la raison et le programme d'une théorie philosophique des types de rationalité', *Le Débat*, 49 (1988), 141–63.
3 R. Rorty, *Consequences of Pragmatism* (Minneapolis: Univerity of Minnesota Press, 1987), and 'Pragmatism and Philosophy', in K. Baynes, J. Bohman and T.A. McCarthy (eds), *After Philosophy: End or Transformation?* (Cambridge, Mass.: MIT Press, 1987), 26–66.
4 M. Heidegger, *Sein und Zeit* (Halle: Niemeyer, 1941), 86.
5 *Ibid.*, 89 ff.

CONSTITUTING MEANING AND JUSTIFYING VALIDITY 121

6 *Ibid.*, 205.
7 E. Husserl, *Die Krisis der europäischen Wissenschaften und die transzendentale Phänomenologie* (The Hague: Nijhoff, 1962).
8 M. Heidegger, *Sein und Zeit*, § 35.
9 *Ibid.*, 208.
10 *Ibid.*, 207 ff.
11 *Ibid.*, 208.
12 M. Heidegger, *Kant und das Problem der Metaphysik* (Frankfurt a. M: Kostermann, 1951).
13 *Ibid.*, 159 ff.
14 In his first book on Kant, Heidegger claimed 'that the I, the pure reason, in its essence is temporal' (*ibid.*, 174); after the *Kehre*, 'reason', as it is understood by occidental philosophy, is conceived as an epochal and hence restrictively valid result of the 'history of being'.
15 Gadamer, *Wahrheit und Methode*, preface to the second edition (Tübingen: Mohr & Siebeck, 1965), xv ff.
16 *Ibid.*, part 3.
17 For the history of this *topos* cf. Apel, *Die Idee der Sprache in der Tradition des Humanismus von Dante bis Vico* (Bonn: Bouvier, 1963, 1980), 321 ff., and 'Das "Verstehen" (eine Begriffsgeschichte als Problemgeschichte)', *Archiv für Begriffsgeschichte*, 1 (Bonn: Bouvier, 1955), 142–99.
18 Apel, 'Szientismus oder transzendentale Hermeneutik?', in *Transformation der Philosophie* (Frankfurt a. M.: Suhrkamp, 1973), vol. 2, 178–219; English translation: *Towards a Transformation of Philosophy* (London: Routledge & Kegan Paul, 1980); cf. Apel, *Der Denkweg von Charles Sanders Peirce* (Frankfurt a. M.: Suhrkamp, 1975).
19 Apel, 'Linguistic Meaning and Intentionality: the Compatibility of the "Linguistic Turn" and the "Pragmatic Turn" of Meaning-theory within the Framework of a Transcendental Semiotics', in H.J. Silverman and D. Welton (eds), *Critical and Dialectical Phenomenology* (Albany: State University of New York Press, 1987), 2–53.
20 Apel, 'Fallibilismus, Konsenstheorie der Wahrheit und Letztbegründung', in Forum für Philosophie Bad Homburg (ed.), *Philosophie und Begründung* (Frankfurt a. M.: Suhrkamp, 1987), 116–211.
21 Apel, 'Die Logosauszeichnung der menschlichen Sprache: die philosophische Relevanz der Sprechakttheorie', in H.-G. Bosshardt (ed.), *Perspektiven auf Sprache* (Berlin and New York: De Gruyter, 1986), 45–87.

The question of the subject: Heidegger and the transcendental tradition*

DAVID CARR
Department of Philosophy, Emory University, Atlanta, GA 30322, USA

Recent Continental European philosophy has converged on the rejection of the subject, or more broadly of the metaphysics of subjectivity. Though this rejection is most commonly associated with French Post-structuralism, it is equally important in Habermas' work. Habermas disagrees with French views on humanism, rationality and the enlightenment, but he joins them in their opposition to what he calls the philosophy of consciousness. A recent anthology by a group of French thinkers (Cadava, Connor and Nancy, 1991) bears the title: *Who Comes After the Subject?*[1] suggesting that the battle against the subject has been fought and won, the opponent vanquished for good. Where, its editors seem to ask, do we go from here?

What exactly is the metaphysics of the subject, that is so resoundingly rejected by such diverse thinkers? It is generally portrayed as nothing less than the entire mainstream of modern philosophy, beginning with Descartes and culminating in its most extreme form in phenomenology and existentialism. It is centered in such notions as the cogito, the 'I think,' consciousness, self-consciousness, self-transparency, self-determination. In spite of its dominance, this tradition is thought to have been gradually undermined in the course of our century when philosophers began to take seriously some powerful ideas from outside the philosophical mainstream, notably those of false consciousness (Marx) the unconscious (Freud) and structuralist conceptions of language.

By themselves, however, these extra-philosophical intrusions would not have been enough to bring on the full-scale repudiation of the mainstream tradition. Merleau-Ponty and Ricoeur, among others, have made valiant attempts to intergrate them into the mainstream. What was decisive, I think, in combination with the influences already mentioned, was the work of the

---

* A version of this paper was delivered as The Aaron Gurwitsch Memorial Lecture at the annual meeting of the Society for Phenomenology and Existential Philosophy in New Orleans, October 1993.

later Heidegger. There is a well-known irony in this: Heidegger betrays no acquaintance with Freud or structuralist theory, and acknowledges Marx only seldom and grudgingly. Unlike them, he is the ultimate philosophical insider, preoccupied primarily with the canon of philosophical history.

Nevertheless Heidegger's attack on the modern tradition has been thought compatible with these other counter-currents, at least by some. But it is also in many ways broader and deeper. If Freud, Marx and structuralism call into question the modern understanding of human beings, Heidegger links this understanding to that of being as such. He attacks not just the philosophical anthropology of modern philosophy, but the underlying ontology or metaphysics on which it is based. Furthermore, his account of the connection between philosophy, science and technology adds a dimension which is totally lacking in Freud and structuralism, and it is much more sophisticated, in the eyes of many, than the one found in Marx. And in any case Marx has been discredited for political reasons in French philosophy now for more than a decade.

Thus it is Heidegger's later work, and in particular his reading of the history of modern philosophy, which has been the dominant influence in the attack on the metaphysics of the subject. In this paper I want to reopen the question of the subject by critically examining Heidegger's reading. In particular, I want to claim that Heidegger ignores the distinction between the metaphysical and the transcendental traditions in modern philosophy, and that he does this by misreading the work of Kant and Husserl. I shall first recount the main features of Heidegger's reading. Then I shall try to show what is wrong with it by advancing an alternative reading of my own.

1. Heidegger's reading of modern philosophy

For the late Heidegger all philosophy is ontology or metaphysics, whose task it to think about beings as a whole with respect to their being (EdP 61).[1] For ancient and medieval philosophy, this thinking finds its expression in the concept of substance as *hypokeimenon*, *substantia* or *subjectum*. Substance is the underlying, persisting foundation which supports everything else. To be is either to *be* a substance or to be a property or predicate of a substance. Substance exists in the primary sense, everything else exists "in" substance and thus has a merely secondary and dependent way of existing.

Modern metaphysics is a variation on this theme, with an important difference. Beginning with Descartes, the human or conscious "subject," the cogito, assumes the role of substance or primary existence. As Heidegger puts it in the Nietzsche lectures, all metaphysics is charactized by "subjectity," but in modern philosophy this is transformed into "subjectivity" [N 450ff.]. To be is either to *be* such a subject or to exist "in" such a subject, and thus again to have a secondary and derivative mode of being. But to exist "in" a subject is now not so much to be a predicate or property of it, as to be an object or representation for it. In virtue of the principle of self-consciousness the subject even has the status of object or representation for itself. And primary being or subjectivity, following Leibniz, Hegel and Nietzsche, is conceived as the activity, striving or will, which takes over all being by objectifying it and reducing it to calculable representations, framing it within a world-picture which is a product of subjective (human) activity.

This notion of activity is embodied in various notions of method or procedure, from Descartes' *Discours* and *Regulae* through Hegel's dialectical method, and finds its expression as well in such notions as scientific method, research, and experimental and technical procedure. Modern philosophy culminates in the development and success of technology. "The end of philosophy reveals itself as the triumph of the manipulable arrangement of a scientific-technical world." ("Das Ende der Philosophie zeigt sich als der Triumph der steuerbaren Einrichtung einer wissenschaftlich-technischen Welt...") [EdP 65]

How do Kant and Husserl fit into this picture? In keeping with his reading of all the modern philosophers, Heidegger asserts that Kant's doctrine in the first Critique is really metaphysical rather than epistemological or critical [K 13f.]. In his early work (*Being and Time* and *Kant and the Problem of Metaphysics*) Heidegger subjects Kant to the same sort of critique he directs at other modern philosophers. They understand the being of beings in general as substantiality or *Vorhandenheit*, which is bad enough, and go on to make the much more serious mistake of interpreting the being of *Dasein* in the same way. Thus, in spite of the rich ontological possibilities to be found in his work, Kant contributes to the misunderstanding of human existence which Heidegger seeks to put right with his fundamental ontology.

In his later work, Heidegger's critical reading of Kant developes parallel to his reading of the other figures of modern philosophy. For one thing, the attempt to find in Kant's work positive steps toward a genuine ontology, is practically abandoned. Kant is treated along with Descartes et al. as a representative of the modern "metaphysics and ontology" which Heidegger studies in order to overcome.

In a sense, then, we could say that it is only the negative side of Kant that now interests Heidegger; but the negative side has also subtly changed. The issue is no longer the misunderstanding of *Dasein*, but rather Kant's participation in the metaphysics of the subject. Again denying any distinction between ontology and epistemology or (in Kantian terms) Critique, Heidegger calls "Transcendentalphilosophie" simply "the modern form of ontology" ("die neuzeitliche Gestalt der Ontologie") [UdM 74]. The claim that Kant substantivizes the human being remains part of this, of course, but equally important is the more general notion that "the beingness of beings is thought as presence *for* the securing representation. Beingness is now objectivity" ("die Seiendheit des Seienden als die Anwesenheit *für* das sicherstellende Vorstellen gedacht wird. Seiendheit ist jetzt Gegenständigkeit.") [74f.] Heidegger seizes on the term *Vorstellen* in order to express the connection, in modern philosophy as a whole, between representation and technology, and *Vorstellen* is a central Kantian term. Given the importance of language for Heidegger, Kant could be seen to have played a central role in modern metaphysics by this terminological choice alone. The development that begins with Descartes, whereby the essence of reality (*Wirklichkeit*) is seen as the "Gegenständlichkeit des Gegenstandes (Objecktivität des Objekts)," is fully grasped in all clarity only by Kant. [N 433] (. . . erst von Kant in aller Klarheit . . .begriffen.) In his notion of the "original synthetic unity of transcendental apperception" (as Heidegger styles it, N 463), Kant also fully articulates the principle of self-consciousness originally formulated by Descartes.

Equally important is the manner in which Kant goes beyond Leibniz in portraying knowledge as an activity and objects known as something like its products [see FndD 142–3]. "Das Vorstellen erwirkt die Zustellung des Entgegenstehens des Gegenstandes." [N 433; Heidegger warns us not to interpret this to mean the object is a psychological product.] What is more, Heidegger emphasizes that Kant calls the understanding a faculty of rules (Vermögen der Regeln), and even as source of rules [FndD 147], which ties in with the modern conception of knowledge as procedure or method. This is a crucial step on the way to the conception of subjectivity as will to power.

In one of Heidegger's last publications, Husserl is drawn into this picture as well. Heidegger's relation to Husserl was always, to say the least, complicated. *Being and Time* is of course dedicated to Husserl, and contains references to him which are almost exclusively positive. The lectures of the 1920s document better than *Being and Time* Heidegger's critical stance toward Husserl's conception of phenomenology, but even they are veiled in the kind of deference Heidegger obviously thought he owed to his mentor. It is clear that he found Husserl's transcendental turn, after the *Logical Investigations*, a perversion of the genuine idea of phenomenology. And Heidegger's critique of Kant's substantivization of the subject was probably aimed at Husserl's "transcendental ego" as well.

When Heidegger turns in the mid-1930s to his more historical preoccupations, Husserl practically vanishes from his pages along with others who were frequently cited in his earlier works, such as Jaspers, Scheler, Cassirer, and Dilthey. These philosophers were contemporaries from whom Heidegger wished to distance himself, some had become politically unmentionable (including Husserl); and in any case they were not taken to belong to the history of metaphysics, with which Heidegger was now preoccupied. This history was supposed to have come to an end with Nietzsche.

It is thus all the more interesting that Husserl should turn up in the 1964 text "Das Ende der Philosophie un die Aufgabe des Denkens," where he is given a place of honor alongside Hegel as a representative of modern metaphysics. To be sure, this is an honor which Husserl and Hegel might not have accepted with a great deal of pleasure, since what they supposedly represent is a mode of thinking which has now come (or is coming) to an end and needs to be replaced. The point here is to seek for a task still reserved for thinking after the end of philosophy. "Welche Aufgabe bleibt dem Denken noch vorbehalten am Ende der Philosophie?" [66].

It is in this context that Husserl now enters the scene, along with Hegel, as a representative of modern philosophy. Heidegger is himself in search of "die Sache des Denkens" – the matter or the issue of thinking *after* philosophy, and he turns to these two thinkers for what they said about the "Sache" of philosophy. Each of these thinkers called philosophy back "zur Sache" or "zu den Sachen selbst." What did they think the "Sache" of philosophy was, what did they think philosophy was really *about*?

Though he admits that there are great differences between Hegel and Husserl, Heidegger thinks they both conceive of philosophy in terms of the connection between subjectivity and method. Thus they conform to the familiar and unified picture developed by Heidegger for modern philosophy as a whole. The matter of philosophy is really decided in advance for both philosophers in virtue of their belonging to the modern tradition. The "subjectivity of consciousness" (p. 69) is what both of them are after, and both conceive of their task as that of developing a procedure for bringing subjectivity "to certifiable givenness" ("zur ausweisbaren Gegebenheit.") (p. 69) Heidegger mentions Husserl's "Principle of all principles" from *Ideas I*, which is embodied in the transcendental reduction (p. 70). Through it Husserl seeks to ground "the objectivity of all objects" -- which Heidegger equates with "das Sein des Seienden" -- in and through subjectivity.

Thus Heidegger presents Husserl as conforming perfectly to the pattern of the tradition, as yet another variation on the theme of modern metaphysics. Like everyone else, whether he realizes it or not Husserl is "really" trying to think the being of beings. In the first instance, to be is to be an object of representation. "Gegebenheit" is just Husserl's version of *Anwesenheit* or *Vorhandenheit*. But this in turn means to be an object or representation *for* the subject; and of course the subject even has this status for itself. The latter is thus being in the primary sense, or as Husserl himself says, "das einzige absolute Seiende" (p. 70). Transcendental subjectivity is just the latest version of the ancient *hypokeimenon*.

What is more, Husserl shares with his modern predecessors the preoccupation with *method*. Through the phenomenological *epoche*, after all, any independence the object might have is taken away. The method is described as a *reduction*: it reduces the world to the status of intentional object or representation. In the process transcendental subjectivity achieves full *Gegebenheit* to itself. Though he does not say it, Heidegger might have characterized Husserl's method, as he does that of the other modern philosophers, as a roundabout way of describing the technological subjugation of the world.

2. An alternative reading

Having laid out in broad outlines Heidegger's story of modern philosophy, I would like now to suggest ways of opening a critical perspective on it. Precisely with respect to its central focus, the concept of the subject or subjectivity, Heidegger's account seems to me to overlook a major difference in modern philosophy, that between metaphysics and the critique of metaphysics, and the closely related difference between the ontological and the transcendental traditions. In recounting Heidegger's reading of the moderns, I singled out his interpretations of Kant and of Husserl, who for me are the chief representatives of the latter tradition. I want to show that Heidegger has misread what is central to their thought and what distinguishes them from the rest of modern philosophy.

There are a couple of rather obvious things about Kant that Heidegger seems almost blatantly to ignore. To consider Kant's theory a metaphysics of the subject is to ignore that such a metaphysics is one of Kant's primary targets in the First Critique. The section entitled Paralogisms of Pure Reason attacks precisely those philosophers who treat the epistemological subject as substance and try to build a metaphysics upon it. They have failed to distinguish, Kant says in effect, between the self as it turns up in experience as the bearer of psychological properties, and the "I think" that functions as condition of the possibility of that very experience. While the former may be considered substance in the limited phenomenal sense, the latter certainly cannot.

That the transcendental "I think" may *not* be treated as a substance in any metaphysical sense, is clearly enunciated in the First Critique. While Kant speaks of transcendental apperception or self-consciousness, the "I" is not conscious of itself as an object, as something *vorhanden* or *anwesend* to itself. One of the great puzzles of the Transcendental Deduction, one which practically scandalized Kant's contemporaries, is that the self-awareness which constitutes the supreme condition of the possibility of experience, cannot be considered an instance of self-knowledge. In saying this Kant denies precisely what is most important about Descartes' *cogito*. This was intolerable to Fichte, for example: how could the fundamental principle of the system of knowledge not itself by known? It seems not to have occurred to him that Kant was not seeking in the self the same metaphysical *fundamentum inconcussum* sought by other modern philosophers, that he was not really a foundationalist in the same way they were. And it seems not to have occurred to Heidegger either.

Furthermore, the relation of the "I think" to its objects, if relation it can be called, cannot be construed as a relation between a thing and its properties, or even as a relation à la Leibniz between a subject and its representations. To construe it in this way seems to me to attribute to Kant precisely the view he is most at pains to deny. I am referring to what Kant calls *Erfahrung*, experience, which is equivalent for him to empirical knowledge. We actually do have experience in this sense, as Kant tells us repeatedly, and the question is, how is it possible? But Kant raises this question based on a very definite conception of what experience is.

The "I think" expresses, in the idiom of later period, an intentional directedness. To think is to think of something or about something or that something is the case. Experience in Kant's sense is of course a particular kind of thinking, that is, the kind embodied in our knowledge of the sensible world. This knowledge requires that out thinking be linked with sense-representations or intuitions. But what is the nature of this link? One might expect that, since thought requires an object, it is sense-representations that serve this function, that they are what experience is *about*.

But this is precisely *not* what Kant is saying. In fact, his rejection of such a notion is a decisive aspect of his own doctrine in relation to his predecessors.

Kant rejects the so-called "way of ideas" expressed notoriously by Locke when he said that the term "idea" "serves bet to stand for whatsoever is the *object* of the understanding when a man thinks" (Locke, 1956: 17). Kant indeed uses the term *Vorstellung* – usually rendered "representation" in English, in a way that corresponds roughly to the term "idea" in English and its cognates in French and Latin, as used by Locke and other early modern philosophers. And he believes that such representation, in the form of sensations or "impressions" (*Eindrücke*, A 50, B 74)[2] are necessarily involved in our knowledge of the sensible world. *But* these representations are "mere determination of the mind" (ibid). Our knowledge of the sensible world is not *about* our mind or its contents or determinations; it is precisely *about* the sensible world, or rather about *objects* in the sensible world. All experience "contains[s], in addition to the intuition of the senses through which something is given, a *concept* of an object as being thereby given, that is to say, as appearing." (A 93, B 126). Experience requires that a manifold of intuition be united, *not* in the subject that has or receives them, but rather in an object

– i.e., something whose very concept is that of being *other* than and independent of the subject.

What functions as the supreme condition of the possibility of experience, then, transcendental apperception, is a self-consciousness, but not of the subject as metaphysical substance conversant only with its own ideas. This would be the Berkeleyan soul or the Leibnizian monad. It may also correspond to Kant's conception of the self given in empirical self-consciousness: a thing in the world with its psychological properties. Instead, this transcendental subject transcends itself toward its objects and toward the world. But his means it is also limited by the world.

Kant's notion of the understanding "as it were, . . . prescribing law to nature" (*der Natur gleichsam das Gesetz vorzuschreiben*) might seem to support perfectly the Heideggerian interpretation, but that notion must be taken together with that of the receptivity of the knowing subject. If the understanding determines what counts as an object of knowledge, it does not create its objects [A 92, B 125] but must wait for them to be given. This is one side of its finitude. The other is expressed in the doctrine of transcendental idealism according to which the world may be more than or other than it is under the conditions governing its appearance to us. To be sure this doctrine is so difficult and troublesome that it was rejected from the start, and is rejected to this day, even by some of Kant's strongest supporters. But Kant insists on it. And its deepest sense is that of the finitude of the subject.

In Kant the subject may seem, in its cognitive guise, to legislate to nature, just as, in its moral guise, it may seem to legislate to itself. But in fact both its spontaneity and its freedom can never be shown to be anything more than necessary assumptions under which alone it can think and act. The transcendental unity of apperception is, in the cognitive sphere, the self-consciousness in which this assumption is made. This is far indeed from an indubitable self-presence or self-knowledge. When the self becomes an object to itself the apperception becomes empirical, the "I" loses its transcendental status, and it becomes an item in the world.

Clearly the transcendental "I" is not a thing in the world. But even less is it a substance which reduces the rest of the world to part of itself. Instead it is a kind of pure relation to a world that transcends it.

It is a similar consideration which governs Husserl's use of the term "transcendental." Of course this is a term which he takes over from Kant. His definition of it is different from Kant's, but it seems to me to be a good expression of Kant's deepest intentions. In the *Cartesian Meditations* he introduces the "concept of the transcendental and its correlate, the concept of the transcendent," in the following way:

> Just as the reduced Ego is not a piece of the world, so, conversely, neither the world nor any worldly Object is a piece of my Ego, to be found in my

conscious life as a really inherent part, as a complex of data of sensation or a complex of acts. This *"transcendence"* is part of the intrinsic sense of anything worldly ... The Ego ... necessarily presupposed by this sense, is legitimately called *transcendental*, in the phenomenological sense. Accordingly the philosophical problems arising from this correlation are called transcendental-philosophical (Husserl, 1962: 26).

This statement, from a relatively late work, tells us that the very notion of transcendental philosophy derives from the transcendence of the world, its non-reducibility to consciousness. It confirms an aspect of Husserl's phenomenology which goes right back to the *Logical Investigations* and the attack on psychologism. Broadly speaking, this attack is directed at the tendency of empiricism to collapse into subjective idealism by reducing objective structures to contents of the mind. The opening move, so to speak, of phenomenology, is a realist move, and it is preserved throughout in the very notion of intentionality. Consciousness is consciousness *of* something, and the of-ness of that relation, or quasi-relation, is irreducible and not explainable in terms of anything else. In being *of* something, consciousness distinguishes itself and its own features, whatever they may be, from that thing, whatever it is.

The concept of intentionality, as Husserl uses it, is meant to counter all attempts to reduce the object of consciousness to part of consciousness or a property of consciousness. For this reason, Husserl's use of the term "reduction" is misleading. Transcendence, that is, irreducibility to consciousness, belongs to the intrinsic *sense* of the objective or the worldly, he tells us. The purpose of the phenomenological "reduction" is precisely to *preserve* that sense and understand it. Hence the realism of phenomenology's opening move does not remain naive; it is not content simply to assert the transcendence of the world, but wants to know what it means to assert it or to believe it. Understanding this sense will, among other things, prevent its being transformed into something else by a philosophical theory laden with metaphysical assumptions, such as empiricism.

The naive and unreflected belief in the transcendence of the world is what Husserl calls the natural attitude. Later, in the *Crisis*, he calls it the world-life of consciousness, whose always pre-given horizon is the life-world. The phenomenological reduction suspends the validity of the natural attitude, puts it out of play. There is no doubt that Husserl considers this fundamental change in attitude the fulfillment of all philosophy's dreams, and as is well known, he even compares it to a religious conversion (Husserl, 1970: 137). But its sole purpose is to understand the very naivete it has left behind, suspends the natural attitude, the better to understand it.

There are two senses in which the natural attitude is never really left behind in Husserl's phenomenology. First, if the purpose of the reduction is to understand the natural attitude, then this attitude is in a sense the source of phenomenological descriptions. All the sciences, including the *Geisteswissenschaften*, are based on the natural attitude, or, as he says later, arise on the basis of the pre-given life-world. A phenomenological clarification of the sciences involves understanding how the undifferentiated natural standpoint gets narrowed into the naturalistic attitude of the natural sciences, on the one hand, and the personalistic attitude of the human sciences, on the other. (This is a distinction made already in *Ideas II*.) Clearly such an understanding is not possible unless the phenomenologist continues in some sense to live in the natural attitude which is being described. Presumable because it is impossible to live in the natural attitude and to observe it phenomenologically at the same time, Husserl often characterizes this pattern of investigation as a zig-zag.

Continuing to live in the natural attitude is not something we need great effort to do. It is, after all, natural to us, and it is its suspension that requires the effort. This is the second sense in which the natural attitude is not really left behind in phenomenology. Husserl repeatedly warns us against falling back into it, as if it exerted a kind of gravitational pull against which we had constantly to struggle. It is the phenomenological reduction that goes against the grain, and Husserl even goes so far as to call it "artificial" (Husserl, 1989: 189). Thus phenomenology, which attempts to satisfy the demands of philosophy by suspending the natural attitude, can never really forget its origins in the natural attitude; nor should it, since by doing so it would be derived of content. In phenomenology consciousness turns back upon itself; but what it finds there, and attempts to describe and understand, is a consciousness immersed naively in the world.

This idea that phenomenology is forever poised on the line between the natural and the transcendental attitudes is borne out in the distinction between transcendental and empirical subjectivity. In the *Crisis* Husserl (1970: 178) calls it the paradox of subjectivity: clearly I am somehow both an object *in* the world and subject *for* the world: how can this be? Again this is an idea taken over from Kant and given a somewhat different account by Husserl. As in Kant, this distinction corresponds to that between two different modes of self-consciousness or apperception; Husserl speaks of natural vs. transcendental reflection. In the one case I take myself and the events of my mental life, intentional an non-intentional, simply to co-exist with all the other things and events in the world. Here the relation between consciousness and the world, whatever else it may be (e.g., causal), is essentially a part-whole relation.

To consider myself as subject for the world, in the full transcendental sense, by contrast, means that the events of my mental life relate to other events and things — whether physical, mental, or ideal — *purely* intentionally.

That is, the latter figure solely as objects for me in the sense that they have meaning for me or make sense to me. Here I relate to the world not a part to whole but rather as consciousness to its horizon of possible intentional objects.

Husserl speaks of a resolution of the paradox of subjectivity when we realize that transcendental subjectivity objectifies or constitutes itself just as it constitutes the world. But the empirical ego is no more surmounted or eliminate thereby than is the natural attitude to which it belongs. Unlike the subjective idealism of a Berkeley, or the absolute idealism of a Hegel, the transcendental idealism of Kant and Husserl does not attempt to triumph over the otherness of the world by incorporating it into the subject. The transcendental is not a subject in the sense of a substance in which everything else inheres. This may be why, in his latest work, Husserl speaks less of the transcendental ego and more simply of transcendental subjectivity.

3. The insubstantial subject

The foregoing discussion of Kant and Husserl has made it possible, I hope, to inaugurate a rereading of what I am calling the transcendental tradition. This new reading differs significantly, it seems to me, from that advanced by the later Heidegger, though it is by no means exclusive to him. Whether influenced by Heidegger or not it has become the standard picture, which tries to assimilate transcendental philosophy to the absolute idealism which in fact followed historically upon Kant and drew on many of his ideas. This same reading has been applied to Husserl, primarily by his detractors, who see him as something of a reincarnation of Fichte. In this concluding section I want to bring together the main elements of my alternative reading of Kant and Husserl as transcendental philosophers.

There are two features of the transcendental tradition, arising out of the foregoing discussion, that I want to stress. The first is the transcendence of the world. This is a vulnerable element in the interpretation of transcendental philosophy since it seems to run counter to the basic insight which gets the whole thing going. Kant's great innovation, after all, is the idea that the mind, instead of passively mirroring an independent and self-sufficient world, is active and productive. It is world-structuring, even world-engendering, if we think of "world" as Kant thought of nature, i.e., as the order and connection of phenomena. Husserl's term is constitution, and both thinkers stress the notion of consciousness as synthesis.

Yet for all that, the mind is not world-creating. True, some read this as a last reluctant concession by Kant to his pietist commitments, as if he would have human reason replacing God in all but the creation of prime matter.

This is of course suggested by the role of sense in his epistemology: Kant himself calls it the raw material to be shaped and fashioned by the understanding [A 1]. And the early Husserl employs the notion of hyletic data brought to life by an animating intention. All of this fits Heidegger's critique, which is in some ways that of the outraged Catholic confronted with blasphemy: man replaces God as source of the world.

Yet the unformed matter of sensation is not, for either of these two philosophers, the genuine mark of human finitude and of the transcendence of the world. If for both thinkers the mind does not create the world, it is not because some kernel of uncreated, pregiven stuff is required for the mix. It is because what the mind genuinely does produce is not existence at all but meaning. And the primary meaning it generates and articulates is that of objectivity and transcendence of the world. The attempt to absorb that transcendence into subjectivity, à la Fichte and Hegel, would be for Kant and Husserl to confuse meaning with being. Furthermore, the meaning generated by subjectivity is itself finite in the sense that it does not exhaust all the possibilities of being. This is the sense of Kant's transcendental idealism: there is more to the world than is captured in our conceptual net. And this is the reason Husserl's phenomenological reduction does not overcome or replace but only thematizes the natural attitude.

The second feature of the transcendental tradition that I want to stress, after the transcendence of the world, has to do with the peculiar ontological status of the transcendental subject. We have seen that Heidegger interprets it not only as substance but as the fundamental substance, primary existence on which all other existence is metaphysically dependent. But how accurate is this? If we begin to look closely at Kant and Husserl with this question in mind we begin to wonder in what sense, if indeed any, the transcendental subject can be said to *be* at all.

We have already noted that there is a sense in which for Kant the transcendental subject cannot be known. In what sense, then can it be said to exist? Kant expresses himself in a way that seems contradictory on this point. On the one hand he says that in transcendental apperception I am conscious *that* I am, that in the "I think" "existence is already given thereby" (B 157 and n). Yet he also says that "this representation is a *thought*, not an *intuition*" (bid). Intuition would be required for knowledge of existence, but the only intuition of self is that of inner sense; this yields knowledge of the empirical self, which is an item in the world, not the supreme condition for knowledge of the world. The chief characteristic of the transcendental subject is spontaneity, but it seems spontaneity cannot be sensed and consequently cannot be know to exist. It seems that the supreme transcendental condition of the possibility of empirical knowledge is that I *take* myself to be a spontaneous subject; yet I cannot *know* myself to be such. The transcendental subject thus aquires something of the *als ob* status associated with the moral subject. Henry Allison (1989: 190) has noted the parallel between the moral agent and the knowing subject, as well as the somewhat tentative character of both: "just as we can act only under the idea of freedom, so we can think only under the idea of spontaneity."

On this reading, the transcendental subject, far from being a fundamental existent, begins to look something like a *fiction*, albeit a necessary one. There would be some historical irony in this, since "fiction" is of course the term favored by Hume (1961: 230) to describe, among other things, "the notion of a *soul* and *self* and *substance*" lying behind our changing perceptions. Kant is generally taken to be attempting a refutation of Hume's sceptical fictionalism, yet at the very most, with respect to notions like self, substance and causality, he seems to be substituting necessary fictions for fictions that are merely useful or convenient.

The idea of necessary fiction may sound like a contradiction in terms, since "fiction" is linked with feigning or pretending, and is thus associated with the freedom of our imagination or fantasy. Even well-known scientific fictions, like Newton's inertial motion, though somehow more than merely useful, are hardly necessary. Yet a convinced Newtonian would say that the notion *is* required *if* we want to understand nature correctly. Thus it makes sense to imagine a conceptual scheme which requires, in a very fundamental way, fictional elements.

Turning to Husserl, both Aron Gurwitsch (1961: 287–200) and Jean-Paul Sartre (1957) have argued that the only concept of an ego truly consistent with phenomenology is that of the empirical ego. Consciousness conceived as intentional (and transcendental) has its own internal unity which does not need and in fact would be compromised by a substantial underlying self. Sartre's affirmation "there is no I" in "The Transcendence of the Ego" leads directly to his conception of consciousness as "nothingness" (le Neant) in his major early work. Thomas Nagel (1986), outlining a conception of the "I" that he explicitly compares with Husserl's, speaks of "The view from Nowhere."

This idea of the transcendental subject as fictional or non-existent should not be taken too far, or understood in the wrong sense. Hume's original fictionalism may be understood, in the context of his religious scepticism, as an attempt to dispense with the immortal soul as a serious contender for philosophical attention. In somewhat the same spirit the contemporary materialist Daniel Dennett seizes on the notion of fiction as a way of dealing with the self as an element of "folk psychology." Whereas Hume begins with the empiricist principle and reports that he is unable to find the self among his experiences, Dennett (1988: 17) begins with the materialist premise that what exists must be "an atom or subatomic particle or . . . other physical item in the world," and then affirms, uncontroversially, that the brain contains no such item that we could call the self. Seeking to appear more generous than Hume, however, Dennett reserves a place for the self by imagining that the brain, like a computer, could generate biographical stories. The central character these stories are about would be the self. But stories don't have to be about real people, as we know from novels and the like. The self can be considered a fictional character just as Sherlock Holmes is a fictional character!

For a materialist like Dennett, of course, this is something like a grand slam. He has not only denied the existence of the self by declaring it fictional, he has explained it away by accounting for its origins. Where Dennett goes wrong is in his notion that brains or computers could generate stories. Of course it is quite conceivable that computers could generate print-outs that could be read and interpreted as stories, just as participants in a party-game, to use another of his examples, can supply random bits of information that can be hilariously combined into stories (Dennett, 1991: 10). But they have to be so combined by *someone*, just as the print-out has to be read and interpreted by *someone*, in order to become a story. Like a deconstructionist eagerly announcing the death of the author, Dennett discovers that we can dispense with the writers and tellers of stories. But we cannot dispense with the reader-hearer-interpreters who are the very meaning-bestowing conscious selves he is trying to explain away (He also speaks of the self as the "central meaner") (Dennett, 1991: 228). Without them we have nothing but dried ink-marks, throbbing vocal chords and wagging tongues. Dennett's literary materialism is a valiant attempt: instead of reducing the self to a bit of matter he tries to reduce it right out of existence, by making it a figment of the imagination. But he seems not to notice that this presupposes consciousness in precisely its most sophisticated form, not dumb sensation reacting to worldly stimuli but the capacity to conjure up non-existent worlds and persons.

It is this capacity, consciousness as origin of meaning, which is the central pivot of the transcendental tradition. The philosophers of that tradition would agree with Dennett on one point: subjectivity is not a thing in the world. And perhaps with another: Dennett (1991: 101) says, "Wherever there is a conscious mind there is a *point of view*. This is one of the most fundamental ideas we have about minds – or about consciousness." But a point of view is a point of view on something or toward something. In other words, in Husserl's language it is intentional. Now you or I can have a point of view on this landscape or that house, or more broadly on this or that topic. But the general point is that to be a subject is to have or to be a point of view in general – toward what? Toward the world as a whole.

This is how the term "world" is used by the phenomenologist: not just "all there is" but "all there is – as experienced from a particular point of view."

Having or being a point of view on the world is hard to square with being an item in the world. This is what Husserl calls the paradox of subjectivity, the paradox to which Nagel's *The View From Nowhere* is devoted. This is why the term "transcendental subjectivity" is used, and why Husserl and Kant, like Sartre and Nagel after them, *resist* substantializing the self. In my view this is the key to what I am calling the transcendental tradition, which Heidegger wrongly characterizes as having substantialized the subject. In fact, ironically, it is the key to Heidegger's own concept of *Dasein* in his early work: human existence as meaning - and world-engendering intentionality.

Notes

1. I shall be referring to the following texts of Heidegger's by means of the indicated abbreviations. The translations are my own. EdP = "Das Ende der Philosophie und die Aufgabe des Denkens" in *Zur Sache des Denkens* (Tübingen: Max Niemeyer Verlan, 1969), pp. 61–80; FndD = *Die Frage nach dem Ding* (Tübingen: Max Niemeyer Verlag, 1962); K = *Kant und das Problem der Metaphysik* (Frankfurt: Vittorio Klostermann. 1951); N = *Nietzsche*, Vol. II (Pfullingen: Neske, 1961); UdM = Überwindung der Metaphysik" in *Vorträge und Aufsätze* (Pfullingen: Neske, 1954), pp. 71–99.
2. I refer in the standard way to the marginal pagination in Kant.

References

Allison, J. (1989). Kant's refutation of materialism. *The Monist* 72 (2)
Cadava, E., Connor, P. and Nancy, J.L. (Eds). (1991). *Who comes after the subject?* New York: Routledge.
Dennett, D. (1988). Why everone is a novelist. *Times Literary Supplement.* September.
Dennett, D.C. (1991). *Consciousness explained.* Boston: Little Brown.
Gurwitsch, A. (1966). A non-egological conception of consciousness. In *Studies in phenomenology and psychology.* Evanston: Northwestern University Press.
Heidegger, M. (1951). *Die Frage nach dem Ding.* Tübingen: Max Niemeyer Verlag.
Heidegger, M. (1951). *Kant und das Problem der Metaphysik.* Frankfurt; Vittorio Klostermann.
Heidegger, M. (1954). Überwindung der Metaphysik. In *Vortäge und Aufsätze.* Pfullingen: Neske.
Heidegger, M. (1961). *Nietzsche, Vol. II.* Pfullingen: Neske
Heidegger, M. (1969). Das Ende der Philosophie un die Aufgabe des Denkens. In *Zur Sache des Denkens.* Tübingen: Max Niemeyer Verlag.
Hume, D. (1961). *A treatise of human nature.* New York: Dolphin Books
Husserl, E. (1962). *Cartesian meditations.* Trans. D. Cairns. The Hague: Martinus Nijhoff
Husserl, E. (1970). *The crisis of European sciences and transcendental phenomenology.* Trans. D. Carr. Evanston: Northwestern University Press.
Husserl, E. (1989). *Ideas pertaining to a pure phenomenology and to a pure phenomenological philosophy.* Second book. Trans. R. Rojcewics and A. Schuwer. Dordrecht: Kluwer.

Kant, E. (1965). *Critique of pure reason*. Trans. N. Kemp, Smith. New York: St Martin's Press.
Locke, J. (1956). *An essay concerning human understanding*. Chicago: Henry Regnery.
Nagel, T. (1986). *The view from nowhere*. New York: Oxford University Press.
Sartre, J-P. (1957). *The transcendence of the ego*. Trans. F. Williams and R. Kirkpatrick. New York: Farrar, Straus.

Heideggerean Postmodernism and Metaphysical Politics

Robert B. Pippin

I

In the following, I shall mostly be concerned to do two things. One is to explain, in so far as I understand it, some aspects of Martin Heidegger's attack on the classical German philosophical tradition, 'German' or 'post-Kantian Idealism'.

I want especially to understand his account of the one essay he seems to regard as the death-knell for this Kantian programme, and thereby, he insists, a death-knell for all the aspirations of modern philosophy itself. This account is given in the lectures Heidegger gave in the 1936 Summer semester in Freiburg on Schelling's 1809 'Treatise on the Essence of Human Freedom', the last essay Schelling personally prepared for publication (even though he was to live and lecture for over forty more years).

As already implied, for Heidegger, the stakes are very high in what appears to be a very abstract topic. The fact (if it is a fact) that the post-Kantian notions of subjectivity, self-consciousness, freedom, etc., could not be defended or saved from various objections, is for Heidegger a reflection on the far deeper insufficiencies of *all* modern philosophy itself, and, indeed, *those* deficiencies reflect the inevitable nihilism of all post-Platonic philosophy. (Heidegger famously interpreted all of modernism and especially the German philosophical version as a failed attempt at human autonomy, an inevitable collapse into a meaningless willfulness he often summarizes with the single word that devours Plato, Descartes and even Nietzsche in its condemnation: 'technology'.)

In that context, the second thing I want to show is how the form of Heidegger's attack, or here the appropriation of Schelling's initial anti-idealism, should be understood as a kind of paradigmatic attack on what is itself a paradigmatic version of philosophical modernism (German Idealism), repeated many times after Heidegger, and that understanding the structure of this attack helps clarify its power, as well as its weaknesses and dangers. Heidegger was quite right to seize on Schelling as the first to appreciate this problem (which, as we shall see, is indeed a serious one), but that fact also helps one to identify what I think is the blind Schellingean alley Heidegger begins to wander into with his own doctrine of historicity, or the inevitably situated 'happening' of any 'thinking'.

More simply: for the sake of argument I shall agree with Heidegger when he claims (later, in a 1941 seminar) that 'Schelling's treatise is the acme of the metaphysics of German Idealism'; and so the 'highest expression of philosophical modernism'; even that 'the essential core of all of Western metaphysics can be delineated in complete clarity in terms of this treatise',[1] but will argue that when Heidegger begins to formulate his response to the problems Schelling identifies, he misreads his opponents and so 'mis-reacts' in what remains a Schellingean form.

Straightforwardly then, the simple question is: in what sense is modern philosophy supposed to have failed? I take my bearings from Heidegger because (i) his expression of dissatisfaction has been extremely influential for European thought after him, and itself echoes deep, persistent strains in the German and European counter-Enlightenment and (ii) because I think that this Heideggerean and counter-Enlightenment reaction misidentifies its target, and so in some sense mis-reacts.

Before beginning, I should also note the context for my remarks about Heidegger's view: what could be called the complex problem of the *political influence* of Heidegger, or even the emergence of what might be called 'left Heideggereans'.

With that label, I mean to identify a certain form of opposition to a number of central aspects of European modernity, or, if you like, to modern bourgeois culture; an opposition to such things as – the very highly authoritative cognitive status of modern natural science (and the growing dependence of modern societies on the technologies made possible by such science); the supreme moral authority of individual conscience and so individual responsibility; the political authority of rights-based, liberal democratic institutions; or the general European Enlightenment hope that the modern revolution would make possible a secular, an essentially rational, foundation for a collective life that could be safely and rightly relied on.

Heidegger's attack on philosophical modernism has recently taken on new meaning in this context, a putative postmodern political agenda (one supposedly not linked to the universalist aspirations of European modernism). At the very least, this sort of approach involves a radical dissatisfaction with the official culture of Western modernity, a dissatisfaction not tied to an analysis of modernity as essentially the culture of a self-contradicting capitalism, but more concerned to link all the universalist, moral aspirations of European modernism with a merely contingent, even necessarily contingent expression of mere self-assertion, 'power', cultural imperialism, Euro-centrism, etc. To be sure, the people that might be linked together under this left-Heideggerean label have profound differences, but the attack on the Idealist 'philosophy of the subject', and 'of reason', on any possible 'first philosophy', and the insistence on some sort of acknowledgement of the historicity or contingency of institutional life, even of truth itself, do shape some common agenda for Rorty, Foucault, Reiner Schürmann, Jean-Luc Nancy, Philippe Lacoue-Labarthe, Gianni Vattimo and others.[2]

Now there are a number of ways to express some sort of dissatisfaction with the putative 'subjectivism' of modern philosophy; the way modern philosophy,

---

© Blackwell Publishers Ltd. 1996

after Descartes, seems to have retreated from any attempt at an account of the world, or 'the whole', and instead concentrated only on the thinkability or representability of possible objects, as if, in Kant's famous phrase, the human mind can know only itself. The inevitable threat of scepticism and psychologism so generated also produced Frege's and Husserl's realism. But I am here treating Heidegger's statement of the philosophical issues in such an anti-subjectivism and anti-humanism as in a way canonical for a certain tradition of later thinkers, however much they disagree with Heidegger or with each other.

II

In these 1936 Freiburg lectures, as Heidegger struggles to explain the significance of the failure of German Idealism to Third Reich university students, one can find one of the most compressed and clearest of Heidegger's many accounts of the history of Enlightenment thought, all in formulations that make it clear where contemporary 'anti-humanisms' get their start.[3] The Enlightenment is to be understood

> ... as a liberation of man to himself. But what man is as himself, wherein his being a self should consist, is determined only in his liberation and by the definitely oriented history of this liberation. Human 'thinking', which here means the forming powers of man, becomes the fundamental law of things themselves. The conquest of the world in knowledge and actions begins . . . Commerce and economy turn into powers of their own in the most narrow, reciprocal connection with the origin of technology, which is something different from the previous invention and use of tools. Art becomes the decisive manner of self-development of human creativity and at the same time its own way of conquering the world for eye and ear . . . The idea of 'sovereignty' brings a new formation of the state and a new kind of political thought and requirement.[4]

In particular, Heidegger emphasizes frequently, Schelling, in his 1809 essay, focused on what he regarded as the 'metaphysical reality' most inconsistent with the idealist notion of freedom as autonomy and self-grounding, and so with the Idealist (or all modernist) hope for a systematic or comprehensive account of any claim for the reality of freedom: *the reality of evil*, a topic I shall return to in the concluding section of this paper.

Understanding and contesting such claims will require two large preliminary steps. One concerns Heidegger's own project and the distinctive character of his claim about historicity or the presuppositions of his treatment of Schelling. The other involves some attempt at understanding at least the aspirations of the post-Kantian idealist tradition which Heidegger, through Schelling, is attacking.

© Blackwell Publishers Ltd. 1996

III

We must first, in other words, give Heidegger his due. His own attempt to suggest the futility of giving ultimate priority to the reflecting, self-determining subject, his account of the futility of attempting to render the mind or the logical structure of thought, absolutely translucent to itself, depends on what he calls the problem of historicity, the locatedness of human subjects in time. That account is radically different from the nineteenth-century versions of historicism with which Heidegger is often associated. These latter doctrines simply extend the subjectivism characteristic of all modern thought as Heidegger reads it. That is, they attempt to transform claims like

> These A's are B's;
> X-actions are good;
> Y's are beautiful;

into

> *We are so minded that*:
> A's count for us as B's;
> we count X-actions as good, or Y's as beautiful.

Instead of a psychologistic theory of such like-mindedness, or a transcendental or Hegelian theory of this possible like-mindedness, conventional historicism just gives historical and often social accounts of such like-mindedness and Heidegger was always infuriated to see what he regarded as a profound attack on such collective subjectivism read as just that theory.[5] Understanding the radicality of his attack on modern thought requires some summary of his theory.

Heidegger's 1927 masterwork, *Being and Time*, was published only as a fragment, yet there is something deeply fitting about the question which ends the published version of the book. Its last sentence is: 'Does *time* itself manifest itself as the horizon of *Being*?'[6] The very title of the work already indicates that Heidegger had all along intended to offer an affirmative answer to this question, to defend a claim about the 'historicity' of human existence and of 'truth' itself, and therewith to begin the destruction of all Western metaphysics, a tradition understood by Heidegger to consist essentially in a refusal to acknowledge such a historicity.[7]

Yet, to frame immediately the question at issue in all 'postmodern' appropriations of Heidegger: what *would* it mean to *acknowledge* such historicity and radical contingency, and so, if we follow Heidegger, *not* to think metaphysically, or subjectively, even 'philosophically', but in some new way informed by such an acknowledgment? If we pursue this issue in Heidegger's

© Blackwell Publishers Ltd. 1996

thought, we find mostly, over and over again, warnings, hesitations, indirections, allusions, neologisms, quotations from the pre-Socratics, and from Hölderlin. Heidegger never tired of reminding his readers of just how profoundly difficult it was to understand what he wanted to say about historicity (*Geschichtlichkeit*) (even to the point of pointing out that his own formulations were necessarily 'concealing', or deceptive).

He is certainly clear enough about the consequences of avoiding or forgetting the ontological dimensions of historicity and of aspiring to be the complete, self-determining subject of one's deeds and thoughts. 'The essence of modernity,' he writes in a typical claim, 'is fulfilled in the age of consummate meaninglessness.'[8] Such a meaningless essence is said to involve 'The securing of supreme and absolute self-development of all the capacities of mankind for absolute dominion over the entire earth.' This impulse at a kind of predatory dominance is said to be the 'secret goad' that 'prods modern man again and again to new resurgences, a goad that forces him into commitments that secure for him the surety of his actions and the certainty of his aims.'[9] The modern aspiration for an enlightened future, the hope that a secular foundation for moral and political life could be formulated and safely relied on, and that a kind of collective, self-legislating autonomy could be achieved, have all failed, according to Heidegger. The totality of 'the essential possibilities of metaphysics' have thereby been 'exhausted', and 'European nihilism', most visible in Nietzsche's 'culmination' of the tradition, is the result.

These claims all obviously depend on Heidegger's distinctive formulation of the basic problem of philosophy. 'The question of Being' (*die Seinsfrage*) is Heidegger's question and in *Being and Time* especially, that question is understood as the question of 'the *meaning* of Being in general'. The question is not be be confused with the metaphysical questions of substance or degrees of reality or necessity, nor with traditional ontological questions: the kinds of beings there are, the basic categories necessary to articulate whatever there is. 'Fundamental ontology' is the theme, some prereflexive and everywhere presupposed 'sense' of anything's 'being' at all. This requires at all costs respecting what Heidegger calls the 'ontological difference', or not confusing this question of the meaning of Being with any question about beings or entities. This amounts to the problem of the possibility of our somehow always already being 'oriented' in the world, originally having bearings of a sort.[10]

As noted already, this way of framing the issue will lead Heidegger to the famous answer embodied in the book's title: 'time' is the horizon of all possible such significance; the meaning of human being, all Being, is radically historical; the familiarity or disclosedness of 'what is' *happens* (is a '*Geschehen*'), even though what happens is not a result of the beliefs or representations of subjects, or norms held in common, or of any sort of a subjective event or meaning conferral. How such meaning or orientation happens, and why it cannot be some sort of result, or some event of matter-of-fact like-mindedness with sources, causes, explanations, etc. is one of the great constant themes in Heidegger. (In fact, his position is so radical that even this fairly neutral language is misleading; 'what' is disclosed is not a 'what' but the utterly contingent event of the disclosedness itself, what Heidegger calls *'Ereignis'.*' since 1936,' he wrote, 'the leading word of my thinking.'[11])

In *Being and Time* and in many other works, Heidegger claims that the fact that we are somehow intuitively inclined to ask about our deepest pre-reflexive familiarity with the world by asking: what is the *source* of this sense making? how do *we* render the world originally sensible, begin by trying to *make* sense out of it? and so forth, has had disastrous consequences since Plato. Being is taken *to be disclosed, rendered* intelligible, by or because of us and so is made into a kind of standing or enduring presence by being so 'measured' in our terms. We thus forget everything we would need to remember if we were to 'think' fundamentally.[12]

Perhaps the best way to put this is to say that Heidegger's conviction about the extraordinary elusiveness of the basic question for human thought means that any meditations inspired by the question must finally be distinctly nonphilosophical, not 'directed' by a subject towards an end, not a problem to be solved, not an aporia to be addressed, or an opaque meaning to be clarified by some activity of ours. Heidegger's notion of historicity is thus not comparable to similar claims in the social or moral sciences, and this alone makes it (and his influence on the postmodernity discussion) extremely hard to understand. He is not trying to offer some transcendental case for the necessary conditionedness of thought, nor to point to contingent social determinants or interests behind or motivating the authority of various intellectual practices. He realizes that we inevitably take him to be offering a thesis about the historicity of truth and he wages a life-long battle to disabuse us of that response, claiming that his founding idea about ontological difference would thereby be ignored. He keeps insisting that he is actually trying *to think historically*, not to think about history. He knows we intuitively assume that an argument for the latter is necessary to justify the former, but that, he keeps saying, is the great error. There is no such argument, no place from which it could be made. There *is* just historizing thinking, whether acknowledged or not, whether in argument form or not. The key issue turns out to be the mode of acknowledgment. So, in *Kant and the Problem of Metaphysics*, in commenting on his own writing about the problem of finitude, he writes,

> . . . the *working out* of the innermost essence of metaphysics must *itself* always be basically finite and can never become absolute. The only conclusion one can draw from this is that *reflection* on finitude, always to be renewed, can never succeed, through a mutual playing off, or meditating equalization of standpoints in order finally and in spite of everything to give us absolute knowledge of finitude, a knowledge that is surreptitiously posited as being 'true in itself.'[13] (My emphases.)

(This is not to say that Heidegger is not interested in motivating his own acknowledgment of this historicity, or that he just 'poeticizes' historically. The

© Blackwell Publishers Ltd. 1996

acknowledgment begun by *Being and Time* is said to be provoked, even made necessary, by the 'completion of metaphysics' in Nietzschean nihilism.[14] A very great deal thereby hangs on the sufficiency of Heidegger's narrative of 'modern thought', as is the case, I believe, with all 'postmodernisms'.[15])

Heidegger's own interrogative stance is thus itself some sort of expectation or an attentive waiting, or, in a frequent, obscure phrase, 'repetition', not a thought or proposal in the traditional sense. (The later fascination with the *Dichten-Denken*, and *Danken-Denken* relation is also crucial here, as is the formulation: *Gelassenheit*.) It could thus itself be called a poetic or theologico-political *engagement* of a sort, rather than the theory that would drive an engagement.

IV

It will not be difficult to contrast such a fundamental ontology with the original idealist aspiration. Put in their own intoxicating language, the modern problem at issue for the idealist tradition is the possibility and status of freedom, and the possible final realization of freedom in the world. The idealism of German idealism has little to do with ideas or representations in the rationalist or empiricist sense. The ideal is human freedom, understood as being a law wholly unto oneself. The enemy, the enemy of modernism simply (whether in the name of pre- or postmodernism), its other, is *dogmatism*: the reliance on anything not redeemed by some rational justification or by a reflexive account of the possibility of any such reliance, defending it against possible objections. Their case is for what they called the reality, finally the 'absolute reality', of such a self-determination, or freedom; a claim that such a fully reflexive self-grounding could be realized systematically and in practical life.[16] Coming to a final understanding of such a reality, and appreciating its 'living' potential in the emerging modern social and political world, is, for the classical German tradition, the unimpeachable, irrevocable achievement of modernity.

In that tradition, the possibility of such freedom is linked both to the possibility of a wholly self-authorizing or self-grounding reason (and thereby to the final destruction of dogmatism, and the realization of reason's complete or 'absolute' self-reliance and so 'maturity'), and to the possibility of a practical rationality, and therewith practical autonomy or self-legislation. As understood by Kant, the early Fichte and Schelling, and Hegel and the left Hegelians, the modern enterprise is thus also inextricably tied to a kind of 'metaphysical politics.' Philosophy is one dimension of a practical engagement, as it is for Heidegger, but where Heidegger strives for a kind of poetic acknowledgement, the Idealists strive for a complete, universal, self-authorization. For the moment, we can understand this as a demand for a kind of free self-determination, what Fichte called an *active* 'positing' of one's stance toward nature and towards one's desires not originally determined or caused by one's relation to nature or to such

© Blackwell Publishers Ltd. 1996

desires. Such activity was understood as a 'norm-governed spontaneity', supposed to be ontologically prior, or 'the condition for the possibility' of all possible relations to nature.

In cognitive terms, the claim is a denial of the view that we can successfully explain the mind's intentional content, its holding possibly true or false knowledge claims, by appeals to the mind's being-determined by some independent content. In the simplest terms, in being aware that something is (or even could be) so-and-so, *I am holding* that it is; *taking* it to be so-and-so; making up my mind; taking a stand. The subject *is* not in a relation to the world; it takes itself to be, and so is always in absolute command of its conceivings and concludings. The same logic applies to action: I can never be said to act *for* a pressing interest or desire, but only on the condition that I determine such interests or desires to merit acting on. In the extraordinary language soon developed: the I's relation to itself is 'The Absolute'; the unconditioned possibility of which explains the possible intelligibility of all else.

Now, none of this insistence on a subject's establishing its relation to the world, especially on its doing so freely or spontaneously, nor my own characterization of such a priority for agency and activity as a kind of metaphysical politics, should be taken to imply that the door opened by Kant did or must lead to some measureless field of possible sorts of activities, to some creativity, to relativisms or historicisms, etc. It may be the most controversial and difficult to understand aspect of this tradition, but the original argument was always that such a central 'spontaneity' *must* be conceived as law or norm governed, as itself possible (or possibly establishing any intentional relation to objects, or responsible activity) *only if* normatively constrained.[17]

This argument form – that the mind-world relation must be 'spontaneously established' and in what must be a norm-governed way (or the argument that such an original spontaneity *could* make experience or a practically intelligible life possible *only if* realized as law, principle, categorical imperative, a *sensus communis* in the aesthetic domain); all in a way that displaces rationalist, empiricist, and naturalist alternatives – was an argument form that was to have many incarnations and reinscriptions, from Hegel's *Logic* to Lukács' reformulation of Kantian spontaneity as productive labour. But it is the argument form most at stake, most in need of attention, I think, in assessments of a possibly modern philosophy. And this is especially true of the concept at the centre of everything, a notion of activity or of human doings and engagings and comportings not, supposedly, itself an empirical or material event, and not a non-empirical or immaterial event, a condition not resistant to naturalist accounts because unnatural but because a different sort of philosophical *explicans* altogether.

(Another way to put this would be: the idealist turn is not a turn to some matter of fact or to some special sort of mental activity as constitutive, but is an argument for the autonomy and irreducibility of the normative dimension in our discursive and ethical practices. To make a claim is to extend a commitment or undertake an obligation, and we could never be said simply to *be* directed to such a claim *by* experience, and it could never be rightly understood as how the human brain concludes things or how we collectively go on.)

To a degree still unappreciated, I think, the young Schelling quickly realized that the whole approach, however interpreted, necessarily generated a basic problem. It was one whose logic would first appear in the German counter-Enlightenment (especially in Jacobi) and then in many, many forms later (certainly in Kierkegaard, later in Nietzsche's account of 'life', and thanks to Heidegger, in thinkers such as Gadamer and Derrida.) The task had been: to think through the implications of the claim that *being in* any cognitive relation to the world, to have disclosed any sense (or being the true subject of one's deeds) is necessarily *to have assumed such a relation actively*, to have determined *oneself* to be in such a relation. This does indeed make all the contents or objects of such a relation necessarily the results of some self-conscious self-determining. Yet we, as embodied agents in the world, are already natural or at least pre-volitionally situated beings, already thinking in a certain way, with a certain inheritance, with certain capacities we clearly share with non-human animals (like perception). It is only *in* being a kind of being, within a certain sort of world with kinds of beings, at a certain historical time, that we *could* be the particular self-determining subjects or agents that we are. To view the issue of *this* sort of pre-reflective situation as itself a result, or in terms of 'what we must *think*' to make sense of 'our' conditions of intelligibility, is to miss the point profoundly.

There *is* indeed something about the radicality of the insistence on the autonomy of this normative or self-authorizing dimension which clearly invites such worries about finitude, whether expressed in religious terms, like Jacobi's, or systematic worries, like Schelling's. It also invites the predictable counter response: that any restriction based on an acknowledgment of such finitude or embodiment or subjection to the laws of neuro-biology, is still something like the self-imposition of a norm, and so is still within the space of reasons. There is nothing, not even das Nichts, 'outside' such a space. And this is the ping-pong game European philosophy has been playing since the original Kant–Hegel vs. Schelling–Kierkegaard version, up to and including the Gadamer–Habermas controversy.

V

As we have already seen, in Heidegger's appropriation of Schelling's rejection of any such 'priority' for subjective self-determination, some sort of lived acknowledgement of such an original situation is at issue, not a new intellectual realization or a different sort of system (all this to avoid the Hegelian rejoinder suggested above). In passages like #74 of *Being and Time* (about 'The Basic Constitution of Historicity'), the possibility of such acknowledgement is tied to anxiety, not to insight, or to systematic philosophy. *Angst* is Heidegger's early figure for the sorts of practical, lived dislocations, or breakdowns, which *make*

© Blackwell Publishers Ltd. 1996

just 'going on' as usual impossible (as if functioning anti-methodologically like Husserl's 'bracketing' of the natural attitude). Boredom, the violence of poetic language, world historical crises, and, as we shall see below, radical evil itself, can all function this way. One *is* displaced in one's being-towards-death; one does not just see something, and the acknowledgement is discussed as both a 'taking over' of one's factual possibilities, and a 'handing down to oneself' of what has been handed down to one, a 'Dasein existing fatefully in the resoluteness which hands itself down.'[18] This will make assessing Heidegger's 'reaction' to modernism extremely difficult. He tries so hard to make his position a 'non-position', itself an 'event', that he defines himself out of that game mentioned above. But I do think that a general point can be made and explored in terms of the topic Heidegger himself focused on in 1936. That requires turning to the topic Schelling introduces to make his point against the subjectivism of modern philosophy, the problem of evil.

For Kant, Fichte and Hegel, moral evil is generally understood as a supreme affirmation of an individual subjectivity, as if I alone am supremely 'real'; and all else counts for nothing. Such acts are themselves considered intelligible against the assumption of, and by contrast with, what free agency really consists in. And of course, in this tradition, morality is a matter of practical rationality; the realization of the highest value, freedom, being the realization of rationality. Immoral acts are themselves free, but only imperfectly, incompletely, and are in some way contrary to, conflicting with, one's own agency. Such acts appear within such a systematic understanding as a *failure* to realize true freedom, and so as unfreedom, a deficit, a failure to be who you really are. (In fact, in Hegel's most notorious extension of this logic, the criminal actually wills *not* the crime itself, alone, but also, implicitly, his own punishment. He must so 'will' on the assumptions necessary for him to be the subject of his own act.) Various possible realizations of freedom are, on such a view, obviously resisted or rejected by subjects, but this is due to ignorance, weakness, historical conditions (which can reach a point where an inseparability between good and evil is inevitable, as in tragic contexts), etc. Such acts remain evil, even if intelligible, but can never be described as absolute negations. There is and can be no 'absolute' evil in the world.

Schelling categorically rejects such a version of what he calls the *malum metaphysicum*, and insists that

> ... the basis of evil must therefore not only be founded on something inherently positive, but rather on the highest positive being which nature contains.[19]

This extraordinary claim implies a notion of 'freedom *for* good and evil' or the claim that evil acting is not a kind of mismeasuring 'through a glass darkly', or a failure, but a completely unmeasurable, or even unconditioned, unintelligible even if depressingly real human and metaphysical potential. (I should note immediately that even though Schelling formulates the issue often as a radical

© Blackwell Publishers Ltd. 1996

choice for good and evil, he has in mind no standard voluntarist picture. Such a 'choice' enacts or evinces or in some sense merely expresses a pre-voluntary structure of significance or 'Absolute'.)

And Heidegger joins Schelling in the general worry about any comprehensively intelligible idealism, particularly as revealed by the problem of evil. In fact he goes quite far in his affirmative and sympathetic summaries. He writes,

> To demonstrate the possibility of evil means to show how man must be, and what it means that man is. After all this it becomes clear that the ground of evil is nothing less than the ground of being human. But this ground must be in God's innermost center. The ground of evil is thus something positive in the highest sense.[20]

Now it is quite likely that Heidegger is not much concerned here with traditional (say, to cite one of his heroes, Augustinean) problems with moral evil. It is more important to him to insist on some notion of radical possibility in his account of historical happenings and of the pre-subjective origin of our collective practices and self-monitorings. Evil figures for him throughout these discussions as something necessarily unrecognizable as ours, and not a finite and incomplete failure to fit in to how we go on.[21] Not acknowledging such a wholly negative possibility would be like regarding the nihilism crisis itself as still incomplete rationalization, or one's impending death as a possibility that will happen someday but not soon, or the failure of meaning in profound boredom as an accidental or pathological aberration in the meaning-structures that are authoritative. In Heidegger's Schellingean version of such responses, we are always trying to re-inscribe within the sovereign realm of the subject a phenomenon that actually wholly undermines the possibility of any such sovereignty.

So here again we have a version of Schelling's worries about the absolute status of a self-determining subjectivity, supposedly the source or condition for the intelligibility of all human thinkings and doings. Evil, so goes the largely implicit argument, cannot be rightly understood on such an assumption, as the privation or failure of practical rationality, without denying its status as evil (the assumption being that weakness, ignorance or the mere influence of our passions fail to account for the reality of evil). For there to be evil, our capacity for evil must be original, not derivative from a potentially fully free agency; and for such evil to be an original possibility, self-determining subjects cannot be 'absolute'. The Heideggerean 'event' of Being must manifest itself originally both 'positively' and 'negatively'.

Although the language is obscure, the intuition behind such disaffection is not hard to understand. On the Idealist assumptions we have been discussing, and on many other modern secularist assumptions, if what ought to be done is fundamentally a matter of what we collectively institute, esteem, authorize ourselves to hold each other to, what was traditionally viewed as evil will look like only a falling away from our norms, just not going on as we do. Heidegger

© Blackwell Publishers Ltd. 1996

and Schelling are trying to evoke some deeper sense of the complete breakdown of 'how we go on', a violation which can highlight the artificiality and incompleteness of any such norm.

(I have not been mentioning the many, many political allusions in Heidegger's Schelling lectures, but it becomes ever clearer in the lectures that Heidegger is not anything like a confused bourgeois academic who wandered naively, like many other such academic Mandarins and Catholic intellectuals, into joining the Nazi party. He means to affirm directly and enthusiastically, Germany's revolutionary situation; its massive breakdown into moral and political anarchy, its potential for terrifying evil and complete dislocations, all of which, he hopes, will shake us loose from the subjectivist illusions of liberal democracy and inaugurate a new beginning.)

To return to Schelling's and Heidegger's language, our own determination for good or evil, in other words, must be seen as a kind of phenomenon or appearance; itself possible because of or by reference to 'the self-positing of the Absolute'. Since this origin is not, for the reasons we have been outlining, a possible object of any account, it follows (for Schelling and Heidegger at any rate) that the reality of freedom, or ontological possibility, is absolutely *unlimited*. There can thus be no system, no 'whole', no *'philosophy* of freedom'. (Kant's original argument that the mind must actively bring its thoughts and intentions into unity, and so under a norm, for there to be 'my' thoughts and intentions is thus rejected, since such a spontaneity is argued to require, for its possibility, a dependence on some 'arche' or fundamental principle, some 'Absolute', whose unity or coherence or intelligibility cannot be articulated.[22]) And if we are free in this sense, then Being cannot be accounted for by any notion or norm, and to live freely cannot be a life commonly and justifiably measured by some norm. It must be some sort of *acknowledgement* of what cannot be measured without falsifying, covering-over. A kind of mythic/poetic discourse seems to keep emerging as the appropriate mode of such acknowledgement. (To some extent, as Heidegger shows, Schelling would agree with some formulation of the *nature* of evil as linked with an extreme individuation, but he insists that traditional interpretations of what Heidegger will call the 'attraction' of such individuation have not been accounted for. Schelling, and Heidegger after him, attribute this attraction to the historical self-manifesting or disclosing process *of Being itself*.)[23]

Such claims all hearken back again to the radical dimensions of Heideggerean historicity – that he is not talking about *how we situate ourselves* within a tradition (or how we legislate the norms regulating our lives), but how we are, contingently and ineffably, *situated* in the revealing and concealing process within which 'fundamental' sense is made. Our attempts to master and ground such contingency (to 'conquer' it he frequently says) is defeated in these breakdown situations, like anxiety or evil, wherein 'being the null basis of a nullity' cannot but be acknowledged.

> Schelling's treatise has nothing to do with the question of the freedom of the will, which is ultimately wrongly put and thus not a question at all.

For freedom is here not a property of man, but the other way around. Man is at best the property of freedom.[24]

Or, 'insofar as man is man, he must participate in this determination of Being, and man *is*, in so far as he brings about this participation in freedom.'[25]

VI

The path Heidegger is on, the way in which his distinctive oppositions set a direction for him, will lead to a number of complex, and I think, unresolvable *aporiai*. The most important consequence of the kind of anti-modernism we have been discussing will involve the resources Heidegger will have left himself in accounting for the possibility of the kind of prereflective intelligibility of finitude, the kind which, for him, renders so problematic the Idealist or modernist aspirations. To live 'in' such 'truth' after all is not merely to live truthfully, wholly unreflectively, as if a matter of luck or fact. It is to live *in the light* of the truth, ultimately in the light of the true place or status of human being. And this immediately opens multiple possible alternatives that must be contested: whether as rights bearing individuals, morally responsible agents, a pious, thankful *ens creatum*, or an ontologically disclosive *Volk*. (We are thus back to our first question: how Heidegger can account for our acknowledgement of this historicity without some *self-determination as historical*, and I don't think we find, within Heidegger, a coherent answer.) Contrary to what Heidegger suggests, we do not simply participate or 'dwell' within a 'world' 'framed' by such alternatives. We participate in a world only by also situating ourselves within it, either carrying on or contesting its own narrative about itself. Heidegger often seems to concede this point. He certainly distinguishes between an inauthentic falling within the practices of 'the They', and an authentic resoluteness. And the light images, suggesting such an illuminated self-situating, are his. But he always paints his picture like one of those great seventeenth century achievements, where the light shines from nowhere.

Admittedly, our own subjection to, and revision of, such norms is not easy to account for phenomenologically. We do, of course, inherit and pass on much unreflectively, or at least in a way that makes the language of self-imposition and justification look highly idealized. But the difficulty in stating that issue, and some general, well justified reluctance to think of such norms in a non-historical and non-social way, as if a matter of 'pure practical reason' alone, etc., is no reason to throw the baby out with the bathwater. If we do, we confront immediately the post-Heideggerean dissolution of subjectivity into the reifications of mentalités, epistemes, 'discourses', 'fields or power', etc., terms that always suggest to me an arch, defensive neo-positivism.[26]

© Blackwell Publishers Ltd. 1996

VII

The basic point I am trying to make is that the most important idea of modernity which Heidegger refuses to acknowledge is much broader than anything that can be captured by the Idealist notions of system or even the meaning of Being. It is a great confusion, for example, to treat the requirement within German Idealism for an 'absolute' condition of intelligibility as somehow on a par with the notion of natural-scientific comprehensiveness, or an absolute *explanation*, as Schelling and Heidegger often do. (It is true to say that the Idealist made *das Ich* 'the Absolute'. But that involves a claim for the unavoidability and irreducibility of our normative self-regulation in the possibility of any cognitive claim or action. It is absolute as the supreme condition for thought and action, not itself 'conditioned'. This is a divergence from, not an instance of the metaphysical or scientific notion of ground.) To assume otherwise would be to assume that the Idealist 'threat' to the 'reality' of evil were the same as the putative threat which would be based on some comprehensively informed point of view, where the difference between the agent who acted wrongly and one who didn't could be *explained or predicted*, thus denying the metaphysical reality of evil. (As in: a sick body obeys the laws of nature as much as a healthy one; it is not any less real or incomplete.)

The original animus of the Idealist revolution, though, was so set against the problem of dogmatism that this sort of explanatory ideal could never emerge for it as an issue, and neither could any such realist question about metaphysical evil. We are never in any position to confront or reject or accept *the* reality of evil, and Heidegger's confusion tempts him to the same formulations he admires in Schelling. To comprehend the irruption of absolute subjectivity as a possible moment within, or permanent threat to, our own developing self-comprehension, and to understand it as a failure of such full self-understanding and so as unfreedom, is not to domesticate or deny it. *It is merely not to mystify it*, not to *pose* it as other, not to *determine* oneself in relation to such an event as a *malum metaphysicum*, and then deny such positing, all of which, from the 'Idealist' perspective, is what is being done in Schelling's response.

Hegel himself makes this point in just these terms in his *Lectures on Aesthetics*. In speaking of Greek tragedy in particular, he says, clearly at odds with the Schellingean–Heideggerean treatment: 'For *evil in the abstract has no truth in itself and is of no interest.*'[27] In his earlier discussion of the moral dimensions of tragedies, he had conceded that agents can freely perform monstrous and barbaric acts, and would be thereby unrecognizable as 'like us' and transformed into some malignant, contingent force of nature. (Lear's insanity in the storm is alluded to.) But there is, he also insists in a way that refers to his whole project, '*no truth*' and therewith no 'interest' in such gross injustices.[28] There is only such 'truth' in a more complexly *human* enactment of evil deeds, one in which the possible instability (or mere subjectivity) of the distinctions our norms establish between good and evil is evoked and confronted. (In his *Lectures on Religion*, he

© Blackwell Publishers Ltd. 1996

cites Milton's Satan as paradigmatic of this phenomenon, who is not a malignant force because he is, however evil, still recognizable as one of us.)

A full statement occurs later:

> For the purely negative is in itself dull and flat and therefore either leaves us empty or else repels us, whether it be used as a motive for an action or simply as a means for producing the reaction of another motive. The gruesome and unlucky, the harshness of power, the pitilessness of predominance, may be held together and endured by the imagination if they are elevated and carried by an intrinsically worthy greatness of character and aim; but evil as such, envy, cowardice and baseness are and remain purely repugnant.[29]

This all introduces a number of issues which cannot be pursued here. The central distinction at issue, between a kind of collapse into or the eruption of, the non-human, which contains no 'truth', and a recognizably motivated, complexly 'positive' and 'negative' evil, raises a number of questions. But it is clear that Hegel's approach *does* indeed foreclose the idea of some 'pure' evil, or a 'metaphysical' attraction to it, as evoked by Schelling and Heidegger. But for Hegel, this concedes only that the conditions of human agency itself can 'fail'; a mad, unrecognizably human malevolence can occur. In the same way Hegel would object to the notion of some *absolute Nichts*, or event-like absolute failure of sense, evoked in Heidegger's account of death. Hegel would insist instead that our being towards death is a being towards a kind of death in a kind of community at a kind of time; in the same way he would object to the idea of '*the*' modern' technological will to power, insisting that there is only a kind of technological reliance, within a community for a purpose; so he would object to the way in which Heidegger wants to evoke somehow what is beyond human self-determination or intelligibility as itself some negative measure for the human.

And so on, on into a refusal to mystify the notion of 'what' we *must* face now, '*the*' retreat of the gods, our 'fate', our 'destiny', our 'locatedness', our 'origin', contingency, what we allow each other to get away with saying, '*the*' Other, 'the' language of the Unconscious, 'the' ineffable, textuality, 'the' body, gender, and so on, through the list of postmodern 'realities'. By contrast, the Idealist version of modernism, as I am presenting it, immediately trumps, as it were, or renders suspicious any claim about real origins or about what is putatively 'outside' our comprehension (like evil).

This version of modernism is not an inviting prospect, since it promises a kind of unending contestation about any fixed points or settled results, a modernity necessarily unending and unsettled.[30] It seems to require both a constant 'bootstrapping' (a reflective self-examination which is made possible by criteria themselves suspiciously local, themselves always subject in principle to such reflection), and so a constant dissatisfaction with such incomplete and finite reflection. Working out what such a modernist model of our intellectual and

© Blackwell Publishers Ltd. 1996

ethical practices might look like will obviously not be easy. Finally, it might now seem even more unlikely in this context to invoke the name of Hegel as the champion of such a complete, if also therefore unsatisfying modernism, since he is regularly taken to be the ultimately satisfied, systematically closed thinker. But he does begin to bring his *Science of Logic* to a close with the following:

> The Identity of the Idea with itself is one with the process; the thought which liberates actuality from the illusory show of purposeless mutability and transfigures it into the Idea must not represent this truth of actuality as a dead repose, as a mere picture, lifeless, without impulse or movement, as a genus or number, or an abstract thought; by virtue of the freedom which the Notion attains in the Idea, the Idea possesses within itself also the most stubborn opposition; its repose consists in the security and certainty with which it eternally creates and eternally overcomes that opposition, in it meeting with itself.[31]

Robert B. Pippin
University of Chicago

NOTES

[1] Heidegger (1991a), pp. 2–3. Some of these remarks are translated in the Appendix to Heidegger (1985), p. 165.

[2] Among such others, see Dallmeyer (1991), and (1993); White (1991); Fynsk (1986).

[3] Heidegger's Schelling lectures themselves evince a self-conscious political agenda. For example, Heidegger begins by telling his students that what is at stake in the topic he will pursue, the fate of German Idealism, is not a dispute among academic theorists, but the very 'historical spirit of the Germans'. Heidegger had decided to begin his lecture series as a whole by reminding his students in great detail of the political setting when Schelling wrote and thereby implying that the fate of Germany and metaphysics or philosophy were linked (then and, we are obviously supposed to conclude, again in 1936). He reminds his students that in 1809 'Prussia had disappeared,' that Napoleon had ruled since 1806 ('and that means here, he oppressed and abused Germany'). And Heidegger had remarked on the 'profound untruth' of the famous words Napoleon had spoken to Goethe at their meeting in Erfurt. Napoleon had told Goethe, in trying to persuade him to leave Germany and come to Paris: 'politics is fate.' No, Heidegger tells his students, 'Spirit (*Geist*) is fate and fate spirit. The essence of spirit, however, is freedom.' Heidegger (1985), pp. 1–7; Heidegger (1982b), pp. 1–4.

Such cryptic remarks (wherein Heidegger sides with Schelling's rejection of 'politics' in favour of 'spirit', with his rejection of the idealist notion of freedom, in favour of the pre-institutional, pre-subjective or even pre-political, perhaps *Volk*-ish 'spirit') already point to the way in which some acknowledgment of the historicity of thought is meant in a sense relevant to politics, even in opposition (in the name of 'Spirit') to all traditional public life.

More conventionally, of course, Heidegger sees the 'subjectivist' understanding of freedom in Kant, Fichte and Hegel (itself paradigmatic of modern aspirations), as 'fated'

© Blackwell Publishers Ltd. 1996

to fail, and that Schelling saw and appreciated that failure but could not resolve any of the difficulties caused by it, and so that Schelling's fate presaged the modern failure itself.

[4] Heidegger (1985), p. 31.

[5] Of course, also at stake for Heidegger is the difference between the conventional understanding of temporality in conventional notions of historicism and even of the past, and his own ontological theory. cf. his account of 'das Vergangene' or 'das Vorbeigegangene' and how such a past '. . ." besteht" freilich nicht irgendwo "an sich", sondern ist das eigentlich Geschichtliche im Vergangenen, das Unvergängliche, und das heißt, das anfängliche Gewesene und anfänglich wieder Wesende.' Heidegger (1991), p. 87. Another rich text on these issues: 'Der Spruch des Anaximander' in Heidegger (1972), pp. 296–343.

[6] Heidegger (1972a), p. 435; Heidegger (1962), p. 488.

[7] The relation between the notion of *Geschichtlichkeit*, which Heidegger inherited from Dilthey and transformed, and notions of historicism and history, is a complex one. cf. my discussion in Pippin (1988), pp. 71–3.

[8] Heidegger (1961b), 'Im Zeitalter der vollendeten Sinnlosigkeit erfüllt sich das Wesen der Neuzeit', p. 24; Nietzsche (1987), p. 178.

[9] Heidegger (1961b), p. 145. Heidegger (1982b), p. 99.

[10] In the 1936/7 Nietzsche lectures, Heidegger characterizes the 'entscheidende Frage' at the end of Western philosophy as 'die Frage nach dem "Sinn des Seins", nicht nur nach dem Sein des Seienden; und "Sinn" ist dabei genau in seinem Begriff umgrenzt als dasjenige, von woher und auf Grund wovon das Sein überhaupt als solches offenbar werden und in die Wahrheit kommen kann.' Heidegger (1961a), p. 26. (English translation: Heidegger (1979), p. 18.) For Heidegger's own account of *Sinn*, as 'openness for self-concealment, i.e. truth' or 'openness of Being' (not as sense of a word), see Heidegger (1982), p. 11; Heidegger (1953), pp. 64, 67.

[11] From the *Nachwort* to the Heidegger (1982), p. 512. Perhaps the most radical, and thus clearest formulation is from the end of the Nietzsche lectures:
What happens in the history of Being? We cannot ask the question this way, because then there would be a happening (*Geschehen*) and something which happens (*Geschehendes*). But the happening (*Geschehen*) itself is the only occurrence (*Geschehenis*). Only Being is. What happens? Nothing happens, if we are seeking for something that happens in the happening. Nothing happens; the event e-vents (*das Ereignis er-eignet*). Heidegger (1961b), p. 485 (not translated in the Harper and Row series.)

[12] The most economical summary of his position are the summaries given in the 1941 lecture series on Nietzsche, 'Entwürfe zur Geschichte des Seins als Metaphysik', Heidegger (1961b), pp. 458–80 (notes not translated in the Harper and Row series). For a more extensive discussion of these themes, see Pippin (1994), pp. 327–46.

[13] Heidegger (1962a), p. 245.

[14] It could also be noted that, since such a fundamental ontological orientation is not a result of, or driven by, insight or theories or beliefs, it is also a consequence of such claims that all politics inspired by an attachment to theories, beliefs, principles, or appeals to reason, become suspect as naive, hiding instead of illuminating, falsely locating 'the subject' and its reflecting activity at the centre, all with political consequences which Heidegger wants to summarize in one word: technology. (He goes so far as to claim that the term 'Technik' 'reveals itself in its meaning with the designation: 'completed metaphysics'. 'Überwindung der Metaphysik', (a collection of remarks collected together from 1936–46) in Heidegger (1967), p. 72.) At the 'centre' is rather a pre-subjective

© Blackwell Publishers Ltd. 1996

ontological site or *Lichtung*, a collective orientation, something with important consequences for any rights based or individualist politics, or any which takes as supreme the sovereign, self-conscious, self-determining individual. (Heidegger's language varies in describing the nature of such a collective orientation. For an oft-quoted formulation, see the Hölderlin lectures of 1934/5 especially, and his claim that, 'The Fatherland is Being itself which from the ground up carries and ordains the history of a folk as one that exists.' Heidegger (1982a), p. 121.) Since the meaning of Being *happens*, and happens in common, in a *Volk* (most especially, linguistically), it might be said that Heidegger's own programme is itself an attempt at a kind of 'political' reversal of the traditional priority of metaphysics (which is, for him, itself already a political act, a 'subjectivism'). Metaphysics is characterized as a 'decision' (*Entscheidung*) in the Nietzsche lectures called 'The Will to Power as Knowledge', Heidegger (1961a), p. 476; Heidegger (1987), p. 6 (although, typically, Heidegger will also gloss such a decision as a 'letting' be decided, to avoid the impressions of someone just thinking something up and resolving). What is being displaced is the possibility of any contemplative a priori determination of substance, what has been called the 'mirror of nature' view. Whereas say, for Hegel, any such determination already reflects spirit's practical determination *of itself in relation to the world*, for Heidegger, such a determination is also not primarily contemplative but a derivative expression of some *pre*-reflective mode of practical engagement, 'care' and orientation which comprises the 'event' of Being (as does his own hermeneutics, adding to the complexities). At least, it is with respect to this dimension of his thought that a comparison with Idealist humanism, and the corresponding notion of agency proper to it, can best eventually be made.

The 'mirror of nature' phrase has of course been made popular by Richard Rorty. Any reference to Rorty raises the question of his own answer to the question: *what is* displacing traditional attempts to get the furniture of the universe *right*, particularly those elements not sensibly apprehensive? Rorty rejects both any notion of a search for the normative requirements of some indispensable free activity, and any original 'event of Being', in favour of a Deweyean pragmatism. See especially Rorty (1991). For objections, see Pippin (1991a), p. 70–4.

[15] In the Schelling lectures, this sort of claim is quite explicit. Schelling and Nietzsche (who is called 'the only essential thinker after Schelling') failed, their projects to realize and complete modern philosophy 'fell apart', but this wasn't just a failure. It was the advent of something wholly different, even the 'summer lightning flash' (*Wetterleuchten*) of the 'new beginning of Western philosophy'. Heidegger (1985), p. 3; Heidegger (1982b), p. 5.

[16] All of these claims of course were regarded by Hegel and others as implied by the Kantian revolution even if they would have been vigorously disputed by the historical Kant.

[17] In Kant, the very possibility of a distinction between a 'realm of nature' and a 'realm of freedom' requires a possible distinction between (natural) law-governed and norm-regulated activities. The latter are *constitutive* of freedom, as Robert Brandom notes and explores in interesting, neo-Hegelian ways in Brandom (1979), pp. 187–96. For the Hegelian version of this case, and his objections to Kant, see my Pippin (1991), pp. 99–132, and (1995).

[18] Heidegger (1972a), p. 384; Heidegger (1962), p. 435. Derrida accuses Heidegger of such a nostalgia for an arche, or first principle, but my own view is that that charge is hasty and unfair to Heidegger, as if what Schürmann calls the an-archic nature of Heideggerean thinking is to be trumped by the debating trick of calling the anarchic the

© Blackwell Publishers Ltd. 1996

Heideggerean arche. cf. Derrida (1982), pp. 1–27; and Schürmann (1987), and the criticisms in Pippin (1991a), pp. 142–7; 156–64.

[19] Schelling (1860), p. 369.

[20] Heidegger (1985), p. 119; Heidegger (1982b), p. 208.

[21] His extremely compressed formulation of this point (italicized in the original): *'Die Größe eines Daseins zeigt sich zuerst daran, ob es im Stande ist, den es überrangended großen Widerstand seines Wesens zu entdecken und festzuhalten.'* Heidegger (1985), 105; Heidegger (1982), p. 183.

[22] My own view is that the most important thing to appreciate about Hegel's project after 1807 is that he does not reject this Kantian beginning, as Schelling does, but tries to 'realize' it. See Pippin (1989).

[23] cf. Heidegger (1985), pp. 152–6; Heidegger (1982b), pp. 264–71. Obviously in most of these passages, Heidegger is evoking his own claims about the inevitably 'covering over' aspect of any 'uncovering'.

[24] Heidegger (1985), p. 9; Heidegger (1982b), p. 15.

[25] ibid.

[26] Such a reification and neo-dogmatism is not foreign to Heidegger either:

Only a few, and they rarely, attain the deepest point of the highest expanse of self-knowledge in the decidedness of one's own being . . . That means that decidedness does not contract one's own being to an empty point of mere staring at one's own ego, but decidedness of one's own being is only what it is as resoluteness. By this we mean standing within the openness of the truth of history, the perdurance (*Inständigkeit*) which carries out what it must carry out, unattainable and prior to all calculation and reckoning. (Heidegger (1985), p. 155; Heidegger (1982b), p. 269.)

For a different, but compelling criticism of 'Heidegger's positivism' (p. 294) compare Rosen (1993). Rosen 'reverses' Heidegger in the name of Plato, but not the textbook Plato of the ancient and modern schoolmen. See especially the first chapter, 'Platonism is Aristotelianism', pp. 3–45.

[27] Hegel (1970), p. 543; Hegel (1975), p. 1212. My emphasis.

[28] Hegel (1970), pp. 276–7; Hegel (1975), 212.

[29] Hegel (1970), p. 288; Hegel (1975), 222.

[30] I discuss this notion in more detail in the last chapter of Pippin (1991a), and in a response to comments and criticisms of this book, Pippin (1995a).

[31] Hegel (1969a), p. 412; Hegel (1969), p. 759.

REFERENCES

Brandom, R. (1979), 'Freedom and Constraint by Norms', in *American Philosophical Quarterly* 16 (July 1979), pp. 187–96.

Dallmeyer, F. (1991), *Between Frankfurt and Freiburg: Toward a Critical Ontology*. Amherst: The University of Massachusetts Press.

Dallmeyer, F. (1993), *The Other Heidegger*. Ithaca: Cornell University Press.

Derrida, J. (1982), 'Différance,' in *Margins of Philosophy*, transl. Alan Bass. Chicago: University of Chicago Press.

Fynsk, C. (1986), *Heidegger: Thought and Historicity*. Ithaca: Cornell University Press.

Hegel, G. W. F. (1969), *Hegel's Science of Logic*, transl. Hegel (1975). W. V. Miller. London: George Allen and Unwin.

© Blackwell Publishers Ltd. 1996

Hegel, G. W. F. (1969a), *Wissenschaft der Logik*, Bd.II. Hamburg: Felix Meiner.
Hegel, G. W. F. (1970), *Vorlesungen über die Ästhetik*, Bd. 15, *Werke in zwanzig Bänden*. Frankfurt a.M.: Suhrkamp.
Hegel, G. W. F. (1975), *Hegel's Aesthetics*, transl. T. M. Knox. Oxford: Oxford University Press.
Heidegger, M. (1953), *Einführung in die Metaphysik*. Tübingen: Niemeyer.
Heidegger, M. (1961a and 1961b), *Nietzsche*, Bds. I and II. Pfullingen: Neske.
Heidegger, M. (1962), *Being and Time*, translated by John Macquarrie and John Robinson. New York: Harper and Row.
Heidegger, M. (1962a), *Kant and the Problem of Metaphysics*, transl. James S. Churchill. Bloomington: Indiana University Press.
Heidegger, M. (1967), *Vorträge and Aufsätze*. Pfullingen: Neske.
Heidegger, M. (1972), *Holzwege*. Frankfurt a.M.: Klostermann.
Heidegger, M. (1972a), *Sein und Zeit*. Tübingen: Niemeyer.
Heidegger, M. (1979), *Nietzsche, Volume I, The Will to Power as Art*, transl. David Farrell Krell. San Francisco: Harper and Row.
Heidegger, M. (1982), *Beiträge zur Philosophie, Gesamtsausgabe*, Bd. 65. Frankfurt: Klostermann.
Heidegger (1982a), *Gesamtsausgabe*, Bd. 39. Frankfurt: Klostermann.
Heidegger, M. (1982b), *Nietzsche, Volume IV, Nihilism*, transl. Frank Hegel (1975). Capuzzi. San Francisco: Harper and Row.
Heidegger, M. (1982b), *Schelling, vom Wesen der menschlichen Freiheit (1809), Gesamtausgabe*, Bd. 42. Frankfurt: Klostermann.
Heidegger, M. (1985), *Schelling's Treatise on the Essence of Human Freedom*, transl. Joan Stambaugh. Athens, Ohio: Ohio University Press.
Heidegger, M. (1987), *Nietzsche, Volume III, The Will to Power as Knowledge and as Metaphysics*, transl. by Joan Stambaugh, David Farrell Krell, Frank Capuzzi. San Francisco: Harper and Row.
Heidegger, M. (1991), *Grundbegriffe, Gesamtausgabe*, Bd. 51. Frankfurt a.M.: Klostermann.
Heidegger, M. (1991a), *Die Metaphysik des deutschen Idealismus, Gesamtausgabe*, Bd. 49. Frankfurt a.M.: Klostermann.
Pippin, R. (1988), 'Marcuse on Hegel and Historicity', in *Marcuse: Critical Theory and the Promise of Utopia*, ed. Robert Pippin, Andrew Feenberg, Charles Webel. London: Macmillan, pp. 71–3.
Pippin, R. (1989), *Hegel's Idealism: The Satisfactions of Self-Consciousness*. Cambridge: Cambridge University Press.
Pippin, R. (1991), 'Hegel, Ethical Reasons, Kantian Rejoinders', in *Philosophical Topics* 19 (Fall 1991), pp. 99–132.
Pippin, R. (1991a), *Modernism as a Philosophical Problem. On the Dissatisfactions of European High Culture*. Oxford: Blackwell.
Pippin, R. (1994), 'On Being Anti-Cartesian; Heidegger, Hegel, Subjectivity and Sociality', in *Vernunftbegriffe in der Moderne*, ed. Hans Friederich Fulda and Rolf-Peter Horstmann. Stuttgart: Klett-Cotta, pp. 327–46.
Pippin, R. (1995), 'Hegel on the Rationality and Priority of Ethical Life', in *Neue Hefte für Philosophie*, vol. 35.
Pippin, R. (1995a), 'Hegelianism as Modernism', in *Inquiry*, forthcoming.
Rorty, R. (1991), 'Heidegger, Contingency, and Pragmatism', and 'Wittgenstein, Heidegger, and the Reification of Language', in *Essays on Heidegger and Others*. Cambridge: Cambridge University Press.

© Blackwell Publishers Ltd. 1996

Rosen, S. (1993), *The Question of Being: A Reversal of Heidegger*. New Haven: Yale University Press.
Schelling, F. W. J. (1860), *Sämtliche Werke*, Bd. 7. Stuttgart und Augsburg: J. G. Cotta.
Schürmann, R. (1987), *Heidegger on Being and Acting: From Principles to Anarchy*. Bloomington, Indiana University Press.
White, S. (1991), *Political Theory and Postmodernism*. Cambridge: Cambridge University Press.

Copyright Acknowledgments

Jean-Luc Marion, "The Ego and Dasein" in *Reduction and Givenness : Investigations of Husserl, Heidegger, and Phenomenology* (Northwestern University Press, 1998): 77–107. Reprinted with the permission of Northwestern University Press.

Stephen Mulhall, "Can There be an Epistemology of Moods?" in *Verstehen and Humane Understanding*, ed. Anthony O'Hear (New York: Cambridge University Press, 1996), 191–210. Reprinted with the permission of Cambridge University Press.

Cristina Lafont, "Die Rolle der Sprache in 'Sein und Zeit'" *Zeitschrift für Philosophische Forschung* 47 (1993): 41–59. Reprinted with the permission of Vittorio Klostermann.

Hans-Georg Gadamer, "*Destruktion* and Deconstruction," in *Dialogue and Deconstruction*, ed. Diane P. Michelfelder and Richard E. Palmer (Albany: SUNY Press, 1989), 102–113. Reprinted with the permission of State University of New York Press.

Charles Spinosa, "Derridian Dispersion and Heideggerian Articulation: General Tendencies in the Practices that Govern Intelligibility," in *The Practice Turn in Contemporary Theory*, ed. Theodore R. Schatzki, Karin Knorr Cetina, Eike Von Savigny (Routledge, 2001). Reprinted with the permission of Routledge.

J. N. Mohanty, "Heidegger on Logic," *Journal of the History of Philosophy* 26 (1988): 107–135. Reprinted with the permission of Emory University.

Mark Wrathall, "The Conditions of Truth in Heidegger and Davidson," *Monist* 82 (1999): 304–323. Copyright 1999, The Monist, Peru, Illinois. Reprinted by permission.

Roderick M. Stewart, "Heidegger and the Intentionality of Language," *American Philosophical Quarterly* 25 (1988): 153–162. Reprinted with the permission of the American Philosophical Quarterly.

Michael Friedman, "Overcoming Metaphysics: Carnap and Heidegger" in *Origins of Logical Empiricism*, ed. Ronald N. Giere (Minneapolis: University of Minnesota Press, 1996), 45–79. Reprinted with the permission of University of Minnesota Press.

Edward Witherspoon, "Logic and the Inexpressible in Frege and

Heidegger," *Journal of the History of Philosophy* 40 (2002): 89–113. Reprinted with the permission of Emory University.

Harrison Hall, "The Other Minds Problem in Early Heidegger," *Human Studies* 1980 (2): 247–254. Reprinted with the permission of Kluwer Academic Publishers.

Charles Guignon, "Philosophy after Wittgenstein and Heidegger" *Philosophy and Phenomenological Research* 50 (1990): 649–672. Reprinted with the permission of the International Phenomenological Society.

Karl-Otto Apel, "Meaning Constitution and Justification of Validity: Has Heidegger Overcome Transcendental Philosophy by History of Being," in *From a Transcendental-Semiotic Point of View* (Manchester: Manchester University Press, 1998), 103–121. Reprinted with the permission of Manchester University Press.

David Carr, "The Question of the Subject: Heidegger and the Transcendental Tradition," *Human Studies* 17 (1995): 403–418. Reprinted with the permission of Kluwer Academic Publishers.

Robert Pippin, "Heideggerean Postmodernism and Metaphysical Politics," *European Journal of Philosophy* 4 (1996): 17–37. Reprinted with the permission of Blackwell Publishers Ltd.